Monitored at Work

Bulletin of Comparative Labour Relations

VOLUME 122

Founding Editor

The series started in 1970 under the dynamic editorship of Professor Roger Blanpain (Belgium), former President of the International Industrial Relations Association. Professor Blanpain, Professor Emeritus of Labour Law, Universities of Leuven and Tilburg, was also General Editor of the International Encyclopedia of Laws (with more than 1,600 collaborators worldwide) and President of the Association of Educative and Scientific Authors Authors. He passed away in October 2016.

General Editor

In 2015 Frank Hendrickx, Professor of labour law at the Faculty of Law of the University of Leuven (Belgium) joined as a co-Editor. Frank Hendrickx has published numerous articles and books and regularly advises governments, international institutions and private organisations in the area of labour law as well as in sports law. He is the Editor-in-Chief of the European Labour Law Journal and General Editor of the International Encyclopaedia of Laws.

Introduction

The Bulletins constitute a unique source of information and thought-provoking discussion, laying the groundwork for studies of employment relations in the 21st century, involving among much else the effects of globalization, new technologies, migration, and the greying of the population.

Contents/Subjects

Amongst other subjects the Bulletins frequently include the proceedings of international or regional conferences; reports from comparative projects devoted to salient issues in industrial relations, human resources management, and/or labour law; and specific issues underlying the multicultural aspects of our industrial societies.

Objective

The Bulletins offer a platform of expression and discussion on labour relations to scholars and practitioners worldwide, often featuring special guest editors.

The titles published in this series are listed at the end of this volume.

BULLETIN OF COMPARATIVE LABOUR RELATIONS - 122

Monitored at Work

The Legitimate Exercise of the Employer's Monitoring Power in the Age of Artificial Intelligence and the Internet of Things

Michele Molè

Wolters Kluwer

Published by:
Kluwer Law International B.V.
PO Box 316
2400 AH Alphen aan den Rijn
The Netherlands
E-mail: lrs-sales@wolterskluwer.com
Website: www.wolterskluwer.com/en/solutions/kluwerlawinternational

Sold and distributed by:
Wolters Kluwer Legal & Regulatory U.S.
920 Links Avenue
Landisville, PA 17538
United States of America
E-mail: customer.service@wolterskluwer.com

ISBN 978-94-035-4426-7

e-Book: ISBN 978-94-035-4436-6
web-PDF: ISBN 978-94-035-4456-4

Printed in the Netherlands.

About the Author

Michele Molè holds a PhD in Law from the University of Groningen (the Netherlands) and a Master's in Law from the University of Milan (Italy). His research focuses on workplace surveillance and on the impact of the market for new technologies on employers' powers and workers' rights. He has carried out research stays at the Katholieke Universiteit Leuven (Belgium), the European Trade Union Institute (Belgium), and the University of Warsaw (Poland). His work focuses on European labour law and technology law, Italian labour law, and has appeared in leading international journals, including the *Comparative Labour Law & Policy Journal* and the *European Labour Law Journal*. In 2022, he founded and coordinated the Panoptiwork research group, through which he organised a seminar series and an international conference, edited an interdisciplinary special issue for the *Italian Labour Law e-Journal*, all focused on the intersections of work and digitalisation.

Table of Contents

About the Author v

Funding Acknowledgements xv

List of Abbreviations xvii

List of Tables xix

CHAPTER 1
Introduction 1
1 The Spread of Digital Technologies to Monitor the Workforce 1
2 The Use of Monitoring Technologies and Its Potential Consequences for Work, Employees and Their Rights 3
3 Problem Statement 5
3.1 Research Objective(s) 5
3.2 Research Question(s) 6
4 Relation to Existing Literature and Originality 7
5 Delimitation of the Research 11
5.1 Subordinate Employment 11
5.2 Selection of Employees' Fundamental Rights 12
5.3 Analysis of the EU Legislation: GDPR, AI Act, PWD 13
6 Terminology 14
6.1 Employees and Workers 14
6.2 Monitoring and Surveillance 15
7 Methodology 15
8 Structure of the Book 17

CHAPTER 2
Between Mirrors and Sensors: On the Origins of the Employer's Monitoring Power 19
1 Introduction: The Rise of the Employer's Monitoring Power During the Industrial Revolutions 19
2 The Origins of Industrial Labour: Monitoring the Presence of Workers and Security 20
3 Taylorism: Pacing the Rhythm of Working Tasks 23
4 Fordism and Company Towns: A Step into Workers' Personal Characteristics 24
5 Discussion: From an Unregulated to a Regulated Monitoring Power 26
6 Conclusions: Origins of the Employer's Monitoring Power and Its 'Juridification' 28

CHAPTER 3
On the Legitimate Exercise of the Employer's Monitoring Power in the European Fundamental Rights Framework 31
1 Introduction: The Employer's Monitoring Power in the European Union Legal Framework 31
2 The Employer's Monitoring Power as an Element of Subordinate Employment 32
3 The Open-Ended Nature of the Employer's Monitoring Power 33
4 The Employer's Monitoring Power in EU Labour Law 34
5 The EU Member States Legislation on the Employer's Monitoring Power: A Diverse Landscape 35
6 The Boundaries of a Legitimate Exercise of the Employer's Monitoring Power: The European Fundamental Rights Framework 36
6.1 Privacy and Data Protection 39
6.1.1 Restrictions to Employees' Right to Privacy and Data Protection 41
6.1.2 Landmark Case *Bărbulescu*: Procedural Safeguards for Employer's Monitoring of Employees 43
6.2 Freedom of Expression 45
6.2.1 Restrictions to Employees' Freedom of Expression 46
6.3 Freedom of Assembly, Association and the Right of Collective Bargaining and Action 49
6.3.1 Restrictions to Employees' Freedoms of Assembly, Association and the Right of Collective Bargaining and Action 52
6.4 Non-discrimination 53
6.4.1 Restrictions to Employees' Right to Non-discrimination 54
7 A Legitimate Exercise of the Employer's Monitoring Power: Monitoring Practices Respectful of Employees' Fundamental Rights 56
8 Conclusions 58

CHAPTER 4
The Impact of AI and IoT-Enabled Technologies on the Exercise of the Employer's Monitoring Power 59
1 Introduction 59
2 The Datafication of the Employer's Monitoring Power: Artificial Intelligence and Internet of Things 59
2.1 Artificial Intelligence (AI) at Work 61
2.2 Internet of Things (IoT) at Work 62
3 The AI and IoT-Enabled Employer's Monitoring Power: Cases 64
3.1 Monitoring Employers' Properties and Employees' Access 64
3.1.1 Access into the Company Premises and Employee Safety and Health 64
3.1.2 Cybersecurity in Organisations 65
3.2 Monitoring Employees' Performance 66
3.2.1 Monitoring Work Performance for Blue Collars 66
3.2.2 Monitoring Work Performance for White Collars 67
3.3 Monitoring of Employees' Personal Characteristics and Behaviours 68
3.3.1 Monitoring of Employees' Social Interactions 68
3.3.2 Monitoring Health and Personal Lifestyle 69
4 Reflection: AI and IoT-Enabled Technologies Reshaping the Employer's Monitoring Power 70
4.1 The Role of Technology Providers 70
4.2 How the Data Analysis Features of AI and IoT-Enabled Technologies Reshape the Exercise of the Employer's Monitoring Power 72
4.2.1 The Descriptive and Diagnostic Analytical Features 72
4.2.2 The Predictive and Prescriptive Analytical Features 73
5 Conclusions 74

CHAPTER 5
A Fundamental Rights Assessment of the Exercise of an AI and IoT-Enabled Employer's Monitoring Power 77
1 Introduction: Employees' Rights and the AI and IoT-Enabled Monitoring Power 77
2 Assessing the Legitimate Exercise of an AI and IoT-Enabled Employer's Monitoring Power 78
2.1 Monitoring Employers' Properties and Employees' Access: Employee OSH and Cybersecurity Standards 78
2.1.1 The Right to Privacy and Data Protection 79
2.1.2 Freedom of Expression 82
2.2 Monitoring Work Performance 83
2.2.1 The Right to Privacy and Data Protection 84
2.2.2 Non-discrimination 85

2.3 Monitoring Personal Characteristics (Physical or Behavioural Traits) 87
2.3.1 The Right to Privacy and Data Protection 88
2.3.2 Freedom of Expression and of Performing Trade Union Activities 90
2.3.3 Non-discrimination 91
3 Conclusions 92

CHAPTER 6
Putting the GDPR to Work: Requirements for a Legitimate Exercise of the Employer's Monitoring Power via AI and IoT-Enabled Technologies 95
1 Introduction 95
2 History of Data Protection Laws at Work: From the 1989 CoE Recommendation to the GDPR 96
2.1 CoE Convention 108, CoE Recommendation No. R(89)2 on the Protection of Personal Data Used for Employment Purposes, and the ILO 1996 Code of Practice 96
2.2 EU Directive 95/46/EC on Personal Data: Employee Monitoring Is Data Processing 98
2.3 After the DPD: Towards a Dedicated Framework for Data Processing at Work? 100
2.4 Reasons for a Missing Framework on Data Processing at Work 102
3 Putting the GDPR to Work: The Employer's Monitoring Power as Data Processing in the GDPR (Articles 1-4 GDPR) 103
3.1 Data Controllers, Data Subjects and Processors, aka: Employers, Employees, Providers 104
3.2 Principles and Obligations Relating to the Processing of Employees' Personal Data (Articles 5, 24, 25 GDPR) 105
3.2.1 Obligations for the Employer 105
3.2.2 Lawfulness, Fairness and Transparency 107
3.2.3 Purpose Limitation 109
3.2.4 Data Minimisation 111
3.2.5 Storage Limitation 112
3.2.6 Accuracy 113
3.2.7 Integrity and Confidentiality 113
3.3 Lawfulness of Processing (Articles 6-7 GDPR) 114
3.3.1 Consent 114
3.3.2 Performance of a Contract 116
3.3.3 Legal Obligation 117
3.3.4 Legitimate Interest 118
3.4 Processing of Special Categories of Personal Data (Article 9 GDPR) 120
3.5 Data Subjects' Rights as Employees' Rights (Articles 12-22 GDPR) 121
3.5.1 Transparency, Information and Access to Personal Data (Articles 12-15 GDPR) 122
3.5.2 Rectification and Erasure (Articles 16-18 GDPR) 124

3.5.3 Right to Object and Not to Be Subject to Automated Decision-Making (Articles 21-22 GDPR) 125
3.6 Data Protection Impact Assessment and the Data Protection Officer (Articles 35-39 GDPR) 128
3.7 Employment as Special Category of Data Processing (Article 88 GDPR) 131
4 Analysis of the GDPR in Employment Contexts: Employers' Obligations, Employees' Rights and AI and IoT-Enabled Technologies 134
5 Conclusions 136

CHAPTER 7
Applying the AI Act to the Employment Context: Requirements for a Legitimate Exercise of the Employer's Monitoring Power via AI and IoT-Enabled Technologies 137
1 Introduction 137
2 AI Act: Scope, Legal Bases, and Aim 139
3 Deployers and Providers 140
4 A Risk-Based Approach to AI Systems: Prohibitions and Requirements for Providers 142
5 Prohibited Artificial Intelligence Practices (Article 5 AI Act) 143
5.1 Article 5(1)(b): AI Systems Exploiting Social and Economic Circumstances 143
5.2 Article 5(1)(c): Social Scoring 144
5.3 Article 5(1)(f): Infer Emotions at Work 145
5.4 Article 5(1)(g): Categorising Natural Persons Through Biometric Data to Deduce or Infer Beliefs and Trade Union Membership 147
6 'High-Risk' AI Systems and Employment Contexts (Articles 6, 7 AI Act) 148
6.1 Obligations for Providers of High-Risk AI Systems 150
6.1.1 Risk Management and Training Duties for High-Risk AI Systems 151
6.1.2 Transparency and Human Oversight 152
6.1.3 Post-market Monitoring 153
6.2 Obligations for Deployers of High-Risk AI Systems 154
6.2.1 Responsible Use and Oversight from Deployers 154
6.2.2 Information and Consultation Duties for Employers 155
6.2.3 Connections with the DPIA and (Limited) Obligation to Conduct an FRIA 156
7 Employees' Individual Rights under the AI Act 157
8 Analysis of the AI Act in the Employment Context: Employers' Obligations, Employees' Rights and AI and IoT-Enabled Technologies 159
9 Conclusions 163

CHAPTER 8
The Limitations of the GDPR and AI Act in the Employment Context 165
1 Introduction 165

2 Performance of a Contract and Legitimate Interests: Interpretative Leeway of GDPR's Legal Grounds in the Context of AI and IoT-Enabled Technologies 166
2.1 Necessity under Article 6(1)(b) GDPR: Performance of a Contract as a Gateway for AI and IoT-Enabled Technologies 167
2.2 Legitimate Interest and Employees' Fundamental Rights: Risks of Overreach in AI and IoT-Enabled Employer Monitoring under Article 6(1)(f) GDPR 170
3 The Limits of Data Subject Rights: Assumptions of Autonomy and Agency and Their Impact on the Employment Relationship 173
3.1 Who Is the Data Subject in the GDPR 174
3.2 The Implications for Labour Law Protection 178
4 The Role of GDPR Processors and AI Act Providers: Employers Deploying AI and IoT-Enabled Technologies and Informational Asymmetries 180
4.1 The Role and Duties of Processors Towards Data Controllers 181
4.2 Bridging the Information Gap: The AI Act's Provider Obligations 184
5 Article 5 AI Act and Its Uncertain Scope in Employment Contexts 185
5.1 The Vague Wording of Article 5(1)(b) and 5(1)(c) AI Act and of the Draft EU Commissions Guidelines 185
5.2 Employers' Capacity to Oversee Complex AI Systems: The Case of Article 5(1)(f) AI Act Exception 187
6 Conclusions 190

CHAPTER 9
Existing Avenues Within the Current EU Legal Framework to Address an Illegitimate Exercise of the AI and IoT-Enabled Employer's Monitoring Power 193
1 Introduction 193
2 Preventing an Illegitimate Exercise of the Employer's Monitoring Power: Strengthening the DPIA Through the AI Act and the Role for Employees' Representatives 194
2.1 How the AI Act Enhances the GDPR's DPIA 195
2.2 Impact Assessments: Relevant Normative Framework 196
2.3 Empowering Employees' Representatives: Using Articles 77 and 80(1) GDPR to Address Violations in the DPIA Process 198
2.4 Connecting DPIA, AI Act, and Employees' Representatives Within the Framework Agreement on Digitalisation 200
3 The Added Value of National Labour Laws in Conjunction with Article 88 GDPR: Another Avenue for Addressing an Illegitimate Exercise of the Employer's Monitoring Power 201
4 Looking Ahead: The Platform Work Directive as a Blueprint for Tailored EU Legislation on Employee Monitoring 203
5 Conclusions 206

CHAPTER 10
Conclusion 209
1 Introduction 209
2 Finding 1: The Employer's Monitoring Power Remains Constant in Purposes, but Its methods and Impact over Employees Evolve over Time 210
3 Finding 2: AI and IoT-Enabled Monitoring Technologies Fail to Meet the Criteria for a Legitimate Exercise of the Employer's Monitoring Power and Violate Employees' Fundamental Rights 211
4 Finding 3: The GDPR and AI Act Impose Requirements for the Legitimate Exercise of the Employer's Monitoring Power, but Fall Short of Providing Protection Suitable to Subordinate Employment 213
4.1 Problem 1: Employers' Interpretative Leeway in Basing Data Processing on Necessity for Performance of a Contract and Legitimate Interest under Article 6(1)(b) and (f) GDPR 214
4.2 Problem 2: Employees as Data Subjects, Employers as Data Controllers: Power Imbalances and Regulatory Challenges in the GDPR 215
4.3 Problem 3: Uncertain Scope of Article 5 AI Act and Human Oversight in Employment Contexts 216
5 Finding 4: When the GDPR and AI Act Work (Well) Together: DPIA, High-Risk AI Systems Requirements and Employees' Representatives for a Legitimate Exercise of the Employer's Monitoring Power 217
6 Conclusion 219
7 Further Research 219

Bibliography 221

Table of Cases 245

Table of Legislation 249

Funding Acknowledgements

The writing of this research was supported by the Cybersecurity Noord Nederland (CSNN) project (2019-2025), co-funded by the Province of Groningen, through the programme Provincie Groningen Ruimtelijk Economisch Programma ZuiderZeeLijn (REP-ZZL).

I am grateful to Prof. S.S.M. Peters and Prof. G.P. Mifsud Bonnici for their valuable guidance in the writing of this book.

List of Abbreviations

AI	Artificial Intelligence
AI Act	Artificial Intelligence Act
BusinessEurope	Confederation of European Business
CCTV	Closed-Circuit Television
CFREU	Charter of Fundamental Rights of the European Union
CoE	Council of Europe
DPA	Data Protection Authority
DPD	Data Protection Directive
DPIA	Data Protection Impact Assessment
DPO	Data Protection Officer
ECHR	European Convention on Human Rights
ECJ	European Court of Justice
ECLI	European Case Law Identifier
ECtHR	European Court of Human Rights
EDPB	European Data Protection Board
EDPS	European Data Protection Supervisor
ENISA	European Union Agency for Cybersecurity
ETUC	European Trade Union Confederation
ETUI	European Trade Union Institute
EU	European Union
EU Reg.	European Union Regulation
EU-OSHA	European Agency for Safety and Health at Work
EUROFOUND	European Foundation for the Improvement of Living and Working Conditions
FRIA	Fundamental Rights Impact Assessment
GDPR	General Data Protection Regulation

GPS	Global Positioning System
ILO	International Labour Organization
IoT	Internet of Things
IT	Information Technology
NGO	Non-governmental Organisation
OSH	Occupational Safety and Health
PWD	Platform Work Directive
TEU	Treaty on the European Union
TFEU	Treaty on the Functioning of the European Union
TUC	Trades Union Congress of United Kingdom
UNI Europa	Union Network International Europe
UNICE	Union of Industrial and Employers' Confederations of Europe
WP29	Article 29 Data Protection Working Party

List of Tables

Table 3.1 Criteria for a Legitimate Exercise of the Employer's Monitoring Power

Table 7.1 Article 5 AI Act, Prohibited AI Practices Relevant to Employment Contexts

Table 7.2 Obligations for AI Providers and AI Deployers/Employers

CHAPTER 1

Introduction

1 THE SPREAD OF DIGITAL TECHNOLOGIES TO MONITOR THE WORKFORCE

Anyone who has ever worked in a restaurant knows it is a job built on constant interaction with coworkers, the restaurant manager, and customers. Waiters and waitresses ensure tables are free and ready, seat new customers, and take and serve orders promptly. Some mix drinks at the bar, others deliver food, or take turns handling payments at the cash register. These activities unfold under the eyes of the restaurant manager, whose role is to monitor all these tasks and ensure a smooth service. At its core, working in a restaurant is a deeply relational job – a very old profession – rooted in cooperation and attentive service to its patrons.

At first glance, the relational and hands-on nature of restaurant work may seem worlds apart from the changes driven by Artificial Intelligence (AI). Yet, companies like the Georgian-Spanish firm *Neurospot* are bridging this gap by introducing AI systems specifically designed to monitor waiters and waitresses while working.[1] This AI-enabled camera tracks employee activities in real time, with a focus on detecting fraud and assessing waiting staff performance. For instance, if drinks are improperly mixed or fail to meet their quality standards, the AI system notifies managers' dashboard of any corrective action needed. Cash register transactions are under scrutiny, with the system capturing most actions, from counting cash to deleting receipts.

Employers, including restaurant owners, have the right to monitor employees. That right is derived from the employment contract. By signing an employment contract, employees agree to follow directives and accept a degree of monitoring while performing their duties. However, as the *Neurospot* case illustrates, new technologies are changing how employers exercise their monitoring powers by integrating digital

1. Neurospot.tech, 'Neurospot: Restaurant Solutions' https://neurospot.tech/en/solutions/restaurant/ accessed 22 October 2025.

tools alongside traditional human oversight. These technologies allow employers to collect data on employees' behaviour and work performance, and their use is increasing. The 2019 *European Company Survey* by EUROFOUND reported that 51% of the 21,869 European companies surveyed employed data analytics in their work processes, with 22% specifically using these tools to monitor employees.[2] Similarly, a 2019 Gartner survey found that 50% of large corporations used 'non-traditional employee tracking methods'.[3] In April 2020, during the COVID-19 pandemic, the global demand for these technologies surged by 108%.[4]

The market for monitoring technologies continues to grow. Since 2021, the NGO CoWorker.org has maintained the *Little Tech Database* cataloguing hundreds of AI-enabled technologies designed for workplaces, including both software and hardware, developed by various companies.[5] Additionally, platforms like Amazon Web Services (AWS) Marketplace provide employers with access to a wide array of solutions.[6] A simple search for 'Workforce Management' on AWS Marketplace returns over four hundred specialised technologies designed for tracking, evaluating, and monitoring employees.[7] These tools are developed and sold to employers to serve various purposes: improving occupational safety and health (OSH) standards,[8] cybersecurity,[9] monitoring employee performance,[10] or monitoring remote employees' activities at home.[11] As these technologies spread in workplaces, they (re)shape businesses' organisation and, most importantly, enable employers to monitor the unfolding of employees' working activities.

---

2. Sara Riso, *Employee Monitoring and Surveillance: The Challenges of Digitalisation* (Publications Office of the European Union 2020) 25.
3. Kristie Ball, 'Electronic Monitoring and Surveillance in the Workplace: Literature Review and Policy Recommendations' (European Union Publications Office 2021) 12 https://data.europa.eu/doi/10.2760/451453 accessed 22 October 2025.
4. *Ibid.*
5. Wilneida Negrón, 'Bossware and Employment Tech Database' (2021) https://home.coworker.org/worktech/ accessed 22 October 2025; Wilneida Negrón, 'Little Tech Is Coming for Workers: A Framework for Reclaiming and Building Worker Power' (*CoWorker.org*, 2021) https://home.coworker.org/wp-content/uploads/2021/11/Little-Tech-Is-Coming-for-Workers.pdf accessed 22 October 2025.
6. 'Amazon Web Services Marketplace' https://aws.amazon.com/marketplace accessed 22 October 2025; *see also* other marketplaces 'Microsoft Azure Marketplace' https://azure.microsoft.com/en-us/ accessed 22 October 2025; 'Google Cloud Marketplace' https://cloud.google.com/ accessed 22 October 2025; 'IBM Cloud Catalog' https://www.ibm.com/consulting/cloud accessed 22 October 2025.
7. 'AWS Search for "Workforce Management" (426 Results)' https://aws.amazon.com/marketplace/search/results?searchTerms=workforce+management accessed 22 October 2025.
8. European Agency for Safety and Health at Work, 'Smart Digital Monitoring Systems for Occupational Safety and Health: Opportunities and Challenges' (2023) https://osha.europa.eu/en/publications/smart-digital-monitoring-systems-occupational-safety-and-health-opportunities-and-challenges accessed 22 October 2025.
9. European Union Agency for Cybersecurity, 'ENISA Threat Landscape 2021: April 2020 to Mid July 2021' (Publications Office 2021) https://data.europa.eu/doi/10.2824/324797 accessed 22 October 2025.
10. Riso (n 2).
11. Antonio Aloisi and Valerio De Stefano, 'Essential Jobs, Remote Work and Digital Surveillance: Addressing the COVID-19 Pandemic Panopticon' (2022) 161 International Labour Review 289 https://doi.org/10.1111/ilr.12219 accessed 22 October 2025.

2 THE USE OF MONITORING TECHNOLOGIES AND ITS POTENTIAL CONSEQUENCES FOR WORK, EMPLOYEES AND THEIR RIGHTS

The *Neurospot* case illustrates the use of AI-enabled technologies through a network of interconnected devices (e.g., cameras), commonly referred to as the Internet of Things (IoT). The introduction of these technologies influences the organisation of work in various ways. Smart cameras like *Intenseye* can help prevent accidents on factory floors by alerting employees to potential risks. According to its manufacturer, this AI-enabled camera network reduces incidents related to employees not wearing hard hats by 89% and can predict and notify of falling objects in warehouses.[12]

The widespread use of laptops, smartphones, and other digital devices in the service sector facilitates remote work via internet connectivity. While this provides employees with greater flexibility, it also exposes work activities to potential cybersecurity risks. Monitoring technologies such as *Controlio* track employee activity on company devices and use AI models to detect potential cybersecurity threats to corporate systems.[13] The *Microsoft Office 365* package offers a different suite of services through its Workplace Analytics tools.[14] These tools allow employers to evaluate how well connected an individual is within the company and conduct team performance analysis based on data from emails, calendars, calls, and chats.

Examples from practice, along with specialised literature, show that the use of these technologies is becoming a routine part of workplace management.[15] This normalisation benefits organisations, and it also normalises the collection of employees' personal data for various purposes.[16] Tools like *Neurospot* and *Intenseye*, for instance, collect and process data on employees' movements to function effectively, while systems like *Controlio* and *Microsoft Workforce Analytics* track employees' online histories, communications, and other device activities.

12. Intenseye; Koçtaş Case Study (*Intenseye: Transforming Workplace Safety with Computer Vision AI*) https://www.intenseye.com/case-studies/koctas-managing-missing-ppe-and-work-at-height-risks-with-ai accessed 22 October 2025.
13. Negrón, 'Little Tech Is Coming for Workers: A Framework for Reclaiming and Building Worker Power' (n 5) 63.
14. Sandy JJ Gould, 'Measuring Work Is Hard. Subcontracting It Won't Help. Explainable AI Won't Help' in Aida Ponce Del Castillo (ed.), *Artificial Intelligence, Labour and Society* (European Trade Union Institute (ETUI) 2024) 109 https://www.etui.org/publications/artificial-intelligence-labour-and-society accessed 22 October 2025.
15. Alex J Wood, 'Algorithmic Management. Consequences for Work and Organisation and Working Conditions' (European Commission 2021) https://publications.jrc.ec.europa.eu/repository/handle/JRC124874 accessed 22 October 2025; Kirstie Ball, 'Workplace Surveillance: An Overview' (2010) 51 Labor History 87 https://doi.org/10.1080/00236561003654776 accessed 22 October 2025; Robert D Sprague, 'From Taylorism to the Omnipticon: Expanding Employee Surveillance Beyond the Workplace' (2007) 25 Journal of Computer & Information Law 1.
16. According to the European General Data Protection Regulation (EU Reg. 2016/679), Article 4(1) personal data is: any information relating to an identified or identifiable natural person ('data subject'); an identifiable natural person is one who can be identified, directly or indirectly, in particular by reference to an identifier such as a name, an identification number, location data, an online identifier or to one or more factors specific to the physical, physiological, genetic, mental, economic, cultural or social identity of that natural person.

Employee monitoring is not a new concept (*see* Chapter 2 on the origins and development of the employer's monitoring power). What distinguishes AI and IoT-enabled technologies is their ability to collect more detailed information, such as tracking employee movements, and process in real time to generate additional insights, e.g., alerts for dropped objects or non-compliant cash register actions. These innovations enable employers to monitor employees with greater precision, potentially amplifying the typical information and power asymmetry present in employment relationships.

The asymmetry in employment contracts arises from the inherent power imbalance between employers and employees. Employers establish businesses, hire staff under employment contracts, and retain the right to monitor employees to ensure compliance with company goals, performance standards, and safety regulations. This asymmetry is rooted in the fact that employers generally hold greater economic and organisational power than employees.[17] By signing the contract, employees typically accept these conditions, which often include a certain level of monitoring of their activities.[18]

This asymmetry, extensively discussed in both sociological and legal scholarship, may be further intensified by employers' increasing access to monitoring technologies. Employees may have limited insight into how their data is collected, processed, and used, while employers can gain highly detailed knowledge of employees' behaviours, often beyond what employees may be aware of.[19] In this regard, the Article 29 Data Protection Working Party (WP29)[20] has, already in 2017, highlighted that employers' right to monitor is reaching new extents and scopes, which may have implications for the enjoyment of fundamental rights at work, including employees' right to privacy, freedom of association, or the ability to organise, hold meetings, and communicate confidentially among peers.[21] The WP29 holds that monitoring employees in real time or retrospectively reconstructing their activities through data analysis may discriminate or deter them from freely expressing concerns, engaging in collective action, or

17. Hugh Collins, 'Market Power, Bureaucratic Power, and the Contract of Employment' (1986) 15 Industrial Law Journal 1 https://doi.org/10.1093/ilj/15.1.1 accessed 22 October 2025.
18. Guy Davidov, Mark Freedland and Nicola Countouris, 'The Subjects of Labor Law: "Employees" and Other Workers' in Matthew Finkin and Guy Mundlak (eds), *Comparative Labor Law Handbook* (Edward Elgar Publishing 2015) http://www.elgaronline.com/view/97817810001 20.xml accessed 22 October 2025.
19. Aiha Nguyen, 'The Constant Boss: Labor under Digital Surveillance' (Data & Society Research Institute 2021) https://datasociety.net/library/the-constant-boss/ accessed 22 October 2025; Ifeoma Ajunwa, Kate Crawford and Jason Schultz, 'Limitless Worker Surveillance' (2017) 735 California Law Review 101.
20. The Article 29 Working Party (WP29) was an independent EU advisory body on data protection and privacy, comprising representatives from each Member State's data protection authority, the European Data Protection Supervisor, and the European Commission. Established under Article 29 of the Data Protection Directive (95/46/EC) in 1996, it was replaced by the European Data Protection Board (EDPB) on 25 May 2018 under the GDPR (Regulation (EU) 2016/679). WP29 opinions, recommendations and guidelines remain authoritative also for the GDPR. Both WP29 and EDPB guidelines are not legally binding.
21. On this point, *see*: Article 29 Data Protection Working Party, 'Opinion 02/2017 on Data Processing at Work' 9-10 https://ec.europa.eu/newsroom/article29/items/610169/en accessed 22 October 2025.

seeking information about their rights.[22] According to the literature, the use of monitoring technologies beyond traditional workplace boundaries, such as in the case of remote working, may encroach employees' personal spaces and private lives.[23] The widespread adoption of these technologies raises important questions about the legitimate exercise of the employer's monitoring power and employees' ability to enjoy their rights in these working environments characterised by monitoring technologies.

3 PROBLEM STATEMENT

3.1 Research Objective(s)

This research aims to examine how AI and IoT-enabled technologies reshape the exercise of the employer's monitoring power and whether their use impacts the enjoyment of employees' fundamental rights in the European legal framework. I aim to assess whether existing EU legislation provides safeguards to ensure that employers using these technologies exercise their monitoring powers legitimately.

My main research objectives are to:

- analyse the origins of the employer's monitoring power through a historical overview. This perspective enables me to trace how, from the earliest employment relationships, technological developments influenced employers' interests in monitoring and how the law has responded to these changes;
- map the boundaries of the legitimate exercise of the employer's monitoring power, considering its implications across various European fundamental rights as expressed in the judgments of the European Court of Human Rights (ECtHR) and European Court of Justice (ECJ);
- assess whether the use of AI and IoT-enabled technologies crosses the boundaries of a legitimate exercise of the employer's monitoring power in the considered European fundamental rights framework;
- evaluate whether the relevant EU legislation ensures the legitimate exercise of the employer's monitoring power via AI and IoT-enabled technologies. I analyse the General Data Protection Regulation (GDPR)[24] and the Artificial

22. Cf. with Simitis discussion of the 'well-adjusted' employee: 'The pressure resulting from employees' need to retain their jobs and from the presence of the information system inhibits critical reactions. The employees tend, instead, to conform to the real or assumed expectations of the employer. Hence, although statutes and collective agreements seek to guarantee a minimum of independence, personnel information systems promote a maximum of adjustment.' Spiros Simitis, 'Reviewing Privacy in an Information Society' (1987) 135 University of Pennsylvania Law Review 707, 723 https://doi.org/10.2307/3312079 accessed 22 October 2025.
23. Jonida Milaj, 'Privacy, Surveillance, and the Proportionality Principle: The Need for a Method of Assessing Privacy Implications of Technologies Used for Surveillance' (2016) 30 International Review of Law, Computers & Technology 115 https://doi.org/10.1080/13600869.2015.1076993 accessed 22 October 2025; Aloisi and De Stefano, 'Essential Jobs, Remote Work and Digital Surveillance' (n 11).
24. Regulation (EU) 2016/679 of the European Parliament and of the Council of 27 April 2016 on the protection of natural persons with regard to the processing of personal data and on the free movement of such data, and repealing Directive 95/46/EC (General Data Protection Regulation).

Intelligence Act.[25] The GDPR is applicable as it regulates the processing of personal data, including employee data. The AI Act is also applicable because it applies to AI systems used for employee monitoring.

3.2 Research Question(s)

To address these research objectives, my *main research question* is:

> What are the effects of the use of AI and IoT-enabled technologies on the exercise of the employer's monitoring power, and can the existing EU legal framework ensure the legitimacy of this exercise?

To address this central question comprehensively, the research is structured around several sub-questions:

- *Sub-question 1: What are the origins of the employer's monitoring power?* This question explores the historical and conceptual roots of this employer power, tracing its rise and development alongside the evolution of industrial labour and master-servant relationships, beginning with the Industrial Revolutions of 18th-century Europe. By adopting a sociological and historical lens, I introduce the fundamental reasons and interests that drove employers to monitor their workforces, laying the groundwork for understanding the transformation of this employer power in modern workplaces.
- *Sub-question 2: What is a legitimate exercise of the employer's monitoring power in the European fundamental rights framework?* This question analyses the concept of the employer's monitoring power as it is considered to be part of the employer's authority that is specific to an employment relationship. Through the case law of the ECtHR and ECJ, I explore the conditions in the European fundamental rights framework under which the exercise of this power can be considered legitimate.
- *Sub-question 3: How do AI and IoT-enabled technologies reshape the exercise of the employer's monitoring power?* Based on literature, I introduce definitions and features of AI and IoT-enabled technologies and analyse how they change the exercise of the employer's monitoring power, reshaping its practical implementation in the workplace.
- *Sub-question 4: What is a legitimate exercise of the AI and IoT-enabled employer's monitoring power in the European fundamental rights framework?* I answer this sub-question with the findings of sub-questions 2 and 3, ultimately examining whether the deployment of AI and IoT-enabled technologies violates employees' fundamental rights.
- *Sub-questions 5 and 6: What requirements do the GDPR (5.) and the AI Act (6.) impose on the legitimate exercise of the employer's monitoring power via AI and IoT-enabled technologies?* Both regulations impose legal requirements on the

25. Regulation (EU) 2024/1689 of the European Parliament and of the Council of 13 June 2024 laying down harmonised rules on artificial intelligence.

exercise of this power which must be fulfilled in order to be considered legitimate. To answer these sub-questions, I will outline and analyse the relevant provisions of both the GDPR (sub-question 5) and the AI Act (sub-question 6).

- *Sub-question 7: Can the GDPR and AI Act ensure the legitimate exercise of the AI and IoT-enabled employer's monitoring power?* By answering this question, I identify shortcomings in the legal protection of employees provided by the GDPR and AI Act against an illegitimate exercise of the employer's monitoring power.
- *Sub-question 8: What pathways exist within the current EU legal framework to address an illegitimate exercise of the AI and IoT-enabled employer's monitoring power?* Through this sub-question, I analyse the strengths of certain provisions of the GDPR and AI Act, which could prevent an illegitimate exercise of the employer's monitoring power. I also discuss how the Platform Work Directive could inspire a future tailored EU legislation focused on employee monitoring through AI and IoT-enabled technologies.

4 RELATION TO EXISTING LITERATURE AND ORIGINALITY

The existing literature on this research topic focuses mainly on the regulatory issues of 'algorithmic management'.[26] This concept is defined by Baiocco and others as the use of 'computer-programmed procedures for the coordination of labour input in an organisation'.[27] Accordingly, legal scholarship in this field explores how various digital technologies, such as AI and IoT-enabled technologies, shape employers' authority and impact employees' rights.[28] This includes analysing employers' managerial, monitoring, and disciplinary powers within employment relationships.[29] Traditionally, labour law scholarship does not analyse these powers in isolation but rather considers their exercise as different expressions of employers' authority, assessing their combined

26. Wood (n 15); *see also*: Antonio Aloisi, 'Regulating Algorithmic Management at Work in the European Union: Data Protection, Non-discrimination and Collective Rights' (2024) 40 International Journal of Comparative Labour Law and Industrial Relations 37 https://doi.org/10.54648/ijcl2024001 accessed 22 October 2025; Halefom H. Abraha, 'Regulating Algorithmic Employment Decisions Through Data Protection Law' (2023) 14 European Labour Law Journal 117 https://doi.org/10.1177/20319525231167317 accessed 22 October 2025.
27. Sara Baiocco et al., 'The Algorithmic Management of Work and Its Implications in Different Contexts' (European Commission 2022) 9 https://publications.jrc.ec.europa.eu/repository/handle/JRC129749 accessed 22 October 2025.
28. Jeremias Adams-Prassl, 'What If Your Boss Was an Algorithm? Economic Incentives, Legal Challenges, and the Rise of Artificial Intelligence at Work' (2019) 41 Comparative Labor Law & Policy Journal 123; Antonio Aloisi and Valerio De Stefano, *Your Boss Is an Algorithm: Artificial Intelligence, Platform Work and Labour* (Hart Publishing, an imprint of Bloomsbury Publishing 2022).
29. *See* further in section 5 of this chapter on delimitation of research, more specifically section 5.1 on subordinate employment.

impact on employees' rights.[30] Some studies specifically investigate how AI and IoT-enabled technologies reshape these dimensions of authority.[31]

The impact of AI and IoT-enabled technologies on employees' fundamental rights has been primarily examined through the lens of privacy and data protection.[32] This focus stems from two main factors. First, these technologies collect and process large amounts of personal data, making the intersection between labour law and privacy regulations particularly relevant. Second, the European Court of Human Rights (ECtHR) has developed a substantial body of case law on Article 8 ECHR, which clarifies the boundaries of privacy rights in the workplace. Scholars have extensively analysed this case law to assess how technological advancements shape employer authority by defining the limits of workplace privacy.[33] While privacy remains the dominant focus, some scholars also examine the impact of AI and IoT-enabled technologies on other fundamental rights, such as freedom of expression, trade union rights, and non-discrimination. However, the analysis of these rights remains fragmented, with studies often addressing them in isolation rather than within a broader framework of workplace protections.[34]

In the context of EU legislation, most studies have focused on the GDPR (and, before that, the Data Protection Directive)[35] to assess whether compliance with data

---

30. Alan Bogg and Cynthia Estlund, 'Between Authority and Domination: Taming the Managerial Prerogative' (2024) 44 Comparative Labor Law & Policy Journal 237; Davidov, Freedland and Countouris (n 18); Bob Hepple and Bruno Veneziani (eds), *The Transformation of Labour Law in Europe: A Comparative Study of 15 Countries, 1945-2004* (Hart Publishing 2009).
31. Aida Ponce Del Castillo (ed.), *Artificial Intelligence, Labour and Society* (European Trade Union Institute (ETUI) 2024) https://www.etui.org/publications/artificial-intelligence-labour-and-society accessed 22 October 2025; Stefania Marassi and John Bolte, 'Leveraging Data Protection Law for Protecting Workers' Fundamental Right to Health and Safety in the Workplace: The Amazon Case' (2024) 10 International Labor Rights Case Law 263 https://doi.org/10.1163/24056901-10020021 accessed 22 October 2025; Pauline T Kim and Matthew T Bodie, 'Artificial Intelligence and the Challenges of Workplace Discrimination and Privacy' (2021) 35 Journal of Labor and Employment Law 289.
32. Frank Hendrickx, 'Privacy 4.0 at Work: Regulating Employment, Technology and Automation, Artificial Intelligence, & Labor Law' (2019) 41 Comparative Labor Law & Policy Journal 147; David Mangan, 'Beyond Procedural Protection: Information Technology, Privacy and the Workplace' [2019] European Law Review 559.
33. Marta Otto, *The Right to Privacy in Employment: A Comparative Analysis* (Hart Publishing 2016); *see also*: Frank Hendrickx, *Protection of Workers' Personal Data: General Principles* (International Labour Organization ed., ILO 2022); Frank Hendrickx and Aline Van Bever, 'Article 8 ECHR: Judicial Patterns of Employment Privacy Protection' in Filip Dorssemont, Klaus Lörcher and Isabelle Schömann (eds), *European Convention on Human Rights and the Employment Relation* (Hart Publishing 2013).
34. Elisa Parodi, 'Discrimination in the Automated Targeting of Job Advertising: The Role of the General Data Protection Regulation' (2024) 16 European Labour Law Journal 109 https://doi.org/10.1177/20319525241285424 accessed 22 October 2025; Kim and Bodie (n 31); Virginia Mantouvalou, 'I Lost My Job over a Facebook Post: Was That Fair? Discipline and Dismissal for Social Media Activity' (2019) 35 International Journal of Comparative Labour Law and Industrial Relations 101 https://doi.org/10.54648/ijcl2019005 accessed 22 October 2025; Aloisi (n 26).
35. Directive 95/46/EC of the European Parliament and of the Council of 24 October 1995 on the protection of individuals with regard to the processing of personal data and on the free movement of such data. *See*: M Freedland et al., *Data Protection and Employment in the European Union: An Analytical Study of the Law and Practice of Data Protection and the Employment Relationship in the EU and Its Member States* (EC 1999) https://books.google.co.

protection laws can balance employers' monitoring interests with employees' rights.[36] More recently, research has turned to the AI Act as a new relevant legal framework for the deployment of AI-enabled technologies in the workplace.[37] Beyond data protection and AI governance, some scholars emphasise the role of collective actors, such as trade unions and works councils, in co-determining the purposes and procedures for implementing monitoring technologies.[38] Adam-Prassl and others call instead for new EU legislation,[39] proposing provisions similar to those on algorithmic management in Chapter III of the Platform Work Directive[40] (and thus applicable only in the specific realm of platform work).[41] Overall, existing scholarship focusing on EU legislation in this area can be divided into two main approaches. The first focuses on compliance with data protection and AI Acts as a means of ensuring a legitimate exercise of employer powers in the digital age. The second advocates for an EU labour law-specific regulation, either through the involvement of collective actors or by proposing new legislation addressing the structural asymmetries in employment relationships.

uk/books?id = v-VNtwAACAAJ accessed 22 October 2025; Mark Jeffery, 'Information Technology and Workers' Privacy: Introduction' (2002) 23 Comparative Labor Law & Policy Journal 251.

36. Frank Hendrickx, David Mangan and Elena Gramano (eds), *Privacy@Work* (Wolters Kluwer 2023); Abraha, 'Regulating Algorithmic Employment Decisions Through Data Protection Law' (n 26); Emanuele Dagnino, 'People Analytics: Work and Labour Protection in the Era of HRM Through Big Data' (2017) 3 Labour Law & Issues 1; Otto (n 33).
37. Cf. with Chiara Cristofolini, 'Navigating the Impact of AI Systems in the Workplace: Strengths and Loopholes of the EU AI Act from a Labour Perspective' (2024) 17 Italian Labour Law e-Journal 75; Ponce Del Castillo (n 31); Antonio Aloisi and Valerio De Stefano, 'Between Risk Mitigation and Labour Rights Enforcement: Assessing the Transatlantic Race to Govern AI-Driven Decision-Making Through a Comparative Lens' (2023) 14 European Labour Law Journal 283 https://doi.org/10.1177/20319525231167982 accessed 22 October 2025.
38. Valerio De Stefano and Simon Taes, 'Algorithmic Management and Collective Bargaining' (2023) 29 Transfer: European Review of Labour and Research 21 https://doi.org/10.1177/10242589221141055 accessed 22 October 2025; Zoe Adams and Johanna Wenckebach, 'Collective Regulation of Algorithmic Management' (2023) 14 European Labour Law Journal 211 https://doi.org/10.1177/20319525231167477 accessed 22 October 2025; Dan Calacci and Jake Stein, 'From Access to Understanding: Collective Data Governance for Workers' (2023) 14 European Labour Law Journal 253 https://doi.org/10.1177/20319525231167981 accessed 22 October 2025; Emanuele Dagnino and Ilaria Armaroli, 'A Seat at the Table: Negotiating Data Processing in the Workplace. A National Case Study and Comparative Insights' (2019) 41 Comparative Labor Law & Policy Journal https://www.ssrn.com/abstract=3403729 & https://doi.org/10.2139/ssrn.3403729 accessed 22 October 2025; Valerio De Stefano, 'Negotiating the Algorithm: Automation, Artificial Intelligence and Labour Protection' (2018) 41 Comparative Labor Law & Policy Journal https://www.ssrn.com/abstract=3178233 & https://doi.org/10.2139/ssrn.3178233 accessed 22 October 2025.
39. Jeremias Adams-Prassl et al., 'Regulating Algorithmic Management: A Blueprint' (2023) 14 European Labour Law Journal 124 https://doi.org/10.1177/20319525231167299 accessed 22 October 2025.
40. Directive (EU) 2024/2831 of the European Parliament and of the Council of 23 October 2024 on improving working conditions in platform work.
41. Nastazja Potocka-Sionek and Antonio Aloisi, 'The Spillover Effect of Algorithmic Management and How (Not) to Tame It', in Kurt Vandaele and Silvia Rainone (eds), *The Elgar Companion to Regulating Platform Work. Insights from the Food Delivery Sector* (Edward Elgar Publishing 2024) http://dx.doi.org/10.2139/ssrn.4738680 accessed 22 October 2025; Antonio Aloisi and Nastazja Potocka-Sionek, 'De-Gigging the Labour Market? An Analysis of the "Algorithmic Management" Provisions in the Proposed Platform Work Directive' (2022) 15 Italian Labour Law e-Journal 29.

The present research contributes to the existing literature with the study of the employer's monitoring power as a distinct element of employer authority. I seek to examine in greater detail its origins, development, and legitimacy, drawing on historical literature. By adopting a historical approach, I explore an overlooked aspect in the labour law scholarship, tracing the evolution of the employer's monitoring power from the Industrial Revolution to its current exercise through AI- and IoT-enabled technologies.[42] I highlight key technological shifts, their impact on both monitoring practices and legislation, thus emphasising continuities and changes in the exercise of this particular aspect of employer authority.

After tracing its origins and evolutions, I define the conditions for the legitimate exercise of the employer's monitoring power in the European fundamental rights framework. In this part of my research, I go beyond the existing focus on privacy by assessing the impact of AI and IoT-enabled technologies on a broader range of fundamental rights, such as non-discrimination, freedom of expression, assembly and association. By taking a comprehensive rights-based approach, this study provides a more holistic assessment, moving beyond the sole privacy paradigm to address broader concerns on employees' rights. This approach offers an in-depth understanding of the evolving scope of the employer's monitoring power and its legitimate exercise in alignment with fundamental rights.

This research, finally, bridges the diverse perspectives in existing scholarship on the GDPR and AI Act by offering a comprehensive and critical examination of these frameworks. Existing studies have not systematically assessed whether and how these regulations fall short in regulating the employer's monitoring power, and, more generally, the asymmetries typical of employment relationships. Existing scholarship on the GDPR and AI Act also does not thoroughly address the role of AI and IoT technology providers, who develop, sell, and maintain these monitoring technologies for employers.[43] As employers increasingly rely on third-party providers, they may have limited transparency or control over how their monitoring power is exercised.[44] This shift creates a new asymmetry that requires closer examination to determine whether the GDPR and AI Act adequately address it. Ultimately, the present research moves beyond compliance-based approaches and critically examines the strengths and limitations of the current EU secondary legislation.

42. Despite the lack of specific research on the legal and historical roots of monitoring at work, De Stefano and Countouris have recently argued that early labour laws were conceived to justify the rising industrial model during the Second Industrial Revolution. They thus emphasise that employer powers have been shaped by public law intervention. Valerio De Stefano and Nicola Countouris, '"Lifting the Private-Law Veil": Employer Authority and the "Contractual Coating" of Worker Subordination' (2024) 44 Comparative Labor Law & Policy Journal 274; *see also*: Valerio De Stefano et al., 'Does Labour Law Trust Workers? Questioning Underlying Assumptions Behind Managerial Prerogatives' (2023) 53 Industrial Law Journal 206 https://doi.org/10.1093/indlaw/dwad022 accessed 22 October 2025.
43. Hendrickx, Mangan and Gramano (n 36); Cristofolini (n 37).
44. The NGO CoWorker.org in 2021 for the first time highlighted this under-researched issue: Negrón, 'Little Tech Is Coming for Workers: A Framework for Reclaiming and Building Worker Power' (n 5).

5 DELIMITATION OF THE RESEARCH

5.1 Subordinate Employment

This research focuses on the employment contract as regulated by labour laws and the rights and duties it establishes for employers and employees. National and EU labour laws grant employers a specific authority, known as employer authority, which defines their relationship with employees as one of subordination. As part of this authority, employers possess the power to monitor employees, referred to as the employer's monitoring power.[45]

Determining a European notion of subordination, however, is not a straightforward matter. According to Countouris, given the diversity among Member State labour laws, the EU has refrained from imposing a uniform definition, respecting the unique jurisdictions of each country.[46] EU labour law does not provide for a comprehensive definition of subordinate employment;[47] it mainly consists of fragmented pieces of legislation that address various facets of the employment relationship and, more broadly, the realm of social policy.[48] The EU Platform Work Directive (PWD) 2024/2831, in Articles 4 and 5, for the first time provides for some elements to identify subordinate employment, marking an important step towards an EU notion of subordination.[49]

The understanding of subordination I propose in this research builds on EU case law[50] and secondary literature,[51] which together provide commonly shared elements of subordinate employment in most EU Member States. This perspective typically characterises employment relationships as those in which the employee operates under the employer's direction, particularly in terms of the time, place, and nature of work

45. Thomas Erhag and Frans Pennings, 'European Union Law and the Protection of Precarious Workers' in Teun Jaspers, Frans Pennings and Saskia Peters (eds), *European Labour Law* (Intersentia 2024).
46. Nicola Countouris, *The Changing Law of the Employment Relationship: Comparative Analyses in the European Context* (Routledge 2016) 15-55 https://www.taylorfrancis.com/books/e/9781315614472 accessed 22 October 2025. *See also* Judy Fudge, 'Labour as a "Fictive Commodity": Radically Reconceptualizing Labour Law' in Guy Davidov and Brian Langille (eds), *The Idea of Labour Law* (Oxford University Press 2011) https://oxford.universitypressscholarship.com/view/10.1093/acprof:oso/9780199693610.001.0001/acprof-9780199693610-chapter-9 accessed 22 October 2025.
47. Catherine Barnard, *EU Employment Law* (4th edn, Oxford University Press 2012) 47.
48. The Directives relevant to the employment relationship address various issues: work-life balance for parents and carers; transparent and predictable working conditions in the European Union; equal treatment; adequate minimum wages in the European Union; employees' involvement (information and consultation, European Works Council, collective redundancies, transfer of undertakings). For a more comprehensive overview of the EU employment strategy: https://ec.europa.eu/social/main.jsp?catId=707&langId=en accessed 22 October 2025.
49. Article 4 PWD ('Determination of correct employment status'), Article 5 PWD ('Legal presumption').
50. Case C-256/01 *Debra Allonby v. Accrington & Rossendale College*, [2004] ECR I-00873, para. 72; Case C-232/09 *Dita Danosa v. LKB Līzings SIA*, [2010] ECR I-11405, paras 38-42.
51. Bernd Waas and G Heerma van Voss (eds), *Restatement of Labour Law in Europe: The Concept of the Employee*, vol 1 (Hart Publishing 2017).

performed.[52] The Court of Luxembourg, in the *Lawrie-Blum* case, frames subordination in employment as a reciprocal exchange: the employee commits to work a portion of his or her time (working hours) under the direction and authority of another party (the employer), in return for remuneration.[53] This exchange grants the employer a degree of control, including the right to impose discipline and set working conditions. This research, ultimately, focuses on one of the three employers' powers – the monitoring power – usually identified in European case law,[54] the literature,[55] as well as the International Labour Office:[56] managerial, monitoring and disciplinary power. Since the law gives the employer, as party to the employment contract, the prerogative to determine working performance, working time, workplace and remuneration, accordingly, it confers on the employer the power to monitor the employee's performance in order to verify the proper fulfilment thereof, and monitor other aspects such as security of company premises and Occupational Safety and Health (OSH).

5.2 Selection of Employees' Fundamental Rights

For reasons of feasibility and focus, in this research, I have selected a limited number of fundamental rights included in both the European Convention on Human Rights (ECHR) and the Charter of Fundamental Rights of the European Union (CFREU). The rights I focus on are: *privacy and data protection; freedom of expression; freedom of assembly, association and the right of collective bargaining and action, and the right to non-discrimination*.[57] In my view, these rights are the most relevant for analysing the

52. Nicola Countouris, 'The Concept of "Worker" in European Labour Law: Fragmentation, Autonomy and Scope', (2018) 47 Industrial Law Journal 192-225, https://doi.org/10.1093/indlaw/dwx014 accessed 22 October 2025.
53. Case C-66/85 *Deborah Lawrie-Blum v. Land Baden-Württemberg* [1986] ECR 2121. The Dutch *Burgerlijk Wetboek* (Civil Code) in Article 7:610 CC describes that *een arbeidsovereenkomst* (a contract of employment) is a contract whereby one party, *de werknemer* (the employee), undertakes during a given period to perform work in the service of the other party, *de werkgever* (the employer), for remuneration; Antoine TJM Jacobs, *Labour Law in the Netherlands* (3rd edn, Kluwer Law International BV 2020) 63. The same definition is given, for example, in France (Cass. soc., 13 novembre 1996, Bull. civ., V, n° 386; *pourvoi* n°94-1318), Germany (§611a para. 1 German Civil Code), Italy (Article No 2094 Italian Civil Code).
54. Martin E Risak and Thomas Dullinger, *The Concept of 'Worker' in EU Law: Status Quo and Potential for Change* (ETUI 2018) 54-64.
55. Bruno Veneziani, 'The Evolution of the Employment Relationship' in Bob Hepple (ed.), *The Making of Labour Law in Europe: A Comparative Study of Nine Countries up to 1945* (Mansell 1986) 100-128; Davidov, Freedland and Countouris (n 18) 2-8.
56. International Labour Conference and Internationales Arbeitsamt (eds), *The Employment Relationship: La Relation de Travail: International Labour Conference, 95th Session 2006* (International Labour Organization 2006) 7.
57. *See*: Filip Dorssemont et al. (eds), *The Charter of Fundamental Rights of the European Union and the Employment Relation* (Hart Publishing 2019); Oliver De Schutter, 'The European Social Charter as the Social Constitution of Europe' in Niklas Bruun et al. (eds), *The European Social Charter and the Employment Relation* (Hart Publishing 2017); Filip Dorssemont, Klaus Lörcher and Isabelle Schömann (eds), *European Convention on Human Rights and the Employment Relation* (Hart Publishing 2013).

legitimate exercise of the employer's monitoring power in the age of AI- and IoT-enabled technologies. I will examine these selected rights and explain their relevance to this analysis in Chapter 3 (sections 6 and 7) and Chapter 5 (section 2).

I have not included in my core selection the right to working conditions that respect workers' health, safety, and dignity (Article 31(1) CFREU).[58] There is no direct equivalent of this right in the ECHR, and I have opted to focus my analysis on rights that are common to both Fundamental Rights Charters. As noted in recent literature, monitoring through AI and IoT-enabled technologies may not only improve workers' health, safety, and dignity but also contribute to stress, anxiety, and other negative effects that may fall within the scope of occupational safety and health (OSH) concerns.[59] These aspects are therefore addressed throughout Chapters 3 and 5 whenever they intersect with the selected fundamental rights.

5.3 Analysis of the EU Legislation: GDPR, AI Act, PWD

In my analysis of whether the EU legislation ensures a legitimate exercise of the AI and IoT-enabled employer's monitoring power (sub-questions 5, 6, 7, 8), I focus on the GDPR and the AI Act. In that analysis, I do not include the Platform Work Directive (PWD), in force since 1 December 2024.[60] Chapter III of the PWD, titled 'Algorithmic Management', includes nine detailed articles with provisions setting boundaries and conditions for the legitimate exercise of this employer power over platform workers. These provisions provide for special protections against discrimination, the misuse of sensitive data, specific bans, and interference with trade union representation. It also provides for information and consultation with unions. Despite its relevance to the employer's monitoring power, the PWD does not feature in my analysis because it does not apply universally to European employees.

The scope of the PWD is limited to certain employers, workers, and employees. According to Article 1(a) PWD, its applicability is restricted to employers that qualify as 'digital labour platforms',[61] and Article 1(b) PWD further confines its provisions to

58. This article provides that: '(1) Every worker has the right to working conditions which respect his or her health, safety and dignity.' *See also*: Klaus Lörcher, 'Article 31: Fair and Just Working Conditions' in Filip Dorssemont et al. (eds), *The Charter of Fundamental Rights of the European Union and the Employment Relation* (Hart 2019).

59. Stefania Marassi and Mária Éva Földes, 'From Healthcare to Employment: Tackling the Regulatory Challenges of in-Body Wearable Devices at Work in the European Union' (2025) 16 European Labour Law Journal 195 https://doi.org/10.1177/20319525241312163 accessed 22 October 2025; Johannes Warter, 'The Legitimacy of Modern Data Processing in the Workplace' (2025) 16 European Labour Law Journal 179, 188 https://doi.org/10.1177/20319525251332923 accessed 22 October 2025.

60. Directive (EU) 2024/2831 of the European Parliament and of the Council of 23 October 2024 on improving working conditions in platform work.

61. Article 1(a) PWD: 'digital labour platform' means a natural or legal person providing a service which meets all of the following requirements: (i) it is provided, at least in part, at a distance by electronic means, such as by means of a website or a mobile application; (ii) it is provided at the request of a recipient of the service; (iii) it involves, as a necessary and essential component, the organisation of work performed by individuals in return for payment, irrespective of whether

those workers engaged in 'platform work'.[62] Article 1(c) PWD further provides that a 'person performing platform work' refers exclusively to individuals engaged in this kind of work, regardless of the nature or designation of their contractual relationship. The scope of the PWD is thus limited to platform work as a specific and non-standard form of employment. This limitation excludes the vast majority of European employees outside the platform economy, making the PWD less relevant to my broader examination of the employer's monitoring power across traditional employment relationships. Consequently, my focus is on the GDPR and AI Act, which provide a more comprehensive framework applicable to all European employees and workers.

Nevertheless, the PWD remains relevant to my research. Chapter III PWD on algorithmic management offers key elements for developing a legislation covering a broad range of employment contexts. When answering sub-question 8, I will refer to these provisions in the PWD to consider how such protections can be extended to subordinate employment.

6 TERMINOLOGY

In this section, I describe the meaning of certain important terms used in this research.

6.1 Employees and Workers

In this research, I refer to *employees* as individuals engaged in an employment relationship governed by a contract of employment. This relationship involves the subordination of the employee to the employer, where the employer has authority over the employee's tasks, working conditions, and can issue directives. The rights and protections that labour law offers employees, such as those related to unfair dismissal, remuneration, and benefits, are central to this contract and distinguish them from other workers.[63] I use the term *workers* to refer to individuals whose status falls between that of an employee and a self-employed person, often in parts where I mention platform work. Workers might receive some protections depending on the Member States' law, like minimum wage and paid holidays, but lack full employment rights as granted by labour law to employees, such as protection against unfair dismissal. They may have more flexibility and autonomy, though they remain somewhat dependent on the employer.[64] Additionally, I use the term *workers* when discussing the historical development of the employer's monitoring power during the Industrial Revolutions, before the establishment of modern employment relationships.

that work is performed online or in a certain location; (iv) it involves the use of automated monitoring systems or automated decision-making systems.

62. Article 1(b) PWD: 'platform work' means work organised through a digital labour platform and performed in the Union by an individual on the basis of a contractual relationship between the digital labour platform or an intermediary and the individual, irrespective of whether there is a contractual relationship between the individual or an intermediary and the recipient of the service.
63. Veneziani (n 55).
64. Countouris (n 52); Davidov, Freedland and Countouris (n 18).

6.2 Monitoring and Surveillance

In this section, I define the use of four key terms in my research: *employer's monitoring power, monitoring and surveillance technologies, AI and IoT-enabled monitoring power,* and *monitoring/to monitor.*

The term *employer's monitoring power* is used to describe the competence granted to employers by employment contracts and labour laws to monitor their employees, particularly in the European context.[65] This concept encompasses the employer's right to control, assess, and evaluate employees' work, to be balanced against employees' rights. My analysis of its origins in the Industrial Revolutions, its legitimate exercise in the European fundamental rights framework, and relevant EU regulations, predominantly uses *employer's monitoring power* to describe this contractual prerogative as outlined by the (past and present) laws. Hence, *employer's monitoring power* reflects the formalised, legal dimensions of this power in the context of modern labour law and employment contracts.

With the term *monitoring technologies*, I indicate any tool, system, or technique used to monitor, track, collect, and analyse information about individuals or groups of individuals. *Monitoring technologies* may include, among others, cameras, biometric scanners, GPS trackers, data analytics tools, etc. Each of these monitoring technologies can also be AI and IoT-enabled. I will refer to the latter as *AI and IoT-enabled technologies*. I will instead use the term *surveillance technologies* when referring to AI and IoT-enabled technologies that have a potentially intrusive nature, which enable constant observation of working activities and collect and process large amounts of employees' data.[66] The term *AI and IoT-enabled employer's monitoring power* refers to the employer's exercise of his or her competence through AI and IoT-enabled technologies.

Finally, I also use the terms *monitoring/to monitor*. This term refers to all the activities an employer may enact in practice – controlling, observing, assessing, evaluating employees' work, etc. – when exercising his or her authority to monitor, i.e., his or her employer's monitoring power.

7 METHODOLOGY

This research is a legal doctrinal study primarily focused on European labour law, EU data protection law, and regulation of AI systems. However, the research also has an interdisciplinary component, as several chapters draw on historical and sociological literature.

In Chapter 2, I analyse historical and sociological literature focusing on the emergence of industrial labour. This historical analysis draws on manuscripts by Frederick W. Taylor and Henry Ford in which they present their organisational

65. Risak and Dullinger (n 54) 54-64.
66. *See* the distinction between monitoring and surveillance elaborated by Riso: Riso (n 2) 3. *See also*: Ball (n 3); Ball (n 15).

theories.[67] I also include research articles, monographs and edited collections by historians and sociologists, both from that historical phase[68] and from more recent times,[69] which explore the origins and evolution of hierarchies in industrial labour. In Chapter 4, the discussion on AI and IoT-enabled technologies is based on specialised literature from sociology and data science (monographs, edited collections and research articles).[70]

In Chapters 3 and 5, I analyse the case law of the ECtHR and the ECJ. Case law research has been conducted by identifying and analysing ECtHR and ECJ decisions relevant to monitoring at work. I consulted the Eur-Lex and Curia databases for the ECJ decisions and the HUDOC database for the ECtHR ones. To reconstruct the overall conclusions drawn by the Courts on specific legal matters (e.g., the protections afforded to employees regarding their freedom of expression at work), I draw on concurring or dissenting opinions in ECtHR rulings that might provide additional insights and Advocate General opinions for ECJ. Additionally, secondary sources including commentaries in edited collections and journal articles were consulted for further interpretation and analysis. The secondary sources consulted were mainly from European labour law, fundamental rights at work and privacy, data protection and AI scholarship.

For Chapters 6, 7, and 8, I conduct extensive research into the applicable EU legislation, focusing on the text of the GDPR and AI Act as they apply in the employment context. These chapters also contain an analysis of EU documents (available on public online databases) from the European Commission Directorate General Employment (1997-2012) to reconstruct the legislative history leading to the Data Protection Directive (DPD) and GDPR. In analysing the GDPR and AI Act, I examine key rules and principles, comparing them with the characteristics of the employment relationship. This analysis is supported by literature (research articles, edited collections and monographs), ECJ case law, guidelines, and opinions from relevant Authorities such as the WP29, European Data Protection Board, and, where applicable, decisions and guidelines from Data Protection Authorities. Finally, in Chapter 9, I develop an analysis of the strengths of the current EU secondary legislation based on the findings of the previous chapters and on a comprehensive literature review in the fields of European labour and data protection law. In doing so, I critically

67. Frederick W Taylor, *The Principles of Scientific Management* (Harper & Brothers 1919) https://archive.org/details/principlesofscie00taylrich/page/n5/mode/2up?view=theater&q=rate accessed 22 October 2025; Henry Ford, *My Philosophy of Industry* (Coward-McCann 1929) https://hdl.handle.net/2027/mdp.39015071144326 accessed 22 October 2025.

68. George Dodd, *Days at the Factories: Or, the Manufacturing Industry of Great Britain Described* (Charles Knight 1843) https://books.google.nl/books/about/Days_at_the_Factories.html?id=1hQLAQAAIAAJ&redir_esc=y accessed 22 October 2025.

69. Christopher Dandeker, *Surveillance, Power and Modernity: Bureaucracy and Discipline from 1700 to the Present Day* (Polity 1990); Thomas S Ashton, *The Industrial Revolution, 1760-1830* (1997 ed., Oxford University Press 1997).

70. *See*, for instance: Wood (n 15); Anurag Singh, Hardeep Singh and Ashutosh Singh, 'People Analytics: Augmenting Horizon from Predictive Analytics to Prescriptive Analytics' in P Mary Jeyanthi et al. (eds), *Decision Intelligence Analytics and the Implementation of Strategic Business Management* (Springer International Publishing 2022) https://doi.org/10.1007/978-3-030-82763-2_13 accessed 22 October 2025.

examine the GDPR, AI Act and the PWD. This discussion incorporates scholarly analyses in labour law and data protection, alongside insights drawn from my own analysis.

8 STRUCTURE OF THE BOOK

To answer the central research question as posed in this first chapter, this book consists of nine more chapters, each addressing a sub-question.

Chapter 2 titled 'Between Mirrors and Sensors: On the Origins of the Employer's Monitoring Power' answers research sub-question 1 ('What are the origins of the employer's monitoring power?'). Drawing on historical and sociological literature, I analyse the origins of industrial labour and how this shaped the employers' power to monitor the workforce and its (earliest form of) regulation. The analysis continues in *Chapter 3,* titled 'On the Legitimate Exercise of the Employer's Monitoring Power in the European Fundamental Rights Framework', and deals with the research sub-question 2 ('What is a legitimate exercise of the employer's monitoring power in the European fundamental rights framework?'). It establishes what is a legitimate exercise of the employer's monitoring power in the European fundamental rights framework by looking at EU labour law and fundamental rights charters.

Chapter 4, titled 'The Impact of AI and IoT-Enabled Technologies on the Exercise of the Employer's Monitoring Power', explores research sub-question 3 ('How do AI and IoT-enabled technologies reshape the exercise of the employer's monitoring power?'). The chapter addresses this question by examining the principal advancements in AI and IoT-enabled technologies, and, by its conclusion, outlines how AI systems, data science, and IoT are changing employers' monitoring capabilities. The discussion on AI and IoT-enabled technologies deployed for employee monitoring continues in *Chapter 5,* titled 'A Fundamental Rights Assessment of the Exercise of an AI and IoT-Enabled Employer's Monitoring Power'. This chapter further discusses the findings of sub-questions 2 and 3 and answers the research sub-question 4 ('What is a legitimate exercise of the AI and IoT-enabled employer's monitoring power in the European fundamental rights framework?'). More specifically, it juxtaposes the protection standards outlined by the ECtHR and ECJ's case law on a legitimate exercise of the employer's monitoring power with the features of the AI and IoT-enabled technologies.

Chapter 6 opens the analysis of the EU secondary legislation with a focus on the GDPR's application in the employment contexts. It is titled 'Putting the GDPR to Work: Requirements For a Legitimate Exercise of the Employer's Monitoring Power via AI and IoT-Enabled Technologies' and addresses research sub-question 5 ('What requirements does the GDPR impose on the legitimate exercise of the employer's monitoring power via AI and IoT-enabled technologies?'). This chapter examines the safeguards the GDPR provides for employees under monitoring and the obligations it imposes on employers deploying AI and IoT-enabled technologies. *Chapter 7* focuses instead on the AI Act, and it is titled 'Applying the AI Act to the Employment Context: Requirements for a Legitimate Exercise of the Employer's Monitoring Power via AI and IoT-Enabled

Technologies'. This chapter answers the research sub-question 6 ('What requirements does the AI Act impose on the legitimate exercise of the employer's monitoring power via AI and IoT-enabled technologies?') by analysing the requirements for AI providers and the safeguards provided for employers deploying AI-enabled technologies at work.

Chapter 8, titled 'The Limitations of the GDPR and AI Act in the Employment Context' follows up to Chapters 6 and 7 by exploring the research sub-question 7 ('Can the GDPR and AI Act ensure the legitimate exercise of the AI and IoT-enabled employer's monitoring power?'), where I identify and analyse the systematic limitations and gaps in employees' protection in the EU legislation on personal data and AI systems. *Chapter 9*, instead, discusses the strengths of the GDPR and AI Act, and it is titled 'Existing Avenues Within the Current EU Legal Framework to Address an Illegitimate Exercise of the AI and IoT-Enabled Employer's Monitoring Power'. This chapter answers the research sub-question 8 ('What pathways exist within the current EU legal framework to address an illegitimate exercise of the AI and IoT-enabled employer's monitoring power?'). There, I discuss the Data Protection Impact Assessment (Article 35 GDPR) and its connections with high-risk AI systems requirements, to determine if this could constitute a stronger *ex ante* assessment to prevent an illegitimate exercise of the employer's monitoring power. I will also discuss how the PWD could be used as a blueprint for a future EU legislation on employee monitoring.

Finally, the concluding *Chapter 10* brings together the research results from the previous chapters and formulates an answer to the main question: *What are the effects of the use of AI and IoT-enabled technologies on the exercise of the employer's monitoring power and can the existing EU legal framework ensure the legitimacy of this exercise?* The chapter concludes by outlining potential solutions for overcoming the limitations identified and with an indication of gaps that could be subject to further research.

CHAPTER 2

Between Mirrors and Sensors: On the Origins of the Employer's Monitoring Power

1 INTRODUCTION: THE RISE OF THE EMPLOYER'S MONITORING POWER DURING THE INDUSTRIAL REVOLUTIONS

In the 19th century, at Crossley's Dean Clough Mill in Halifax (UK), the owner's elderly mother had a mirror installed in her room so that she could secretly inspect the crowds of workers entering and leaving her son's business on a daily basis (1840-1860 ca.). As a result, she could spot any theft of company goods or unruly behaviour.[71] In the 21st century, in the UK, Barclays (2020) introduced the AI and IoT-enabled technology *OccupEye* in some of its premises.[72] Such a software uses sensors installed at each desk to monitor whether or not an employee is sitting at his or her desk. The software, created by US company Sapience Analytics, helps the employer to identify those who fall behind targets, suggest muting an employee's phone, and send chat pop-ups for breaks lasting longer than twenty minutes.[73] Admittedly, few comparisons might be drawn between the working conditions of 19th-century English mill workers and 21st-century bank employees. Yet it is possible to follow a long, important thread of monitoring capabilities between a mirror and a sensor. Whether through mirrors or sensors, monitoring involves coordinating and evaluating the workforce, making

71. Richard Biernacki, *Fabrication of Labor: Germany and Britain, 1640-1914* (University of California Press 2018) 123.
72. Kalyeena Makortoff, 'Barclays Using "Big Brother" Tactics to Spy on Staff, Says TUC' (*The Guardian*, 20 February 2020) https://www.theguardian.com/business/2020/feb/20/barlays-using-dytopian-big-brother-tactics-to-spy-on-staff-says-tuc accessed 22 October 2025.
73. Trade Union Congress, 'Technology Managing People: The Worker Experience' (2020) 29 https://www.tuc.org.uk/research-analysis/reports/technology-managing-people-worker-experience accessed 22 October 2025.

labour processes efficient, controlling working locations, protecting company property from theft or abuse, and ensuring the health and safety of employees.[74]

This chapter examines the employer's monitoring power first as an unregulated one, then as a form of contractual power regulated by labour law. In order to answer research sub-question 1 'What are the origins of the employer's monitoring power?', I explore the origins of this power in the then newly industrialised society of the 18th century.

My analysis is based on three cases: the early textile industries in the United Kingdom (section 2),[75] then the Taylorist (section 3)[76] and Fordist's factories (section 4).[77] Since the introduction of the factory (18th and 19th centuries) and its developments through Taylorism, Fordism and company towns (19th and 20th centuries), monitoring has emerged as an unregulated and highly influential employer power over salaried workers.[78] Anderson describes the then-new power as 'private government', namely as an arbitrary, unaccountable power over those it governs.[79] I shall explore the development of such an unregulated 'private government' in this section, before analysing the legal framework that emerged at the end of the Second Industrial Revolution.

The origin and development of the employer's monitoring power were linked to the industrial model's need to fulfil three main purposes: (1) to concentrate artisans and peasants in large plants, (2) to pace the rhythm of production, (3) or oversee workers' personal characteristics. In section 5, I further discuss these needs that drove employers to monitor workers' activities and behaviours, as well as how these practices were introduced and regulated by early labour laws. This historical perspective provides a valuable foundation for my following analysis of how modern surveillance technologies present similar challenges. In section 6, I address the research sub-question 1 and provide concluding remarks on the transition from an unregulated employer power towards a contractual prerogative granted by the law.

2 THE ORIGINS OF INDUSTRIAL LABOUR: MONITORING THE PRESENCE OF WORKERS AND SECURITY

Accustoming the former rural population to factory work was the need that prompted the early stages of the First Industrial Revolution (1760-1830). The rise of the industrial model radically transformed both working organisation and conditions by concentrating large masses of workers receiving a salary (from now, salaried workers) under the first large capitalist entrepreneurs.[80] The adaptation of the existing rural population to

74. Ball (n 15).
75. Eric J Hobsbawm, 'The Machine Breakers' (1952) 1 Past and Present 57 https://doi.org/10.1093/past/1.1.57 accessed 22 October 2025.
76. Sprague (n 15).
77. Ajunwa, Crawford and Schultz (n 19).
78. Ashton (n 69) 87.
79. Elizabeth Anderson and Stephen Macedo, *Private Government: How Employers Rule Our Lives (and Why We Don't Talk about It)* (Princeton University Press 2017) 44-45.
80. Ashton (n 69) 87.

industrial settings was gradual, evolving over time due to technological advancements and the choices made by pioneering entrepreneurs. The newly established factory shifts, up to fourteen or sixteen hours a day, were distant from the working routine followed in pre-industrial environments.[81] Between the 14th and 18th centuries, an adult male villager (farmer, casual labourer, miner) worked between 1,440 and 1,980 hours a year.[82] With the advent of the factory (from the 18th and 19th centuries), the new salaried workers had to get used to an estimated 3,100 to 3,650 hours of work a year.[83] Hence, the pace of the new industrial technologies clashed with blocks of leisure time rooted in the local cultures of continental Europe and the United Kingdom.[84]

The first capitalist entrepreneurs thus needed to train former farmers and casual workers as salaried workers adapted to the new industrial methods. To facilitate this, they trained a further category of salaried worker: the supervisor. Additionally, they implemented systems of fines for behaviours such as drunkenness, gambling, or tardiness for assigned shifts.[85] Historical literature reports that the clock was used as a tool for marking out the rhythm of shifts; most of the early British and Russian industrial plants had indeed a central clock tower.[86] Then, the introduction of artificial lighting with gas lamps allowed the plants to run at night for the first time since the 18th century.[87] Particularly, the textile merchants sought to bring previously scattered textile homeworkers into a centralised workspace, leading to the development of the factory system.[88] By concentrating production in a single location, they could better monitor the labour process. Historians and sociologists describe this transition as part of a broader effort by early capitalist entrepreneurs to reshape social order. The shift to

81. Eric J Hobsbawm, *The Age of Revolution: Europe 1789-1848* (Repr, Abacus 2007) 27; Edward Palmer Thompson, 'Time, Work-Discipline, and Industrial Capitalism' [1967] Past & Present 56 https://doi.org/10.1093/past/38.1.56 accessed 22 October 2025.
82. Douglas Knoop and GP Jones, *The Medieval Mason* (Barnes and Noble 1967) 105 https://historyofeconomicthought.mcmaster.ca/knoop/MediaevalMason.pdf accessed 22 October 2025.
83. Joseph S Zeisel, 'The Workweek in American Industry 1850-1956' (1958) 81 Monthly Labor Review 23; Wladimir S Woytinsky, 'Hours of Labour', *Encyclopedia of the Social Sciences* (Macmillan 1935).
84. Edith C Rodgers, *Discussion of Holidays in the Later Middle Ages*, Studies in History, Economics and Public Law (AMS Press, 1967), 10-11, https://books.google.it/books/about/Discussion_of_Holidays_in_the_Later_Midd.html?id=bBQoAQAAMAAJ&redir_esc=y accessed 22 October 2025; 'Rules for the Observance of Feast-Days in Medieval England', (1 November 1961) 34(90) Historical Research, 117-147 https://doi.org/10.1111/j.1468-2281.1961.tb02090.x accessed 22 October 2025.
85. Ashton (n 69) 85.
86. Edward Palmer Thompson (1967): 56-97.
87. Ian West, 'Industrializing Light: The Development and Deployment of Artificial Lighting in Early Factories' in Costas Papadopoulos and Holley Moyes (eds), Ian West, *The Oxford Handbook of Light in Archaeology* (Oxford University Press 2017) https://oxfordhandbooks.com/view/10.1093/oxfordhb/9780198788218.001.0001/oxfordhb-9780198788218-e-23 accessed 22 October 2025.
88. Richard Edwards, *Contested Terrain: The Transformation of the Workplace in the Twentieth Century* (Nachdr, Basic Books 1996) 113.

factory-based work required integrating individuals from diverse cultural and occupational backgrounds – such as former farmers, hand-loom weavers, stockingers, and nail-makers – into a structured and disciplined industrial workforce.[89]

The role of monitoring in shaping industrialised society was first analysed by Michael Foucault in his seminal work 'Discipline and Punish: The Birth of the Prison'. Foucault outlines his analysis in relation to Jeremy Bentham's imaginary prison, the Panopticon (1791). Bentham's Panopticon defined an observation system – a circular prison with a shadowy tower in the middle – where prisoners were to be placed under the possibility of monitoring without knowing whether they were actually being watched.[90] Such an architecture was meant for use in prisons, schools, hospitals and the new factories: Bentham's ideas represented precisely that need of the shift in governance, from pre-industrial societies towards industrialised ones.[91] Thus, in the primitive phase of the employer's monitoring power, the main purpose was a social ordering architecturally designed – according to Foucault's analysis – to concentrate the workforce under a few supervisors scrutinising through elevated workstations, mirrors, lamps, gates, clocks and bells to make the workforce visible.[92]

In the eyes of the contemporary reader, the deployment of these technologies would hardly be considered as ground-breaking, yet it should not be overlooked that the debate at the time – preceding any regulation of labour – actually dealt with a new ability of employers to increasingly monitor workers' workdays. The very phenomenon called Luddism[93] represented precisely the labour force's concern about being over-exposed to the scrutiny of the first employers.[94] The demand of former textile homeworkers, for instance, was to preserve their individual autonomy, producing according to their needs while being able to control the hours and intensity of work. What was opposed was not the new textile technologies themselves, but rather the ongoing monitoring in the new factories.[95] Luddism and other protests were contesting the unregulated ability of the first entrepreneurs to monitor the attendance of workers.[96] Ultimately, my analysis above on the very origins of this employer power at the rise of the First Industrial Revolution shows how the main purpose of monitoring was

89. *Ibid.*
90. Michel Foucault, *Surveiller Et Punir: Naissance De La Prison* (Gallimard 1975) 167.
91. Barry Wellman, *Networks in the Global Village: Life in Contemporary Communities* (Barry Wellman ed., 1st edn, Routledge 2018) 1-47 https://www.taylorfrancis.com/books/9780429967269 accessed 22 October 2025.
92. Dodd (n 68) 285. 'On the summit of the building, at a considerable elevation, is a small square room, provided with windows on all four sides. From this an extensive view may be obtained in every direction.'
93. According to the main historical literature, the Luddites were an organisation of English textile workers in the 19th century with the aim of destroying new textile machinery. The protests against the manufacturers were linked to their fear that machines would replace their role in industry. Frank Ongley Darvall, *Popular Disturbances and Public Order in Regency England: Being an Account of the Luddite and Other Disorders in England during the Years 1811-1817 and of the Attitude and Activity of the Authorities* (Oxford University Press 1969).
94. Hobsbawm (n 75) 57-60; John H Plumb, *England in the Eighteenth Century* (Reprinted, Penguin Books 1986) 150.
95. Ira Katznelson and Aristide R Zolberg (eds), *Working-Class Formation: Nineteenth-Century Patterns in Western Europe and the United States* (Princeton University Press 1986) 72-74.
96. Jan Lucassen, *The Story of Work: A New History of Humankind* (Yale University Press 2021) 302.

social ordering to establish working routines and suppressing any security risks (e.g., theft, riots).[97]

3 TAYLORISM: PACING THE RHYTHM OF WORKING TASKS

The evolution of the employer's monitoring power continued during the Second Industrial Revolution (1870-1914). Technological innovation at that time meant advances in manufacturing and systems such as telegraph and railway networks, gas and water supply, sewage systems, electrical power and telephones. The factory of the late 19th and early 20th century was epitomised by Frederick W. Taylor's scientific management, an organisational doctrine that, although limited in actual implementation, had a profound impact on the conception of monitoring at work.[98] By means of precise instructions on movements and timing for each specific gesture, scientific management aimed to create the most efficient way for every single working task, in Taylor's words, identified as:

> Perhaps the most prominent single element in modern scientific management is the task idea. The work of every workman is fully planned out by the management at least one day in advance and each man receives in most cases complete written instructions, describing in detail the task which he is to accomplish, as well as the means to be used in doing the work [...] This task specifies not only what is to be done but how it is to be done and the exact time allowed for doing it.[99]

Taylor's conception extends beyond merely monitoring workers' arrivals and departures from the factory. His idea of monitoring is instead ingrained in the very operations of the factory, specifically in the tasks assigned to the workers. Looking back at the case of textile production, workers' expertise and knowledge were still tied to their individual backgrounds, as monitoring focused mainly on attendance at the company's premises. Taylor instead broke down workers' expertise into smaller tasks. This meant that individual workers no longer needed to know how to produce an entire garment.[100] The aim of scientific management was to expand monitoring beyond working rhythms up to the understanding of production processes.[101] The workforce was no longer expected to possess craftsmanship skills; instead, they were to function

97. Katznelson and Zolberg (n 95) 85. The protests were fierce: it was reported that the police often intervened to forcibly move people from rural areas to modern housing near the factories. It happened, in France, that in response streetlights were destroyed, accused of being police eyes.
98. Jonathan M Woodham, *Twentieth Century Design* (Oxford University Press 1997) 12; Hugh GJ Aitken, *Taylorism at Watertown Arsenal: Scientific Management in Action 1908-1915* (Harvard University Press 1960) 50.
99. Taylor (n 67) 39.
100. Robert Kanigel, 'Taylor-Made: How the World's First Efficiency Expert Refashioned Modern Life in His Image' (1997) 37 The Science 19 http://www.ams.sunysb.edu/~weinig/Taylor-made.pdf accessed 22 October 2025.
101. Harry Braverman, *Labor and Monopoly Capital: The Degradation of Work in the Twentieth Century* (25th anniversary ed., Monthly Review Press 1998) 62.

like cogs in a complex machine monitored by the manager.[102] With Taylor, it is possible then to point to the second main purpose of the employer's monitoring power: to monitor the working performance.

4 FORDISM AND COMPANY TOWNS: A STEP INTO WORKERS' PERSONAL CHARACTERISTICS

Among the most renowned appliers of Taylor's scientific management was Henry Ford, founder of the Ford Motor Company in 1903. Ford, however, applied it in a particular way compared to other industries, which is why Fordism is often referred to as a different organisational theory from Taylorism. Where Taylorism fragmented tasks and assigned them to workers, Fordism not only fragmented tasks but also aimed to transform the workforce into a single, fast, human machine.[103] The peculiarity of Ford's monitoring paradigm is denoted by the human workforce as part of one large machine that would function harmoniously.[104] Hence, to achieve such an integration, in his words:

> Just as a clean factory, clean tools, accurate gauges and precise methods of manufacture produce a smooth working, efficient machine, so clear thinking, clean living, spare dealing make of an industrial or domestic life a successful one, smooth running and helpful to everyone concerned.[105]

Monitoring with Ford extends beyond mere observation or assigning specific tasks; it delves into the personal characteristics of the workforce, aiming to create the human-machine organisation envisioned by Ford. In this respect, Ford's factories had a Sociological Department to which inspectors were assigned: they inspected workers' private homes to check compliance with the living conditions set by the Ford Motor Company.[106] The inspections concerned families' spending habits, marital relationships, or alcohol consumption. If those conditions were not found to be adequate, the worker's daily wage was halved from USD 5 to USD 2.50.[107] The overall aim of the inspections was to ensure that only 'Model Americans' were working at the Ford Motor

102. Taylor (n 67) 83. 'All of those, who, after proper teaching, either will not or cannot work in accordance with the new methods and at the highest speed must be discharged by the management.'
103. Henry Ford, *My Life and Work* (Open Road Integrated Media 2015) 80 https://search.ebscohost.com/login.aspx?direct=true&scope=site&db=nlebk&db=nlabk&AN=1058736 accessed 22 October 2025. 'The first step forward in assembly came when we began taking the work to the man instead of the men to the work. We now have two general principles in all operations – that a man shall never have to take more than one step, if possibly it can be avoided, and no man need ever stoop over.'
104. David A Hounshell, 'Ford Automates: Technology and Organization in Theory and Practice' (1995) 24 Business and Economic History 59, 69.
105. Ford (n 67) 37.
106. Ajunwa, Crawford and Schultz (n 19) 107-108.
107. Daniele Linhart, *La commedia umana del lavoro: dal taylorismo al management neoliberale* (Mimesis Edizioni 2021) 77.

company, therefore the need to impose standards of living.[108] The inspectors' intervention could not only be punitive but also corrective. Some of them were able to inspect the diet followed by the worker and check how personal savings were managed.[109]

Similar monitoring of workers' personal life developed in the 19th-20th century through the so-called Model villages or Company towns,[110] such as in the case of the UNESCO World Heritage Site Crespi d'Adda (Lombardy, Italy),[111] Bournville (Birmingham, UK),[112] or Pullmann (Chicago, US).[113] Employers aimed to enhance workers' living conditions by establishing villages integrated with industrial plants, providing decent housing, schools, and recreational activities. The goal was to divert the working class from vices like drunkenness and gambling. They anticipated disciplined workers who would avoid these pitfalls and, crucially, resist the influence of union organisers.[114] Literature points out that company towns constituted a system of imposition of morality to be kept in factory villages, which often resulted in disciplinary sanctions.[115] Company towns thus allowed companies to shape the lifestyle and activities of their workers to serve their own interests.

Monitoring, resulting from Fordism and European/US company towns, does not aim to check adherence to given directives. Even in Taylor's system, the employer's direct instructions became secondary; workers were expected to perform repetitive tasks in sync with the pace set by industrial production, rather than responding to individual orders.[116] What Fordism and company towns introduced was a more expansive and modern form of monitoring. Employers extended their monitoring to workers' personal lives, aiming at shaping an ideal and morally acceptable working class. This marked the emergence of a third dimension of the employer's monitoring power: monitoring of workers' personal characteristics, reinforcing control over their behaviours even outside the workplace.[117]

At the end of the Second Industrial Revolution, it is therefore possible to identify three purposes, which were pursued in an unregulated labour relationship:

---

108. Ifeoma Ajunwa, *The Quantified Worker: Law and Technology in the Modern Workplace* (Cambridge University Press 2023) 185.
109. *Ibid.* The diet recommended to employees was vegetarianism, as the one followed by Ford himself.
110. Margaret Crawford, *Building the Workingman's Paradise: The Design of American Company Towns* (Verso 1995).
111. Valerio Varini, 'Building an Industrial Society: Welfare Capitalism in the "City of Factories", Sesto San Giovanni, Italy' (2016) 23 European Review of History: Revue européenne d'histoire 724 https://doi.org/10.1080/13507486.2016.1154928 accessed 22 October 2025.
112. KC Parsons, 'The Model Company Town: Urban Design Through Private Enterprise in Nineteenth-Century New England by John S. Garner' (1985) 58 The New England Quarterly 639 https://doi.org/10.2307/365575 accessed 22 October 2025.
113. Stanley Buder, *Pullman: An Experiment in Industrial Order and Community Planning, 1880-1930* (Oxford University Press 1980).
114. Linda Carlson, *Company Towns of the Pacific Northwest* (University of Washington Press 2003) 190.
115. Carlson (n 114); Crawford (n 110); Parsons (n 112); Thompson (n 81).
116. Taylor (n 67) 83.
117. Ajunwa, Crawford and Schultz (n 19).

(1) to monitor employers' properties and workers' accesses;
(2) to monitor workers' performance;
(3) to monitor workers' personal characteristics and behaviours.

5 DISCUSSION: FROM AN UNREGULATED TO A REGULATED MONITORING POWER

Eventually, by the end of the Second Industrial Revolution, there was a shift from employer power being entirely governed by contractual freedom to employer power as a contractual prerogative regulated by law – a gradual transition that coincided with the working-class struggle to secure the first labour regulations in Europe and the United States. As part of this process, the introduction of early labour laws began to include elements of regulation governing the exercise of previously unregulated employer power, including the monitoring power.

Following the Second International in 1889, the demand of European and American workers, supported by riots and strikes, was to reduce working hours and limit monitoring over workers' private lives, hence the Eight-Hour Workday Movement.[118] Among the first demands for labour protection was the one 'to protect continuous blocks of time from employer work or the control of employers and to create a regular pattern of work and leisure time'.[119] Working days could indeed vary between twelve and sixteen hours, with a wide margin of discretion on the part of the employer as no regulation of working hours was present.[120] Internationally, the eight-hour movement was the strongest and most supported by workers' organisations. At the national level, however, legislation began to emerge to formalise and limit employers' monitoring activities.[121]

Simitis, in his essay on the 'juridification' of labour relations,[122] highlights that the recognition of working conditions as a societal issue in need of regulation has not followed the same path in all countries.[123] With regard to monitoring, in the UK, early worker protections were introduced sector by sector, such as the Coal Miners Act of 1908, which established a maximum of eight working hours, and the Trade Board Act

118. The Second International (1889-1916), an organisation of socialist and labour parties established on 14 July 1889, played an important role in introducing the demand for an eight-hour workday into the international discourse. Katznelson and Zolberg (n 95).
119. Gary S Cross, 'The Quest for Leisure: Reassessing the Eight-Hour Day in France' (1984) 18 Journal of Social History 195, 208 https://doi.org/10.1353/jsh/18.2.195 accessed 22 October 2025.
120. Lucassen (n 96) 367-369.
121. De Stefano et al. recently noted how the first labour laws in Europe were serving mostly the interests of employers, therefore further justifying the authority of employers over workers (e.g., keeping booklets, legally imposing discipline in the company premises). De Stefano et al. (n 42) 12.
122. Simitis describes 'Juridification of labor relations' as the process through which 'substantial elements of labor relations are one after another subjected to conditions included in a scheme imposed by the state, deliberately interfering with individual relationships and displacing personal agreements by mandatory rules of behavior'. Spiros Simitis, 'The Juridification of Labor Relations' (1986) 7 Comparative Labor Law & Policy Journal 93, 100.
123. *Ibid.*, 95.

of 1909, establishing boards which could set minimum wages protections in four industries: chain-making, ready-made tailoring, paper-box making, machine-made lace making, and finishing trades.[124] In contrast, countries like France, during the same period, chose to implement cross-sectoral regulations on wages and working hours that applied universally, regardless of the type of work.[125] Similarly, in 1896, the Belgian legislator approved the *Loi sur les règlements d'atelier* which was mandating employers to publish at company level the rules to be respected at work, allowing workers and their representatives to comment and discuss them at company level. Despite the legal framework in the 19th-century European countries being fragmented and often still very punitive towards workers,[126] their demands gained further strength with the founding, in 1900 in Bern, of the International Association for Labour Legislation, which advocated, among other demands, for the autonomy of the working individual and a right to family life outside the factories.[127]

At the end of the First World War, it was no coincidence that the Treaty of Versailles (1919, Article 427) and the first convention of the newly founded International Labour Organization (1919, Convention No. C001) stipulated that the hours of 'work shall not exceed eight in the day and forty-eight in the week'. The first international labour standard thus accommodated the most pressing demand that arose from the Second Industrial Revolution.[128] Although it was a debate that lasted decades and had many facets, it is useful to look at it as the first major labour regulation transforming limitless monitoring practices into a regulated monitoring power; to protect a minimum sphere of personal autonomy and dignity, for a long time not covered in the unregulated labour markets. Thus, looking at the debate of the time, the eight-hour working day as an international standard represented a minimum level of guarantees to avoid inhuman working conditions.[129]

After the ILO Convention C001 and World War II, the contemporary regulatory approach to labour law protection began to appear in the European countries[130] – also

124. Sheila Blackburn, 'Ideology and Social Policy: The Origins of the Trade Boards Act' (1991) 34 The Historical Journal 43 https://doi.org/10.1017/s0018246x00013923 accessed 22 October 2025.
125. Simitis, 'The Juridification of Labor Relations' (n 122) 96.
126. With the Trade Union Act (1871) in the UK, the Trade Unions were legalised; until then workers could have been prosecuted according to the Masters and Servants Act of 1823, which provided imprisonment or forced labour in case of insubordination to the master/employer. There is evidence and even after 1871, trade union activity was prosecuted in English Courts. Suresh Naidu and Noam Yuchtman, 'Coercive Contract Enforcement: Law and the Labor Market in Nineteenth Century Industrial Britain' (2013) 103 American Economic Review 107 https://doi.org/10.1257/aer.103.1.107 accessed 22 October 2025.
127. Justin Godart, 'Les clauses du travail dans le traité de Versailles (28 juin 1919) les décisions de la conférence de Washington (novembre 1919)' (Dunod 1920) 5-13.
128. Kari Tapiola, 'What Happened to International Labour Standards and Human Rights at Work?' in Tarja Halonen and Ulla Liukkunen (eds), *International Labour Organization and Global Social Governance* (Springer International Publishing 2021) https://doi.org/10.1007/978-3-030-55400-2_3 accessed 22 October 2025.
129. *Ibid.*, 66.
130. For an overview of the employment contract evolution (in the UK context): Simon F Deakin and Frank Wilkinson, *The Law of the Labour Market: Industrialization, Employment, and Legal Evolution* (Oxford University Press 2005) 41.

with regard to the employer's monitoring power.[131] The ILO Declaration of Philadelphia (10 May 1944, 'Declaration concerning the aims and purposes of the International Labour Organisation') further strengthened the principle that labour is not a commodity and that its regulation aims to fair policies on wages, working hours and other working conditions (Article III, letter b); to achieve the goal of social justice imposed by the ILO in the 1919 Treaty of Versailles (Article II).[132]

In the newly established regulatory framework, the power to monitor workers is no longer a master-subordinate relationship but a contractual prerogative, shaped by international standards and domestic labour laws.[133] This process shifts the previously unchecked authority of employers towards a system of legal norms that balance the rights and responsibilities of both parties. The employer's monitoring power becomes a competence integrated into the modern employment contract, subjected to the scrutiny of both state-imposed regulations and international labour standards norms.[134]

In this context, labour relations are no longer seen as purely individual affairs. The modern state restricts previously accepted contractual freedoms by imposing binding conditions of work.[135] This shift marks a broader recognition of social justice, which was notably advanced by the Treaty of Versailles and further reinforced later on by instruments like the European Convention on Human Rights.[136] These frameworks have been instrumental in establishing the rule of law at work, rather than left to the discretion of individual parties. Thus, the employer's right to monitor employees, and the extent of such monitoring, is now a subject for regulation, completing the juridification process described by Simitis.[137]

6 CONCLUSIONS: ORIGINS OF THE EMPLOYER'S MONITORING POWER AND ITS 'JURIDIFICATION'

This chapter provides an answer to research sub-question 1: *what are the origins of the employer's monitoring power?* By examining the development of this power during the rise of industrial society, I highlighted its three original functions: to monitor employers' properties and workers' access; to monitor workers' performance; to monitor workers' personal characteristics. Initially, this power was exercised within a master-subordinate relationship grounded in private agreements. Workers had no protection in the law against the employer's exercise of this power.

131. *See*, for instance, the discussion throughout the 1960s (then converged into the Italian Workers' Statue) to ban covert workplace surveillance unless necessary for health and safety purposes. Lord Wedderburn, 'The Italian Workers' Statute: Some British Reflections' (1990) 19 Industrial Law Journal 154, 169 https://doi.org/10.1093/ilj/19.3.154 accessed 22 October 2025.
132. International Labour Organization, 'Declaration Concerning the Aims and Purposes of the International Labour Organisation' https://www.ilo.org/static/english/inwork/cb-policy-guide/declarationofPhiladelphia1944.pdf accessed 22 October 2025.
133. Simitis, 'The Juridification of Labor Relations' (n 122) 103.
134. *Ibid.*, 93-94.
135. *Ibid.*, 107.
136. Tapiola (n 128).
137. Simitis, 'The Juridification of Labor Relations' (n 122) 100.

As industrialisation progressed, efforts to regulate labour relations (and thus the employer's monitoring power) emerged, which ultimately led to what Simitis described as the 'juridification' of labour relations: i.e., the process through which 'substantial elements of labor relations are one after another subjected to conditions included in a scheme imposed by the state, deliberately interfering with individual relationships and displacing personal agreements by mandatory rules of behavior'.[138] The movement for an eight-hour workday, supported by strikes and legislative efforts, sought to establish a division between work and private life. This objective was reflected in national regulations, such as the Coal Mines Act (1908) and the Trade Board Act (1909) in the UK, as well as cross-sectoral labour laws in France or Belgium. Internationally, the International Labour Organization (1919) formalised these efforts. The Treaty of Versailles (1919) and ILO Convention C001 established the first binding international standard limiting working hours, reflecting growing recognition of the need to regulate unregulated employer authority.

In this context, the transition from employer discretion to state-imposed regulations illustrates the process of 'juridification' of labour relations. What had initially been an unregulated exercise of employer power based on private agreements gradually became subject to legal norms. As early labour laws were introduced, the scope of regulation expanded to include the employer's monitoring power, transforming it from an unregulated power into one governed by state-imposed legal norms. The employer's monitoring power becomes an element of the employment contract, constrained by domestic and international standards. The next chapter aims to map the boundaries established by the European fundamental rights framework for the legitimate exercise of the employer's monitoring power.

138. *Ibid.*

CHAPTER 3

On the Legitimate Exercise of the Employer's Monitoring Power in the European Fundamental Rights Framework

1 INTRODUCTION: THE EMPLOYER'S MONITORING POWER IN THE EUROPEAN UNION LEGAL FRAMEWORK

In this chapter, I analyse the employer's monitoring power as a power embedded in employment contracts and regulated by the law. More specifically, I explore the conditions for its legitimate exercise in the European fundamental rights framework. I answer the research sub-question 2: *What is a legitimate exercise of the employer's monitoring power in the European fundamental rights framework?*

The structure of this chapter is as follows. In section 2, I elaborate on the employer's monitoring power as an element of subordinate employment in labour law. This power remains inherently flexible (section 3), as it, for instance, allows the employer to organise and manage the company. Its open-ended nature makes it challenging to find delineated definitions of what is a legitimate exercise of the employer's monitoring power in the law. This is reflected in both the domestic law of EU Member States and EU law. Some Member States explicitly define in domestic laws what a legitimate exercise of this employer power is; others have no specific regulations and rely on data protection law, showing a rather different approach on what is allowed to monitor at work.[139] This lack of harmonisation, as I shall discuss in sections 4 and 5, is mainly due to the European legislative action focusing only on certain aspects of employment contracts, leaving to domestic laws a greater role in determining working conditions, employers' obligations and employees' rights. Such a diverse regulatory landscape is also influenced by the fact that employers' decisions are

139. For an overview of the regulation of the employer's monitoring power in the European Member States: Riso (n 2) 9-16.

inherently dynamic, evolving through the ongoing collaboration between employers and employees. In sections 6 and 7, I therefore provide an analysis based on a fundamental rights framework that is common to all EU Member States, as enshrined in Article 6 of the Treaty on European Union (TEU). This framework consists of the Charter of Fundamental Rights of the European Union (CFREU) and the European Convention on Human Rights (ECHR). Fundamental rights impose *general criteria* to be respected by EU and Member States' laws, and these criteria will base my analysis for understanding what is a legitimate exercise of the employer's monitoring power in that framework. By outlining these *general criteria*, I define the exercise of the employer's monitoring power as legitimate when the monitoring of employee activities by employers complies with them and is thus respectful of the employees' fundamental rights. In section 8, I answer research sub-question 2 by outlining the conditions for a legitimate exercise of this employer's power under the European fundamental rights framework.

2 THE EMPLOYER'S MONITORING POWER AS AN ELEMENT OF SUBORDINATE EMPLOYMENT

Labour laws have a peculiar nature: through employment contracts, they allow for hierarchical relationships between individuals who, outside the workplace, are otherwise considered equals.[140] Within these hierarchical relationships, employees' subordination allows the employer to determine and control key aspects of work-related activities – such as task assignments, workflows, breaks, supervision, and workplace policies – which the employee is expected to follow.[141] When an employee signs an employment contract, s(he) becomes part of the employers' structured 'bureaucratic organization'.[142] Employers define the employee's role through policies that they freely establish within the boundaries of applicable laws (e.g., labour laws, OSH regulations, and privacy laws).[143] European case law,[144] literature,[145] as well as the International Labour Office,[146] consistently describe employers' authority as composed of three powers: managerial, monitoring and disciplinary. As the law vests employers with the prerogative to determine working performance, working time, workplace and remuneration, accordingly, it confers on the employer the hierarchical superiority to exercise managerial (or directive) power to instruct the employee to perform the tasks assigned. In addition, it confers on the employer the power to monitor the employee, an open-ended and flexible power that encompasses observing the traits, behaviours, and performance of the workforce, which is what I call the employer's monitoring

140. Cf. Alain Supiot, *Critique du droit du travail* (Presses Universitaires de France 2015) 9.
141. *Ibid.*, 56.
142. Collins, 'Market Power, Bureaucratic Power, and the Contract of Employment' (n 17).
143. Alvin W. Gouldner, *Patterns of Industrial Bureaucracy: A Case Study of Modern Factory Administration* (1. Free Press Paberback ed., New York: The Free Press, 1964), 282.
144. Martin E Risak and Thomas Dullinger, *The Concept of 'Worker' in EU Law: Status Quo and Potential for Change* (ETUI 2018) 54-64.
145. Veneziani (n 55) 100-128; Davidov, Freedland and Countouris (n 18) 2-8.
146. International Labour Conference and Internationales Arbeitsamt (n 56) 7.

power.[147] Finally, the disciplinary power that – within the limits of the law – allows sanctioning the employee for non-compliance with the contractually agreed duties (e.g., oral counselling, written warning notices, suspension without pay, termination of employment).[148] These open-ended powers adapt over time to employers' needs and constitute the unequal power framework that is typical of subordination: the employer can decide at will how and when to exercise his or her managerial, monitoring and disciplinary power.[149]

Labour laws balance this power asymmetry by establishing standards that compensate for the socio-economic inequality between the employer and the employee, limit the employer's authority and protect the employee from unfavourable conditions unilaterally imposed by the stronger party (the employer). Key aspects of the contract – such as salary, working hours, and health and safety – are regulated by law in a way that safeguards employees' dignity and autonomy.[150] Tracing precisely the boundaries of a legitimate exercise of the employer's monitoring power remains complex due to its inherent flexibility and the evolving collaboration with employees.

3 THE OPEN-ENDED NATURE OF THE EMPLOYER'S MONITORING POWER

The open-ended nature of the monitoring power is addressed by economic and legal scholarship as the main feature of employers' authority over employees. Ronald Coase in his *The Nature of the Firm* (1937) theorises the firm as a hierarchical organisation resorting to subordinate employment (and not a series of service contracts) to better organise subordinate employees.[151] Although this increases organisational costs, it allows the exercise of management, monitoring and disciplinary powers by the employer. Ultimately, according to Coase, the employment contract itself allows the employer to organise the workforce according to his or her business targets.[152] The monitoring power, then, together with the other employer prerogatives, is necessarily an open-ended contractual term (and thus a unilateral employer power) for the good performance of the contract itself. Part of the legal scholarship relates the open-ended

147. Cf. with Chapter 1, section 6.2 'Monitoring and Surveillance'.
148. For an extensive analysis of the relationship between monitoring, managerial and disciplinary power, *see*: Richard Edwards, *Contested Terrain: The Transformation of the Workplace in the Twentieth Century*, Nachdr (New York: Basic Books, 1996), 111-162.
149. Guy Davidov, *A Purposive Approach to Labour Law* (Oxford University Press 2016) 54.
150. *Ibid.*, 39.
151. Ronald H Coase, 'The Nature of the Firm' (1937) 4 Economica 386 https://doi.org/10.2307/2626876 accessed 22 October 2025.
152. Antonio Aloisi and Valerio Stefano, 'Regulation and the Future of Work: The Employment Relationship as an Innovation Facilitator' (2020) 159 International Labour Review 47 https://doi.org/10.1111/ilr.12160 accessed 22 October 2025; OECD, 'Algorithms and Collusion: Competition Policy in the Digital Age' (2017) https://www.oecd.org/content/dam/oecd/en/publications/reports/2017/05/algorithms-and-collusion-competition-policy-in-the-digital-age_02371a73/258dcb14-en.pdf accessed 22 October 2025.

nature of such a contractual term to the relational nature of the employment contract.[153] As such, it reflects an ongoing relationship that involves incremental changes. Collins, in this regard, theorises that the contract serves as a formal framework for a relationship that evolves naturally through cooperation,[154] although such cooperation does not eliminate conflicting interests or the employee's subordination to the employer.[155] Instead, the commitment to cooperate rests on the assumption that the authoritative relationship to which the employee is subjected is inherently 'evolutionary' in nature.[156]

These insights suggest that the employer's monitoring power, as part of the employer's authority, must be understood as an evolving and open-ended aspect of the employment relationship that adapts over time in response to business needs, technological developments, and legal constraints. This perspective highlights why the scope of the employer's monitoring power cannot be regulated by rigid contractual terms, thus requiring further investigation into the conditions for its legitimate exercise in the law. In the next section, I analyse the employer's monitoring power in EU labour law.

4 THE EMPLOYER'S MONITORING POWER IN EU LABOUR LAW

European Union legislation does not explicitly define subordinate employment or establish clear parameters for the legitimate exercise of the employer's monitoring power. EU labour law, in fact, mainly consists of a patchwork of legislation that addresses various facets of the employment relationship and, more broadly, the realm of social policy.[157] This body of law is largely shaped by secondary legislation, especially Directives.[158] The absence of a definition is often attributed in mainstream literature to the EU's reluctance to interfere with the diverse labour law legislations of Member States.[159] Defining what constitutes a legitimate exercise of the employer's monitoring power at the EU level is thus a challenging task. Nonetheless, certain essential elements can be inferred from European case law.

153. Mark Freedland, *The Personal Employment Contract* (Oxford University Press 2005) 271 https://academic.oup.com/book/10120 accessed 22 October 2025; Hugh Collins, 'Employment as a Relational Contract' (2021) 137 Law Quarterly Review 426 https://doi.org/10.1080/10383441.2021.1895542 accessed 22 October 2025; Maayan Niezna and Guy Davidov, 'Consent in Contracts of Employment' (2023) 86 The Modern Law Review 1134 https://doi.org/10.1111/1468-2230.12802 accessed 22 October 2025.
154. Collins, 'Employment as a Relational Contract' (n 153) 434-435.
155. Douglas Brodie, 'How Relational Is the Employment Contract?' (2011) 40 Industrial Law Journal 232, 240-241 https://doi.org/10.1093/indlaw/dwr009 accessed 22 October 2025.
156. Collins, 'Employment as a Relational Contract' (n 153) 434-435.
157. The Directives touching upon the employment relationship cover, among others, the following issues: work-life balance for parents and carers; equal treatment; transparent and predictable working conditions in the European Union; adequate minimum wages in the European Union; employees involvement (information and consultation, European Works Council, collective redundancies, transfer of undertakings). For a comprehensive view of the EU employment strategy: https://ec.europa.eu/social/main.jsp?catId=707&langId=en accessed 22 October 2025.
158. Barnard (n 47) 47.
159. Countouris (n 46) 15-55. *See also* Fudge (n 46).

The ECJ provided the European debate with some more details about this open-ended power: one of the essential elements of employment is 'that for a certain period of time a person performs services for and under the direction of another person'.[160] In the *Lawrie-Blum* case, the Court verified the existence of an employment relationship by establishing that the employee (a teacher) was indeed under the (direction and) monitoring of the school. The school acted as an employer by overseeing the tasks performed by the employee as well as by monitoring the start and end of working hours.[161] From this established case law of the ECJ, I deduce that the monitoring power is the power granted by law to the employer to verify legitimately the employee's compliance to the instructions given and of work performance;[162] and that, consequently, the law endows the employer with this open-ended power since work intensity, assessment of its quality and pace, can hardly be totally anticipated in the contractual terms.[163] It follows from this case law that the ECJ also regards the employer's monitoring power as a necessarily open-ended contractual term, as it allows the employer to organise and run his or her business.[164]

As the regulation of labour in the EU largely falls within the domain of domestic laws, I will explore in the next section whether a uniform regulatory approach on the employer's monitoring power exists across Member States' labour laws.

5 THE EU MEMBER STATES LEGISLATION ON THE EMPLOYER'S MONITORING POWER: A DIVERSE LANDSCAPE

Labour laws of the Member States are remarkably diverse with respect to the regulation of the employer's monitoring power.[165] According to the 2020 EUROFOUND report on 'Employee monitoring and surveillance', which mapped domestic labour laws on this matter, these different approaches can be broadly categorised into three main types. On the one hand, EUROFOUND finds States with specific rules legitimising or prohibiting particular implementations of the employer's monitoring power. Legislation in Bulgaria, Italy, Portugal, Romania, and Spain can be seen as limiting the monitoring of

160. Case C-66/85 *Deborah Lawrie-Blum v. Land Baden-Württemberg* [1986] ECR 2121, para. 17. *See also* in this regard similar findings of the ECJ: ECJ in, C-197/86 *Steven Malcolm Brown v. The Secretary of State for Scotland* [1988] ECR 03205, para. 21; ECJ in, C-344/87 Bettray, [1989] ECR 01621, para. 14; C-94/07, *Andrea Raccanelli v. Max-Planck-Gesellschaft zur Förderung der Wissenschaften eV*, [2008] ECR I-05939, para. 34.
161. Case C-66/85 *Deborah Lawrie-Blum v. Land Baden-Württemberg* [1986] ECR 2121, para. 18; Cf. further with Case C-256/01 *Debra Allonby v. Accrington & Rossendale College,* [2004] ECR I-00873 para. 72.
162. *See also* in this regard: Case C-270/13 *Iraklis Haralambidis. v. Calogero Casilli* (CFI 5 June 2014), Opinion of AG Wahl, para. 30.
163. Jo Carby-Hall, 'The Contractual Nature of Social Law' (2003) 45 Managerial Law 23, 34 https://doi.org/10.1108/03090550310770893 accessed 22 October 2025.
164. Risak and Dullinger offer a comprehensive ECJ's case law review on employers' power to monitor employees; they also point to the open-ended nature of the employer's monitoring power, *see*: Risak and Dullinger (n 54) 54-64.
165. European Foundation for the Improvement of Living and Working Conditions, *Employee Monitoring and Surveillance the Challenges of Digitalisation* (2020) 8-16 https://doi.org/10.2806/424580 accessed 22 October 2025.

work performance through cameras or other digital systems for certain purposes, as highlighted in the EUROFOUND report.[166] In these instances, a legitimate exercise of the monitoring power normally lies in the security needs of company property and the health of employees. Any monitoring carried out outside these two purposes is illegal. On the other hand, the EUROFOUND report finds that there are States leaving the regulation of this employer power to national or company level collective bargaining. Austria, Belgium, Germany, Sweden and Norway are characterised by a strong industrial relations system. There works councils or trade unions by law bargain over implementation of monitoring systems. The codetermination system that characterises these countries determines the purposes for which the employer can monitor employees.[167] Finally, according to the report, some countries do not fit into either of the two main categories, as they lack specific legislation or a structured system of industrial relations that systematically regulates the employer's monitoring power. In these cases, data protection laws[168] and Courts play a greater role in determining the boundaries of a lawful employer's monitoring power (among others, from the EUROFOUND report: Ireland, Latvia, Lithuania, Luxembourg, the Netherlands).[169]

The EUROFOUND mapping highlights significant differences in how EU Member States regulate the legitimate exercise of the employer's monitoring power, with no uniform legislative standard across their domestic laws. This regulatory diversity, combined with the absence of a clear definition of what is a legitimate exercise in EU labour law, results in varying levels of employee protection at the national level. This lack of clarity is also reflected in cases challenging existing national frameworks before the European Courts.

6 THE BOUNDARIES OF A LEGITIMATE EXERCISE OF THE EMPLOYER'S MONITORING POWER: THE EUROPEAN FUNDAMENTAL RIGHTS FRAMEWORK

While domestic labour laws may differ significantly among EU Member States, all Member States have ratified the European Convention on Human Rights (ECHR), which establishes a common minimum standard of fundamental rights protection across Europe.[170] The ECHR thus applies universally across the Union and sets

166. The following data are retrieved from the EUROFOUND report. *See*: Bulgaria: The Protection of Personal Data Act 2002 (last amended in 2023); Italy: Workers' Statute, Articles 4 and 8 (Law n. 300 of 1970); Portugal: Labour Code, Articles 20, 21, 22 (Law n. 9 of 2007); Romania: Labour Code (Law n. 53 of 2003 and Law n. 190 of 2018) and Spain (Law n. 3 of 2018).
167. Cf. Virginia Doellgast, Ines Wagner and Sean O'Brady, 'Negotiating Limits on Algorithmic Management in Digitalised Services: Cases from Germany and Norway' (2023) 29 Transfer: European Review of Labour and Research 105 https://doi.org/10.1177/10242589221143044 accessed 22 October 2025.
168. When data processing of employees' data is involved: *See* Chapter 6.
169. European Foundation for the Improvement of Living and Working Conditions (n 165) 8-16.
170. Elena Gerasimova and Elena Sychenko, 'Council of Europe: European Social Charter and European Convention on Human Rights' in Beryl Ter Haar and Attila Kun (eds), *EU Collective Labour Law* (Edward Elgar Publishing 2021) https://china.elgaronline.com/view/edcoll/9781788116381/9781788116381.00012.xml accessed 22 October 2025.

essential standards for regulating the exercise of the employer's monitoring power.[171] This means that domestic laws must be interpreted and applied in a manner consistent with the ECHR. Moreover, when a situation falls within the scope of EU law, it is also subject to the Charter of Fundamental Rights of the European Union (CFREU). Article 6(1) of the Consolidated version of the Treaty on European Union (TEU) provides that the EU recognises the rights, freedoms, and principles set out in the Charter of Fundamental Rights of the European Union (CFREU) of 7 December 2000, which shall have the same legal value as the Treaties. In addition, Article 6(3) TEU affirms that the provisions of the ECHR form an integral part of the EU's fundamental rights framework, as they constitute general principles of Union law.[172]

Article 51(1) CFREU provides that the Charter is addressed to 'institutions, bodies, offices and agencies of the Union'. Therefore, their legal acts must comply with the Charter together with those of the EU Member States 'only when they are implementing Union law'. The Explanations of Article 51[173] clarify that 'implementing' has to be broadly interpreted and that the CFREU provisions apply to the Member States when they 'act in the scope of Union law'.[174] Thus, the CFREU fundamental rights cannot be applied in relation to national legislation if the provisions in EU law (for instance, Directive 2000/78/EC on equal treatment) do not provide particular obligations on Member States regarding a specific situation.[175]

Hence, both EU legislation and the national laws of Member States that implement EU law must comply with the standards of protection established by the CFREU

171. Olivier De Schutter, 'Human Rights in Employment Relationships: Contracts as Powers' in Filip Dorssemont, Klaus Lörcher and Isabelle Schömann (eds), *European Convention on Human Rights and the Employment Relation* (Hart Publishing 2013).
172. Article 6 TEU:

'1. The Union recognises the rights, freedoms and principles set out in the Charter of Fundamental Rights of the European Union of 7 December 2000, as adapted at Strasbourg, on 12 December 2007, which shall have the same legal value as the Treaties. The provisions of the Charter shall not extend in any way the competences of the Union as defined in the Treaties. The rights, freedoms and principles in the Charter shall be interpreted in accordance with the general provisions in Title VII of the Charter governing its interpretation and application and with due regard to the explanations referred to in the Charter, that set out the sources of those provisions.
2. The Union shall accede to the European Convention for the Protection of Human Rights and Fundamental Freedoms. Such accession shall not affect the Union's competences as defined in the Treaties.
3. Fundamental rights, as guaranteed by the European Convention for the Protection of Human Rights and Fundamental Freedoms and as they result from the constitutional traditions common to the Member States, shall constitute general principles of the Union's law.'

173. The CFREU is accompanied by Explanatory Notes provided by the authors of the Charter to clarify its provisions. Explanations are not binding but, according to Article 6(1) TEU, they shall be given due regard while interpreting and applying the Charter.
174. Cf. with Article 51(1) CFREU Explanations, which refer to the ECJ case law establishing 'that the requirement to respect fundamental rights defined in the context of the Union is only binding on the Member States when they act in the scope of Union law (…)'.
175. Marta Otto, Frans Pennings and Saskia Peters, 'Fundamental Social Rights in European Union Law' in Teun Jaspers, Frans Pennings and Saskia Peters (eds), *European Labour Law* (2nd edn, Intersentia 2024) 113.

and ECHR.[176] While the EU has not yet acceded to the ECHR,[177] Article 6(3) TEU recognises the ECHR as part of the Union's fundamental rights framework. As such, the ECHR plays a key interpretative role in shaping the content and application of EU law, as well as of national legislation that falls within its scope.[178]

As the European Court of Human Rights (ECtHR) established in *Young, James and Webster v. the United Kingdom* (1981), the obligations arising under the ECHR extend to the regulation of private employment relationships.[179] Even where a dispute involves only private actors, the State remains responsible for ensuring that the legal framework adequately protects the employees' fundamental rights at stake. In this context, the employment relationship, though a private relationship, must be governed by legislation that aligns with the EU's fundamental rights framework.[180] Employees must be protected by provisions that uphold the rights enshrined in the CFREU and the ECHR. At the same time, the legal framework that regulates employer powers – such as the monitoring one – must also be designed and applied in a manner that is consistent with these fundamental rights. Both the CFREU and the ECHR impose negative and positive obligations on Member States: they must not only refrain from interfering with fundamental rights but also take active measures to secure their enjoyment, including in relationships between private parties such as employers and employees.[181] The CFREU and the ECHR therefore function as normative references that shape both the protective obligations owed to employees and the limits within which employer prerogatives must be exercised. In this sense, laws regulating the employer's monitoring power must be consistent with the standards set out in both the CFREU and the ECHR.

In the analysis that follows, I examine *general criteria* that EU law and its national implementations must satisfy to ensure that the employer's monitoring power is exercised in a manner that is legitimate, that is, in full respect of employees' fundamental rights. As I have already explained in Chapter 1 (section 5.2), I focus my analysis on the following selection of fundamental rights and freedoms: *right to privacy and data protection, freedom of expression, freedom of assembly, association, the right to collective bargaining and action, and the right to non-discrimination.* Where the case law of the ECJ is absent or limited, I rely on the jurisprudence of the ECtHR to interpret

176. Under certain conditions and within the scope of EU law, the provisions of the CFREU may have a direct effect on horizontal employment relationships. It is essential that the Charter provision confers a subjective right which can be invoked as such. This is not however my focus in this discussion. On the horizontal effect of fundamental rights, *see*: *ibid.*, 122.

177. 'Major Progress on the Path to EU Accession to the ECHR: Negotiations Concluded at Technical Level in Strasbourg' *Delegation of the European Union to the Council of Europe* (31 March 2023) https://www.eeas.europa.eu/delegations/council-europe/major-progress-path-eu-accession-echr-negotiations-concluded-technical-level-strasbourg_en?s=51 accessed 22 October 2025.

178. De Schutter, 'Human Rights in Employment Relationships: Contracts as Powers' (n 171).

179. *Young, James and Webster v. UK* App(s) Nos 7601/76 and 7806/77 (ECtHR, 13 August 1981) para. 49.

180. In this research, I focus on the exercise of monitoring power by private employers.

181. Olivier De Schutter, 'The CFREU and Its Specific Role to Protect Fundamental Social Rights' in Filip Dorssemont et al. (eds), *The Charter of Fundamental Rights of the European Union and the Employment Relation* (Hart 2019); De Schutter, 'Human Rights in Employment Relationships: Contracts as Powers' (n 171).

and give substance to the fundamental rights that EU law incorporates. Ultimately, in this section, I will look at these rights and their interpretation by the ECJ and the ECtHR in applying the considered rights and freedoms. I aim to understand what is a legitimate exercise of the employer's monitoring power and the standards of protection from a fundamental rights perspective.

6.1 Privacy and Data Protection

The most frequent reference to the employer's monitoring power comes from the ECtHR's case law dealing with Article 8 ECHR ('Right to respect for private and family life').[182] The ECJ, to date, has not dealt with cases on the enjoyment of the right to privacy in relation to the employer's monitoring power.[183]

Article 8(1) ECHR provides that 'Everyone has the right to respect for his private and family life, his home and his correspondence', whereas Article 7 CFREU provides that 'Everyone has the right to respect for his or her private and family life, home and communications.' The right to privacy, also known as 'the right to be left alone', establishes the right for each individual to have a life away from the public sphere.[184] The ECtHR accepts that privacy protection does not simply imply the right not to have external interferences with one's private life. The ECtHR offers a more nuanced idea of private life, acknowledging that there are 'zone[s] of interaction of a person with others, even in a public context, which may fall within the scope of "private life"'.[185] In other words, there are contexts not strictly private where the right to private life and the protection of one's personal data fall under the protection of Article 8(1) ECHR. The right to data protection, distinct from the right to privacy, is recognised in both Article 8 ECHR and Article 8(1) CFREU ('Everyone has the right to the protection of personal data concerning him or her'). The ECtHR stresses that the protection of personal data is often complementary to a person's enjoyment of his or her right to privacy. For instance, in the case *Satakunnan Markkinapörssi Oy and Satamedia Oy v. Finland*, the ECtHR found that Article 8 ECHR includes a right to data protection, enabling individuals to invoke their rights concerning data that, while neutral in isolation, may fall within the scope of Article 8 ECHR when collected, processed, and disseminated in a manner that affects their private life.[186]

The first case in which the right to privacy and data protection at work was recognised under Article 8 ECHR was *Niemietz v. Germany* (1992) of the ECtHR.[187]

182. 'Factsheet: Surveillance at Workplace' (European Court of Human Rights 2023) https://www.echr.coe.int/Documents/FS_Workplace_surveillance_ENG.pdf accessed 22 October 2025.
183. David Mangan, 'From Monitoring of the Workplace to Surveillance of the Workforce' in Tamas Gyulavári and Emanuele Menegatti (eds), *Decent Work in the Digital Age* (Hart Publishing 2022) 321.
184. The 'right to privacy' was first conceptualised by Warren and Braindeis in 1890, *see*: Samuel D Warren and Louis D Brandeis, 'The Right to Privacy' (1890) 4 Harvard Law Review 193 https://doi.org/10.2307/1321160 accessed 22 October 2025.
185. *PG and JH v. UK* (2001) ECHR 546 para. 56.
186. *Satakunnan Markkinapörssi Oy and Satamedia Oy v. Finland* App No 931/13 (ECtHR, 27 June 2017) para. 137.
187. *Niemietz v. Germany* (1992) App No 13710/88 (ECtHR, 16 December 1992).

There, the Court found that although an individual has a contractual duty in a workplace to interact with colleagues and supervisors, the protection of private life persists for employees.[188] In working lives, most people have a significant, if not the greatest, opportunity to develop relationships with the outside world (paragraph 29). In other words, the Court recognised that most people work and that every employee is a unique individual with a work and a private life (paragraph 30). Hence, the protection of private life even within a public context like the workplace falls under the scope of Article 8 ECHR (paragraph 33). However, it is not always possible to make a priori distinctions as to when certain activities performed in the workplace are work-related (e.g., work-related phone call) or non-work-related (e.g., phone call to a family member). Consequently, there could be grounds to limit the right to privacy, such as allowing employers to overhear personal phone calls to relatives without violating the right to privacy. A proper balance between employer needs and employees' rights, according to the Court, is essential (paragraph 29).

In *Sidabras and Dziautas v. Lithuania* (2004), the ECtHR further stressed that privacy and data protection at work extend beyond traditional civil rights.[189] In employment contexts, these rights serve as social rights because their violations can directly affect other fundamental aspects of employment, such as the right to work and fair working conditions. This distinction from the ECtHR suggests that privacy and data protection at work are not solely about individual autonomy and private life but also about securing stable and fair employment. Hendrickx and Van Bever understand privacy violations at work as violations that may have broader repercussions, including risks of unemployment, damage to one's reputation, or unhealthy working conditions; i.e., privacy and data protection could act as protection of the social and economic standing of employees.[190]

Ultimately, the employer's monitoring power (and its legitimate exercise), according to the ECtHR's case law on privacy at work, is an employer's right 'to engage in monitoring [of working activities], including the corresponding disciplinary powers, in order to ensure the smooth operation of the company'.[191] This employer's right is not absolute because it must be balanced with employees' right to enjoy private situations or locations, safeguarded from external interference.[192] Employees also enjoy a right to keep their private sphere under their own control and to decide when and how to

188. *Ibid.*, para. 29.
189. *Sidabras and Dziautas v. Lithuania*, App Nos 55480/00 and 59330/00 (ECtHR, 27 July 2004) paras 57-58. The Court stresses that there is no watertight separation between social and economic rights and the scope of Article 8 ECHR. *See also*: Mangan (n 183) 317.
190. Hendrickx and Van Bever (n 33) 206.
191. *Bărbulescu v. Romania* [2017] App No 61496/08 (ECtHR, 5 September 2017), para. 124.
192. Oskar J Gstrein and Anne Beaulieu, 'How to Protect Privacy in a Datafied Society? A Presentation of Multiple Legal and Conceptual Approaches' (2022) 35 Philosophy & Technology 10 https://link.springer.com/10.1007/s13347-022-00497-4 & https://doi.org/10.1007/s13347-022-00497-4 accessed 22 October 2025.

interact with the rest of society.[193] In the next section, I analyse the conditions which allow for a legitimate interference with employees' privacy rights.

6.1.1 *Restrictions to Employees' Right to Privacy and Data Protection*

Restrictions to employees' rights to privacy and data protection may be permissible under both Article 8(2) ECHR and Articles 7 and 8 of the Charter of Fundamental Rights of the European Union (CFREU) under the conditions posed by Article 52(1) CFREU.

Under Article 8(2) ECHR, any interference by a public authority must 'in accordance with the law' pursue one or more legitimate aims – such as public safety, the prevention of crime, or the protection of the rights and freedoms of others – and be 'necessary in a democratic society', which entails a strict proportionality test to assess whether the restriction on the exercise of the fundamental right is justified.[194] The ECtHR in *Malone v. UK* regards these requirements as preventing the arbitrary exercise of (public or private) power[195] and empowering citizens to reasonably foresee the consequences of their actions.[196] The exception referring to the 'protection of the rights and freedoms of others' suggests that employers have interest and might find legitimate grounds in limiting employees' privacy. Yet, for instance, an employer's right to monitor an employee's work email is not absolute and has to be 'necessary in a democratic society', as clarified by the case *Handyside v. United Kingdom.*[197] Moreover, the proportionality principle requires a connection between a legitimate objective pursued (an employer's interest) and the means used to achieve it (limitation to the right to privacy). Therefore, any limitation to employees' privacy rights under Article 8 ECHR must not only be in accordance with the law and pursue a legitimate aim but also respond to a pressing social need and be strictly proportionate to that aim, thus ensuring that the employer's interference is not merely useful or reasonable, but truly necessary in a democratic society.[198]

Similarly, Article 52(1) CFREU allows for limitations on the rights recognised in Articles 7 CFREU ('Respect for private and family life') and 8 CFREU ('Protection of personal data'), but only if such limitations are provided for by law, respect the essence of the rights, and comply with the principle of proportionality. The protection of the essence of a right implies that even when a legitimate aim is pursued, the core content of the right must remain intact.[199] A limitation that nullifies or renders the right

193. Jeanne Pia Mifsud Bonnici, 'Exploring the Non-absolute Nature of the Right to Data Protection' (2014) 28 International Review of Law, Computers & Technology 131, 133-134 https://doi.org/10.1080/13600869.2013.801590 accessed 22 October 2025.
194. Hendrickx and Van Bever (n 33) 197.
195. *Malone v. the United Kingdom* (1984) App No 8691/79 (ECtHR, 26 April 1985).
196. *Sunday Times v. the United Kingdom* (1980) App No 6538/74 (ECtHR, 6 November 1980).
197. *Handyside v. United Kingdom* (1976) App No 5493/72 (ECtHR, 7 December 1976), paras 48-49.
198. Janneke Gerards, 'How to Improve the Necessity Test of the European Court of Human Rights' (2013) 11 International Journal of Constitutional Law 466 https://doi.org/10.1093/icon/mot004 accessed 22 October 2025.
199. Maja Brkan, 'In Search of the Concept of Essence of EU Fundamental Rights Through the Prism of Data Privacy' [2017] SSRN Electronic Journal http://www.ssrn.com/abstract=2900281 & https://doi.org/10.2139/ssrn.2900281 accessed 22 October 2025.

ineffective would violate the essence of the right and cannot be justified, regardless of its proportionality. In the employment context, this means that employer monitoring – whether for OSH, cybersecurity, or business efficiency – is legitimate only if it is legally grounded, strictly necessary for a legitimate aim, and proportionate in its scope and impact on employees' fundamental rights, taking into account the essence of privacy and data protection rights.

The ECtHR, unlike the ECJ, has a significant thread of case law regarding the restriction of privacy and data protection rights at work.[200] Through this case law, I can highlight how the Court applies these criteria to determine the legitimate exercise of the employer's monitoring power.

For instance, in *Halford* (1997), the Court found that intercepting the applicant's work and private calls violated Article 8 ECHR.[201] The monitoring of Ms Halford's work performance and behaviours was intended to gather evidence against her in an internal procedure related to a missed promotion she had contested. The Court determined that this monitoring was neither lawful nor could it be justified under any of the exceptions in Article 8(2) ECHR concerning the right to respect for private life. Similar findings were made in the 2007 *Copland* case, where monitoring of internet and email use at work was deemed neither legitimate under English law nor necessary in a democratic society.[202] The Court in particular did not deny that monitoring work performance may be (a) 'necessary [monitoring purpose] in a democratic society' (paragraph 48), but confirmed that in the absence of such a strict element of necessity, internet and email monitoring for its own sake is in breach of Article 8 ECHR. In the case *Antović and Mirković v. Montenegro* (2018), the Court confirmed this approach.[203] This case concerned a university installing cameras in teaching rooms for reasons of 'safety of property and people' (paragraph 8). The domestic law (Montenegro 'Personal Data Protection Act') provided for the installation of cameras in workplaces for safety and security of company property, but only if the aims pursued, notably the safety of people or property or the protection of confidential data, cannot be achieved in any other way (paragraph 59). The ECtHR noted, in this regard, that teaching rooms serve as workplaces for teachers, where they interact with students, develop relationships, and shape their social identity (paragraph 44). It followed, according to the Court, that constantly recording employees' actions in their working space was beyond the allowed monitoring and constituted a disproportionate and unnecessary reduction of their right to private life, as 'the interference in question was not in accordance with the law, a fact that suffices to constitute a violation of Article 8' (paragraph 60).

The ECtHR has nevertheless taken less protective stances towards employees when monitoring is aimed at protecting company assets. In the cases *Florindo* (2022), *Lopez Ribalda* (2019) and *Köpke* (2010), the ECtHR held that the right of the employer to protect an economic activity from unlawful activities with covert monitoring falls under the exception of Article 8(2) ECHR 'for the protection of the rights and freedoms

200. Mangan (n 183) 321.
201. *Halford v. United Kingdom* (1997) App No 20605/92 (ECtHR, 25 June 1997).
202. *Copland v. United Kingdom* (2007) App No 62617/00 (ECtHR, 3 April 2007).
203. *Antović and Mirković v. Montenegro* (2018) App No 70838/13 (ECtHR, 28 November 2017).

of others'.[204] These decisions concern employees' stealing at work in the case of *Lopez Ribalda* or *Köpke* and personal use of company tools as in the case of *Florindo*. The Court in all those cases found that the employer's right to property was correctly considered and that a reduction in the privacy of the employees involved was necessary and proportionate.[205] Covert monitoring to protect company property therefore, according to the Strasbourg Court, may be a legitimate exercise of the employer's monitoring power, even if employers had violated domestic laws providing for procedural elements prior to and during the monitoring activity, such as prior notification of the monitoring measure to the employee.[206]

Ultimately, the ECtHR case law on Article 8 ECHR illustrates that the legitimate exercise of the employer's monitoring power depends on compliance with the criteria set out in Article 8(2) ECHR. Any interference with employees' right to privacy must be lawful, necessary, and proportionate to a legitimate aim. The above-mentioned decisions underscore that the employer's monitoring power, even when linked to business interests or workplace security, must be carefully assessed in relation to employees' fundamental right to privacy.

In the next subsection, I analyse the case *Bărbulescu v. Romania* where the Court developed a comprehensive test to assess the legitimate exercise of the employer's monitoring power in relation to employees' right to private life.[207]

6.1.2 *Landmark Case* **Bărbulescu***: Procedural Safeguards for Employer's Monitoring of Employees*

Mr Bărbulescu was dismissed by a private company after disciplinary proceedings. The company found the applicant using his chat business account for personal purposes. Although Mr Bărbulescu was aware of the company policy prohibiting the use of company laptops and internet connection for personal purposes, he was not specifically informed that he had been monitored while having conversations, with either customers or relatives. The Court held that the applicant was unaware of the full extent and specific activities of the employer's monitoring (paragraph 133). While recognising the employer's right to determine the internal policies on how to use corporate tools, the Court acknowledged that the assessment of necessity and proportionality of any monitoring activity should always take into account the protection of private social life in the workplace: 'an employer's instructions cannot reduce private social life in the workplace to zero. Respect for private life and for the privacy of correspondence continues to exist, even if these may be restricted in so far as necessary'.[208] In

204. *Florindo De Almeida Vasconcelos Gramaxo v. Portugal* (2022) App No 26968/16 (ECtHR, 13 December 2022); *López Ribalda and Others v. Spain*, App No 1874/13 and 8567/13 (ECtHR, 17 October 2019); *Köpke v. Germany* (2010) App No 420/07 (ECtHR, 5 October 2010).
205. Michele Molè and David Mangan, '"Just More Surveillance": The ECtHR and Workplace Monitoring' (2023) 14 European Labour Law Journal 694 https://doi.org/10.1177/20319525231201274 accessed 22 October 2025.
206. *Ibid.*
207. *Bărbulescu v. Romania* (2017) App No 61496/08 (ECtHR, 5 September 2017).
208. *Ibid.*, para. 80.

paragraph 118, the ECtHR observes that labour regulation differs in the domestic law of the Council of Europe's States Parties; therefore, no European consensus on the issue is evident in the comparative-law material available to the Court. The CoE States Parties should then be afforded a broad margin of appreciation in regulating how employers can restrict non-professional communications by their employees. Yet, such a discretion is not without limits. CoE States Parties, according to the Court, must ensure that any monitoring measures implemented by employers, regardless of their extent and duration, are accompanied by adequate safeguards against potential abuse (paragraphs 119-120). This requirement aligns with precedents recalled by the Court.[209]

The Court in the Bărbulescu case describes in detail how a State Party should fulfil its positive obligation to ensure the proper application of the employees' right to privacy under Article 8 ECHR. While States retain a certain margin of appreciation, the Court establishes a number of procedural elements to prevent an arbitrary exercise of the employer's monitoring power: the so-called Bărbulescu test.[210] Such a procedural focus established by the Court stresses the importance of the positive obligations side of Article 8 ECHR. It sheds light on the fact that a legitimate exercise of the employer's monitoring power is not just about refraining from interferences with the private sphere of employees, but informing and empowering the subjects under monitoring. In paragraph 121, the Court sets out six key factors to determine whether the intrusion into employees' private life is legitimate, establishing that the domestic authorities should treat the following factors as relevant:

(i) whether the employee has been notified of the possibility that the employer might take measures to monitor correspondence and other communications, and of the implementation of such measures (*Ex ante notification*);

(ii) the extent of the monitoring and the degree of intrusion into the employee's privacy: the Court makes a distinction between monitoring the flow of communications and their content. Whether all communications or only part of them have been monitored should also be taken into account, as should the question of whether the monitoring was limited in time and the number of people who had access to the results. The same applies to the spatial limits to the monitoring. The extent of monitoring and degree of intrusion depend on the context and the purposes pursued by the employer (*Extent of monitoring*);

(iii) whether the employer has provided legitimate reasons to justify monitoring the communications and accessing their actual content. The Court explicitly refers to the fact that '[since] monitoring of the content of communications is by nature a distinctly more invasive method, it requires weightier justification' (*Legitimate reasons*);

209. *Roman Zakharov v. Russia* [GC], App No 47143/06, (ECtHR, 4 December 2015) paras 232-234; *Klass and Others v. Germany*, App No 5029/71 (ECtHR, 6 September 1978) para. 50.
210. Mangan (n 32).

(iv) whether it would have been possible to establish a monitoring system based on less intrusive methods and measures than directly accessing the content of the employee's communications. In this connection, there should be an assessment in the light of the particular circumstances of each case of whether the aim pursued by the employer could have been achieved without directly accessing the full contents of the employee's communications (*Less invasive methods*);

(v) the consequences of the monitoring for the employee subjected to it, and the use made by the employer of the results of the monitoring operation, in particular whether the results were used to achieve the declared aim of the measure (*Impact on the employee*);

(vi) whether the employee was provided with adequate safeguards, especially in the case of highly intrusive monitoring operations. According to the Court, 'such safeguards should in particular ensure that the employer cannot access the actual content of the communications concerned unless the employee has been notified in advance of that eventuality' (*Provision of adequate safeguards*).

The *Bărbulescu* case is a landmark in defining the boundaries of a legitimate exercise of the employer's monitoring power under Article 8 ECHR. It establishes a clear procedural framework that domestic authorities must follow to balance the privacy rights of employees with employers' interests. As already argued in the scholarship, if consistently applied, this test could offer actionable guidelines to State Parties for regulating the introduction of new surveillance technologies at work, mindful of both employees' rights and employer interests.[211]

6.2 Freedom of Expression

Freedom of expression is a second fundamental right that provides important standards of protection and outlines what constitutes a legitimate exercise of the employer's monitoring power. Article 10(1) ECHR and Article 11(1) CFREU provide that 'Everyone has the right to freedom of expression. This right shall include freedom to hold opinions and to receive and impart information and ideas without interference by public authority and regardless of frontiers.' Freedom of expression is considered by the ECtHR a fundamental aspect of a democratic society and essential for individual self-fulfilment.[212] The ECtHR has upheld the rights of employees to be protected from disciplinary actions or dismissal based on their political views,[213] critical comments about the employer or colleagues,[214] and has provided strong protection for

211. *See* in this regard: Mangan (n 183); Mangan (n 32); Molè and Mangan (n 205).
212. *Lingens v. Austria* (1986) 8 EHRR 407, para. 41.
213. *Vogt v. Germany* (1995) App No 17851/91 (ECtHR, 30 November 1995) para. 61.
214. *Fuentes Bobo v. Spain* App No 39293/98 (ECtHR, 29 February 2000); *Vellutini and Michel v. France* App No 32820/09 (ECtHR, 6 October 2011).

whistle-blowers.[215] This underscores the idea that an individual's right to express themselves should not be unduly restricted by an employer's power – such as the monitoring one. This analysis is based on both ECtHR and ECJ case law, particularly on the ECJ *Connolly v. Commission* case (2001).[216] This case law provided for important elements in assessing what is a legitimate interference with employees' freedom of expression at work.

Both the ECtHR and the ECJ agree that the scope of this freedom covers any 'information' or 'ideas' that are not only favourably received or regarded as inoffensive or as a matter of indifference but also those that 'offend, shock or disturb'.[217] Therefore, any individual employee statement, whether true, false, expressing an opinion or a judgment through any means of communication, may fall under the scope of this freedom.

The case law focuses predominantly on two employer's monitoring power purposes: monitoring employees' performance and behaviours. Monitoring activities are usually aimed at checking statements made publicly by employees on social networks (such as *Facebook, X, LinkedIn* and so on).[218] As private individuals, we frequently write personal opinions or judgments on our public profiles. In some circumstances, an employer may have a legitimate interest in protecting himself or herself from these opinions (among others, protecting his or her reputation).[219] Hence, more and more cases of disciplinary sanctions (even dismissals) for opinions or judgments expressed publicly on social networks, even if expressed outside working hours, are under the scrutiny of the European Courts.[220]

6.2.1 Restrictions to Employees' Freedom of Expression

Freedom of expression, like many fundamental rights, is not absolute and can be subject to limitations. Article 10(2) ECHR stipulates that any restrictions on this freedom must be prescribed by law and necessary in a democratic society, for the protection of the rights and freedoms of others, among other protected general

215. *Heinisch v. Germany* App No 28274/08 (ECtHR, 21 July 2011). Since 2019 a Directive on whistleblowing is enforced in the European Union. Directive (EU) 2019/1937 of the European Parliament and of the Council of 23 October 2019 on the protection of persons who report breaches of Union law.
216. Case C-274/99P, *Connolly v. Commission* [2001].
217. *Handyside v. United Kingdom* (1976) App No 5493/72 (ECtHR, 7 December 1976), para. 49; Case C-274/99P, *Connolly v. Commission* [2001] para. 43. The freedom of expression has also a collective dimension, which closely connects with freedom of assembly and association at work. I will elaborate further on it in the next section (6.3). Here it is worth emphasising that the freedom of expression is an essential component of trade union freedoms. The exercise of rights such as the right to receive information and be consulted and to bargain collectively (Article 27 CFREU, Article 28 CFREU) or to form and join a trade union (Article 11 ECHR, Article 12 CFREU) is complemented by this freedom.
218. Martin E Risak, 'Employer Acquisition and Use of the Contents of Employee Social Media: An Overview' (2018) 39 Comparative Labor Law & Policy Journal 441.
219. Diego Alvarez Alonso, 'Social Media in the Employment Relationship Context: A Typology of Emerging Conflicts' (2018) 39 Comparative Labor Law & Policy Journal 287, 289.
220. Mantouvalou (n 34).

interests.[221] Limiting the enjoyment of this freedom undergoes the same conditions imposed by Article 8(2) ECHR on the right to privacy and data protection: the restriction must not only be in accordance with the law and pursue a legitimate aim but also respond to a pressing social need and be strictly proportionate to that aim, thus ensuring that the employer's interference is not merely useful or reasonable, but truly necessary in a democratic society. Article 52(1) CFREU provides that the same criteria apply to the limitations to freedom of expression (Article 11 CFREU), with the addition that the essence of a right (such as employees' freedom of expression) must remain intact even when a legitimate aim is pursued. This means that if any restriction respecting the three criteria (prescribed by law, pursuing a legitimate aim, necessary and proportionate) still promotes a 'chilling effect' in the enjoyment of this right, i.e., a limitation that nullifies or renders the right ineffective, this cannot be justified, regardless of its proportionality.[222] The restriction must be necessary and must genuinely meet objectives of general interest recognised by the Union or protect the rights and freedoms of others.

The ECtHR applies the criteria provided for by Article 10(2) ECHR,[223] and since the *Connolly* case,[224] the ECJ has consistently applied as well the test developed on the basis of Article 10(2) ECHR and Article 52(1) CFREU.[225] Both European Courts, according to Cobbaut, apply the same criteria:[226]

- *must be prescribed by law*. Both Courts find that any restriction of the freedom of expression must be worded precisely in the law or interpreted narrowly.[227] Freedom of expression is typically limited by anti-discrimination directives

221. Article 10(2) ECHR: 'The exercise of these freedoms, since it carries with it duties and responsibilities, may be subject to such formalities, conditions, restrictions or penalties as are prescribed by law and are necessary in a democratic society, in the interests of national security, territorial integrity or public safety, for the prevention of disorder or crime, for the protection of health or morals, for the protection of the reputation or rights of others, for preventing the disclosure of information received in confidence, or for maintaining the authority and impartiality of the judiciary.'
222. Brkan (n 199).
223. *See*, for instance: *Hrachya Harutyunyan v. Armenia* (2014) App No 15028/16 (ECtHR, 27 August 2024); *Herbai v. Hungary* (2019) App No 11608/15 (ECtHR, 5 November 2019); *Marunić v. Croatia* (2017) App No 51706/11 (ECtHR, 28 March 2017); *Kharlamov v. Russia*, App No 27447/07 (ECtHR, 8 October 2015); *Heinisch v. Germany* (2011) App No 28274/08 (ECtHR, 21 July 2011).
224. Connolly was suspended in September 1995 as an official of the European Unions and then dismissed the following February on the grounds that he had failed to secure the necessary permission from his superiors for the publication of the book he wrote during unpaid leave. The ECJ held that the sanction was a disproportionate reduction of his freedom of expression. *See*: Case C-274/99P, *Connolly v. Commission* [2001] para. 43.
225. Article 52(2) of the Charter of Fundamental Rights of the European Union adds an extra step in assessing limitations on rights. It requires the court to first check if the essence of a right is respected before considering the necessity and proportionality of any limitation. If the limitation undermines the core content of the right, the analysis ends. Only if the essence remains intact does the court proceed to assess whether the limitation is justified.
226. Elliot Cobbaut, 'Article 11: Freedom of Expression and Information' in Filip Dorssemont et al. (eds), *The Charter of Fundamental Rights of the European Union and the Employment Relation* (Hart 2019) 305-306.
227. *Ibid.*, 305.

(Directive 2000/43/EC prohibiting discrimination on the grounds of race or ethnic origins; Directive 2000/78/EC establishing a general framework for equal treatment in employment and occupation). Their application ensures that discriminating statements are forbidden in workplaces as well. Other norms provide for confidentiality duties such as in the case of trade secrets (Directive 2016/943 on the protection of undisclosed know-how and business information (trade secrets) against their unlawful acquisition, use and disclosure);

- *must be justified by the legitimate aim of protecting the rights of others*. For example, according to the above-mentioned EU legislation, an employer may have a legitimate interest in monitoring employees' social media activities to prevent certain information relating to his or her economic activity from circulating as provided for by the Trade Secrets Directive (Directive 2016/963). However, it is unlikely that the employer under EU law has a legitimate interest in sanctioning an employee – after monitoring his or her social media activities – for posting on social networks the union activities promoted in his or her workplace.[228] This ultimately means that in the latter case, the employer is not pursuing a legitimate aim and is violating 'the rights of others', such as the employee's freedom of expression on social media on his or her activities;
- *must be necessary and proportionate*. While both the ECJ and the ECtHR assess the proportionality of restrictions on freedom of expression in employment contexts, the ECJ also considers the protection of the essence of fundamental rights. Article 52(1) CFREU states that any limitation on the exercise of rights must respect the essence of those rights. In contrast, Article 10(2) ECHR does not explicitly include this concept. The inclusion of the essence clause signals a stricter threshold: even if a restriction pursues a legitimate aim and is proportionate, it may still be invalid if it compromises the core of the right itself. States must therefore ensure that their domestic legal frameworks align with these standards, upholding both proportionality and the inviolability of the right's essence. In practice, both Courts undertake a contextual analysis of the contested expression and the employer's response. Relevant factors include the employee's role and responsibilities (e.g., managerial or public-facing positions), the form and tone of the expression (e.g., violent or offensive language), and its content. These are balanced against the employer's interests, such as reputational harm or the maintenance of a cohesive workplace, particularly in cases involving the monitoring of employees' social media activity or disciplinary sanctions like dismissal. For instance, the ECtHR has upheld dismissals where an employee holding a high-profile position, such as a public relations manager, made statements that damaged the organisation's reputation.[229] Ultimately, both Courts weigh the seriousness of the harm caused by the expression against the consequences of the restriction or

228. Alonso (n 219) 317.
229. *Obst v. Germany* App No 425/03 and *Schuth v. Germany*, App No 1620/03 (ECtHR, 23 September 2010); *see also Szima v. Hungary* (2012) App No 29723/11 (ECtHR, 9 October 2012).

sanction imposed, ensuring that the measures do not disproportionately impact the employee's fundamental rights.[230]

To conclude this section, using monitoring technologies that limit employees' freedom of expression may pursue a legitimate aim and constitute a legitimate exercise of the employer's monitoring power, may it be for a socially safe working environment or business reputation. The exercise of the employer's monitoring power, including the use of monitoring technologies, should always be carefully assessed to ensure that it is prescribed by the law, pursuing a legitimate aim, and necessary and proportionate to that aim. This applies not only to disciplinary sanctions resulting from monitoring but also to the entire monitoring process itself, ensuring that any interference with employees' freedom of expression remains justified. The application of Article 10(2) ECHR and Article 52 CFREU plays an important role, as it can prevent imposing an employer's moralistic views on how employees should conduct their lives, or prevent the imposition of majority opinions on individuals, minorities or other groups.[231] The function of this right is also closely intertwined with a collective dimension, i.e., protecting the freedom of expression of groups of people at work, such as trade unions.

6.3 Freedom of Assembly, Association and the Right of Collective Bargaining and Action

Freedom of expression, in its collective dimension, is closely intertwined with the so-called trade union freedoms, i.e., the freedom of assembly and association in trade union organisations.[232] Article 11 ECHR and Article 12 CFREU provide that everyone can freely and peacefully assemble and associate with others, with a specific reference to the right to form and to join trade unions for the protection of employees' interests.[233] Given the explicit reference in these Articles, there is a unanimous consensus that they establish rights to form and to join or not to join trade unions.[234] Moreover, Article 28 CFREU ('Right of collective bargaining and action') provides that 'Workers and employers, or their respective organisations, have, in accordance with Union law and national laws and practices, the right to negotiate and conclude

230. *See* more specifically: T-76/03, *Herber Meister v. OHMI* [2004] paras 167-168.
231. Mantouvalou (n 34) 125.
232. *See,* among others: *Paolomo Sanchez and others v. Spain* (2012) App No 28955/06 (ECtHR, 12 September 2011). Antoine Jacobs, 'Article 12: Freedom of Assembly and of Association' in Filip Dorssemont et al. (eds), *The Charter of Fundamental Rights of the European Union and the Employment Relation* (Hart 2019) 318.
233. Article 11(1) ECHR: 'Everyone has the right to freedom of peaceful assembly and to freedom of association with others, including the right to form and to join trade unions for the protection of his interests.' Article 12(1) CFREU: 'Everyone has the right to freedom of peaceful assembly and to freedom of association at all levels, in particular in political, trade union and civic matters, which implies the right of everyone to form and to join trade unions for the protection of his or her interests.'
234. Jacobs, 'Article 12: Freedom of Assembly and of Association' (n 232) 321.

collective agreements at the appropriate levels and, in cases of conflicts of interest, to take collective action to defend their interests, including strike action.'[235]

Whether collective bargaining and action is also protected under Article 11 ECHR has been the subject of extensive debate in case law and academic literature, reflecting the tension between fundamental social rights and economic freedoms within the ECHR.[236] The ECtHR has in fact granted a wide margin of appreciation to the State Parties to define what actions trade unions can pursue to defend their interests. In the *Schmidt and Dahlström* case, the ECtHR stressed that it is up to the single CoE State Party to determine the means through which the trade unions can defend their interests (right of collective action, right to strike, right to bargain collectively).[237] On the ECJ's side, the so-called Viking-Laval Quartet[238] found in four different cases that the extent and exercise of collective labour rights (such as the right to bargain collectively and the right to strike) is to be balanced against the free movement of services in the EU and the right to conduct a business (Article 16 CFREU).[239] In these four cases, trade unions took collective actions (striking and requests of collective bargaining) against the industrial plans of the companies that – otherwise – would have harmed employees' rights. The ECJ jurisprudence, in more recent years, has confirmed that Article 16 CFREU (Right to conduct a business) should always be read together with fundamental labour rights, specifying that starting a business is not an absolute right and a fair balance with employees' rights is necessary.[240]

Following the above-mentioned ECJ jurisprudence, the ECtHR delivered two important rulings on collective action and collective bargaining as fundamental rights guaranteed by the European Charters, including Article 11 ECHR.[241] In the *Demir and*

235. Filip Dorssemont and Marco Rocca, 'Article 28: Right to Collective Bargaining and Action' in Filip Dorssemont et al. (eds), *The Charter of Fundamental Rights of the European Union and the Employment Relation* (Hart 2019).
236. Antoine Jacobs, 'Article 11 ECHR: The Right to Bargain Collectively under Article 11 ECHR' in Filip Dorssemont, Klaus Lörcher and Isabelle Schömann (eds), *European Convention on Human Rights and the Employment Relation* (Hart Publishing 2013); Filip Dorssemont, 'The Right to Take Collective Action under Article 11 ECHR' in Filip Dorssemont, Klaus Lörcher and Isabelle Schömann (eds), *European Convention on Human Rights and the Employment Relation* (Hart Publishing 2013); Gerasimova and Sychenko (n 170).
237. *Schmidt And Dahlström v. Sweden* (1976) App No 5589/72 (ECtHR, 6 February 1976).
238. Case C-438/05 *The International Transport Workers' Federation and The Finnish Seamen's Union v. Viking Line ABP and OÜ Viking Line Eesti* [2007] ECLI:EU:C:2007:772; Case C-341/05 *Laval un Partneri Ltd v. Svenska Byggnadsarbetareförbundet, Svenska Byggnadsarbetareförbundets avdelning 1, Byggettan and Svenska Elektrikerförbundet* [2007] ECLI:EU:C:2007:809; Case C-346/06 *Dirk Rüffert v. Land Niedersachsen* [2008] ECLI:EU:C:2008:189; Case C-51/08 *European Commission v. Grand Duchy of Luxemburg* [2011] ECLI:EU:C:2011:336.
239. Christian Joerges and Florian Rödl, 'Informal Politics, Formalised Law and the "Social Deficit" of European Integration: Reflections after the Judgments of the ECJ in *Viking* and *Laval*' (2009) 15 European Law Journal 1 https://doi.org/10.1111/j.1468-0386.2008.00448.x accessed 22 October 2025.
240. Case C-201/15 *Anonymi Geniki Etairia Tsimenton Iraklis (AGET Iraklis) v. Ypourgos Ergasias, Koinonikis Asfalisis kai Koinonikis Allilengyis* [2016] ECLI:EU:C:2016:972. *See also*: Antoine Jacobs, 'The Future of the Charter on Fundamental Rights of the European Union' in Filip Dorssemont et al. (eds), *The Charter of Fundamental Rights of the European Union and the Employment Relation* (Hart 2019) 40-41.
241. Klaus Lörcher, 'The New Social Dimension of the Jurisprudence of the European Court of Human Rights (ECtHR): The Demir and Baykara Judgement, Its Methodology and Follow-Up'

Baykara (2008) and *Enerji Yapi-Yol Sen* (2009) judgments,[242] the Strasbourg Court moved away from its previous restrictive view on the material scope of Article 11 ECHR and held that the right to bargain collectively and the right to strike (and more broadly a right to collective action) are foundational and intrinsic elements of the right to form and join trade unions.[243] The *Demir* and *Enerji* cases are often referred to as the cases that brought the social turn of the ECtHR – traditionally oriented towards the protection of civil and political rights/freedoms.[244] The ECtHR based its new interpretation of Article 11 ECHR on ILO Conventions 87, 98 and 151, providing for minimum standards on collective bargaining and freedom of trade union organisations.[245]

From this overview of ECtHR and ECJ case law, I can conclude that there exist essential standards of protection concerning these freedoms in relation to the employer's monitoring power. National laws that allow employers to monitor trade union membership or activities must balance employers' interests with the rights established in Articles 11 ECHR and 12 CFREU. For instance, the ECtHR has found that employer's monitoring of union membership and employees' union activities may violate Article 11 ECHR, but only if this disclosure concretely prevents trade union activities from happening. If the employer's access to this information is for retaliation against union members, that could constitute a disproportionate interference with Article 11 ECHR.[246] According to Jacobs, monitoring practices that discourage union participation or create a chilling effect on the right of association might be deemed unlawful, as they undermine the protections envisaged by these articles.[247]

While the ECtHR acknowledges a margin of appreciation for CoE State Parties in regulating trade union activities and employer's interference on them, it has also recognised that monitoring of union membership or activities may violate Article 11 ECHR if it discourages participation in those activities, thus creating, as noticed by Jacobs, a chilling effect. The employer's access to such information must be justified by a legitimate aim and be necessary and proportionate to that aim. If monitoring practices are used to retaliate against union members or restrict their ability to take collective

---

in Filip Dorssemont, Klaus Lörcher and Isabelle Schömann (eds), *European Convention on Human Rights and the Employment Relation* (Hart Publishing 2013).

242. *Demir and Baykara v. Turkey* (2008) App No 34503/97 (ECtHR, 12 November 2008); *Enerji Yapi-Yol Sen v. Turkey* (2009) App No 68959/01 (ECtHR, 21 April 2009).

243. In the case of *Demir* and *Baykara*, the Court found that the invalidation of a collective agreement by the employer (the Turkish government) was against a right to collectively bargain under Article 11 ECHR. This principle was further reaffirmed in the *Enerji Yapi-Yol Sen v. Turkey* case, where trade union members received disciplinary sanctions following a strike. The Court emphasised that a right to collective action is a constitutional element of any existing trade union. Dorssemont (n 236) 336-339; Jacobs, 'Article 12: Freedom of Assembly and of Association' (n 232) 321; Jacobs, 'Article 11 ECHR: The Right to Bargain Collectively under Article 11 ECHR' (n 236) 312.

244. Lörcher (n 241).

245. *Ibid.*, 6-7; Vincenzo Pietrogiovanni, 'Collective Bargaining: (Not Just) a Fundamental Right' in Beryl Ter Haar and Attila Kun (eds), *EU Collective Labour Law* (Edward Elgar Publishing 2021) 76-77 https://china.elgaronline.com/view/edcoll/9781788116381/9781788116381.00010.xml accessed 22 October 2025.

246. *National Association of Teachers in Further and Higher Education v. UK* (1998) App No 28910/95 (ECtHR, 16 April 1998).

247. Jacobs, 'Article 12: Freedom of Assembly and of Association' (n 232).

action, they would likely constitute an unlawful interference with trade union rights. Therefore, any monitoring measures must be carefully balanced to ensure they do not undermine employees' ability to organise and advocate for their interests.

6.3.1 Restrictions to Employees' Freedoms of Assembly, Association and the Right of Collective Bargaining and Action

Article 11(2) ECHR lays down the same conditions as for Articles 8 and 10 of the Convention: any restrictions on trade union freedoms must be prescribed by law, must pursue a legitimate aim, and must be necessary and proportionate to the objective pursued. As discussed in the previous sections, Article 52(1) CFREU provides the same conditions for limiting the enjoyment of the corresponding rights of Article 12 CFREU, with the additional requirement that any limitation must respect the essence of those rights and freedoms.

It is worth noting how in the *Demir* case the ECtHR affirmed that restrictions on the enjoyment of the rights under Article 11 ECHR 'must not impair the very essence of the right to organise'.[248] I emphasise that this principle establishes a clear threshold: absolute bans on collective bargaining or strike action cannot be justified under any of the exceptions listed in Article 11(2) ECHR, as they undermine the essence of the right to join and form trade unions. In *Demir*, the Court found that sanctioning employees for engaging in collective action was not a proportionate means of achieving the employer's stated aim - protecting the public interest (both cases involved civil servants). Despite recognising a broad margin of appreciation for states in regulating collective labour rights, the ECtHR concluded that such restrictions must nonetheless respect the core content of the rights at stake. This position aligns with the standard under Article 52(1) CFREU, which similarly prohibits limitations that compromise the essence of fundamental rights and freedoms.

By applying Article 11(2) ECHR, the reasoning in *Demir*, and Article 52(1) CFREU to the monitoring of trade union activities, it becomes clear that any restrictions on collective rights must be lawful, necessary, proportionate to a legitimate aim. Moreover, any limitation to these fundamental freedoms must respect the essence of those rights and freedoms, without which they would be devoid of substance. The exercise of an employer's monitoring power that results in a chilling effect on trade union rights would likely fail this test, as it undermines the core of the right to collective action. The importance of protecting the essence of these rights was also stressed in 2017, when the WP29 emphasised in its opinion on data processing at work that any exercise of the employer's monitoring power through surveillance technologies would likely strengthen a chilling effect, undermining employees' ability to engage in confidential communication about trade union activities and to participate in employees'

248. *Demir and Baykara v. Turkey* (2008) App No 34503/97 (ECtHR, 12 November 2008), para. 97. *See also* para. 144: 'the Court does not accept restrictions that affect the essential elements of trade-union freedom, without which that freedom would become devoid of substance'.

associations.[249] On this basis, any monitoring not respectful of the criteria established by the ECHR (as interpreted by the ECtHR) and CFREU is to be regarded as an illegitimate exercise of power if it disproportionately interferes with employees' rights to assemble and associate. For instance, an employer might implement GPS tracking devices on company vehicles or mobile apps that monitor the location and activity of employees during non-working hours. If the employer were to use this data to identify employees attending trade union activities or protests, this constitutes an illegitimate exercise of the employer's monitoring power. Employers' monitoring practices over trade union activities could be justified, for instance, by security reasons if there is strong evidence that the collective actions are aimed solely at harming economic activity in an unreasonable manner. However, it is essential to stress that strikes and other forms of collective action that cause economic disruption may still be legitimate expressions of employees' rights.[250]

Finally, violations of trade union freedoms may co-occur with violations of employees' right to privacy or freedom of expression and are therefore assessed using the relevant tests analysed in the previous sections. For example, an employer investigating employees' trade union membership is eligible for a violation of the right to privacy, or an employee sanctioned for distributing electoral propaganda may invoke freedom of expression in conjunction with his or her right to non-discrimination, which I analyse in the next section.[251]

6.4 Non-discrimination

The principle of non-discrimination serves as an important limitation for the legitimate exercise of an employer's monitoring power. Article 14 ECHR and Articles 20-21 CFREU, in fact, prohibit any form of discrimination based on 'sex, race, colour, language, religion, political or other opinion, national or social origin, association with a national minority, property, birth or other status'. Although Article 14 contains a list of discrimination grounds, it is not to be interpreted as a closed list; the case law, as analysed by McGoldrick, has systematically included discriminatory grounds not mentioned in the Convention, such as sexual orientation (mentioned in Article 21 CFREU) or trade union membership.[252]

Both Directives 2000/78/EC and 2000/43/EC regard the right to non-discrimination as a 'universal right' in their respective recitals.[253] Its application is

249. Article 29 Data Protection Working Party, 'Opinion 02/2017 on Data Processing at Work' (n 21) 9.
250. Dorssemont (n 236) 343; Jacobs, 'The Future of the Charter on Fundamental Rights of the European Union' (n 240) 40-41.
251. Mantouvalou (n 34) 123-124.
252. Dominic McGoldrick, 'The Development and Status of Sexual Orientation Discrimination under International Human Rights Law' (2016) 16 Human Rights Law Review 613 https://doi.org/10.1093/hrlr/ngw030 accessed 22 October 2025.
253. Council Directive 2000/78/EC of 27 November 2000 establishing a general framework for equal treatment in employment and occupation; Council Directive 2000/43/EC of 29 June 2000 implementing the principle of equal treatment between persons irrespective of racial or ethnic origin.

deeply rooted in the Treaties of the European Union. Article 2 TEU prescribes that the Union is founded on the respect of human dignity, equality, the rule of law and the rights of persons belonging to minorities. The obligations imposed on Member States by Articles 14 ECHR and 20-21 CFREU encompass both negative and positive dimensions. Therefore, Member States are prevented from engaging in any unjustified discrimination and shall fulfil their negative obligation to refrain from actions that undermine equality. However, they are also required to undertake positive measures to promote and achieve equality. This dual obligation ensures that non-discrimination is not only a protective right but also an active commitment to fostering an inclusive environment for all individuals.[254]

The literature usually differentiates between direct and indirect discrimination.[255] Direct discrimination occurs when employees are subjected to different monitoring measures based on a discriminatory ground, like trade union membership. Therefore, monitoring communications specifically of trade union members would constitute direct discrimination in workplace monitoring.[256] However, when a seemingly neutral monitoring policy disproportionately impacts a specific group, indirect discrimination occurs. For instance, implementing productivity monitoring that inadvertently disadvantages employees with disabilities could constitute indirect discrimination and ultimately an illegitimate exercise of the employer's monitoring power.[257]

The right to non-discrimination is closely intertwined with the other fundamental rights discussed here. Monitoring confidential conversations of trade unionists could potentially violate the right to privacy or infringe upon the right to freedom of expression if employers penalise trade unionists for publicly expressing their views on corporate matters. In *Danilenko and others v. Russia*, for example, the ECtHR found that following a collective action initiated by a trade union, an employer had systematically monitored and penalised his employees who were also members of this trade union in the annual evaluations or dismissed them in collective dismissal procedures. The Court concluded for a joint violation of Articles 11 and 14 ECHR because Russia had failed to provide judicial protection against discrimination on the basis of trade union membership.[258]

6.4.1 Restrictions to Employees' Right to Non-discrimination

Both the ECJ and the ECtHR in their case law hold that employees in comparable situations must not be treated differently and that different situations must not be

254. Niklas Bruun, 'Articles 20 and 21: Equality and Non-discrimination' in Filip Dorssemont et al. (eds), *The Charter of Fundamental Rights of the European Union and the Employment Relation* (Hart 2019) 385.
255. Sandra Fredman, *Discrimination Law* (3rd edn, Oxford University Press 2022) 247-313; Bruun (n 254) 396; Niklas Bruun, 'Prohibition of Discrimination under Article 14 European Convention on Human Rights' in Filip Dorssemont, Klaus Lörcher and Isabelle Schömann (eds), *European Convention on Human Rights and the Employment Relation* (Hart Publishing 2013).
256. Fredman (n 255) 250.
257. *Ibid.*, 248-249.
258. *Danilenko and others v. Russia* (2005) App No 67336/01 (ECtHR, 6 July 2005).

treated in the same way.[259] Where it can be shown that a particular practice places persons with specific characteristics at a particular disadvantage compared to others, it is necessary to assess whether the employer can objectively justify that practice. This requires the employer to demonstrate that any differential treatment pursues a legitimate aim.[260] According to ECJ case law, employers may rely on a range of legitimate aims, including, for example, encouraging recruitment or promoting labour market flexibility.[261] The objective justification test requires then the assessment of whether the measures adopted are both 'appropriate' and 'necessary' in pursuing those legitimate aims, in line with the principle of proportionality. Necessity, more specifically, requires the recognition of whether other measures would have prevented the discriminatory impact.[262]

In this context, if the employer's monitoring activities result in different treatment of employees, this treatment must be justified by being grounded in a legitimate aim, such as ensuring workplace security or performance standards, and an assessment of whether the concrete measures adopted are appropriate and necessary in pursuing those aims. Discrimination arising from monitoring that cannot be objectively justified under this test (for instance, the differential treatment is solely based on explicitly forbidden discrimination grounds) would be considered unlawful, as it undermines employees' rights to non-discrimination.[263]

For example, a highly specialised employee who is required to keep industrial or state secrets may be subject to closer tracking and monitoring of his or her communications compared to colleagues who do not have access to confidential information. This would be justified as a form of differential treatment based on the specific requirements of their role.[264] The Trade Secrets Directive acknowledges that confidentiality duties may be imposed on certain employees to protect secret information.[265] However, when there is an insufficient link with the legitimate business interest of the employer and the means used, such an exercise of the employer's monitoring power may be considered discriminatory.[266] Discrimination also occurs when it is established that there is no reasonable relationship of proportionality between the monitoring

259. Bruun (n 254) 389. *See* among others: *Thlimmenos v. Greece* (2000) App No 34369/97 (ECtHR, 6 April 2000); Case C-303/05 *Advocaten voor de Wereld VZW* ECLI:EU:C:2007:261.
260. *Runkee and White v. UK* (2007) Apps nos 42949/98 and 51134/99 (ECtHR, 10 May 2007), para. 35.
261. Case C-335/11 and C-337/11 *HK Danmark v. Dansk almennyttigt Boligselskab* and *HK Danmark v. Dansk Arbejdsgiverforening*, ECLI:EU:C:2013:222, para. 82; Case C-270/16, *Carlos Enrique Ruiz Conejero v. Ferroser Servicios Auxiliares SA and Ministerio Fiscal*, ECLI:EU:C:2018:17, para. 44.
262. Mark Bell and Ann Numhauser-Henning, 'Equal Treatment' in Teun Jaspers, Frans Pennings and Saskia Peters (eds), *European Labour Law* (2nd edn, Intersentia 2024) 284-286.
263. Cf. with Janneke Gerards, 'The Discrimination Grounds of Article 14 of the European Convention on Human Rights' (2013) 13 Human Rights Law Review 99 https://doi.org/10.1093/hrlr/ngs044 accessed 22 October 2025.
264. Alonso (n 219) 309.
265. Directive (EU) 2016/943 of the European Parliament and of the Council of 8 June 2016 on the protection of undisclosed know-how and business information (trade secrets) against their unlawful acquisition, use and disclosure.
266. *I.B. v. Greece* (2013) App No 552/10 (ECtHR, 3 October 2013) *Emel Boyraz v. Turkey* (2014) App No 61960/08 (ECtHR, 2 December 2014).

measure and the aims pursued.[267] Thus, monitoring employees' communications - particularly when that employee has confidentiality obligations - could be deemed disproportionate if, for instance, the extent of monitoring differs based on an unjustified employer's belief in each employee's ability to maintain business secrets.

Ultimately, to have a legitimate exercise of the employer's monitoring power, any deviation from the prohibition of discrimination must meet specific criteria: it must not be solely based on an explicitly forbidden discriminatory ground, it must comply with the requirement of legality (i.e., the law permits differences in treatment), pursue a legitimate aim, and undergo an assessment of the necessity and proportionality of the measures taken in relation to that aim. This ensures that any distinctions made are aligned with the overarching principles of non-discrimination, ultimately ensuring a legitimate exercise of the employer's monitoring power.

7 A LEGITIMATE EXERCISE OF THE EMPLOYER'S MONITORING POWER: MONITORING PRACTICES RESPECTFUL OF EMPLOYEES' FUNDAMENTAL RIGHTS

Despite the fact that the employer's monitoring power is loosely defined in EU labour law and that the Member States apply varying regulatory approaches, important standards and conditions for its legitimate exercise can be found in the European fundamental rights framework. As mentioned above, by 'legitimate' I mean that monitoring practices must respect the fundamental rights of employees, including privacy and data protection, freedom of expression, freedom of assembly and association, the right to collective bargaining and action, and non-discrimination. Monitoring that fails to respect these rights cannot be deemed legitimate.

The following *general criteria*, established by the ECHR and CFREU and interpreted by the respective Courts, require that any limitation to the above analysed rights and freedoms must be:

- *prescribed by law*;
- *pursue a legitimate aim*, such as public safety, protection of the rights and freedoms of others;
- *necessary and proportionate*: the measure must be necessary in a democratic society and proportionate to the aim pursued;
- *respecting the essence of those rights and freedoms:* Article 52(1) CFREU provides that any restriction to CFREU rights must not affect the core content or fundamental nature of the right in question, even when it pursues a legitimate aim and it is necessary and proportionate.

In the previous subsections (6.1 to 6.4), I identified more structured elaborations of these *general criteria* for each fundamental right in a work context, as developed through ECtHR and ECJ case law. These elaborations tailor the overarching principles - such as legality, legitimate aim, necessity, and proportionality - to the specific

267. Bruun (n 255) 374.

contours of each right or freedom, providing a more precise framework for assessing what constitutes a legitimate restriction on employees' enjoyment of those rights in the context of employee monitoring. I summarise them in Table 3.1.

Table 3.1 Criteria for a Legitimate Exercise of the Employer's Monitoring Power

Fundamental Right	*Legal Basis*	*Additional Notes/Right-Specific Criteria*
Privacy and Data Protection	Article 8 ECHR, Articles 7, 8 CFREU	The ECtHR's *Bărbulescu v. Romania* judgment introduced more specific criteria that need to be taken into account for assessing proportionality and procedural guarantees against arbitrariness, including: 1. *ex ante* notification; 2. extent of monitoring; 3. legitimate reasons; 4. less invasive methods; 5. impact on the employee; 6. provision of adequate safeguards.
Freedom of Expression	Article 10 ECHR, Article 11 CFREU	Both the ECtHR and the ECJ require that any interference with this fundamental right strictly meets the 'prescribed by law' criterion, meaning that the legal basis must be sufficiently clear, accessible, and foreseeable to avoid arbitrary interference. This means that restrictions be precisely worded in law or, where ambiguities exist, be interpreted narrowly to safeguard against abuse.
Freedom of Assembly, Association and the Right of Collective Bargaining and Action	Article 11 ECHR, Article 12 CFREU	The ECHR has recognised the right to bargain collectively and the right to take collective action under Article 11 ECHR, as they are part of the essence of the freedom of assembly and association (*Demir* case).
Non-discrimination	Article 14 ECHR, Article 21 CFREU	The assessment through the *general criteria* by the ECtHR and ECJ takes the form of an objective justification test, meaning that any differential treatment must be prescribed by law, pursue a legitimate aim (therefore, not be based solely on forbidden grounds, e.g., race, gender, trade union activity), necessary and proportionate.

The four *general criteria*, and their more structured elaboration for each fundamental right in the ECtHR and ECJ case law outlined in the table, constitute the framework I will apply in Chapter 5 to assess whether AI and IoT-enabled technologies respect employees' fundamental rights. This framework serves as the basis for determining whether the deployment of these technologies amounts to a legitimate exercise of the employer's monitoring power.

8 CONCLUSIONS

In this chapter, I assessed the legitimate exercise of the employer's monitoring power in relation to fundamental rights at work. I addressed the following research question (n. 2): *What is a legitimate exercise of the employer's monitoring power in the European fundamental rights framework?*

Defining what constitutes a legitimate exercise of the employer's monitoring power is particularly complex in the EU context. While employment relationships are primarily regulated at the national level, the exercise of the employer's monitoring power must nonetheless comply with European standards for fundamental rights protection. I conceptualised this power as an open-ended and flexible prerogative, rooted in the employer's right to organise the business and protect its property, that authorises the observation of employees' behaviours, traits, and performance within the workplace. It is a relational and dynamic form of authority, embedded in the subordination inherent to the employment relationship.

This power is not absolute. It is subject to substantive and procedural limits derived from the Charter of Fundamental Rights of the European Union (CFREU) and the European Convention on Human Rights (ECHR), as incorporated into EU law via Article 6 TEU. Through the case law of the ECtHR and the ECJ, I identified a set of *general criteria* to determine what constitutes a legitimate exercise of this employer power. As I explained in sections 6 and 7, these include: the requirement that any monitoring be *prescribed by law* with a clear legal basis; that it pursues a *legitimate aim*, such as safeguarding company property, ensuring safety, or meeting legal obligations; that it must be *necessary and proportionate* in light of the aim pursued; and that *it respects the essence of the fundamental rights involved*, in accordance with Article 52(1) CFREU.

However, I found that a legitimate exercise of the employer's monitoring power within the European fundamental rights framework is not just one that complies with the above *general criteria* but also meets additional, right-specific standards developed in European case law. The ECtHR and ECJ have established that, in the employment context, legitimacy must be assessed in light of how monitoring affects employees' enjoyment of rights such as privacy, freedom of expression, freedom of assembly and association, the right to collective bargaining and action, and non-discrimination. Additional criteria – such as the Bărbulescu test, safeguards against abuses and chilling effects (in relation to the freedom of expression/assembly and association), and the need to objectively justify differential treatment – establish a contextualised and more demanding standard for assessing the legitimacy of employer monitoring.

This framework will serve as the benchmark for assessing AI and IoT-enabled monitoring practices in the chapters that follow. In Chapter 4, I will analyse how AI and IoT-enabled technologies are impacting the exercise of the employer's monitoring power, potentially challenging the application of the legitimacy standards identified here.

CHAPTER 4

The Impact of AI and IoT-Enabled Technologies on the Exercise of the Employer's Monitoring Power

1 INTRODUCTION

This chapter answers the research sub-question 3: *How do AI and IoT-enabled technologies reshape the exercise of the employer's monitoring power?* Section 2 introduces AI systems and IoT networks as monitoring technologies that have the potential to reshape how employers exercise their monitoring power. By collecting and processing vast amounts of real-time data, these technologies offer unprecedented insights into employee behaviour, performance, and the use of company property. Section 3 analyses how these technologies are implemented, breaking down the analysis according to the specific purposes they serve. The discussion unfolds across the three key purposes identified in Chapter 2: monitoring company property and employees' access, monitoring employees' performance, monitoring employees' personal characteristics and behaviours. Section 4 continues the analysis by reflecting on how the involvement of third-party technology providers complicates traditional workplace power dynamics and how the data analysis employed by AI and IoT-enabled technologies reshapes monitoring practices. Section 5 concludes by answering the research sub-question.

2 THE DATAFICATION OF THE EMPLOYER'S MONITORING POWER: ARTIFICIAL INTELLIGENCE AND INTERNET OF THINGS

Employers are increasingly turning to the market for surveillance technologies to enhance their monitoring capabilities. As mentioned in the introduction of this book,[268]

268. Cf. with section 1, Chapter 1.

the Little Tech Database produced by the American NGO CoWorker.org collected more than 550 products for workforce monitoring and management developed by specialised companies.[269] According to the 2019 European Company Survey conducted by EUROFOUND, 51 % of the European companies surveyed (21,869) employ data analytics in their work processes, and 22 % of them more specifically use some form of data analytics on employees.[270] A Gartner survey in 2019 found that 50 % of surveyed large corporations utilised 'non-traditional employee tracking'.[271] The COVID-19 pandemic further accelerated this trend, with global demand for employee monitoring software surging by 108 % in April 2020.[272] During the pandemic, concerns grew as companies, like *Teleperformance*, used webcams to capture remote employees' activities, prompting a survey of the TUC (a federation of English Trade Unions) which found one in seven British employees being monitored by digital technologies during the pandemic.[273]

The spread of laptops, smartphones, tablets, smartwatches and other surveillance technologies is reshaping monitoring into a ubiquitous collection and processing of data, often connected to the 'big data' infrastructures.[274] To better understand the reach of the employer's monitoring power and its impact on employees, it is useful to use the concept of 'datafication', i.e., the understanding of objects, people, processes and environments through the data collected by hardware and processed by software.[275]

Gstrein and Beaulieu describe datafication as a process that makes (inter)personal relationships and activities always quantifiable and analysable, in order to – for instance – derive behavioural patterns.[276] Interactions with other colleagues, with objects or environments, are meticulously observed and analysed to get the full value out of the three purposes of the employer's monitoring power. Smartwatches constantly track an employee's movements and reconstruct his or her whereabouts in the event of the theft of company goods. In the event of a cyber-attack, corporate cybersecurity relies on software tracking any action taken online by the employee. Wearables inform the employer how quickly an employee completes a task, with whom the employee interacts and the quality of conversation with colleagues. *Cogito*,

269. Negrón, 'Little Tech Is Coming for Workers: A Framework for Reclaiming and Building Worker Power' (n 5) 24.
270. Riso (n 2) 25.
271. Ball (n 3) 12.
272. *Ibid.*
273. Trade Union Congress (n 73).
274. I refer to big data infrastructures as a set of practices involving the collection, processing and analysis of large data sets through digital technologies. Big data is also used as a catch-all term for economic value generated through the processing of information and the monetisation of knowledge. *See*: Mirko Tobias Schäfer and Karin Es, van (eds), *The Datafied Society. Studying Culture Through Data* (Amsterdam University Press 2017) 13 https://library.oapen.org/handle/20.500.12657/31843 accessed 22 October 2025; Maddalena Favaretto et al., 'What Is Your Definition of Big Data? Researchers' Understanding of the Phenomenon of the Decade' (2020) 15 PLOS ONE e0228987 https://doi.org/10.1371/journal.pone.0228987 accessed 22 October 2025.
275. Gstrein and Beaulieu (n 192) 3.
276. *Ibid.*, 3-4.

a popular software in call centres, advises the employee in real time how to correctly modulate the tone of voice. Cameras with facial recognition software decide on promotions and recruitment, or recommend appropriate breaks to drivers.[277]

This data-driven understanding of reality is enabled by newly developed monitoring technologies, particularly by AI and IoT-enabled technologies processing and analysing vast amounts of information.[278] The use of these technologies impacts business organisations and ways of working, and most importantly, how the employer exercises his or her monitoring power. To understand how the large-scale collection and correlation of employee data reshape the exercise of the employer's monitoring power, I explore in this section the different features of AI systems and IoT networks.

2.1 Artificial Intelligence (AI) at Work

In this study, I adopt the definition of 'AI system' as outlined in Article 3(1) of the European Union AI Act:

> 'AI system' means a machine-based system designed to operate with varying levels of autonomy and that may exhibit adaptiveness after deployment and that, for explicit or implicit objectives, infers, from the input it receives, how to generate outputs such as predictions, content, recommendations, or decisions that can influence physical or virtual environments.

Recital 12 AI Act further clarifies that AI systems have the capability to infer, generate predictions, content, recommendations, or decisions that influence their environment. Their autonomy can range from minimal to fully independent operation, with some systems exhibiting adaptiveness, meaning they can learn and evolve after deployment. AI systems may function as standalone solutions or as embedded or non-embedded components within products.[279] Therefore, AI systems can be programmed to simulate human behaviour from a restricted range of parameters and contexts, with specific objectives (e.g., enforcing cybersecurity policies, performance assessments, OSH measures, labour processes optimisation). When deployed by employers, AI-enabled surveillance technologies promise improvements in organisational efficiency, security, and other operational aspects.[280] A clear example in this sense is *Cogito*, whose AI model listens in real time to the employee's telephone conversation with the customer. By analysing the tone of voice, conversation content

277. Valerio De Stefano and Mathias Wouters, 'AI and Digital Tools in Workplace Management and Evaluation: An Assessment of the EU's Legal Framework' (European Parliament 2022) https://doi.org/10.2861/305539 accessed 22 October 2025.
278. Alexandra Mateescu and Aiha Nguyen, 'Explainer: Workplace Monitoring & Surveillance' (Data & Society Research Institute 2019) https://datasociety.net/library/explainer-workplace-monitoring-surveillance/ accessed 22 October 2025.
279. Dimitra Kamarinou, Christopher Millard and Jatinder Singh, 'Machine Learning with Personal Data', *Data Protection and Privacy. The Age of Intelligent Machines* (Hart Publishing 2017) https://www-bloomsburycollections-com.proxy-ub.rug.nl/book/data-protection-and-privacy-the-age-of-intelligent-machines/ch4-machine-learning-with-personal-data-this-paper-has-been-produced-by-members-of-the-microsoft-cloud-computing-research-centre-a-collaboration-betwe?from=search accessed 22 October 2025.
280. OECD (n 152).

and interaction patterns, the AI system is able to analyse more than two hundred voice signals in tandem with the conversational context to improve results during calls. It also notifies supervisors when agents currently under their supervision fail to meet business evaluation parameters during challenging calls. Live pop-up notifications with emoticons indicate the progress of the conversation: a heart (empathetic response), a coffee cup (less empathetic response), and so on.[281]

To sum up, an AI system employs various data science techniques to make sense of large quantities of data.[282] Its introduction at work, as in the case of *Cogito*, allows for a permanent and detailed monitoring of employees and their activities.

2.2 Internet of Things (IoT) at Work

IoT refers to a network of interconnected objects and spaces, each equipped with processors and wireless connections, allowing them to communicate and function autonomously via the Internet.[283] These objects can include wearable devices, sensors embedded in machinery, smart cameras, and even workplace furniture with tracking capabilities. According to Peppet's taxonomy, any IoT device must have the following features:[284]

- generating or collecting data;
- processing data;
- sending and receiving data;
- identifying itself.

Hence, objects or spaces can communicate with each other independently of human intervention; each device connected to the network constantly collects data on a wide variety of elements. Generating and sending data, identifying themselves in relation to the environments and agents involved, are connotations that lead software

281. 'Cogito: Real-Time AI Coaching & Guidance for Contact Centers' https://cogitocorp.com accessed 22 October 2025.
282. Phoebe V Moore, 'Artificial Intelligence: What Everyone Needs to Know' (2019) 40 Organization Studies 466. On big data and their societal impact: Jianqing Fan, Fang Han and Han Liu, 'Challenges of Big Data Analysis' (2014) 1 National Science Review 293 https://doi.org/10.1093/nsr/nwt032 accessed 22 October 2025; Jie Liu, Jigui Sun and Shengsheng Wang, 'Pattern Recognition: An Overview' (2006) 6 International Journal of Computer Science and Network Security 57.
283. According to the classification proposed by CISCO, when intelligent connection involves people, processes, data and things, it would be more appropriate to speak of the Internet of Everything. The IoE connects physical things with virtual things in a *unicum*. This goes beyond just talking between devices; it is more about enabling everything (living, non-living, virtual) to talk to each other. This virtual unison, according to CISCO, is missing from the commonly adopted definition of the Internet of Things, which is based on Smart Objects and not on non-physical entities.
284. Scott R Peppet, 'Regulating the Internet of Things: First Steps Toward Managing Discrimination, Privacy, Security & Consent' [2014] University of Colorado Law School Legal Studies Research Paper Series 12-25.

engineering research to define the combined use of AI and IoT as 'embedding intelligence' into objects or environments.[285]

IoT networks enhance AI system deployment in workplaces by collecting employees' personal data through sensors and connected devices, feeding AI systems with real-time insights on employees' behaviour and performance. AI systems may process employee data alongside other sources, such as publicly available datasets, organisational records, and synthetic data, as well as images, text, audio, and sensor inputs, depending on their functions. By integrating these various data streams, AI-enabled technologies can analyse, predict, and influence employee actions, making IoT networks a crucial element of AI-enabled monitoring.[286] An example of an AI and IoT-enabled monitoring could be a smart office system that uses IoT sensors to monitor employee movements and AI to analyse and predict behaviour. For instance, motion sensors, wearable trackers, and smart cameras could collect data on where employees are located, how long they stay at their desks, how often they leave their workstations. This data would then be processed by an AI system to analyse patterns, such as determining an employee's productivity based on their movement or the frequency of breaks. The AI system could also make predictions, such as identifying employees who may be disengaged or overworked, suggesting interventions like offering breaks or reallocating workloads.

To provide a complete framework on the functionalities of these technologies, it is important to stress that AI systems and IoT networks can also operate independently. For instance, in the case of AI systems analysing publicly available online information about employees, such as social media.[287] Conversely, IoT networks can function without AI involvement, as seen in workplaces equipped with automated features like motion sensors that regulate lighting or control door access. These sensors operate based on pre-programmed, rule-based responses rather than intelligent decision-making.[288] Unlike AI systems, which analyse data over time, adapt to patterns, and make complex decisions, these IoT systems primarily focus on automating mechanical processes such as energy efficiency and workspace coordination. While they do collect and analyse data, such as movement patterns or light intensity, their purpose is not behavioural analysis but rather optimising environmental conditions and operational efficiency. In such cases, IoT networks serve purely as an automation technology rather than a mechanism for behavioural analysis.

285. Robert P Dick et al., 'Embedded Intelligence in the Internet-of-Things' (2020) 37 IEEE Design & Test 7 https://doi.org/10.1109/mdat.2019.2957352 accessed 22 October 2025.
286. Training data is the initial dataset used to train machine learning algorithms. Models create and refine their rules using this data. It is a set of data samples used to fit the parameters of a machine learning model to train it by example. Christian Janiesch, Patrick Zschech and Kai Heinric,. 'Machine Learning and Deep Learning'. (2021) 31 Electron Markets 685-695 https://doi-org.proxy-ub.rug.nl/10.1007/s12525-021-00475-2 accessed 22 October 2025.
287. Negrón, 'Little Tech Is Coming for Workers: A Framework for Reclaiming and Building Worker Power' (n 5) 63-64.
288. Alireza Jaribion, Siavash H Khajavi and Jan Holmstrom, 'IoT-Enabled Workplaces: A Case Study of Energy Management and Data Analytics', *IECON 2019 – 45th Annual Conference of the IEEE Industrial Electronics Society* (IEEE 2019) https://ieeexplore.ieee.org/document/8927003/ accessed 22 October 2025.

3 THE AI AND IOT-ENABLED EMPLOYER'S MONITORING POWER: CASES

In this section, I analyse a few examples of AI and IoT-enabled technologies for employee monitoring. The objective of this analysis is to examine how AI and IoT-enabled technologies are deployed for the three main purposes or dimensions of the employer's monitoring power identified in Chapter 2,[289] namely to monitor:

- employers' properties and employees' access;
- employees' performance;
- employees' personal characteristics and behaviours.

Building on this, I assess how these technologies reshape monitoring methods.

3.1 Monitoring Employers' Properties and Employees' Access

3.1.1 Access into the Company Premises and Employee Safety and Health

One of the main purposes of monitoring is overseeing employee access to company property.[290] This is today facilitated by self-tracking technologies. Employers can monitor access to the workplace in real time by leveraging the devices they provide to employees, such as smartphones, laptops, smartwatches, and tablets. AI-enabled cameras further enhance access control by recognising vehicle plates at entry and exit points, allowing for automated authorisation and security screening.[291]

The same AI and IoT-enabled technologies that regulate access control can also contribute to the improvement of occupational safety and health (OSH).[292] These technologies are commonly used to identify potential risks to employees. For example, *Intenseye* can detect when an employee has fallen, is near hazardous equipment, or is not wearing required protective gear, such as gloves. During the COVID-19 pandemic, the developers of this technology introduced a new function to monitor and notify managers of non-compliance with social distancing measures.[293]

The integration of AI and IoT-enabled technologies into OSH measures has been recognised by the EU-OSHA as a means to enhance workplace safety standards.[294] These technologies facilitate immediate reporting of emergencies and hazards through features like fall detection and panic alerts,[295] helping to prevent accidents, improve rescue operations, and address underreporting of OSH issues.[296] Notably, these AI and

289. Cf. with section 4 of Chapter 2.
290. European Foundation for the Improvement of Living and Working Conditions (n 165) 29.
291. Deborah Lupton, *The Quantified Self: A Sociology of Self-Tracking* (Polity 2016).
292. Ball (n 3) 27.
293. 'Intenseye' https://www.intenseye.com accessed 22 October 2025.
294. European Agency for Safety and Health at Work (n 8).
295. *Ibid.*, 5.
296. European Agency for Safety and Health at Work (n 8); Lucia Kilic, et al., 'Smart Digital Monitoring Systems for Occupational Safety and Health: Uses and Challenges' (European

IoT-enabled technologies reshape the exercise of the employer's monitoring power for both security and health and safety purposes.

3.1.2 Cybersecurity in Organisations

Monitoring cybersecurity risks falls within the employers' purpose of monitoring company property and controlling employee access. Just as physical access to workplaces is monitored to prevent unauthorised entry, digital access must also be safeguarded to protect a company's digital assets. Online activities can create vulnerabilities, such as unauthorised data access, phishing attacks, or malware intrusions, which threaten corporate security. To mitigate these risks, employers deploy cybersecurity monitoring tools that track employees' network activity, detect suspicious behaviour, and enforce access controls, ensuring both physical and digital assets remain secure.[297] For example, employees accessing company networks from unsecured devices or public Wi-Fi can expose sensitive data to cyber threats. To mitigate these threats, employers deploy AI and IoT-enabled technologies that detect unusual login patterns, flag suspicious email activity, and restrict access to potentially harmful websites.[298] Employers, moreover, must also ensure compliance with cybersecurity standards set by national laws implementing the NIS2 Directive (Directive (EU) 2022/2555) and the GDPR, which establish requirements for risk management, incident reporting, and data protection.[299] The increase in teleworking following the COVID-19 pandemic has further expanded companies' exposure to cyber threats, thus increasing the adoption of surveillance technologies to increase cybersecurity standards.[300]

AI and IoT-enabled technologies such as *Controlio* and *Interguard* track activities on corporate devices, including smartphones, smartwatches, wearables, tablets, and laptops, detecting and reporting security risks associated with employee online behaviour.[301] These technologies store and log webpages accessed on corporate devices, while technologies like *FlexiSpy* can record conversations, private messages, geolocation data, and downloaded photo libraries.[302] As with physical access control and

Agency for Safety and Health at Work 2023) https://osha.europa.eu/en/publications/smart-digital-monitoring-systems-occupational-safety-and-health-uses-and-challenges accessed 22 October 2025; Daniel Podgórski (ed.), *New Opportunities and Challenges in Occupational Safety and Health Management* (7th edn, CRC Press 2020).

297. Isabella Corradini, *Building a Cybersecurity Culture in Organizations* (Springer 2020) 37-42.
298. Clay Posey and Mindy Shoss, 'Research: Why Employees Violate Cybersecurity Policies' (*Harvard Business Review,* 20 January 2022) https://hbr.org/2022/01/research-why-employees-violate-cybersecurity-policies accessed 22 October 2025; European Union Agency for Cybersecurity (n 9).
299. Directive (EU) 2022/2555 of the European Parliament and of the Council of 14 December 2022 on measures for a high common level of cybersecurity across the Union, amending Regulation (EU) No 910/2014 and Directive (EU) 2018/1972, and repealing Directive (EU) 2016/1148 (NIS 2 Directive).
300. European Union Agency for Cybersecurity (n 9) 7.
301. Negrón, 'Little Tech Is Coming for Workers: A Framework for Reclaiming and Building Worker Power' (n 5) 63-64.
302. *Ibid.*

workplace safety monitoring, these technologies collect, store, and analyse employee activity data to identify potential risks.[303]

In this context, the use of AI and IoT-enabled technologies extends employer's monitoring activities beyond physical access control to encompass the monitoring of digital activities. Employers can now ensure that employee behaviours, both online and offline, are continuously monitored to safeguard company assets, comply with OSH regulatory requirements, and mitigate cybersecurity threats.

3.2 Monitoring Employees' Performance

3.2.1 Monitoring Work Performance for Blue Collars

One of the sectors exemplifying the impact of AI and IoT-enabled technologies on blue collars is logistics.[304] Companies in this sector often use 'organised disorder'[305] depot methods: goods are not organised by categories into their warehouses but arranged according to the purchasing preferences of consumers.[306] Thus, the warehouse employee must follow the indications emitted by devices and wearables provided by the company, unwinding through the 'apparent chaos' of the warehouse. The employee is therefore totally dependent on surveillance technologies. To function, the organisational model must track where the employees are physically, how many breaks they take and for how long, how long it takes them to perform a specific task.[307] Further on the case of logistics, delivery trucks can be equipped with AI-enabled cameras to give advice on the best driving behaviours. They can, for example, warn the employee and inform the manager in cases of non-agreed breaks.[308]

Beyond logistics, in retail, there is a popular management system called *RetailNext*.[309] This network of cameras and cash counters enable the collection and analysis of data from employees working in retail. Using direction mapping and other techniques, *RetailNext* analyses the employee's movements, customer interactions, and

303. Markus Christen et al., 'A Review of Value-Conflicts in Cybersecurity' (2017) 1 The ORBIT Journal 1 https://doi.org/10.29297/orbit.v1i1.28 accessed 22 October 2025.
304. A blue-collar employee is an individual performing manual work, often in industries but also services, such as delivery of goods.
305. Prince Vijai and GV Muralidhara, 'Inside Amazon: Chaotic Storage System' (IBS Center for Management Research 2016) https://www.thecasecentre.org/main/products/view?id=138531 accessed 22 October 2025.
306. Wood (n 15) 3.
307. Thomas De Lombaert et al., 'Mass Collection of Workers' Data in Warehouse Facilities: Reflections on Privacy and Workforce Well-Being' (2024) 17 Italian Labour Law e-Journal 145; Heiko Diefenbach, Eric H Grosse and Christoph H Glock, 'Human-and-Cost-Centric Storage Assignment Optimization in Picker-to-Parts Warehouses' (2024) 315 European Journal of Operational Research 1049 https://doi.org/10.1016/j.ejor.2024.01.033 accessed 22 October 2025.
308. Annie Palmer, 'Amazon Is Using AI-Equipped Cameras in Delivery Vans and Some Drivers Are Concerned about Privacy' (*CNBC*, 3 February 2021) https://www.cnbc.com/2021/02/03/amazon-using-ai-equipped-cameras-in-delivery-vans.html accessed 22 October 2025.
309. 'RetailNext' https://retailnext.net accessed 22 October 2025; the Little Tech database reports that Retailnext is used by several multinational retail companies: Negrón, 'Bossware and Employment Tech Database' (n 5).

store layouts to gain insight into store operations. This technology also captures frequent, high-resolution snapshots of the store environment and employees performing their daily tasks, including cash operations. This allows an employer to accurately monitor the actions performed and to monitor collective and individual performance accordingly.[310]

3.2.2 Monitoring Work Performance for White Collars

Surveillance technologies for white collars usually involve sensors and tracking systems on corporate devices.[311] This involves closely analysing individual tasks, often extending to aspects of daily routines. This can include monitoring not only the time spent on work-related activities but also the frequency and duration of breaks, such as bathroom or coffee breaks, as well as the occupancy levels of an employee's desk over a specific period. For example, technologies like *Occupeye* can track desk occupancy to gauge how often and how long an employee is present at his or her workstation. By examining these granular details, employers gain insights into work patterns, allowing for more precise assessments of productivity.[312] *Genome*, among others, is used to calculate the average time to complete a specific task on the laptop. This software alerts team leaders when projects are behind schedule. *RescueTime*, with similar functions, aims to reduce distractions that may be impacting employees' productivity.[313] *HubStaff* enables geofencing (a virtual perimeter of a real geographic area) of employees' laptops and other devices they carry with them (e.g., smartphones); employees - such as teleworkers - connected via these devices can thus be recommended certain routes and breaks, and it is possible to track how much time they spent at each location and how much time they took to complete specific tasks.[314]

Monitoring the work performance can focus on the behavioural traits of employees. For instance, the use of biometric data can detect emotional statuses such as anger, contempt, disgust, engagement, joy, sadness, and so on; this data collected through AI-monitored virtual meetings can give insights to the employer and adjust working schedules or working shifts accordingly.[315]

These AI and IoT-enabled technologies fundamentally reshape the exercise of the employer's monitoring power by providing a highly detailed and real-time view of employees' activities, both on and off the job. Employers can now monitor not just

---

310. Mohammad Hossein Jarrahi et al., 'Algorithmic Management in a Work Context' (2021) 8 Big Data & Society 3 http://journals.sagepub.com/doi/10.1177/20539517211020332 accessed 22 October 2025.
311. A white-collar employee is an individual performing work in offices or other professional environment. Riso (n 2) 30-33; Mateescu and Nguyen (n 278).
312. James Bloodworth, *Hired: Six Months Undercover in Low-Wage Britain* (Revised and updated edition, Atlantic Books 2019).
313. Wood (n 15) 5.
314. Negrón, 'Little Tech Is Coming for Workers: A Framework for Reclaiming and Building Worker Power' (n 5) 63-64.
315. Oliver Behn, Michael Leyer and Deniz Iren, 'Employees' Acceptance of AI-Based Emotion Analytics from Speech on a Group Level in Virtual Meetings' (2024) 76 Technology in Society 102466 https://doi.org/10.1016/j.techsoc.2024.102466 accessed 22 October 2025.

work-related tasks but also personal behaviours that are linked to performance assessment, such as break times, desk occupancy, and emotional states. By analysing these granular data points, employers gain detail insights into individual performance.

3.3 Monitoring of Employees' Personal Characteristics and Behaviours

3.3.1 Monitoring of Employees' Social Interactions

AI and IoT-enabled technologies can be used to process employees' personal characteristics (physical or behavioural) to further integrate them into the company organisation. One major development in this regard is looking at the social interactions among employees while performing their tasks or interacting with peers. For instance, through devices such as smartphones, laptops, smartwatches, it is possible to identify groups of employees who interact frequently, connect their personal communications to their actual productivity and deduce whether these acquaintances are potentially harmful or profitable to the company.[316] These features are mainly known from *Google Workspace* or the *Microsoft Teams* platform.[317] These business management packages offered by Big Tech companies provide dashboards capable of charting the activities and relationships of employees and tracking optimal collaboration patterns (these features are also present on *Controlio* and *Interguard* as discussed in section 3.1).[318]

Chat tools for internal use are often AI moderated, detecting the mood of the workforce through language and communication patterns.[319] In the case of *Cogito*, the software analyses the employee's voice during calls and provides real-time feedback to call centre operators. When it detects an 'altered emotional state', the system displays feedback on the screen, prompting operators to adjust their tone of voice and modify their approach to the conversation.[320] These examples show a growing intersection between personal characteristics and productivity evaluation, which is also reflected in gamification.[321] Gamification refers to the application of AI-enabled gaming interfaces to monitor employees' performances or personal characteristics and to put them in competition.[322] AI-enabled recruiting systems with gaming interfaces can highlight where employees' skills excel or need improvement. Thus, such a technology looks for the personal characteristics desired by the recruiters, such as perseverance, customer focus, willingness to take risks and interpersonal skills.[323] The data inferred from

316. Paul Leonardi and Noshir Contractor, 'Better People Analytics Measure Who They Know, Not Just Who They Are' [2018] Harvard Business Review 70.
317. Gould (n 14) 110.
318. De Stefano and Wouters (n 277) 13.
319. Katharina Lix et al., 'Expressly Different: Discursive Diversity and Team Performance' [2019] Research Papers 3773, Stanford University, Graduate School of Business https://ideas-repec-org.proxy-ub.rug.nl/p/ecl/stabus/3773.html accessed 22 October 2025.
320. Wood (n 15) 6.
321. Steve Dale, 'Gamification: Making Work Fun, or Making Fun of Work?' (2014) 31 Business information review 82 https://doi.org/10.1177/0266382114538350 accessed 22 October 2025.
322. Mateescu and Nguyen (n 278).
323. Hadary Mallafi and Dwi H. Widyantoro, 'Prediction Modelling in Career Management', *2016 International Conference on Computational Intelligence and Cybernetics* (2016).

gaming activities, then, can be cross-referenced with the employee's salary and benefits, hours worked, number and age of children, marital status and health information.[324] Through these data, gamification offers analyses of skill development and the 'probability of success' of each employee.[325]

Monitoring employees' social interactions implies that the AI and IoT-enabled technology can analyse the workforce collective behaviours and detect potential threats from them. *Perceptyx*, for instance, is a survey tool that gauges employee satisfaction. It utilises a 'union vulnerability index', which compares the responses to a database of twelve million survey responses from other clients, to predict the likelihood of employees seeking unionisation at a given company. Other companies like *Worktango* and *Littler Mendelson* offer similar functionalities.[326]

Finally, AI and IoT-enabled technologies in some instances can forecast patterns of choices of each employee, before the employee in question can even conceive them.[327] This includes generating 'high-flight risk' ratings that identify in advance those employees who are most likely to resign,[328] as well as predicting the development of particular skills by cross-referencing data from the devices used by the employee and his or her social acquaintances in the company.

3.3.2 Monitoring Health and Personal Lifestyle

In this subsection, I focus specifically on the monitoring of employees' lifestyle and health beyond the mandatory OSH standards for employers, which I addressed earlier in section 3.1. Here, my aim is to explore the growing and rapidly evolving trend of monitoring employees' personal lifestyles, particularly their health-related choices and living conditions.[329] With the advancement of AI and IoT-enabled technologies, employers now have the capability to easily track and influence employees' lifestyle decisions through health programmes and wearable devices that collect data on physical activity, sleep patterns, and other health metrics.[330] The American company

324. Katharina Simbeck, 'HR Analytics and Ethics' (2019) 63 IBM Journal of Research and Development 9 https://doi.org/10.1147/jrd.2019.2915067 accessed 22 October 2025; Ulrich Leicht-Deobald et al., 'The Challenges of Algorithm-Based HR Decision-Making for Personal Integrity' (2019) 160 Journal of Business Ethics 377 https://doi.org/10.1007/s10551-019-04204-w accessed 22 October 2025.
325. Negrón, 'Little Tech Is Coming for Workers: A Framework for Reclaiming and Building Worker Power' (n 5) 63-64.
326. *Ibid.*
327. Valerio De Stefano and Simon Taes, 'Algorithmic Management and Collective Bargaining' (European Trade Union Institute (ETUI)) 10 https://www.etui.org/publications/algorithmic-management-and-collective-bargaining accessed 22 October 2025; De Stefano and Wouters (n 277).
328. Weihuang Dai and Zijiang Zhu, 'Employee Resignation Prediction Model Based on Machine Learning' in Jemal H Abawajy et al. (eds), *2020 International Conference on Applications and Techniques in Cyber Intelligence*, vol 1244 (Springer International Publishing 2021) http://link.springer.com/10.1007/978-3-030-53980-1_55 accessed 22 October 2025.
329. Negrón, 'Little Tech Is Coming for Workers: A Framework for Reclaiming and Building Worker Power' (n 5) 25; Nguyen (n 19) 19.
330. European Foundation for the Improvement of Living and Working Conditions (n 165) 31; Matthew T. Bodie et al., 'The Law and Policy of People Analytics' 88 University of Colorado

Fitbit, which specialises in consumer electronics and fitness products, introduced *Fitbit Care*, a platform that targets employer-based wellness programmes. Fitbit-like devices gather a steady flow of personal information, which can be sent to third-party organisations such as insurance companies. This data can be used to adjust health insurance premiums based on personal health information or behaviour. This practice is prevalent in the United States, but technology companies are also entering the healthcare sector in Europe.[331]

A further development involving AI and IoT-enabled technologies is the analysis of employees' sedentary lifestyles in what are known as Living Labs. These are 'living laboratories' and offices equipped with various sensors related to room usage, the measurement of each employee's sitting time (sedentary index), and the amount of coffee a specific employee consumes (based on the activation of the coffee machine with their company badge). By cross-referencing this data, a company can provide advice on work routines and promote a healthier, less sedentary lifestyle.[332]

Ultimately, monitoring the health of employees as part of corporate wellness programmes is an increasingly common practice, and AI and IoT-enabled technologies can help make it more efficient and consistent over time, even predicting the likelihood of non-work-related health issues.[333]

These advancements highlight how these technologies reshape the exercise of the employer's monitoring power by enabling more granular, real-time tracking of employees' personal characteristics and behaviours. This allows employers to assess aspects of employees' private lives, such as social interactions and health choices, in a way that was previously not possible. The integration of AI and IoT-enabled technologies allows for predictive insights, facilitating proactive decision-making and personalised interventions.

4 REFLECTION: AI AND IOT-ENABLED TECHNOLOGIES RESHAPING THE EMPLOYER'S MONITORING POWER

4.1 The Role of Technology Providers

The increasing reliance on AI and IoT-enabled technologies has consequences for how employers exercise their monitoring power. One key consequence is the growing dependence of employers on third-party technology providers. Most surveillance technologies are developed by specialised producers and suppliers, extending beyond the so-called Big Tech companies. In 2021, the *Little Tech Database* report found that

Law Review 961 https://ssrn.com/abstract=2769980 accessed 22 October 2025; Erik Brynjolfsson and Tom Mitchell, 'What Can Machine Learning Do? Workforce Implications' (2017) 358 Science 1530 https://doi.org/10.1126/science.aap8062 accessed 22 October 2025.

331. Riso (n 2) 31.
332. Hamed S Alavi, Denis Lalanne and Yvonne Rogers, 'The Five Strands of Living Lab: A Literature Study of the Evolution of Living Lab Concepts in HCI' (2020) 27 ACM Transactions on Computer-Human Interaction 1 https://doi.org/10.1145/3380958 accessed 22 October 2025.
333. Bodie et al. (n 330).

while firms like *Amazon, Apple, Google, Meta,* and *Microsoft* play a significant role in this market,[334] a broader range of providers - including small or medium-sized commercial companies, business intelligence companies, military companies, start-ups, data brokers, and app developers - offer monitoring technologies tailored to various workplace needs.[335] Analysing the employer's monitoring power today must take into account that employers increasingly follow the design choices of providers rather than directing the use of monitoring technologies to meet actual monitoring needs.[336] In some cases, companies such as *Amazon* develop and manage AI and IoT-enabled technologies in-house, but this remains the exception.[337] More commonly, the involvement of third-party providers embeds external actors into the corporate structure by tasking them with maintaining the monitoring technology and retaining critical knowledge of its operation. This dynamic underscores how technology providers shape not only how technologies function but also how employers exercise their monitoring power in the workplace.[338]

As these technologies mediate how data is collected, processed, and presented, the employer's role increasingly resembles that of a user rather than a direct controller. The ability to understand and act upon employee data often depends on the software and dashboards provided by the technology, which means that meaningful insights can only be accessed through the infrastructure controlled by the provider.[339] This shift raises fundamental questions about accountability. When the exercise of monitoring power results in potential violations of employees' fundamental rights - such as privacy, freedom of association, or non-discrimination - it is no longer evident whether employers may fully control or even understand the extent to which these technologies impact fundamental rights.[340] If employers cannot fully understand or control how monitoring technologies operate, ensuring compliance with legal standards, such as those required by data protection and labour laws, this may require specific accountability frameworks in the relationship between employers and technology providers.[341]

334. Negrón, 'Bossware and Employment Tech Database' (n 5).
335. Negrón, 'Little Tech Is Coming for Workers: A Framework for Reclaiming and Building Worker Power' (n 5).
336. Cf. with Albin reflections in this regard: Einat Albin, 'Channelling Technologies to Benefit Employees via Labour Law' in Nicolas Bueno, Beryl Ter Haar and Nuna Zekic (eds), *Labour Law Utopias* (1st edn, Oxford University Press Oxford 2024) https://academic.oup.com/book/58011/chapter/477420515 accessed 22 October 2025.
337. Alessandro Delfanti, 'Machinic Dispossession and Augmented Despotism: Digital Work in an Amazon Warehouse' (2021) 23 New Media & Society 39 https://doi.org/10.1177/1461444819891613 accessed 22 October 2025.
338. André Gorz, *Métamorphoses du travail: critique de la raison économique* (Gallimard 2004) 90.
339. On this point: Sandy JJ Gould, 'Stochastic Machine Witnesses at Work: Today's Critiques of Taylorism Are Inadequate for Workplace Surveillance Epistemologies of the Future' [2024] Proceedings of the CHI Conference on Human Factors in Computing Systems 1 https://doi.org/10.1145/3613904.3642206 accessed 22 October 2025; Gould (n 14); Michele Molè, 'Commodified, Outsourced Authority: A Research Agenda for Algorithmic Management at Work' (2024) 17 Italian Labour Law e-Journal 169.
340. *See* in this regard Chapter 8, section 4. I also discuss these shifts in accountability here: Molè, 'Commodified, Outsourced Authority: A Research Agenda for Algorithmic Management at Work' (n 339) 183-184.
341. On this point *see* Chapter 7 on the AI Act and the requirements for AI providers.

4.2 How the Data Analysis Features of AI and IoT-Enabled Technologies Reshape the Exercise of the Employer's Monitoring Power

The second key reflection relates to how the use of AI and IoT-enabled technologies expands the reach and enhances the effectiveness of the employer's monitoring power. These technologies, for instance, enable more consistent and pervasive spatial monitoring, meaning that they allow employers to track a wider range of areas, events, and data points. Moreover, they facilitate continuous data collection and analysis, providing insights that extend beyond real-time observation to include employees' historical patterns and potential future behaviours. This transformation allows employers to monitor not just immediate workplace activities but also the broader context of employees' actions over time.

This development does not create a new form of employer power. Rather, it reshapes and enhances the effectiveness of the employer's monitoring power within the identified monitoring purposes of protecting corporate assets, managing workforce performance, and monitoring personal characteristics. In this section, I will illustrate how this reshaping occurs by examining four key categories of data analytics – *descriptive, diagnostic, predictive*, and *prescriptive* – that AI and IoT-enabled technologies employ.[342]

4.2.1 *The Descriptive and Diagnostic Analytical Features*

AI and IoT-enabled technologies allow for a *descriptive* analysis of employees' data. Whether for security systems, workforce management, or analysing personal characteristics for organisational needs, this descriptive function sorts and classifies data collected from various IoT devices. It helps employers understand past and real-time situations related to specific purposes. This can take the form of data visualisations such as charts, graphs, reports and dashboards.[343] For example, *Controlio*, *Interguard*, and *Flexispy* provide detailed descriptions of online activity on devices connected to the corporate IT infrastructure.[344] In workforce management, *Hubstaff* allows geofencing to pace working rhythms,[345] while specific ID cards trace and reconstruct social relationships among employees to assist in organising work teams.[346]

342. I use the categorisation outlined by Sharma et al. (2022) where they discuss these categories and how they are employed in decision intelligence analytics to support better decision-making in businesses. This framework leverages data insights – through descriptive, diagnostic, predictive, and prescriptive analytics – to inform, optimise, and implement strategic business decisions. Ashish K Sharma et al., 'Analytics Techniques: Descriptive Analytics, Predictive Analytics, and Prescriptive Analytics' in P Mary Jeyanthi et al. (eds), *Decision Intelligence Analytics and the Implementation of Strategic Business Management* (Springer International Publishing 2022) https://doi.org/10.1007/978-3-030-82763-2_1 accessed 22 October 2025.
343. *Ibid.*, 4; Dagnino (n 36).
344. Negrón, 'Little Tech Is Coming for Workers: A Framework for Reclaiming and Building Worker Power' (n 5) 63-64.
345. *Ibid.*, 64. Geofencing consists of observing users moving from one place to another and how long they stay in those places.
346. Leonardi and Contractor (n 316).

This descriptive function is often complemented by a *diagnostic* analysis aimed at monitoring the root causes of events. Diagnostic analysis helps employers answer the question: why did something happen?[347] Processes such as data discovery[348] and data mining[349] allow employers to delve deeper into the underlying reasons behind workplace events. For instance, *Controlio* and similar software can help explain how malware was introduced into the corporate IT structure by identifying when and which employee clicked on a malicious link.[350] Similarly, *Hubstaff* can reveal where and when an employee logged in using a company device, providing a detailed geolocation chronology.[351]

These *descriptive* and *diagnostic* features improve the reach and effectiveness of the exercise of the monitoring power by allowing the employer to identify and potentially respond to issues with greater insight and accuracy. As a result, these technologies increase both the quantity and quality of information available to inform employers' decision-making and management.

4.2.2 The Predictive and Prescriptive Analytical Features

The descriptive and diagnostic analyses provide historical data, which can then be fed into an AI model that identifies key future trends and patterns. This is where *predictive* analysis comes into play, a feature that enhances the employer's monitoring power by enabling employers to anticipate potential future events based on the patterns observed in historical data.[352] For example, in the context of workplace OSH, tools like *Intenseye* use predictive analytics to foresee safety incidents by analysing employees' actions and environmental factors that precede accidents.[353] Similarly, surveillance technologies can track employees' sedentary habits, using this data to predict potential

347. Singh, Singh and Singh (n 70) 147.
348. Data discovery is a definition from data science scholarship. *See* the previous footnote on this. It refers in particular to the practices of companies in navigating through the history of their data (relating to various indices, including employee performance) and in applying advanced analysis to identify patterns, gain insights, answer highly specific business questions and derive insights from the data collected so far.
349. Data mining is a practice from data science that analyses large data sets to identify patterns and relationships to solve business problems through data analysis.
350. Malware is software designed to cause disruption to a computer, server, or computer network to gain unauthorised access to systems. It is used for espionage or cybercrime activities to extract private information from the victim or to cause the disruption of the proper functioning of systems. Mohd Faizal Ab Razak et al., 'The Rise of "Malware": Bibliometric Analysis of Malware Study' (2016) 75 Journal of Network and Computer Applications 58 https://doi.org/10.1016/j.jnca.2016.08.022 accessed 22 October 2025.
351. Negrón, 'Little Tech Is Coming for Workers: A Framework for Reclaiming and Building Worker Power' (n 5) 63-64.
352. Sharma et al. (n 342) 7; Singh, Singh and Singh (n 70) 147; Prachi S Deshpande, Subhash C Sharma and Sateesh K Peddoju, 'Predictive and Prescriptive Analytics in Big-Data Era' in Prachi S Deshpande, Subhash C Sharma and Sateesh K Peddoju (eds), *Security and Data Storage Aspect in Cloud Computing* (Springer Singapore 2019) https://doi.org/10.1007/978-981-13-6089-3_5 accessed 22 October 2025.
353. 'Intenseye' (n 293).

health issues, such as musculoskeletal disorders or long-term cardiovascular risks.[354] By incorporating predictive analysis, the AI and IoT-enabled monitoring power allows employers to proactively address potential risks. This feature strengthens the employer's ability to mitigate possible issues before they occur, enhancing the effectiveness of their monitoring power.

While predictive analysis focuses on anticipating future events, *prescriptive* analysis takes this a step further by recommending specific actions to prevent these events from occurring.[355] Prescriptive analysis involves processing data to determine the most optimal course of action, considering all relevant factors. This approach produces actionable recommendations that can guide decision-making.[356] Prescriptive analytics thus enhances the employer's ability to not only foresee potential issues but also to intervene effectively in real time. For example, AI and IoT-enabled technologies such as *Intenseye* can predict when an employee is about to approach a dangerous area and automatically issue an alert to prevent an accident.[357] Similarly, in the context of workforce management, prescriptive analytics can inform decisions about future staffing needs, such as adjusting hiring plans in anticipation of potential employee dismissals.[358] Moreover, tools like *Cogito*, which monitor the tone of voice in call centres, offer minute-by-minute guidance on how to interact with customers to ensure optimal outcomes. Through these prescriptive capabilities, employers can shape the employee's behaviour in real time.[359]

Together, *predictive* and *prescriptive* analytics reshape the exercise of the employer's monitoring power into a more dynamic, anticipatory, and responsive form of observation. These advancements ensure that employee behaviours are not only observed but actively shaped and guided according to real-time and anticipated needs.

5 CONCLUSIONS

This chapter addressed the research sub-question 3: *How do AI and IoT-enabled technologies reshape the exercise of the employer's monitoring power?*

While answering this research question, I found that the purposes of the employer's monitoring power have not changed, but its implementation has – particularly through the use of AI and IoT-enabled technologies. AI systems, with varying degrees of autonomy and adaptiveness, enable employers to infer, predict, and decide on employee behaviour and performance. These systems do not merely automate monitoring tasks; they simulate human oversight for specific objectives, such as OSH,

354. Negrón, 'Little Tech Is Coming for Workers: A Framework for Reclaiming and Building Worker Power' (n 5) 67.
355. Singh, Singh and Singh (n 70) 147.
356. Davide Frazzetto et al., 'Prescriptive Analytics: A Survey of Emerging Trends and Technologies' (2019) 28 The VLDB Journal 575 https://doi.org/10.1007/s00778-019-00539-y accessed 22 October 2025; Deshpande, Sharma and Peddoju (n 352).
357. 'Intenseye' (n 293).
358. Negrón, 'Little Tech Is Coming for Workers: A Framework for Reclaiming and Building Worker Power' (n 5) 67.
359. Wood (n 15) 6.

productivity optimisation, or behavioural risk detection. IoT networks reinforce these capabilities by collecting continuous, real-time data from employees via sensors and connected devices. This allows AI systems to dynamically analyse, anticipate, and influence employees' conduct with unprecedented granularity.

AI and IoT-enabled technologies thus reshape the exercise of the employer's monitoring power along several dimensions. First, it transforms monitoring from a reactive and episodic function into a continuous, anticipatory observation. Using descriptive and diagnostic analytics, employers can visualise and understand past and current behaviours; predictive and prescriptive analytics further enable them to anticipate risks or performance issues and recommend or implement interventions automatically. This shift redefines the temporal structure of monitoring power: it becomes data-driven and increasingly pre-emptive.

Second, the employer's role in the monitoring process itself is reshaped. Employers often rely on third-party technology providers who design, update, and manage the AI and IoT-enabled technology. As a result, the technical design choices of providers structure how monitoring occurs in practice. This raises accountability concerns, particularly when the systems used interfere with employees' fundamental rights.

In conclusion, AI and IoT-enabled technologies reshape the employer's monitoring power by expanding its reach across time and space, enhancing its effectiveness through predictive capabilities, and transforming its structure through the involvement of third-party service providers.

In the next chapter, I will investigate whether this reshaped employer's monitoring power can be exercised in a way that respects fundamental rights of employees.

CHAPTER 5

A Fundamental Rights Assessment of the Exercise of an AI and IoT-Enabled Employer's Monitoring Power

1 INTRODUCTION: EMPLOYEES' RIGHTS AND THE AI AND IOT-ENABLED MONITORING POWER

In this chapter, building on my analysis of how AI and IoT-enabled technologies reshape the exercise of the employer's monitoring power, I address the research sub-question 4: *What is a legitimate exercise of the AI and IoT-enabled employer's monitoring power in the European fundamental rights framework?*

The use of AI and IoT-enabled technologies by employers to exercise their monitoring power raises concerns in scholarship,[360] case law[361] and DPAs[362] on the enjoyment of employees' fundamental rights. Fundamental rights play an essential role in protecting our working lives and foster many aspects of our personal, social and economic fulfilment. In Chapter 3, I defined a 'legitimate' exercise of the employer's

360. Council of Europe et al., *Handbook on European Data Protection Law: 2018 Edition* (Publications Office 2019) 330; Antonio Aloisi and Elena Gramano, 'Artificial Intelligence Is Watching You at Work. Digital Surveillance, Employee Monitoring, and Regulatory Issues in the EU Context' (2019) 41 Comparative Labor Law & Policy Journal 95.

361. Mangan (n 183).

362. Article 29 Data Protection Working Party, 'Opinion 02/2017 on Data Processing at Work' (n 21); 'Garante Privacy: Ordinanza Del 10.11.2022: Illegittimo Il Trattamento Di Dati Biometrici per La Rilevazione Delle Presenze' (*Lavorosì*, 11 January 2023) http://www.lavorosi.it/rapporti-di-lavoro/riservatezza/garante-privacy-ordinanza-del-10112022-illegittimo-il-trattamento-di-dati-biometrici-per-la-ri/ accessed 22 October 2025; Garante per la Protezione dei Dati Personali, 'Riders: Italian SA Says No to Algorithms Causing Discrimination A Platform in the Glovo Group Fined EUR 2.6 Million' (2021) https://www.garanteprivacy.it/home/docweb/-/docweb-display/docweb/9677377#english accessed 22 October 2025.

monitoring power as one that respects employees' fundamental rights, including privacy, freedom of expression, trade union freedoms and non-discrimination.[363] Given that AI and IoT-enabled technologies are increasingly used for monitoring purposes, understanding what use can be considered legitimate becomes an important task for research.[364]

In section 2, I analyse the employer's three main monitoring purposes: monitoring employer property and employees' access; monitoring employees' performance; and monitoring employees' personal characteristics and behaviours. I assess the legitimate exercise of an AI- and IoT-enabled employer's monitoring power, via the technologies discussed in Chapter 4, by applying the *general criteria* and their more specific elaborations in the ECtHR and ECJ case law for legitimate restrictions of employees' fundamental rights, as identified in the table in Chapter 3 (section 7). This analysis enables an evaluation of whether and how these technologies interfere with or reinforce employees' fundamental rights. Section 3 concludes by addressing the regulatory challenges emerging from my analysis and answers research sub-question 4.

2 ASSESSING THE LEGITIMATE EXERCISE OF AN AI AND IOT-ENABLED EMPLOYER'S MONITORING POWER

2.1 Monitoring Employers' Properties and Employees' Access: Employee OSH and Cybersecurity Standards

Digital Occupational Safety and Health (OSH) systems offer improved safety standards through a detailed overview of employees' activities, as seen in the case of the AI camera *Intenseye*. Similarly, on the cybersecurity front, software such as *Controlio*, *Interguard*, and *FlexiSpy* record device activities of employees and can prevent or rapidly solve security issues.[365] With them, employers can ensure, and possibly raise, security and safety standards in their businesses. Yet, monitoring of movements on the shopfloor, AI-enabled cameras on drivers, or tracking for cybersecurity purposes, provides refined information about past, current, and future employees' actions. While this can prevent (cyber)accidents, it is worth exploring whether its implementation constitutes a legitimate exercise of the employer's monitoring power.

363. Sections 7 and 8, Chapter 3.

364. *See*, for instance, *López Ribalda and Others v. Spain*, App No 1874/13 and 8567/13 (ECtHR, 17 October 2019), Joint dissenting opinion Judges De Gaetano, Yudkivska and Grozev, para. 2: 'This case demonstrates the growing influence and control that technology has in our world, and more particularly, the collection and use of our personal data in our everyday activities. As a living instrument, the Convention, and therefore the Court, not only needs to recognise the influence of modern technologies, but also has to develop more adequate legal safeguards to secure respect for the private life of individuals.'

365. All the mentioned examples on digital tools for cybersecurity and OSH purposes are taken from my discussion in Chapter 4, section 3.1.

2.1.1 *The Right to Privacy and Data Protection*

While both the European Agency for Safety and Health at Work (EU-OSHA) and the European Union Agency for Cybersecurity (ENISA) have recognised the positive impact of these technologies on OSH and cybersecurity standards in companies,[366] their introduction raises concerns in scholarship about their impact on employees' right to privacy and data protection.[367] The WP29, in its Opinion on data processing at work, warned that these practices can result in *incompatible further processing*.[368] Examples include the use of surveillance technologies for other purposes rather than security, to monitor employees' availability, performance, and customer interactions. The Opinion also cautioned against using CCTV[369] footage to routinely evaluate employees' behaviours and performance or using geolocation data (like Wi-Fi or Bluetooth tracking).[370] Similarly, AI and IoT-enabled technologies such as *Intenseye* and *Controlio* conduct continuous, real-time data collection to support objectives such as OSH or cybersecurity.

Any limitation to employees' right to privacy and data protection must meet the *general criteria* set out in Article 8(2) ECHR and Article 52(1) CFREU.[371] First, the monitoring must be *prescribed by law*, for example, through specific legal provisions on OSH. Second, the monitoring must be strictly limited to achieving a clearly defined and *legitimate aim*. In practice, however, these technologies often extend their reach beyond such aims.[372] A system designed to detect hazardous behaviours might also

366. Cf. European Agency for Safety and Health at Work (n 8); European Union Agency for Cybersecurity (n 9).
367. *See*, for instance, the *Florindo* ECtHR case: Molè and Mangan (n 205); *see also*: Aude Cefaliello, Phoebe V Moore and Robert Donoghue, 'Making Algorithmic Management Safe and Healthy for Workers: Addressing Psychosocial Risks in New Legal Provisions' (2023) 14 European Labour Law Journal 192 https://doi.org/10.1177/20319525231167476 accessed 22 October 2025; Hendrickx (n 32); Marta Otto, 'Workforce Analytics v Fundamental Rights Protection in the EU in the Age of Big Data' (2019) 40 Comparative Labor Law and Policy Journals https://cllpj.law.illinois.edu/ accessed 22 October 2025.
368. Article 29 Data Protection Working Party, 'Opinion 02/2017 on Data Processing at Work' (n 21) 10.
369. Closed-Circuit Television (CCTV) is a system using cameras to transmitting to a specific and closed network for monitoring and security purposes. CCTV signals are not publicly transmitted but are instead sent to designated monitors or recording devices.
370. Article 29 Data Protection Working Party, 'Opinion 02/2017 on Data Processing at Work' (n 21) 10.
371. Cf. with sections 6.1 and 7, Chapter 3.
372. Cybersecurity and OSH monitoring often foster the so-called function creep of surveillance, which, according to Koops, is to be understood as 'an imperceptibly transformative and therewith contestable change in a data-processing system's proper activity'. Cf. Bert-Jaap Koops, 'The Concept of Function Creep' (2021) 13 Law, Innovation and Technology 29 https://doi.org/10.1080/17579961.2021.1898299 accessed 22 October 2025. About repercussions on autonomy and dignity of workers due to excessive monitoring, *see*: Emma Rooksby and Natasha Cica, 'Personal Autonomy and Electronic Monitoring in the Workplace' in John Weckert (ed.), *Electronic Monitoring in the Workplace* (IGI Global 2005) https://www.igi-global.com/chapter/personal-autonomy-electronic-monitoring-workplace/10022 accessed 22 October 2025.

process biometric data or capture non-work-related actions,[373] while cybersecurity monitoring may collect private communications or location data.[374] Third, the interference must be *necessary and proportionate*, meaning that no less intrusive alternative is available to achieve the same aim, and that the scope and duration of monitoring are strictly limited to what is required for the stated purpose.[375] Finally, the monitoring must *respect the essence of the right to privacy*, ensuring that even a necessary and proportionate AI and IoT-enabled monitoring does not undermine the very substance of that right.

As I have discussed in Chapter 3, the ECtHR's judgment in *Bărbulescu v. Romania*[376] identified six additional factors to assess proportionality and procedural guarantees against arbitrariness, which should guide the assessment of whether employee monitoring respects the right to privacy: (1) whether the employee has received an *ex ante notification*; (2) the *extent of monitoring*; (3) the employer's *legitimate reasons*; (4) the possibility of using *less intrusive methods*; (5) the *impact on the employee*; and (6) the presence of *adequate safeguards*:

- The requirement of *ex ante notification* demands that employees must be clearly and specifically informed in advance about the monitoring's scope, purpose, methods, and potential consequences. This proves to be essential in this context, as many AI and IoT-enabled technologies, such as those for OSH or cybersecurity purposes, are based on complex data analysis[377] and operate with limited transparency for employees.
- The *extent of monitoring* and the degree of intrusion must be proportionate to the aim pursued. The ECtHR stressed the need to assess whether monitoring was limited in time, content, access, and space. AI and IoT-enabled technology systems like *Intenseye* and *Controlio*, used for OSH or cybersecurity, exceed these limits. Though the aims may be legitimate, these tools frequently operate continuously and comprehensively, tracking biometric data, behaviours, and even private conversations.[378] Such a monitoring can intrude into employees' private lives, especially when not limited to specific risk contexts. Without clear restrictions in the operation of these technologies, the degree of intrusion becomes disproportionate to the stated safety or security purposes.
- The provided *legitimate reasons* for monitoring, such as ensuring OSH compliance or cybersecurity, require a weightier justification when carried out through distinctly more invasive methods, as stipulated by the ECtHR. AI and

373. Annie Palmer, 'Amazon Is Rolling out Cameras That Can Detect If Warehouse Workers Are Following Social Distancing Rules' (*CNBC*, 16 June 2020) https://www.cnbc.com/2020/06/16/amazon-using-cameras-to-enforce-social-distancing-rules-at-warehouses.html accessed 22 October 2025.
374. Christen et al. (n 303).
375. Jonas Christoffersen, *Fair Balance: Proportionality, Subsidiarity and Primarity in the European Convention on Human Rights* (Martinus Nijhoff Publishers 2009).
376. *See* section 6.1.2, Chapter 3.
377. *See* my discussion on the descriptive, diagnostic, predictive and prescriptive features of AI and IoT-enabled technology data analysis, section 4.2, Chapter 4.
378. *See* Chapter 4, section 3.1. Cf. with the concept of function creep in monitoring: Koops (n 372).

IoT-based tools like *Intenseye* and *Controlio*, though initially introduced for these legitimate purposes, often extend beyond their original scope. For example, *Intenseye* may capture not only hazardous behaviours but also emotional states or personal conduct, while *Controlio* can record keystrokes or screen activity, potentially intercepting private communications. When these systems shift from identifying objective risks to monitoring subjective or unrelated behaviours, the initial justification no longer holds, and the level of intrusion becomes disproportionate.[379]

- The availability of *less intrusive methods* must be considered. Instead of monitoring individual employees, employers could use systems that focus on general workplace conditions (e.g., detecting falling objects or excessive noise levels) while anonymising or aggregating any personal data incidentally collected. Trigger-based monitoring systems, activated only when predefined risk thresholds are met, represent a more proportionate solution. For example, cybersecurity tools could focus on detecting anomalies in sensitive systems rather than continuously logging all activity. AI and IoT-enabled technologies like *Intenseye* and *Controlio* could, in order to be legitimate, adopt these less invasive approaches to achieve the same safety or security objectives. Instead of constantly tracking individual movements, *Intenseye* could limit itself to monitoring workplace safety risks (e.g., identifying hazardous behaviours), while *Controlio* could focus on detecting cybersecurity threats rather than monitoring all employee activities. In line with the ECtHR's reasoning, there should be an assessment in the light of the particular circumstances of each case to determine whether the employer's aim could have been achieved without directly accessing the full contents of the employee's communications or personal data.
- The *impact on the employee* and the employer's use of the monitoring results must also be scrutinised. If the data collected through *Intenseye* or *Controlio* is not strictly used to identify immediate safety hazards or cybersecurity threats, but is instead employed for broader, less defined purposes (e.g., tracking employee productivity or behaviours outside the stated scope), the monitoring would be disproportionate to the original aim. The results of the monitoring should be targeted and used exclusively to address the declared objective, such as improving safety standards or protecting sensitive systems, to avoid disproportionate intrusion into employees' privacy.
- *Adequate safeguards* must be in place to prevent abuse from employers; these safeguards could also include measures like transparent data usage policies and limited data retention periods to ensure that monitoring does not exceed its necessary scope and is fully compliant with privacy protections.

In light of the *Bărbulescu* criteria, the use of AI and IoT-enabled technologies for OSH and cybersecurity purposes must be carefully scrutinised. Unless they meet the

379. *See also*: Article 29 Data Protection Working Party, 'Opinion 02/2017 on Data Processing at Work' (n 21) 23.

above requirements regarding proportionality and procedural safeguards, they do not satisfy the requirements for restricting the right to privacy and data protection at work. Without these essential safeguards, the deployment of these technologies for OSH or cybersecurity purposes constitutes an illegitimate exercise of the employer's monitoring power.

2.1.2 Freedom of Expression

Under Article 10(2) ECHR and Article 52(1) CFREU, restrictions on employees' freedom of expression are permissible only when they comply with the *general criteria*: the restriction must be *prescribed by law, pursue a legitimate aim,* be *necessary and proportionate,* and *respect the essence of the freedom in question.*[380] Based on my analysis of relevant case law from both the ECtHR and ECJ in Chapter 3, I found that the Courts apply these general criteria by permitting restrictions that are narrowly worded in the law, to prevent arbitrary interference and ensure that only those limitations explicitly prescribed by law are imposed on this freedom.[381]

Even if a particular instance of monitoring does not appear to infringe the freedom of expression when assessed individually, constant AI and IoT-enabled monitoring may give rise to a broader structural issue: function creep.[382] As defined by Koops, 'function creep' is 'an expansion or shift in the proper activity of a data-processing system in relation to its purpose or use, which is considered contestable because people insufficiently recognise that it involves a qualitative change'.[383] For example, a system originally introduced to ensure physical security may eventually be used to assess performance, availability, or customer interaction, without proper re-evaluation of its legitimacy, as noted by the WP29 in its Guidelines on data processing at work.[384] The WP29 emphasised a similar risk also for collective forms of expression such as trade union freedoms, as surveillance technologies might facilitate a 'chilling effect on the fundamental rights of employees to organise, set up workers' meetings, and communicate confidentially'.[385] Such technologies can create an environment where employees feel discouraged from expressing opinions or engaging in union activities. This concern echoes a substantial line of European case law recognising that indirect or cumulative forms of interference can still violate fundamental rights, especially in the employment context.[386]

380. On the balancing between cybersecurity and employees' privacy – with specific reference to purpose limitation – *see*: Lilian Mitrou and Maria Karyda, 'Employees' Privacy vs. Employers' Security: Can They Be Balanced?' (2006) 23 Telematics and Informatics 164, 171 https://doi.org/10.1016/j.tele.2005.07.003 accessed 22 October 2025.
381. Cf. with sections 6.2 and 7, Chapter 3.
382. Posey and Shoss (n 298).
383. Koops (n 372) 53.
384. Article 29 Data Protection Working Party, 'Opinion 02/2017 on Data Processing at Work' (n 21) 10.
385. *Ibid.*, 9.
386. On the 'discouraging' measures leading to chilling effects on the enjoyment of fundamental rights: *Wille v. Liechteinstein* (1999) App No 28396/95 (ECtHR, 28 October 1999); *Fuentes Bobo v. Spain* (2000) App No 39293/98 (29 February 2000); *Goodwin v. UK* (2002) App No 28957/95

For instance, the NIS2 Directive obliges certain employers to implement appropriate cybersecurity measures to protect critical infrastructure, thereby pursuing a legitimate aim clearly prescribed by law.[387] However, this obligation does not extend to constant and limitless monitoring of employee communications. If monitoring captures private conversations that may reveal trade union activity, political beliefs, or other sensitive matters, there is a risk that the requirements of necessity and proportionality will be violated, particularly where less intrusive, targeted tools could achieve the same security goals. Monitoring is only lawful to the extent that it responds directly to concrete workplace risks and remains within the boundaries of what is explicitly permitted by law. Measures that fail to do so risk becoming arbitrary interferences, even when framed as efforts to enhance safety or security.[388]

Therefore, to prevent an illegitimate restriction of employees' freedom of expression, employers must not only ensure that AI and IoT-enabled technologies for cybersecurity or OSH monitoring are grounded in law but also assess whether the monitoring measure is necessary and proportionate. This includes adopting privacy-preserving techniques, such as anomaly detection limited to sensitive systems, while avoiding the incidental collection of data unrelated to the risks to be prevented. Implementing strict technical safeguards, such as encryption and access controls, is essential to ensure that monitoring remains confined to its intended purpose and does not spill over into disciplinary uses unrelated to security concerns.[389] Failing to do so makes the AI and IoT-enabled monitoring an illegitimate exercise of the employer's power to monitor his or her employees.

2.2 Monitoring Work Performance

Whether blue-collar or white-collar, monitoring employees' work performance today implies the use of a wide range of AI and IoT-enabled technologies. Sensors and algorithms can learn where employees are physically (desk, shopfloor), how many breaks they take and for how long, and how long it takes them to perform a specific task.[390] They often monitor bathroom breaks, coffee breaks, occupancy levels of the working desk for a given period (such as in the case of *Occupeye*).[391] In short, as seen in the corresponding section 3.2, Chapter 4, for every work performance monitoring need, there is a corresponding software or sensor available from the surveillance technology market.

(11 July 2002); *Guja v. Moldova* (2008) App No 14277/04 (ECtHR, 12 February 2008); *Kudeshkina v. Russia* (2009) App No App No 29492/05 (ECtHR, 26 February 2009).

387. Cf. with section 3.1, Chapter 4. Directive (EU) 2022/2555 of the European Parliament and of the Council of 14 December 2022 on measures for a high common level of cybersecurity across the Union, amending Regulation (EU) No 910/2014 and Directive (EU) 2018/1972, and repealing Directive (EU) 2016/1148 (NIS 2 Directive).
388. Cobbaut (n 226) 305-306.
389. Corradini (n 297); European Agency for Safety and Health at Work (n 8).
390. Delfanti (n 337).
391. Bloodworth (n 312).

2.2.1 The Right to Privacy and Data Protection

Performance assessment is an aspect of the employer's monitoring power, and it is subject to varying regulatory approaches in Member States' labour laws. In this context, to have an AI and IoT-enabled monitoring respectful of privacy and data protection fundamental rights, the implementation of such technologies must comply with the *general criteria* laid down in Article 8(2) ECHR and Article 52(1) CFREU:[392] Monitoring must be *prescribed by law, pursue a legitimate aim, respect the essence of the rights concerned*, and be *necessary and proportionate*. This means that even if AI and IoT-enabled monitoring serves a legitimate aim and is proportionate, it cannot be justified if it undermines the very substance of the fundamental right at stake.

As I have discussed in Chapter 3, the ECtHR's judgment in *Bărbulescu v. Romania*[393] identified six factors that should guide the assessment of proportionality and procedural safeguards against arbitrariness: (1) whether the employee has received ad *ex ante notification*; (2) the *extent of monitoring*; (3) the employer's *legitimate reasons*; (4) the possibility of using *less intrusive methods*; (5) the *impact on the employee*; and (6) the presence of *adequate safeguards*. The ECtHR in the *Bărbulescu* case has also clarified that the balancing of interests between the employee's right to privacy and the employer's right to engage in monitoring for the 'smooth running of the company' must be carefully conducted (paragraph 124).

I observe that since the regulation of performance assessment monitoring differs significantly across domestic legal systems,[394] the requirement to assess necessity and proportionality acquires particular importance in this context.[395] While the 'prescribed by law' criterion ensures a legal basis for monitoring, it may still permit a wide range of practices depending on national legislation. The necessity and proportionality test, by contrast, provides a common standard under the European fundamental rights framework that allows for a more substantive evaluation of whether a specific monitoring measure unjustifiably interferes with employees' rights, regardless of national divergences.

In this regard, the ECtHR's *Florindo* case (2022) and the accompanying dissenting opinion highlight the importance of applying a necessity and proportionality test when assessing the use of modern surveillance technologies for monitoring work performance.[396] Mr Florindo was dismissed for underreporting the kilometres travelled with the company car and for working fewer hours than required. His employer relied on a GPS installed in the car to track his mileage and hours worked. While the ECtHR acknowledged that using GPS data for performance monitoring is unlawful under Portuguese law (Article 20 Labour Code), which restricts monitoring to security and

392. Cf. with sections 6.1 and 7, Chapter 3.
393. *See* section 6.1.2, Chapter 3.
394. Cf. with section 5, Chapter 3, on the various EU Member States legislations on the employer's monitoring power, as mapped by the 2020 EUROFOUND report on monitoring and surveillance at work: Riso (n 2).
395. *Ibid.*
396. *Florindo De Almeida Vasconcelos Gramaxo v. Portugal* (2022) App No 26968/16 (ECtHR, 13 December 2022), para. 124.

safety purposes, the majority of the judges still upheld the dismissal based on both underreporting kilometres and work performance data (working less than the hours contractually agreed). The Court reasoned that the damage caused to company property justified the interference with Mr Florindo, even if the work performance data was unlawfully collected.[397] The dissenting opinion challenged this conclusion, arguing that the Court failed to assess whether less intrusive alternatives could have achieved the same objective (protection of company property) without using work performance data. The Portuguese DPA had previously suggested a less privacy-invasive monitoring method, which the employer (and the Court) disregarded. By overlooking these alternatives, the dissenting judges contended, the Court weakened the necessity test and failed to ensure that monitoring was strictly proportionate to its purpose.

As this case shows by analogy, the use of technologies that enable constant and granular tracking of employees' working performance without clear safeguards regarding their purposes may exceed what is necessary for legitimate monitoring and potentially violate employees' privacy rights under Article 8 ECHR.[398] This concern is amplified by the limited legal clarity surrounding permissible performance monitoring practices, as highlighted in *Florindo*, where the Court did not clearly define the boundary between acceptable monitoring for protecting company property and unnecessary monitoring of work performance.[399] By applying both the general criteria and their elaboration through the Bărbulescu factors – including *ex ante* notification, the extent of monitoring, legitimate reasons, availability of less intrusive alternatives, impact on the employee, and procedural safeguards – the Court could have reached a more robust and transparent assessment of the legitimacy of the monitoring at issue.[400]

This, I conclude, highlights the relevance of strictly adhering to the *Bărbulescu* test when evaluating the use of AI and IoT-enabled technologies for monitoring employees' performance, to prevent an illegitimate exercise of the employer's monitoring power.[401]

2.2.2 Non-discrimination

AI and IoT-enabled technologies can identify which employee (or group of employees) performs best on a specific project, which employees are going to quit or who is more

397. I comment on these discrepancies in the *Florindo* case with David Mangan: Molè and Mangan (n 205) 700.
398. *Ibid.*, 698.
399. In *Antović and Mirković v. Montenegro*, the Court reached an opposite conclusion. It found that continuous camera surveillance of teaching staff was unnecessary, as the legally permissible security objectives could have been met by installing cameras in public areas rather than monitoring teachers' performance in classrooms. *Antović and Mirković v. Montenegro* (2017) App No 70838/13 (ECtHR, 28 November 2017).
400. Molè and Mangan (n 205).
401. Michele Molè, 'The Internet of Things and Artificial Intelligence as Workplace Supervisors: Explaining and Understanding the New Surveillance to Employees Beyond Art. 8 ECHR' (2022) 15 Italian Labour Law e-Journal 87, 90.

promising for promotion. While this represents a legitimate aim, performative evaluations are carried out with data of various kinds, including personal or social connotations.[402] In this regard, AI and IoT-enabled technologies present a structural problem, since they can perpetuate biases, stereotypes and social perceptions.[403] An AI system learning process in fact is based on analysing historical behavioural patterns.[404] In the realm of employment, these patterns may mirror past discrimination instances, such as instances where women are paid less for the same job or are dissuaded from pursuing certain occupations due to on-the-job harassment.[405]

Legal scholarship points to various AI-based job recruitment technologies that systematically perpetuate biases against underrepresented groups by hiring or promoting them less on the basis of nationality, gender, age, health or other personal characteristics.[406] These technologies used to predict the performance of an applicant have been found to generate correlations of a purely random nature without any causal link. For example, a UK dataset revealed that Facebook users who liked 'curly fries' were more likely to have strong computer programming skills than other users. These arbitrary patterns could influence hiring or promotion decisions without any legitimate basis.[407]

Under Article 14 ECHR and Article 52(1) CFREU, any restriction on the right to non-discrimination must meet the *general criteria* outlined in Chapter 3. Specifically, the ECtHR and ECJ apply an *objective justification test*, where any differential treatment must not only be *prescribed by law* and pursue *a legitimate aim* (such as avoiding relying on prohibited grounds such as race, gender, or trade union activity), the differential treatment must be also *necessary and proportionate* to achieve the stated objective, and *respect the essence of the right.*[408]

For instance, in a court case in Bologna, as discussed by Hießl in her case law review, the food delivery platform Deliveroo was found to be using an algorithm to assess riders' 'reliability' and 'participation' based on their logging in for work shifts

402. Wood (n 15) 4; Heiner Heiland, 'Controlling Space, Controlling Labour? Contested Space in Food Delivery Gig Work' (2021) 36 New Technology, Work and Employment 1 https://doi.org/10.1111/ntwe.12183 accessed 22 October 2025; Negrón, 'Little Tech Is Coming for Workers: A Framework for Reclaiming and Building Worker Power' (n 5).
403. Kim and Bodie (n 31).
404. Liu, Sun and Wang (n 282).
405. Kim and Bodie (n 31) 294.
406. *Ibid.*, 299; Sandra Wachter and Brent Mittelstadt, 'A Right to Reasonable Inferences: Re-Thinking Data Protection Law in the Age of Big Data and AI' (2019) Columbia Business Law Review 494 https://doi.org/10.7916/cblr.v2019i2.3424 accessed 22 October 2025; Jarrahi et al. (n 310) 3; Pauline T. Kim, 'Data-Driven Discrimination at Work' (2017) 58 William and Mary Law Review 857 https://scholarship.law.wm.edu/wmlr/vol58/iss3/4 accessed 22 October 2025; Alina Köchling and Marius Claus Wehner, 'Discriminated by an Algorithm: A Systematic Review of Discrimination and Fairness by Algorithmic Decision-Making in the Context of HR Recruitment and HR Development' (2020) 13 Business Research 795 https://doi.org/10.1007/s40685-020-00134-w accessed 22 October 2025.
407. Kim and Bodie (n 31) 299; Wachter and Mittelstadt (n 406).
408. Cf. with sections 6.4 and 7, Chapter 3.

and availability during peak hours.[409] The algorithm by using these indexes determined access to future shifts, favouring those with higher scores. The Court assessed whether this system was indirectly discriminating against riders who participated in trade union activities or had family responsibilities. The Court applied the objective justification test and considered trade union activities as a form of expressing political or philosophical beliefs, which are protected under the prohibition of discrimination based on belief.[410] The algorithm penalised those who engaged in these activities by lowering their reliability and participation scores, thereby discriminating against them based on their political or philosophical beliefs. The Court ruled that this practice violated the prohibition of indirect discrimination based on belief, as outlined in Article 1 of Directive 2000/78/EC. Similarly, the Court found discrimination against employees with family responsibilities, finding a violation of the prohibition of indirect discrimination under Article 14 of the Recast Directive 2006/54/EC and Articles 11-12 of the Work-Life Balance Directive for Parents and Carers (EU) 2019/1158.[411]

While the legitimacy of Deliveroo's aim to ensure rider availability was not contested, the Court found that penalising workers for engaging in trade union activities or having family responsibilities was neither necessary nor proportionate. In practice, this resulted in some riders being assigned fewer shifts due to these factors. Deliveroo failed to prove that these discriminatory practices were essential to achieving its business objectives (assigning shifts and continuity in deliveries). This ruling underscores the relevance of the objective justification test to prevent AI and IoT-enabled monitoring that discriminates, ensuring that even when pursuing a legitimate aim, such as maintaining continuity in deliveries, any differential treatment must be necessary and not disproportionately infringe upon employees' rights.[412]

AI and IoT-enabled technologies, by collecting more information about the workforce and by drawing on behavioural patterns, may facilitate direct or indirect discrimination against employees.[413] To mitigate the risk of discrimination stemming from the exercise of an AI and IoT-enabled employer's monitoring power, regulation must address how these technologies are trained. I will later explore in Chapters 6-9 whether the GDPR and AI Act provide sufficient safeguards to prevent discriminatory outcomes in the context of employee monitoring.

2.3 Monitoring Personal Characteristics (Physical or Behavioural Traits)

Last among the employer's monitoring purposes analysed here is the monitoring of the employee's personal characteristics, such as physical traits or behaviours, to further integrate them into the employer's organisation.[414] These monitored behaviours,

409. Christina Hießl, 'Algorithmic Management in the Workplace: Taking Stock of Case Law and Litigation in Europe' [2022] Hungarian Labour Law eJournal 10 https://hllj.hu/letolt/2022_2_a/01_ChHiessl_hllj_uj_2022_2.pdf accessed 22 October 2025.
410. Article 1 of Directive 2000/78/EC. *ibid.*
411. *Ibid.*, 4.
412. Cf. with section 6.4, Chapter 3. *Ibid.*, 10.
413. Köchling and Wehner (n 406) 838-840.
414. Cf. with section 3.3, Chapter 4.

whether of individuals or groups, are diverse and closely tied to the functionality of specific AI and IoT-enabled technologies. On a more individual level, it is possible to identify employees who interact frequently, connect their personal communications to their productivity,[415] and detect the workforce mood through language and communication patterns.[416] Workforce collective behaviours can be monitored as well. In Chapter 4, I brought the example of *Perceptyx*, a workplace survey tool allegedly predicting the likelihood of employees seeking unionisation.[417] Monitoring personal characteristics, similar to monitoring for security and safety, may have important impacts on the right to privacy, freedom of expression and discrimination.

2.3.1 *The Right to Privacy and Data Protection*

In the 1997 *Halford* case, the ECtHR found that an employer's interception of telephone calls to monitor an employee's private life, with the aim of justifying a professional decision (denying Ms Halford a promotion), did not meet any of the exceptions set out in Article 8(2) ECHR.[418] A similar approach was taken in *Copland*, where the Court acknowledged that monitoring (of telephone and private conversations) could, in certain circumstances, pursue a 'necessary [monitoring purpose] in a democratic society' (paragraph 48).[419] However, in the absence of clear provisions in the law and strict necessity for such measures (e.g., security or safety measures, *see* section 2.1 of this Chapter), monitoring employees' non-work-related behaviour was found by the ECtHR as in violation of Article 8(2) ECHR. These cases demonstrate that while monitoring of employees' personal behaviour is not absolutely prohibited, it must comply with the *general criteria* under Article 8(2) ECHR and Article 52(1) CFREU: it must be *prescribed by law, pursue a legitimate aim*, be *necessary and proportionate*, and *respect the essence of the right to privacy*.

As established in greater detail in the *Bărbulescu* test, this assessment requires balancing the employer's interests with the employee's right to privacy and hinges on proportionality and the existence of procedural guarantees against arbitrariness (paragraph 121). I draw on this test in the analysis that follows to assess whether the deployment of AI and IoT-enabled technologies for monitoring employees' personal characteristics – specifically, the use of AI and IoT-enabled technologies to infer information from employees' social interactions at work[420] – constitutes a legitimate exercise of the employer's monitoring power:

- *Ex ante notification*: Employees must be clearly informed in advance about the deployment of AI and IoT-enabled technologies and the scope of the monitoring. This includes specification of which personal behaviours (e.g., social

415. Leonardi and Contractor (n 316).
416. Lix et al. (n 319).
417. 'Perceptyx' https://www.perceptyx.com accessed 22 October 2025.
418. *Halford v. United Kingdom* (1997) App No 20605/92 (ECtHR, 25 June 1997).
419. *Copland v. United Kingdom* (2007) App No 62617/00 (ECtHR, 3 April 2007).
420. Cf. with section 3.3, Chapter 4, on the use of AI and IoT-enabled technologies for inferring information from employees' personal behaviour in and outside work.

interactions, voice tone, physical proximity) are tracked, for what purposes, the technological methods used, and the potential consequences for the employee.

- *Extent of monitoring*: The employer must demonstrate a lawful purpose for the use of the AI and IoT-enabled technology to monitor personal behaviours, such as workplace (cyber)security or the protection of company assets (*see*, in this regard section 2.1 of this chapter).
- *Legitimate reasons*: The extent of the employer's monitoring power (*see* previous point) must be proportionate to the legitimate aim pursued. According to the ECtHR in *Bărbulescu*, more intrusive forms of monitoring require a correspondingly weightier justification, particularly where private or sensitive aspects of the employee's life are concerned. Accordingly, tracking social interactions among colleagues must be justified by a compelling operational need, such as ensuring workplace safety or addressing serious organisational risks, that outweighs the intrusion into employees' interpersonal dynamics.
- *Less invasive methods*: The employer must consider whether his or her monitoring needs could be achieved through less invasive means. In the case of tracking social interactions at work, the employer should demonstrate that less intrusive means are not available. For instance, if the goal is to enhance teamwork, organising collective training sessions would be a more proportionate approach than tracking individual employees' interactions through wearable devices.[421]
- *Impact on the employee*: Monitoring must not lead to harmful effects, such as excessive psychological pressure, undue interference with autonomy, or biased performance evaluations based on irrelevant personal data. Employers should assess and mitigate any adverse impact on employees' rights and working conditions.
- *Provision of adequate safeguards*: Employees must have access to clear procedures to contest or seek redress against unjustified or arbitrary monitoring. Effective safeguards, such as independent oversight, the right to explanation, and review mechanisms, must be in place to prevent misuse or disproportionate reliance on behavioural data collected through AI and IoT-enabled technologies.

Considering the *Bărbulescu* criteria, the deployment of AI and IoT-enabled technologies to infer employees' behaviours or social interactions is not justified as often the same goals (e.g., enhance teamwork) could be achieved through less intrusive and more proportionate methods that do not involve the systematic data

421. The French DPA found that re-training of employees based on individual devices collecting data was unnecessary and disproportionate, as the same goals could have achieved by looking at output results per unit (groups of employees). Michele Molè, 'Minimised Work Surveillance Exists under the GDPR: Amazon France and the DPA Sanction' (*Global Workplace Law & Policy*, 4 March 2024) https://global-workplace-law-and-policy.kluwerlawonline.com/2024/03/04/minimised-work-surveillance-exists-under-the-gdpr-amazon-france-and-the-dpa-sanction/ accessed 22 October 2025; Marassi and Bolte (n 31).

collection and analysis of employees' individual or interpersonal behaviours. Given that AI and IoT-enabled technologies have the potential to shift the balance towards a disproportionate reduction in the enjoyment of fundamental rights, it is crucial that the law provides for robust procedural guarantees. In particular, the law should ensure that employers' use of these technologies is tightly in line with the *Bărbulescu* criteria, to protect employees' fundamental rights in an increasingly data-driven working environment.

2.3.2 Freedom of Expression and of Performing Trade Union Activities

In April 2022, *Amazon,* following a leak to the press, stopped the development of its internal chat-app *Shout-Out* which was intended for its employees. Some developers disclosed the AI system's model that was intended to monitor employees' communications.[422] The AI system would have blocked a variety of terms that correlate to criticism of Amazon's working conditions and union activities, such as 'Slave labour', 'Representation', 'Union', 'Unite/Unity' and others.[423]

As I have discussed in Chapter 3, under Articles 10(2), 11(2) ECHR, when employers' monitoring activities restrict employees' freedom of expression, assembly and association, any restriction must be *prescribed by law, pursue a legitimate aim*, and meet the requirements of *necessity and proportionality* in a democratic society. Moreover, the restriction *must respect the essence of the right*, as required by Article 52(1) CFREU and by the ECtHR *Demir* case interpreting Article 11(2) ECHR.[424] As regards restricting employees' freedom of expression under Article 10(2) ECHR, I found in Chapter 3 that the ECtHR and ECJ usually allow for restrictions that are precisely worded in law or narrowly interpreted, to avoid arbitrary interference.[425] While anti-discrimination laws and trade secret protections, such as those outlined in Directives 2000/43/EC, 2000/78/EC, and 2016/943/EU, may justify specific and limited restrictions, broad and pre-emptive censorship of work-related discussions as the one imposed by *Amazon Shout-Out* lacks a legitimate aim. Measures that prohibit the use of terms like union, representation, or slave labour exceed the scope of protecting legitimate business interests and instead aim to restrict discussions on workplace rights. Preventing employees from engaging in collective representation or discussing working conditions does not pursue a legitimate aim as required by the European fundamental rights framework. Even where some moderation of content may be justified – that is, where it is prescribed by law and pursues a legitimate aim – the necessity and proportionality of the restriction must still be rigorously assessed in light of Article 10(2) ECHR and Article 52(1) CFREU. This ensures that the restriction does not go beyond what is strictly required and does not impair the essence of the right

422. Ken Klippenstein, 'Leaked: New Amazon Worker Chat App Would Ban Words Like "Union," "Restrooms," "Pay Raise," And "Plantation"' (*The Intercept*, 4 April 2022) https://theintercept.com/2022/04/04/amazon-union-living-wage-restrooms-chat-app/ accessed 22 October 2025.
423. *Ibid.*
424. Cf. with sections 6.2, 6.3 and section 7, Chapter 3.
425. Cf. with section 6.2, Chapter 3.

to freedom of expression. Moreover, the Amazon *Shout-Out* AI system's model, by blocking a wide range of terms, would have significantly limited employees' ability to engage in legally protected activities, particularly the right to join trade unions as protected under Article 11 ECHR.

To give another example, *Perceptyx*, a survey tool designed to gauge employee satisfaction, uses a 'union vulnerability index' based on comparisons with a large external database to predict the likelihood of unionisation.[426] Such monitoring must be prescribed by law and thus require a specific legal provision allowing for it. In the absence of a clear legal basis, monitoring collective behaviours aimed at detecting unionisation efforts is not allowed. Moreover, as discussed in section 6.3 of Chapter 3, the use of such technologies could foster a chilling effect, discouraging employees from exercising their right to unionise. This would directly contradict the obligation to respect the essence of the right to freedom of association under Article 52(1) CFREU and Article 11(2) ECHR, as interpreted by the ECtHR in *Demir*, which established that restrictions undermining the core of trade union rights are not allowed.[427]

Regular monitoring of communications, interactions, and movements grants employers access to information that can directly inhibit assembly efforts and discourage open expression.[428] The ECtHR has affirmed that 'members of a trade union must be able to convey their demands to their employer as a means to improve employee conditions', underlining that depriving a trade union, or any employee, of the ability to express views freely takes away from them a fundamental advocacy tool.[429] Without adequate safeguards, AI- and IoT-enabled monitoring technologies can act as powerful deterrents, discouraging union representatives or employees from advocating for their rights. This risk to the freedoms of expression, assembly, and association was also highlighted by the WP29 in its opinion on data processing at work.[430]

The implementation of AI- and IoT-enabled technologies that restrict employees' ability to form or join trade unions violates Articles 10 and 11 ECHR, and the law must provide for adequate safeguards to employees in this regard.

2.3.3 Non-discrimination

AI and IoT-enabled monitoring of employees' personal characteristics and behaviours can also violate employees' right to non-discrimination. Under Article 14 ECHR and Article 52(1) CFREU, any restriction on the right to non-discrimination must meet the *general criteria* I outlined in Chapter 3. Specifically, the ECtHR and ECJ apply an *objective justification test*, where any differential treatment must not only be *prescribed*

426. Cf. with section 3.3, Chapter 4. *See*: 'Perceptyx' (n 417).
427. Cf. with section 6.3, Chapter 3.
428. De Stefano and Taes (n 327).
429. *Szima v. Hungary* (2012) App No 29723/11 (ECtHR, 9 October 2012) para. 31.
430. 'Technologies that monitor communications can also have a chilling effect on the fundamental rights of employees to organise, set up workers' meetings, and to communicate confidentially (...) Monitoring communications and behaviour will put pressure on employees to conform in order to prevent the detection of what might be perceived as anomalies.' Cf. Article 29 Data Protection Working Party, 'Opinion 02/2017 on Data Processing at Work' (n 21) 9-10.

by law and pursue *a legitimate aim* (such as avoiding relying on prohibited grounds such as race, gender, or trade union activity), the differential treatment must also be *necessary and proportionate* to achieve the stated objective. It must also respect the *essence of the right*, according to Article 52(1) CFREU.[431]

The implementation of technologies such as *Cogito*, which monitors a personal characteristic – the voice – and evaluates the politeness of tone with customers, must also be assessed under the objective justification test.[432] First, the monitoring must be prescribed by law; i.e., a specific legal provision must allow employers to systematically monitor employees for, e.g., performance management purposes. Second, even if the employer could invoke a legitimate aim, such as improving customer service, monitoring the politeness of tone across all employees is not a neutral criterion. It could potentially lead to indirect discrimination. It is unclear whether such a technology can accurately assess and differentiate voices and prosody[433] influenced by personal, linguistic, and cultural nuances.[434] Monitoring voices might therefore constitute a ground for indirect discrimination.[435] The monitoring of politeness based on voice characteristics could lead to indirect discrimination against certain groups, thus resulting in not objectively justified differential treatment. Without a demonstrable necessity for achieving a lawful objective and without proportionate safeguards to prevent discriminatory outcomes, such a monitoring with AI and IoT-enabled technologies would fail the objective justification test, violating employees' non-discrimination rights.

3 CONCLUSIONS

This chapter addressed research sub-question 4: *What is a legitimate exercise of the AI and IoT-enabled employer's monitoring power in the European fundamental rights framework?* I analysed AI and IoT-enabled technologies used for the three employer monitoring purposes identified in Chapter 4: monitoring employer property and employees' access; monitoring employee performance; and monitoring employees' personal characteristics and behaviours.

Building on the definition in Chapter 3, I understand a legitimate exercise of the employer's monitoring power as one that complies with the *general criteria* of legality (prescribed by law), legitimate aim, necessity, and proportionality, and respects the essence of the rights concerned. These criteria have been elaborated through the case law of the ECtHR and the ECJ and apply across different fundamental rights, including

431. Cf. with section 6.4, Chapter 3.
432. Cf. with section 3.3, Chapter 4. *See*: 'Cogito: Real-Time AI Coaching & Guidance for Contact Centers' (n 281).
433. Prosody, as defined by the Merriam-Webster online Dictionary, is 'the rhythmic and intonational aspect of language'.
434. Vered Shakuf et al., 'Processing Emotional Prosody in a Foreign Language: The Case of German and Hebrew' (2022) 6 Journal of Cultural Cognitive Science 251 https://doi.org/10.1007/s41809-022-00107-x accessed 22 October 2025.
435. Wachter and Mittelstadt (n 406).

the rights to privacy and data protection, freedom of expression, freedom of association, and non-discrimination.

With respect to privacy and data protection, I found that the ECtHR's six-point test, developed in *Bărbulescu v. Romania*, is crucial for assessing the legitimacy of restrictions to these employees' fundamental rights. AI and IoT-enabled technologies may pursue legitimate aims, but their continuous, intrusive, and opaque data processing often exceeds what is proportionate, especially when less invasive alternatives are available. As highlighted by the ECtHR *Bărbulescu* case, legitimacy requires not only clear, *ex ante* notification and purpose limitation but also proportionality, minimal intrusiveness, and strict safeguards to ensure that employee monitoring remains justified, targeted, and respectful of fundamental rights.

Regarding the freedom of expression, I concluded that the ECtHR and ECJ apply these general criteria by permitting only those restrictions that are narrowly and explicitly prescribed by law, thus preventing arbitrary interference and ensuring that limitations on freedom of expression are lawful. This approach is essential, given that the WP29 has highlighted the chilling effect monitoring can have on freedom of expression. AI and IoT-enabled monitoring can disproportionately restrict employees' freedom of expression, particularly when it results in function creep – where systems initially deployed for legitimate aims like OSH or cybersecurity are repurposed to monitor behaviours unrelated to those risks. To remain lawful under Article 10(2) ECHR and Article 52(1) CFREU, the restriction must be explicitly prescribed by law, pursue a legitimate aim, and be implemented in a necessary and proportionate manner. This requires, for instance, safeguards as purpose limitation, regular proportionality reviews, and strict safeguards to prevent repurposing.

Concerning the freedom of assembly and association, the ECtHR emphasises that any restriction must not only meet the criteria in Article 11(2) ECHR but also respect the very essence of these freedoms, as articulated in Article 52(1) CFREU. Monitoring tools like *Perceptyx's* 'union vulnerability index', or AI-moderated internal chats banning conversations on unionisation, violate employees' freedom of assembly and association by deterring unionisation and infringing the essence of that right under Article 11(2) ECHR and Article 52(1) CFREU. AI and IoT-enabled technologies that track communications or behaviours related to collective action must be strictly regulated by law and supported by safeguards, as their unregulated use can create a chilling effect on trade union freedoms, a conclusion reached also by the WP29 in its opinion on data processing at work.

In the case of AI and IoT-enabled technologies such as *Cogito*, which monitor and then assess employees' personal characteristics, to prevent violations of non-discrimination rights, I concluded that such monitoring practices are legitimate if they pass an objective justification test as outlined by the European Courts. This means that monitoring practices must be clearly prescribed by law, pursue a legitimate aim, be strictly necessary and proportionate, and respect the essence of the right to non-discrimination. Without these safeguards, the use of AI and IoT-enabled technologies risks violating Articles 14 ECHR and 21 CFREU, and, in cases related to trade union activities, Articles 11 ECHR and 12 CFREU.

In conclusion, assessing the legitimacy of AI and IoT-enabled employer monitoring remains a highly contextual task. Courts adopt a case-by-case approach, weighing the specifics of each workplace and technology, which allows for nuance but creates legal uncertainty. Given the opaque, adaptive, and predictive nature of these technologies, and the involvement of third-party providers which further complicates accountability (*see* section 4.1, Chapter 4), this raises important questions about the safeguards needed to ensure transparency, oversight, and effective protection of employees' rights.

These reflections underscore the need for clear and structured legal safeguards to ensure that AI and IoT-enabled employer monitoring is carried out in a way that respects fundamental rights. In the next chapters, I examine the EU's data protection and AI regulatory frameworks – namely the GDPR and the AI Act – to assess whether they offer the substantive and procedural guarantees necessary to ensure compliance with the European fundamental rights framework.

CHAPTER 6

Putting the GDPR to Work: Requirements for a Legitimate Exercise of the Employer's Monitoring Power via AI and IoT-Enabled Technologies

1 INTRODUCTION

In this chapter, I assess whether the European legislation on data protection, and, more recently, AI systems (*see* following Chapter 7), provides safeguards for the legitimate exercise of the AI and IoT-enabled employer's monitoring power. In this chapter, I will answer research sub-question 5: *What requirements does the GDPR impose on the legitimate exercise of the employer's monitoring power via AI and IoT-enabled technologies?*

To address this question comprehensively, this chapter commences with an introductory section (section 2) that offers a historical perspective on the evolution of European data protection regulations. It explores the reasons behind the lack of specific European legislation on data processing at work. Section 3 examines the GDPR, including its principles, rights, and obligations. I analyse these provisions in light of relevant literature, case law, and guidance from the WP29 and EDPB, including their opinions and recommendations, which, while not legally binding, offer valuable interpretative insight.[436] I specifically explore the roles of data subjects and data controllers, as well as the corresponding data subject's rights, data controllers'

436. The Article 29 Working Party (WP29) was an independent EU advisory body on data protection and privacy, comprising representatives from each Member State's data protection authority, the European Data Protection Supervisor, and the European Commission. Established under Article 29 of the Data Protection Directive (95/46/EC) in 1996, it was replaced by the European Data Protection Board (EDPB) on 25 May 2018 under the GDPR (Regulation (EU) 2016/679). WP29 opinions, recommendations and guidelines remain authoritative also for the GDPR. Both WP29 and EDPB guidelines are not legally binding.

obligations, and data processing principles. In section 4, I analyse the overall obligations arising for employers and the safeguards that employees can find in the GDPR. The analysis focuses on how these provisions apply to the AI and IoT-enabled employer's monitoring power. Section 5 concludes by analysing how the GDPR and its allegedly universal (i.e., applicable to all contexts) regulatory approach can be 'put to work'[437] on the employer-employee relationship to guarantee a legitimate exercise of the employer's monitoring power.

2 HISTORY OF DATA PROTECTION LAWS AT WORK: FROM THE 1989 COE RECOMMENDATION TO THE GDPR

The GDPR is a general regulation that applies to any personal data processing. Before delving into its content, it is important to analyse the factors that led to adopting a general regulation, rather than a labour-specific regulatory framework. This analysis will later help me illustrate the limitations of the current regulatory framework as applied to employment contexts.

2.1 CoE Convention 108, CoE Recommendation No. R(89)2 on the Protection of Personal Data Used for Employment Purposes, and the ILO 1996 Code of Practice

The earliest legislative reference to the protection of personal data processed by automated means dates back to Convention 108 of the Council of Europe (1981). The Convention, which was later updated in 2018 (Convention 108 +), does not refer to employment contexts. It provided, however, the first definitions of the two main protagonists in a digital society (and workplace): the data controller and the data subject. The data controller is:

> The natural or legal person, public authority, agency or any other body who is competent according to the national law to decide what should be the purpose of the automated data file, which categories of personal data should be stored and which operations should be applied to them.[438]

Whereas the data subject is:

> An identified or identifiable individual.[439]

437. I borrow the pun from Philippa Collins, who in her recent monograph analysed whether by putting to work the framework of fundamental rights, workers receive adequate protection from domestic labour law. My approach is similar; I examine whether the GDPR and AI Act, general regulations that are seemingly 'universal', achieve their intended goals when applied to workplace contexts. Philippa M Collins, *Putting Human Rights to Work: Labour Law, the ECHR, and the Employment Relation* (1st edn, Oxford University Press 2022).
438. Article 2(d), Convention for the Protection of Individuals with regard to Automatic Processing of Personal Data (n. 108).
439. Article 2(a) Convention for the Protection of Individuals with regard to Automatic Processing of Personal Data (n. 108).

The employer as a data controller and the employee as a data subject were later specifically addressed in Recommendation No. R(89)2, again by the Council of Europe. The Recommendation highlighted in its preamble how 'the use of automatic data processing methods by employers should be guided by principles which are designed to minimise any risks which such methods could possibly pose for the rights and fundamental freedoms of employees, in particular their right to privacy'.[440] By calling for a regulatory framework tailored to the employment relationship, the Council of Europe set forth two key principles that would later influence subsequent legislation. First, it clarified that employers' monitoring activities qualify as data collection and processing when employees can be identified or are identifiable through this information. Second, by requiring the development of specific principles that minimise risks to employees' fundamental freedoms, it highlighted that data processing in employment settings requires special considerations.[441]

Drawing on the general principles set out in the CoE Convention 108, the Recommendation emphasised that employers must inform and consult employees and their representatives about data collection and processing. It also reaffirmed employees' rights to access and correct their data when necessary.[442] In addition, the Recommendation reiterated the principle of data relevance, requiring that employers collect only data strictly necessary for the intended purposes and store it only for as long as needed.[443] Certain 'Particular categories of data' are also recognised as in need of further protection, such as employees' data on political opinions, trade union membership, religion, or sexual life, which should not be collected except through specific and informed consent from them.[444] The CoE Committee of Ministers updated the Recommendation in 2015 (Recommendation No. CM/Rec(2015)5), which from then on (until the present day) includes specific provisions regarding limitations on the use of biometric data, GPS systems, monitoring of employees' electronic communications, and video surveillance, reaffirming the principles of strict necessity for monitoring, whereby no more data than necessary for the intended purposes should be collected and processed.[445]

Recommendation No. R(89)2 was the pioneering document to introduce these principles in Europe. While it was a Recommendation and not legally binding for Member States, it set the groundwork. In fact, a few years later, in 1996, the International Labour Office (ILO) published its Code of Practice,[446] restating the same

440. Council of Europe, 'Recommendation No. R(89)2 of the Committee of Ministers to Member States on the Protection of Personal Data Used for Employment Purposes' (1989) 1 https://rm.coe.int/1680500b15 accessed 22 October 2025.
441. *Ibid.*, 1, Preamble.
442. *Ibid.*, 2. Points 3, 4, 7, and 12.
443. *Ibid.*, 3. Points 1 and 4.3 (specifically on recruitment).
444. *Ibid.*, 4. Point 10.
445. Council of Europe, 'Recommendation No. CM/Rec(2015)5 of the Committee of Ministers to Member States on the Processing of Personal Data in the Context of Employment' (2015) https://rm.coe.int/cmrec-2015-5-on-the-processing-of-personal-data-in-the-context-of-empl/1680a43b68 accessed 22 October 2025.
446. International Labour Organization, 'Code of Practice: Protection of Workers' Personal Data' https://www.ilo.org/global/topics/safety-and-health-at-work/normative-instruments/code-of-practice/WCMS_107797/lang--en/index.htm accessed 22 October 2025; Hendrickx (n 33) 16.

principles, such as transparency and notification to employees (and their representatives) of automated processing, and collection of strictly relevant and necessary data for the purposes pursued. The ILO code added relevant new principles: continuous monitoring of employees should be avoided except for OSH needs. It also introduced for the first time the right of each employee not to be subject to wholly automated decisions.[447] At the time, the literature often viewed these interventions with scepticism due to their non-binding nature on ILO Member States. Critics argued that they served more as declarations in the international debate rather than effective interventions addressing the issue.[448] However, the aforementioned principles did not remain a dead letter. Some states incorporated the Recommendation into national law, and the principles were later taken up and further developed in the 1995 European Directive on the Protection of Personal Data.

2.2 EU Directive 95/46/EC on Personal Data: Employee Monitoring Is Data Processing

The CoE Convention 108 and the Recommendation R(89)2 played an important role in shaping principles that were later incorporated into general data protection legislation, particularly the European Data Protection Directive 95/46/EC (DPD, now replaced by the GDPR).[449] In the DPD, for the first time, the ratio of employers-employees as data controllers-data subjects is formally acknowledged in EU law. This acknowledgement was present in Article 8 DPD, prohibiting the processing of special categories of data such as 'racial or ethnic origin, political opinions, religious or philosophical beliefs, trade-union membership (...) health or sex life'. More specifically, Article 8(b) DPD allowed the data processing of these special categories as legitimate when this 'is necessary for the purposes of carrying out the obligations and specific rights of the controller in the field of employment law in so far as it is authorised by national law providing for adequate safeguards'. Since the DPD and today through the GDPR, the EU legislation has explicitly identified the workplace as a distinct context where employers collect and process employees' personal data, making them subject to data protection laws.[450]

447. Article 29 Data Protection Working Party, 'Working Document on the Surveillance and Monitoring of Electronic Communications in the Workplace' (2002) 11 https://ec.europa.eu/justice/article-29/documentation/opinion-recommendation/files/2002/wp55_en.pdf accessed 22 October 2025.
448. Spiros Simitis, 'Reconsidering the Premises of Labour Law: Prolegomena to an EU Regulation on the Protection of Employees' Personal Data' (1999) 5 European Law Journal 45, 50-51 https://doi.org/10.1111/1468-0386.00065 accessed 22 October 2025.
449. Cf. with Recital 11 and Article 8 DPD, Directive 95/46/EC of the European Parliament and of the Council of 24 October 1995 on the protection of individuals with regard to the processing of personal data and on the free movement of such data.
450. The labour law scholarship in that decade started indeed to focus on the issue of data processing at work: Frank Hendrickx and Catarina Castro (eds), *Employment Privacy Law in the European Union. Surveillance and Monitoring* (Intersentia 2002); Mark Freedland, 'Data Protection and Employment in the European Union: An Analytical Study of the Law and

Article 8(b) DPD acted as an exception to the ban on the processing of special categories of data, hence, all of these data could not be collected at work, unless specifically provided for by national labour law. Recommendation 1/2001 from WP29 on 'Employee Evaluation Data' further clarified that under the DPD, both raw data collected directly from the employee and data generated during data processing qualify as personal data protected by the Directive.[451] This means that employees' personal data can include subjective evaluations, scores, or ratings by the employer related to the employee's performance or other characteristics.[452]

Under the DPD, employee monitoring required a balance between employer interests and employees' right to personal data protection. The WP29 emphasised that, according to Article 6 DPD, monitoring must be proportionate and address inherent risks in economic activities, such as safety, health, and work process functionality. Any monitoring activity, or data processing, must be fair and lawful, using an appropriate and relevant amount of data without exceeding the employer's stated purposes. Additionally, Articles 10-11 DPD promoted a general principle of transparency. This means that for data processing to be fair and lawful, employees should be informed about, or have access to and the ability to rectify (Article 12 DPD), the data collected and the purposes for which they are used.

According to the WP29, the DPD allowed employees not to 'leave their right to privacy at the door of their workplace every morning'.[453] These principles aimed to minimise the impact of employer activities on employees' privacy and data protection rights. At the same time, they sought to empower employees with a certain level of control, enabling them to access and object to the processing of their data. Moreover, Article 15 DPD, later incorporated into the 1996 ILO Code of Practice, introduced the right for individuals not to be subjected to fully automated decisions that significantly affect them, such as performance evaluations.[454]

Article 7 DPD of the Directive then introduced the legal bases for processing personal data. The WP29's Opinion No 8/2001 highlights how the relevant legal bases in the field of employment were essentially three: processing necessary for the

Practice of Data Protection and the Employment Relationship in the EU and Its Member States' (European Commission 1999); Matthew W Finkin, *Privacy in Employment Law* (Bureau of National Affairs 1995).

451. On the role of the WP29, *see* the first footnote of this chapter.
452. 'Based on the definition of Article 2(a) of Directive 95/46/EC personal data means any information relating to an identifiable or identified person, such as for instance data relating to his/her physical, physiological, mental, economic, cultural or social identity. (…) Personal data includes not only population registry data or information resulting from objective factors which can be verified or rectified, but also any other element, information or circumstance having an information content such as to add to the knowledge of an identified or identifiable person.' Article 29 Data Protection Working Party, 'Recommendation 1/2001 on Employee Evaluation Data' (2001) 2 https://ec.europa.eu/justice/article-29/documentation/opinion-recommendation/files/2001/wp42_en.pdf accessed 22 October 2025.
453. Article 29 Data Protection Working Party, 'Opinion 8/2001 on the Processing of Personal Data in the Employment Context' (2001) 19 https://ec.europa.eu/justice/article-29/documentation/opinion-recommendation/files/2001/wp48_en.pdf accessed 22 October 2025; Article 29 Data Protection Working Party, 'Opinion 02/2017 on Data Processing at Work' (n 21) 8.
454. Article 29 Data Protection Working Party, 'Opinion 02/2017 on Data Processing at Work' (n 21) 8.

performance of a contract (Article 7(1)(b) DPD); processing necessary to comply with a legal obligation (Article 7(1)(c) DPD); processing necessary for the purposes of legitimate interests pursued by the employer, except where fundamental rights of employees prevail (Article 7(1)(f) DPD).[455]

Article 7(1)(a) DPD established the data subject's consent as a legal basis for processing their personal data. However, Opinion No 8/2001 clarified that consent from the data subject, particularly an employee, is often considered 'misleading' as a basis for data processing in the employment context. The WP29's concern was that while it may seem as if individuals can simply refuse certain data processing activities, such as visiting a website, the repercussions in an employment setting can be far more severe than in other contexts. For instance, an employee could face disciplinary action and even lose his or her job if (s)he refuses consent, making the substantial validity of consent structurally questionable. While in the 2001 Opinion the WP29 believed that the consent of the employee could be considered valid only if substantially and genuinely freely given,[456] in Opinion No 2/2017, the WP29 takes a stronger stance: consent as a legal basis for processing employee data is never valid because it is not freely given due to the informational and power asymmetries between employer and employee.[457]

In conclusion, Directive 95/46/EC has since 1995 regarded the employer's monitoring power as the power to collect personal data – potentially also special categories of data (Article 8 DPD) – to which the principles of the DPD and the rights of the data subject apply.

2.3 After the DPD: Towards a Dedicated Framework for Data Processing at Work?

Since 1995 the WP29's Opinions have steered the interpretation of the DPD by highlighting some problematic elements – such as consent – and the need for a constant interaction with EU labour law. Such an interaction, according to its 2001 Opinion on data processing in employment contexts, is necessary since:

> Employment practices rely more and more on the processing of personal data to which general data protection principles apply.[458]

And, most importantly:

> Not all problems that arise in the employment context and involve the processing of personal data are exclusively data protection ones.[459]

455. Article 29 Data Protection Working Party, 'Opinion 8/2001 on the Processing of Personal Data in the Employment Context' (n 453) 15.
456. *Ibid.*, 23.
457. Article 29 Data Protection Working Party, 'Opinion 02/2017 on Data Processing at Work' (n 21) 6-7.
458. Article 29 Data Protection Working Party, 'Opinion 8/2001 on the Processing of Personal Data in the Employment Context' (n 453) 14.
459. *Ibid.*

In its 2001 Opinion, the WP29 emphasised that regulating data processing in the workplace should account for the unique protections required in employment relationships. These required protections, in fact, differ from those provided by general data protection laws. According to the WP29, this recognition should guide the development of regulatory solutions that meaningfully protect employees' interests. The debate at the time had thus already highlighted that the employer-employee relationship is fundamentally different from that of an average data controller and an average data subject.[460] In this Opinion, the WP29 points to the differences between labour and data regulations: labour regulation addresses the economic and social dependence of employees, while data protection laws, by contrast, primarily focus on power and informational asymmetry between data controllers and data subjects. Moreover, as Jeffery pointed out, a shortcoming of the DPD in the context of labour regulation was the limited involvement of employees' representatives, such as trade unions or works councils, in decision-making and consultative processes on matters pertaining to the processing of employees' data.[461]

A few years before the 2001 WP29's Opinion, in 1999, Simitis shared a similar view: while the merit of the DPD was finally to have addressed the regulation of a growing digitalisation of society,[462] additional attention should have been paid to data processing at work, where power and information asymmetries between employers and employees tend to increase with digitalisation.[463] The DPD regulatory approach, Simitis emphasises, was still oriented towards a general regulation, namely an abstract definition of actors (data controller, data subject) interacting in generic data processing and applicable principles.[464] Article 8 had paved the way for more specific regulations by the Member States in certain contexts of data processing, including workplace contexts. Yet, it had already produced some disharmony among different Member States, with particular activism in countries like France, Italy, Germany, and Denmark, which had undertaken specific sectoral regulations already before the DPD.[465] As early as 1997, the European Commission recognised the need for uniform regulation for data processing at work to address the ambiguities arising from the varying implementation

460. *See*: Hendrickx and Castro (n 450); Freedland et al. (n 35).
461. Jeffery (n 35).
462. Simitis, 'Reconsidering the Premises of Labour Law: Prolegomena to an EU Regulation on the Protection of Employees' Personal Data' (n 448) 51.
463. *Ibid.*
464. *Ibid.*
465. *Ibid.*, 49. 'Omnibus' regulations were increasingly supplemented by sector-specific rules. Back in the seventies, legislation, akin to Denmark's, cautiously aimed to make processing principles less abstract by setting up different regulatory frameworks for the public and private sectors. Germany, however, stuck to its initial approach but began to emphasise sector-specific statutes, regulating areas such as the processing activities of social security agencies, police departments, educational institutions, and hospitals. France followed suit in this direction, adopting sector-specific laws and gradually replacing standard rules with simplified procedures overseen by the *Commission Nationale de l'Informatique et des Libertés*. Additionally, the expansion of regulatory tools through codes of conduct endorsed by data protection authorities, as seen in the Netherlands, underscores ongoing efforts to better tailor processing regulations to evolving contexts of personal data usage.

of the Directive by Member States, among which data processing at work.[466] However, such legislation has still not seen the light of day.

2.4 Reasons for a Missing Framework on Data Processing at Work

As thoroughly reconstructed by Abraha, there were at least three unsuccessful attempts (2001, 2004, 2010-2012) prior to the GDPR's approval to introduce a legal framework focused on the employment context.[467]

In 2001, a European Commission consultation with social partners resulted in disagreement, with trade unions supporting an EU Directive on workplace data protection and employers' organisations opposing it.[468] Employers argued that existing legislation, particularly the DPD, was sufficient and that EU action was premature. They favoured first reviewing the Directive's transposition and analysing national implementations. Additionally, they questioned the necessity of a new Directive, citing subsidiarity and proportionality concerns. They also emphasised the need for flexibility, respect for national diversity, and the avoidance of overregulation or excessive burdens on employers.[469]

Then, in 2004, the Directorate-General for Employment and Social Affairs was reported drafting a proposal for a Directive concerning the processing of employees' personal data. Yet, it was not even presented at the Commission due to the divergence among social partners and the lack of political support.[470] Finally, in 2012, during the preparatory works of the GDPR, the Commission proposed the 'establishing [of] detailed and further harmonised rules for specific sectors', including the employment

466. Communication from the Commission on the Social and Labour Market Dimension of the Information Society, Brussels, 23 July 1997, COM(97)390 final.
467. Halefom H Abraha, 'A Pragmatic Compromise? The Role of Article 88 GDPR in Upholding Privacy in the Workplace' (2022) 12 International Data Privacy Law 276, 280 https://doi.org/10.1093/idpl/ipac015 accessed 22 October 2025.
468. European Commission, 'Second Stage Consultation of Social Partners on the Protection of Workers' Personal Data' https://www.eumonitor.nl/9353000/1/j9vvik7m1c3gyxp/vi7jgsu3tgzr accessed 22 October 2025.
469. *See* the reasoning of employers in the reply from UNICE (today: BusinessEurope, employers' association at EU level) to the Consultation with Social Partners opened in 2001, which rejects any room for negotiation on the issue: 'To sum up, European employers are opposed to the specific directive on a European framework aiming at personal data protection in the employment context envisaged by the Commission. As they already explained in their reply to the first-stage consultation, they believe that directives 95/46 and 90/270 already ensure a high degree of protection of workers throughout Europe. Detailing out the application of the general principles of directive 95/46 in the employment context in the way suggested by the Commission would prove counterproductive for both companies and workers. (...) It is also crucial that the diversity of national rules and the balance struck in member states between rights and obligations of both workers and employers is respected.' UNICE, 'Commission's Second-Stage Consultation on the Protection of Workers' Personal Data – UNICE Reply' 3-4 https://www.businesseurope.eu/publications/commissions-second-stage-consultation-on-the-protection-of-workers-personal-data-unices-reply/ accessed 22 October 2025.
470. Paul De Hert and Hans Lammerant, 'Protection of Personal Data in Work-Related Relations' (European Parliament's Committee on Civil Liberties, Justice and Home Affairs 2013) 25 https://eur-lex.europa.eu/resource.html?uri=cellar:cce0203c-caf8-4a7b-a79d-69e279c677c0.0002.06/DOC_1&format=PDF accessed 22 October 2025.

relationship.[471] In its proposal, the Commission envisaged that 'proportionality and legitimacy requirements mentioned in Articles 6 and 7 of Directive 95/46/EC would be regulated in detail for employment relationships'.[472] Yet, some Member States resisted this proposal of harmonising at the EU level specific data processing rules in employment contexts, viewing it as a potential threat to their national laws and impacting their industrial relations systems.[473]

Ultimately, the resistance to an employment-specific EU legislation led to a general regulation, the General Data Protection Regulation, which entered into force on 25 May 2018. In its first recitals (Recital 9 GDPR), it links directly to the DPD, recalling that 'The objectives and principles of Directive 95/46/EC remain sound, but it has not prevented fragmentation in the implementation of data protection across the Union.'

3 PUTTING THE GDPR TO WORK: THE EMPLOYER'S MONITORING POWER AS DATA PROCESSING IN THE GDPR (ARTICLES 1-4 GDPR)

Article 1(2) of the GDPR specifies that the Regulation safeguards the fundamental rights and freedoms of individuals, particularly their right to the protection of personal data. Therefore, the protection of employees' fundamental rights is undoubtedly a priority under the EU's data protection Regulation. Although the GDPR does not systematically refer to employers or employees,[474] its provisions fully apply to the employment relationship. Accordingly, in the following sections, when I refer to employers and employees, these terms correspond to the GDPR's categories of data controllers and data subjects, respectively. In this context, the employer, typically acting as the data controller, processes employees' personal data as part of routine workplace activities. According to Article 4(2) GDPR, such processing includes:

> Any operation or set of operations which is performed on personal data or on sets of personal data, whether or not by automated means, such as collection, recording, organisation, structuring, storage, adaptation or alteration, retrieval, consultation, use, disclosure by transmission, dissemination or otherwise making available, alignment or combination, restriction, erasure or destruction.

471. European Commission, 'Commission Staff Working Paper SEC(2012) 72 Final' 47-48 https://www.europarl.europa.eu/cmsdata/59702/att_20130508ATT65856-1873079025799224642.pdf accessed 22 October 2025.
472. *Ibid.*, 47-48. The EU Commission's intentions, however, were not uniform. In the same preparatory works, at pp. 149 and 150, the topic of data protection in work contexts is later framed as an issue of 'Cost and Price Competitiveness' on which – to avoid excessive costs and damage to the competitiveness of European companies – 'No material changes of data protection rules relating to employment relationships are proposed. Clarification and harmonisation of general data protection concepts will remove divergences and reduce costs caused by fragmentation.'
473. European Commission, 'Second Stage Consultation of Social Partners on the Protection of Workers' Personal Data' (n 468). The EU has in fact limited ('shared' with Member States) legislative competence in employment matters, outlined in Article 153(1) TFEU.
474. With exception of Articles 4(4), 9, 88 GDPR, as I will discuss later in this chapter.

This definition closely mirrors that found in Article 2(b) of the now-repealed DPD and reflects a broad, technology-neutral understanding of data processing.[475] By the time the GDPR was adopted in 2016, the EU legislator was well aware of ongoing advances in data science and the increasing integration of data-driven technologies in the workplace. As a result, Article 4(4) GDPR defines 'profiling' as a data-intensive processing activity used to evaluate or predict, among other things, employees' behaviour or other personal characteristics:

> Profiling means any form of automated processing of personal data consisting of the use of personal data to evaluate certain personal aspects relating to a natural person, in particular to analyse or predict aspects concerning that natural person's performance at work, economic situation, health, personal preferences, interests, reliability, behaviour, location or movements.

With this definition, the GDPR aligns closely with today's mainstream concept of the datafied workplace,[476] where employers understand the workforce and workplace by collecting and processing employees' data.[477] AI and IoT-enabled technologies, used to evaluate employees' performance, behaviour, or other personal traits, thus fall within the material scope of the GDPR.

Having introduced the GDPR's notion of data processing and profiling, I shall now turn to the definitions of the main actors involved in data processing: data controllers, data subjects, and processors.

3.1 Data Controllers, Data Subjects and Processors, aka: Employers, Employees, Providers

An employer collecting data for organisational, performance assessment or security purposes acts as a natural or legal person determining the purposes and means for the processing of employees' personal data (i.e., 'data controller', Article 4 (7) GDPR).[478] The employee, likewise, is reflected in that 'natural person' ('data subject') described as an identifiable natural person, who can be identified, directly or indirectly, through the provided information (Article 4 (1) GDPR).[479] Often, the data controller, when purchasing an AI and IoT-enabled technology, will be joined by the so-called processor, i.e., the

475. Article 2(b) DPD: '"processing of personal data" ("processing") shall mean any operation or set of operations which is performed upon personal data, whether or not by automatic means, such as collection, recording, organization, storage, adaptation or alteration, retrieval, consultation, use, disclosure by transmission, dissemination or otherwise making available, alignment or combination, blocking, erasure or destruction'.
476. On datafication at the workplace, *see* section 2, Chapter 4.
477. Bodie et al. (n 330).
478. Article 4(7), EU Reg. 2016/679: 'controller' means 'the natural or legal person, public authority, agency or other body which, alone or jointly with others, determines the purposes and means of the processing of personal data; where the purposes and means of such processing are determined by Union or Member State law, the controller or the specific criteria for its nomination may be provided for by Union or Member State law'.
479. Article 4(1), EU Reg. 2016/679: '"personal data" means any information relating to an identified or identifiable natural person ("data subject"); an identifiable natural person is one who can be identified, directly or indirectly, in particular by reference to an identifier such as

company developing and selling the technology (Article 4(8) GDPR). The processor acts on behalf of the data controller and is to be identified as a natural or legal person, public authority, agency or other body which processes personal data on behalf of the controller. According to Article 28 GDPR ('Processor'), the data controller has the duty to only use processors that provide 'sufficient guarantees to implement appropriate technical and organisational measures in such a manner that processing will meet the requirements of this Regulation and ensure the protection of the rights of the data subject' (Article 28(1) GDPR).[480] Article 28(3)(a) GDPR further explains that the processor acts only on documented instructions coming from the data controller. When the processor acts independently without the data controller instructions (e.g., determining the employer's monitoring purposes), Article 26 GDPR and the so-called joint controllership will come into operation, meaning that the processor will instead be considered to be a data controller jointly with the employer (with the corresponding obligations).[481]

Conversely, employees are granted a range of individual rights that enable them to monitor the employer's use of their personal data and take action if there is any misuse. In other words, the GDPR results in what has been defined 'a set of individual rights and a set of company obligations' to ensure the protection of personal data in the EU.[482]

More specifically, employers and their processors find in Chapter II (Principles) and IV (Controller and Processor) the principles, procedures and obligations for the legitimate collection and processing of employees' data. An employee, however, will find in Chapter III (Rights of the Data Subject) his or her individual rights. To understand the GDPR's operation, I have outlined its categories and key players. With that foundation laid, I shall turn to the analysis of the principles governing data processing (Article 5 GDPR) and explore the legal bases for data processing (Articles 6-9 GDPR).

3.2 Principles and Obligations Relating to the Processing of Employees' Personal Data (Articles 5, 24, 25 GDPR)

3.2.1 Obligations for the Employer

Article 5 GDPR ('Principles relating to processing of personal data') provides the data controller and processor with dynamic principles, meaning that the EU legislator

a name, an identification number, location data, an online identifier or to one or more factors specific to the physical, physiological, genetic, mental, economic, cultural or social identity of that natural person'.

480. The relationship between the data controller and the processor and their respective obligations are specifically regulated in Chapter IV 'Controller and Processor' of the GDPR.
481. Christopher Millard and Dimitra Kamarinou, 'Article 26 Joint Controllers' in Christopher Kuner et al. (eds), *The EU General Data Protection Regulation (GDPR)* (Oxford University Press, New York 2020) https://academic.oup.com/book/41324/chapter/352299120 accessed 22 October 2025.
482. Meg Leta Jones and Margot E Kaminski, 'An American's Guide to the GDPR' (2020) 98 Denver Law Review 93, 116.

provides methodical and practical indications on how a processing must operate to be considered legitimate. The principles listed in Article 5(1) are: (a) lawfulness, fairness, transparency; (b) purpose limitation; (c) data minimisation; (d) accuracy; (e) storage limitation; (f) integrity and confidentiality. Albeit broad principles, they act as operational indications on how to perform employee monitoring (and its three purposes) when based on collecting and processing of employee data. As emphasised by the EDPB, these principles result in an obligation on the data controller or processor to ensure that they implement them.[483]

Before analysing the principles of Article 5 GDPR in detail, it is worth discussing the general obligations imposed on the data controller. Article 5 GDPR is in fact embedded within a framework of accountability that determines how these principles must be implemented and enforced in practice. Article 24 GDPR ('Responsibility of the controller') provides that the data controller must be able to demonstrate (to a Data Protection Authority, for instance) that the monitoring activities over employees are compliant with the Regulation.[484] The employer must thus adopt 'appropriate technical and organisational measures' to ensure compliance with the principles and obligations arising from the regulation itself. The emphasis on 'appropriateness' means that employers must take steps proportionate to the unique risks involved in each instance of data processing. Similarly, in Article 32 GDPR ('Security of processing'), the concept of appropriateness is recurring in providing for the security of data subjects' information.[485]

Article 25 GDPR provides for a more specific 'obligation to act' for data controllers.[486] The first set of obligations in Article 25(1) is defined as privacy by design. The employer, prior to the processing,[487] must implement appropriate technical and organisational measures designed on the principles of Article 5 GDPR.[488] Article 25(2) GDPR, then, provides for privacy by default, meaning that any software application should work on pre-existing and preselected values. Therefore, the GDPR requires data controllers to run or choose software that are *ex ante* inscribed with the principles

483. European Data Protection Board, 'Guidelines 4/2019 on Article 25 Data Protection by Design and by Default' (2020) 5 https://www.edpb.europa.eu/sites/default/files/files/file1/edpb_guidelines_201904_dataprotection_by_design_and_by_default_v2.0_en.pdf accessed 22 October 2025.
484. *Ibid.*, 9.
485. Katerina Demetzou, 'GDPR and the Concept of Risk: The Role of Risk, the Scope of Risk and the Technology Involved' in Eleni Kosta et al. (eds), *Privacy and Identity Management. Fairness, Accountability, and Transparency in the Age of Big Data*, vol 547 (Springer International Publishing 2019) https://link.springer.com/10.1007/978-3-030-16744-8_10 accessed 22 October 2025.
486. Efstratios Koulierakis, 'The Challenge of Incorporating Legal Rules into Digital Applications: A Theoretical Exploration of Article 25 GDPR' (2022) 18 Illyrius – International Scientific Review 35, 36.
487. Data protection by design shall be implemented 'at the time of determination of the means of processing', Article 25(1) GDPR.
488. Article 25 GDPR explicitly mentions non-exhaustive technical and organisational measures such as pseudonymisation and minimisation. I discuss them below in section 3.2.4.

applicable to the processing of personal data.[489] In other words, privacy by design requires data protection principles are inherent in the design of the processing rather than added later. Privacy by default, however, ensures that by default only the minimum necessary personal data is collected and processed, with the strictest privacy settings applied. All the above-mentioned principles are ultimately summarised in general obligations to comply with the Regulation in Article 24 GDPR ('Responsibility of the data controller') and Article 25 GDPR ('Data protection by default and by design').[490]

What do these Article 5 GDPR principles, which are necessary to fulfil the general obligations outlined in Articles 24 and 25 GDPR, ultimately entail? In the following subsections, I will elaborate on their application in the employment context.

3.2.2 *Lawfulness, Fairness and Transparency*

Article 5(1)(a) GDPR ('Lawfulness, fairness and transparency') provides that personal data must be processed lawfully, fairly and transparently. Whether data are collected directly from the employee or data generated by AI and IoT-enabled technologies (e.g., employee performance evaluation),[491] they must be subject to the condition of *lawfulness*. Regulatory references on what constitutes this 'lawfulness' can come not only from the GDPR itself but also from labour law. For example, in Italy, Article 4 of the Workers' Statute (introduced in 1970 and reformed in 2015) prohibits employers from monitoring employees through technological means, except when necessary for health and safety reasons to protect employees.[492] The interplay of all these regulations can determine in the specific case whether monitoring is lawful.

Fairness is depicted as distinct from *transparency* and *lawfulness*, sparking a significant debate over its precise meaning due to the lack of a clear definition in the

489. European Data Protection Board, 'Guidelines 4/2019 on Article 25 Data Protection by Design and by Default' (n 483) 11.
490. Christopher Docksey, 'Article 24 Responsibility of the Controller' in Christopher Kuner et al. (eds), *The EU General Data Protection Regulation (GDPR)* (Oxford University Press, New York 2020) https://academic.oup.com/book/41324/chapter/352298857 accessed 22 October 2025; Lee A Bygrave, 'Article 25 Data Protection by Design and by Default' in Christopher Kuner et al. (eds), *The EU General Data Protection Regulation (GDPR)* (Oxford University Press, New York 2020) https://academic.oup.com/book/41324/chapter/352299028 accessed 22 October 2025.
491. Employees' performance evaluation as an output of AI and IoT constitutes personal data and is subject to compliance to the GDPR. Article 29 Data Protection Working Party, 'Recommendation 1/2001 on Employee Evaluation Data' (n 452).
492. After a law reform in 2015, Article 4 now provides that the tools necessary for work are not subject to this general prohibition on monitoring employees' performance. Currently, in the Italian labour law literature, there is an intense debate seeking to determine what these necessary tools are. Cf. Alessandra Ingrao, *Il Controllo a Distanza Sui Lavoratori e La Nuova Disciplina Privacy: Una Lettura Integrata* (Cacucci 2018).

GDPR's Recitals.[493] Most of the literature[494] and ECJ case law[495] state that fairness has to do with preventing adverse effects, putting emphasis on non-discrimination protection of data subjects. Therefore, under this perspective, fairness encompasses principles such as non-discrimination and fair balancing between opposing interests (e.g., employers' optimisation of labour processes versus employees' privacy).[496] The ECJ in the *Google Spain* case highlighted that fairness involves balancing the relevant circumstances and interests at stake. Specifically, it noted that this balance depends on factors such as the nature and sensitivity of the information for the individual's privacy, and the public's interest in accessing that information.[497] However, in some instances, the ECJ appears to view fairness more as a procedural safeguard.[498] In this sense, fairness would imply that data controllers also ensure that they implement and demonstrate compliance with the GDPR. In this instance, fairness would imply adhering to certain 'standards of care' such as providing timely information to data subjects and maintaining transparency in their data processing practices.[499]

Transparency is mentioned as the third principle of Article 5(1)(a) GDPR, which, according to Recital 39 GDPR, mandates that all information and communication regarding the handling of personal data should be readily available and easily comprehensible, using clear and straightforward language. In line with Article 5 and its principles governing data processing and monitoring, employers should design and operate their monitoring systems to allow employees easy access to information. This

493. *See*, among others: Gianclaudio Malgieri, 'The Concept of Fairness in the GDPR: A Linguistic and Contextual Interpretation', *Proceedings of the 2020 Conference on Fairness, Accountability, and Transparency* (ACM 2020) https://dl.acm.org/doi/10.1145/3351095.3372868 accessed 22 October 2025; Damian Clifford and Jef Ausloos, 'Data Protection and the Role of Fairness' (2018) 37 Yearbook of European Law 130 https://doi.org/10.1093/yel/yey004 accessed 22 October 2025; Bruno Lepri et al., 'Fair, Transparent, and Accountable Algorithmic Decision-Making Processes: The Premise, the Proposed Solutions, and the Open Challenges' (2018) 31 Philosophy & Technology 611 https://doi.org/10.1007/s13347-017-0279-x accessed 22 October 2025.
494. I refer to the literature review by Malgieri (n 493) 157. *See also* Clifford and Ausloos (n 493) 140-141. The Article 29 Data Protection Working Party associates unfairness to discrimination: 'Profiling may be unfair and create discrimination, for example by denying people access to employment opportunities, credit or insurance, or targeting them with excessively risky or costly financial products', Article 29 Data Protection Working Party, 'Guidelines on Automated Individual Decision-Making and Profiling for the Purposes of Regulation 2016/679' (2018) 10 https://ec.europa.eu/newsroom/article29/items/612053 accessed 22 October 2025.
495. Case C-362/14, *Maximillian Schrems v. Data Protection Commissioner*, joined party: Digital Rights Ireland Ltd, para. 42; Case C-553/07, *College van burgemeester en wethouders van Rotterdam v. M.E.E. Rijkeboer*, 7 May 2009, paras 64, 66. *See also*: Joined Cases C-92/09 and C-93/09, *Volker und Markus Schecke GbR and Hartmut Eifert v. Land Hessen*, 2009; Case C-275/06 *Productores de Música de España (Promusicae) v. Telefónica de España SAU*, 29 January 2008.
496. *See*, among others, the research intersecting fairness in algorithmic management at work and non-discrimination law: Aloisi (n 26).
497. Case C-131/12, *Google Spain SL, Google Inc. v. Agencia Española de Protección de Datos* (AEPD), Mario Costeja González, 13 May 2014, para. 81.
498. Malgieri (n 493) 157. *See also* Clifford and Ausloos (n 493) 154.
499. *See*, for instance, Case C-201/14, Judgment of 1 October 2015, Bara et al., EU:C:2015:638. In this case, the ECJ found that data collected for one purpose (taxation) cannot automatically be reused for another (health insurance) without proper legal basis and informing the data subject.

includes details such as identifying the data controller, understanding the purposes of processing, and providing additional information to ensure fair and transparent handling of personal data.[500]

In the context of the employer's monitoring power, I adopt the prevailing interpretation of fairness as requiring a careful balancing of competing interests, with a particular emphasis on non-discrimination as a foundational principle of data processing.[501] This understanding is especially relevant in light of the growing use of AI and IoT-enabled technologies in the workplace, which can exacerbate risks of bias and unequal treatment. Accordingly, I argue that employers must exercise their monitoring power in a way that takes into account all relevant employees' interests and rights and ensures transparency towards the workforce.

3.2.3 Purpose Limitation

Article 5(1)(b) GDPR ('Purpose limitation') follows by establishing that personal data shall be collected for specified, explicit and legitimate purposes and not further processed in a manner that is incompatible with those purposes. Prior to the introduction of the GDPR, the WP29 defined it as the principle of 'finality'.[502] This means that before an employer purchases a surveillance technology, s(he) must clearly define the purposes for the data processing that will take place once activated.[503] Then, when the processing starts, (s)he must comply with the stated purposes since further processing may be allowed only in specific cases and must be 'compatible' with the original ones. For instance, the data processed by an AI-enabled camera installed on trucks only for safety purposes to monitor the driving behaviours of drivers cannot be then processed to conduct employees' overall performance assessment.

Purpose limitation is of utmost importance to prevent the so-called function creep of monitoring, i.e., the usage of available personal data beyond the purposes for which they were initially collected.[504] Its application is particularly important to prevent the adverse effects of an AI and IoT-enabled employer's monitoring power, being the principle that preserves legal certainty for employees and allows cooperation and trust in an employment relationship.[505] In a greater datafication of workplaces, specification

500. Article 29 Data Protection Working Party, 'Guidelines on Transparency under Regulation 2016/679' (2018) 6-7 https://ec.europa.eu/newsroom/article29/items/622227 accessed 22 October 2025.
501. Aloisi (n 26).
502. Article 29 Data Protection Working Party, 'Opinion 8/2001 on the Processing of Personal Data in the Employment Context' (n 453) 20.
503. In the guidelines pertaining data protection by design and by default, purpose limitation is mentioned among the preconditions to have before starting designing and operating any data processing: European Data Protection Board, 'Guidelines 4/2019 on Article 25 Data Protection by Design and by Default' (n 483) 19-20.
504. For a discussion on the available conceptualisations of 'function creep' of surveillance I refer to: Koops (n 372).
505. Article 29 Data Protection Working Party, 'Opinion 3/2013 on Purpose Limitation' (2013) 56 https://ec.europa.eu/justice/article-29/documentation/opinion-recommendation/files/2013/wp203_en.pdf accessed 22 October 2025; De Stefano et al. (n 42); Collins, 'Employment as a Relational Contract' (n 153).

of purposes is an essential first step to make the application of the GDPR effective. The WP29 defines purpose limitation as a prerequisite for applying any other data quality requirement listed in Articles 5 and 25 GDPR.[506] Such a principle fundamentally reinforces the overall aims of the European regulation, contributing to the transparency, legal certainty and predictability of data processing in the EU. Employers, therefore, in designing their monitoring activities, should determine with minute precision what is the exact purpose. In this book, to conduct my analysis, I group employers' purposes into three broad categories: monitoring the employer's property, monitoring working performance, and monitoring employees' behaviours or characteristics. However, under Article 5(1)(b) GDPR, the principle of purpose limitation requires that employers go beyond such general categories and specify their purposes for data processing with greater precision. This means they must clearly define the specific and concrete objectives behind each monitoring activity – for example, monitoring location data to prevent theft of company vehicles or analysing keystroke patterns to detect cybersecurity threats – rather than relying on overarching justifications.

Purpose limitation, according to the WP29, is divided into two building blocks: *purpose specification* and *compatible use*.[507]

Purpose specification refers to the 'specified, explicit and legitimate purposes' referred to in Article 5(1)(b) GDPR. Collecting data for certain purposes makes these purposes logically the *raison d'être* of the processing itself; therefore, purpose specification is an essential precondition for the data collection since it will specify the scope of the processing operations, the relevant data to be collected, and the duration of the data retention.[508] 'Explicit' fulfils the predictability and legal certainty aims of purpose limitations since it fosters the necessary degree of transparency to have unambiguous and clearly expressed purposes on the side of the workplace supervisors. The explicit formulation of purposes helps all the parties involved in the data processing know how the data can/will be used: for instance, the AI-enabled camera on drivers implemented for driving safety concerns must be explicitly geared towards that specific prediction of risks (e.g., accidents, risks for cyclists).[509] The legitimacy of purposes is to be determined through the balancing test present in Article 6(1)(f) GDPR, on which I will elaborate further in section 3.3.4 of this chapter.

The second building block of purpose limitation is the *compatible use* of the data when the employer embarks on 'further processing'.[510] In other words, the purposes of processing further to collection shall not be incompatible with the purposes as they were originally specified. Determining the compatibility between original and further purposes requires analysing several key factors.[511] The new processing shall be

506. Article 29 Data Protection Working Party, 'Opinion 3/2013 on Purpose Limitation' (n 505) 4.
507. *Ibid.*, 11-13.
508. *Ibid.*, 11-12.
509. *Ibid.*, 17.
510. *Ibid.*, 12.
511. *Ibid.*, 23.

substantially coincident with the original one. The greater the distance between the purposes of collection and the purposes of further processing, the less likely a positive compatibility assessment is. What is substantially overlapping can also be determined by the context in which the data are collected and the reasonable expectations of the employees-data subjects regarding their use.[512] By using the example of an AI camera to monitor driving behaviours for safety purposes, I can conclude that an employer cannot use the camera's recorded data to penalise an employee for taking too many bathroom breaks. The WP29's Opinion 2/2017 refers to a similar scenario where the compatibility test would fail: intelligent surveillance systems installed to identify employee entry cannot be used to gauge employees' friendliness with customers or any other event unrelated to security reasons.[513]

Thus, an employer's monitoring power remains legitimate if it pursues specific, explicit, and lawful purposes and remains consistent with them throughout its operation. This ensures data processing aligns with principles of transparency, legal certainty, and predictability, protecting employees against an illegitimate exercise of this employer's power.

3.2.4 Data Minimisation

Article 5(1)(c) GDPR ('Data minimisation') provides that only adequate, relevant and limited to what is necessary data can be processed to fulfil the purposes for processing. Additional and more specific guidance on implementing data minimisation can be found in Article 25(2) GDPR, which addresses data protection by default.[514]

First, the data controller must consider that s(he) cannot collect more data than necessary for the specific purpose of processing ('amount of personal data collected'); if certain categories of data are not necessary or if it is possible to collect less granular data, that surplus of data should not be collected at all. Borrowing the EDPB words, data minimisation substantiates and operationalises the principle of necessity: the employer has to predetermine which features and parameters supporting his or her business are strictly necessary to the well functioning of the company.[515] The EDPB refers to this operationalisation of minimisation as 'data avoidance', i.e., avoid processing of personal data when this is possible for the relevant purposes pursued.[516]

The same applies to the processing itself ('the extent of their processing', Article 25(2) GDPR); if the same objectives can be achieved with fewer operations on data, this is also part of data minimisation.[517] In a recent case in France involving Amazon, the

512. *Ibid.*, 24.
513. Article 29 Data Protection Working Party, 'Opinion 02/2017 on Data Processing at Work' (n 21) 10.
514. European Data Protection Board, 'Guidelines 4/2019 on Article 25 Data Protection by Design and by Default' (n 483) 12.
515. *Ibid.*, 21.
516. *Ibid.*
517. *Ibid.*, 13.

DPA sanctioned the company for not aggregating[518] a large portion of the performance monitoring data of warehouse employees. There, the DPA did not contest the fact that Amazon collected certain data but rather the fact that it did not aggregate them sufficiently and retained a large amount of them, thus making monitoring 'excessive and intrusive'.[519] The employer was processing an unnecessary amount of data instead of consulting them in the form of aggregated (less detailed) data.

Minimisation also concerns the accessibility of the collected data. Article 25(2) GDPR specifies that not everyone should have access to these data, but only those who need to perform specific operations on it, namely, the data controller (the employer and any collaborators) and, if applicable, the processor.[520] Indeed, data minimisation is closely related to the principle of storage limitation, which I discuss in detail in the next subsection dedicated to Article 5(1)(d) GDPR.

3.2.5 Storage Limitation

Article 5(1)(e) GDPR ('Storage limitation') stipulates that employees' data should be retained in a manner that allows identification for no longer than necessary for the purposes for which the personal data are processed. Data may be stored for longer periods only for public interest, scientific or historical research purposes or statistical purposes. Storage limitation is mentioned also in Article 25(2) GDPR ('the period of their storage') in relation to data protection by default. If the employee's personal data is no longer necessary, it shall be deleted or anonymised by default, i.e., systematically embedded in the processing.[521] How long the storage limitation period should be is to be determined on a case-by-case basis. In the *Amazon* case mentioned earlier, the DPA imposed a sanction due to a thirty-one-day data retention period for all tasks performed by each warehouse employee. This was considered disproportionate and unnecessary by the French DPA. In this specific case, a weekly data retention period, or at most less than a month, would have sufficed for determining employee shifts and evaluations for further training purposes.[522] As this case well demonstrates, if the employer intends to retain employees' data collected for prolonged periods, s(he) must provide justification and develop legal grounds and reasoning to do so.[523] Otherwise, s(he) must systematically proceed with the deletion or complete anonymisation of the data under Articles 5(1)(e) and 25(2) GDPR.

518. Data aggregation is a process where raw data are gathered and expressed in a broader summary form, usually illustrated through statistical analysis.
519. Molè, 'Minimised Work Surveillance Exists under the GDPR: Amazon France and the DPA Sanction' (n 421).
520. European Data Protection Board, 'Guidelines 4/2019 on Article 25 Data Protection by Design and by Default' (n 483) 13.
521. *Ibid.*
522. Molè, 'Minimised Work Surveillance Exists under the GDPR: Amazon France and the DPA Sanction' (n 421).
523. European Data Protection Board, 'Guidelines 4/2019 on Article 25 Data Protection by Design and by Default' (n 483) 25.

3.2.6 *Accuracy*

Article 5(1)(d) GDPR ('Accuracy') requires employers to collect accurate data and to keep them up to date. Inaccurate data, in fact, represent a risk for the data subjects' rights and freedoms according to the EDPB.[524] An example of a risk to the fundamental rights of employees may be performance data that are poorly collected or distorted by automated decision-making systems. In this regard, Recital 65 GDPR relates this principle to the right to rectification and erasure of inaccurate data (Articles 16 and 17 GDPR). The employer will then have to check that the data is correct, including during processing, and if necessary, with the employee himself/herself. Should the employee invoke his or her rights to rectification or erasure, the employer must act without delay.[525] For example, an AI and IoT-enabled technology that classifies and forecasts warehouse employees' shifts based on performance data might not correctly count sick leave and recalculate the performance of employees on the basis of unjustified absence. In this case, the employee would have a right to rectification, and the employer a duty of care to distinguish in his or her recording sick leave from unjustified absences.

3.2.7 *Integrity and Confidentiality*

Article 5(1)(f) GDPR ('Integrity and confidentiality') provides for cybersecurity standards. These principles stress the paramount importance of safeguarding personal information from unauthorised access, loss, or damage. Article 5(1)(f) GDPR, therefore, requires the implementation of robust technical and organisational measures to ensure data security and thus effectively protect employees' privacy rights.[526] Recital 78 and Article 32 GDPR ('Security of processing') underscore the need for continuous assessment and improvement of security measures to address evolving threats and vulnerabilities, especially when sensitive data are involved. These measures, according to the EDPB, encompass risk analysis, access control, secure transfers, storage, and pseudonymisation of employees, or complete anonymisation as much as possible.[527] In particular, risk analysis plays a central role in this framework, requiring a thorough examination of potential threats to personal data security. Employers are required to exercise their monitoring power digitally in a way that protects individuals' rights and minimises vulnerabilities, ensuring that data collection does not expose the workforce to unauthorised or malicious access.[528] The implementation of these measures often entails a certain degree of collaboration from the employee: for example, two-factor authentication via mobile phones, or monitoring software for online activities to prevent/trace how and when a data breach occurred.

---

524. *Ibid.*, 23.
525. *Ibid.*, 23-24.
526. On the complicated balance between privacy and security refer to: Mitrou and Karyda (n 380).
527. European Data Protection Board, 'Guidelines 4/2019 on Article 25 Data Protection by Design and by Default' (n 483) 26.
528. *See*, for instance, the ENISA reports on the cyber risks for companies: European Union Agency for Cybersecurity (n 9); Corradini (n 297).

3.3 Lawfulness of Processing (Articles 6-7 GDPR)

For an employer to legitimately exercise his or her monitoring power through AI and IoT-enabled technologies, s(he) must demonstrate compliance with the principles outlined in Article 5 GDPR, as required by Article 24(1) GDPR.[529] However, for the processing to be lawful, it must also have a valid legal basis under Article 6 GDPR ('Lawfulness of processing').[530]

The employer must therefore meet at least one of the conditions for lawfulness under Article 6(1) GDPR for the processing or profiling of employees: (a) consent given by the employee; (b) the processing is necessary for the performance of a contract; (c) compliance with a legal obligation; (d) processing is necessary in order to protect the vital interests of the data subject; (e) processing is necessary for the performance of a task carried out in the public interest; (f) processing is necessary for the purposes of the legitimate interests pursued by the controller to be balanced with the fundamental rights of the employee.

As stressed by the WP29, the legal basis 'vital interest' and 'public interest' (Article 6(1)(d) and 6(1)(e) GDPR) are 'less likely to be relevant in the employment context'.[531] With exceptions in the employment of civil servants with special responsibilities, these will rarely be valid legal bases for employer's data processing.[532] Conversely, it is commonly accepted in literature and by the WP29 that the main legal bases at the disposal of employers are *consent*, the *performance of a contract*, *legal obligation*, and, finally, *legitimate interest*.[533] I will focus on the latter in the following subsections.

3.3.1 Consent

Article 6(1)(a) GDPR provides that the processing of data subjects' data is lawful if the latter have given consent to the processing of their personal data for one or more specific purposes. To define what consent is, I shall analyse two further Articles in the

529. Article 24(1) GDPR: 'the controller shall implement appropriate technical and organisational measures to ensure and to be able to demonstrate that processing is performed in accordance with this Regulation. Those measures shall be reviewed and updated where necessary'.
530. Waltraut Kotschy, 'Article 6 Lawfulness of Processing' in Christopher Kuner et al. (eds), *The EU General Data Protection Regulation (GDPR)* (Oxford University Press, New York 2020) https://academic.oup.com/book/41324/chapter/352296511 accessed 22 October 2025.
531. Article 29 Data Protection Working Party, 'Opinion 8/2001 on the Processing of Personal Data in the Employment Context' (n 453) 15; Article 29 Data Protection Working Party, 'Opinion 02/2017 on Data Processing at Work' (n 21) 6-8.
532. For the sake of completeness, the legal basis 'public interest' could be invoked by the employer when the employer is a State and its employee holds sensitive functions, for example. This remains an infrequent and irrelevant scenario in legally grounding the monitoring power for most (public and private) employers.
533. *See*, among others: Hendrickx (n 32); Adams-Prassl et al. (n 39); Article 29 Data Protection Working Party, 'Opinion 8/2001 on the Processing of Personal Data in the Employment Context' (n 453) 15; Article 29 Data Protection Working Party, 'Opinion 02/2017 on Data Processing at Work' (n 21) 6-8.

GDPR: Article 4(11) GDPR ('Definitions') and Article 7 GDPR ('Conditions for consent'). Article 4(11) GDPR defines consent as any freely given, specific,[534] informed and unambiguous indication of the data subject's wishes[535] by which s(he), by a statement or by a clear affirmative action,[536] signifies agreement to the processing of personal data relating to him or her. The precondition for valid consent is the genuine free choice and control for individuals regarding their personal data ('freely given'). The EDPB emphasises that consent must be given without coercion or adverse consequences for refusal, and it should not be bundled with terms and conditions.[537] On this, Article 7(4) GDPR underscores the need to scrutinise situations where consent is tied to the performance of contracts or services, ensuring that individuals can freely exercise their rights without coercion. The GDPR acknowledges that power imbalances between data controllers and subjects exist and need careful assessment of any undue pressure or influence exerted on data subjects. This is why Article 7(1) GDPR requires the controller to demonstrate that the data subject has consented to the processing of his or her personal data. The consent must be provided through a specific written declaration, with proof that the request for consent is clear, intelligible, and easily accessible, using plain and straightforward language (Article 7(2) GDPR). Finally, the employee-data subject shall have the right to withdraw his or her consent at any time without consequences.[538]

The presence in the GDPR of such guarantees and conditions for determining valid consent has its roots in an earlier debate. Already with Directive 95/46/EC, the WP29 had pointed to consent as a 'misleading' legal basis in situations where the data controller benefits from power asymmetries that disadvantage the data subject.[539] One

534. Since a service may involve multiple processing operations for more than one purpose, the data subject should be free to choose which purpose to accept. Recital 43 GDPR expressly states that consent is not freely given if data subjects were not allowed to separately consent for the different purposes: European Data Protection Board, 'Guidelines 05/2020 on Consent under Regulation 2016/679' 14 https://edpb.europa.eu/sites/default/files/files/file1/edpb_guidelines_202005_consent_en.pdf accessed 22 October 2025.
535. The EDPB defines *the unambiguous wishes of the data subjects* in relation to Article 2(h) of Directive 95/46/EC, which described consent as an 'indication of wishes by which the data subject signifies his agreement to personal data relating to him being processed'. Article 4(11) GDPR builds on this definition, by clarifying that valid consent requires an unambiguous indication by means of a statement or by a clear affirmative action, in line with previous guidance issued by Opinion 15/2011 on the definition of consent (WP187), p. 12. Unambiguous means also that if the data collection has multiple non-concurrent purposes, the data subject has to consent specifically to all of them with a clear affirmative act, *see*: *ibid.*, 18.
536. The EDPB defines *affirmative act* as a situation where the data subject must have taken a deliberate action to consent to the particular processing. Recital 32 GDPR sets out additional guidance on this. Such action can be collected through a written or (a recorded) oral statement, including by electronic means, *see*: *ibid.*
537. The EDPB specifies that the situation of 'bundling' consent with acceptance of terms or conditions is highly undesirable, and consent should be considered as not freely given: *ibid.*, 10.
538. The controller, according to Recital 42 GDPR, needs to demonstrate that it is possible for the data subject to refuse or withdraw consent without detriment.
539. *See* above section 2.2 in this chapter. Article 29 Data Protection Working Party, 'Opinion 8/2001 on the Processing of Personal Data in the Employment Context' (n 453) 3.

of these situations was typically represented by employment.[540] As early as WP29 Opinion 8/2001, the processing of employees' data on the basis of consent is described as the 'last resort' of the legal bases in Article 7 DPD. The substantive reality around the recourse of consent in employment is depicted as follows:

> The worker is in theory able to refuse consent but the consequence may be the loss of a job opportunity. In such circumstances consent is not freely given and is therefore not valid. The situation is even clearer cut where, as is often the case, all employers impose the same or similar condition of employment.[541]

In its 2001 Opinion, the WP29 concluded that consent is inherently misleading in employment contexts, making it invalid, except in specific situations where the employee can demonstrate a genuine choice without repercussions.[542] In Opinion 2/2017, after the adoption of the GDPR, the WP29 reiterated this position on consent. It emphasised that consent should not serve as the legal basis for processing employee data due to the power imbalance between employers and employees, unless there are strong guarantees that can prove that consent is freely given.[543]

3.3.2 *Performance of a Contract*

Article 6(1)(b) GDPR states that data processing is lawful when it is necessary for the performance of a contract to which the data subject is a party or for taking steps at the data subject's request before entering into a contract. In the employment context, a typical example for the use of this legal basis would be processing an employee's salary and bank account details to facilitate wage payments. This legal ground, according to the WP29, must be interpreted strictly, as it does not apply to situations where the processing is not genuinely necessary for the performance of the contract itself.[544] The 'performance of a contract' as a legal basis thus requires a careful evaluation of the necessity of processing, in line with the principles of purpose limitation and data minimisation. Clarifying the contract's objective and substance is essential to determining whether specific data processing is indispensable for its proper execution.[545]

540. Article 29 Data Protection Working Party, 'Opinion 15/2011 on the Definition of Consent' 13-14 https://ec.europa.eu/justice/article-29/documentation/opinion-recommendation/files/2011/wp187_en.pdf accessed 22 October 2025.
541. Article 29 Data Protection Working Party, 'Opinion 8/2001 on the Processing of Personal Data in the Employment Context' (n 453) 23.
542. *Ibid.* The same view is reflected in the 2002 Working Document on the surveillance of electronic communications in the workplace: Article 29 Data Protection Working Party, 'Working Document on the Surveillance and Monitoring of Electronic Communications in the Workplace' (n 447).
543. Article 29 Data Protection Working Party, 'Opinion 02/2017 on Data Processing at Work' (n 21) 6.
544. Article 29 Data Protection Working Party, 'Opinion 06/2014 on the Notion of Legitimate Interests of the Data Controller under Article 7 of Directive 95/46/EC' (2014) 16 https://ec.europa.eu/justice/article-29/documentation/opinion-recommendation/files/2014/wp217_en.pdf accessed 22 October 2025.
545. *Ibid.*, 17.

In Opinion 06/2014 on the definition of legitimate interest of Article 6(1)(f) GDPR, the WP29, in outlining a notion of contract performance, makes an extensive reference to the monitoring of employees by employers.[546] Monitoring of employees' internet access, email, or telephone usage, as well as video surveillance, extends beyond what is strictly required for performing an employment contract. However, the necessity of such a monitoring may vary depending on the nature of the employment, acknowledging that in some job positions, monitoring might be a precondition to perform the work itself.[547] The WP29 suggests that in the latter instances, legal obligation or the legitimate interests of the data controller shall constitute the most suitable legal grounds. 'Performance of a contract', according to the WP29, shall not encompass subsequent actions during the actual execution of the contract. It follows, then, that this legal ground can be used only with a stricter necessity test showing that the absence of such a data processing would tantamount to the impossibility to conclude the contract of employment; for example, an Amazon warehouse employee who, upon signing his or her employment contract, does not consent to the required monitoring systems would effectively be unable to perform his or her job.[548]

3.3.3 *Legal Obligation*

Data processing by employers may, in some cases, be required by law. In this regard, *Article 6(1)(c)* GDPR stipulates that processing is lawful when it is necessary for compliance with a legal obligation to which the employer (as the data controller) is subject. Labour laws at the national level might require the employer to process certain data. For instance, an employer may have to collect and share with the Authorities employees' personal data about their salaries to comply with fiscal regulations,[549] or to process social security contributions.[550] Another example of a legal obligation to collect employees' data is the OSH framework. According to Directive 89/391/EEC on the introduction of measures to encourage improvements in the safety and health of employees at work,[551] the employer must regularly collect data and information on employees in order to assess working conditions and potential risks, to maintain adequate levels of health and safety required by European legislation from Member

546. *Ibid.*
547. With AI and IoT-enabled technology monitoring this might act as a backdoor since more and more jobs rely on surveillance tools. I will extensively delve into it in Chapter 8 about the limitations of the GDPR in employment contexts.
548. This might allow for a broad scope of the performance of a contract as a legal ground. I focus on this issue in Chapter 8, section 2.1.
549. Article 29 Data Protection Working Party, 'Opinion 02/2017 on Data Processing at Work' (n 21) 7.
550. Article 29 Data Protection Working Party, 'Opinion 8/2001 on the Processing of Personal Data in the Employment Context' (n 453) 15; Article 29 Data Protection Working Party, 'Opinion 06/2014 on the Notion of Legitimate Interests of the Data Controller under Article 7 of Directive 95/46/EC' (n 544) 19.
551. Council Directive 89/391/EEC of 12 June 1989 on the introduction of measures to encourage improvements in the safety and health of workers at work.

States.[552] Article 14 of the Directive further outlines the requirement for implementing health surveillance measures for employees, tailored to the specific risks they face on the job.[553]

3.3.4 *Legitimate Interest*

Last but not least, among the relevant legal grounds for data processing in employment contexts is *Article 6(1)(f)* GDPR. There the GDPR provides that the processing shall be lawful if it is necessary for the purposes of the legitimate interests pursued by the data controller, except where such interests are overridden by the interests or fundamental rights and freedoms of the data subject which require protection of personal data.

The open-ended formulation of this legal ground raises questions on its exact scope and application. The WP29 stressed in its dedicated Opinion that all the other grounds (including the ones analysed here: consent, performance of a contract, legal obligation) have an a priori presumption that the balance between the different rights and interests at stake is satisfied.[554] However, legitimate interests as legal ground require a specific test to assess whether the interests and fundamental rights of the employee-data subjects are adequately considered.[555] This openness has led the WP29 to define more precisely what can be considered an 'interest' and when it can be regarded as legitimate, in order to prevent it from becoming an 'open door' to legitimising all data processing activities that do not fall under any of the other legal grounds.[556] For the WP29, the concept of 'interest' is related but distinct from 'purpose'. Purpose represents the specific reasons for a precise data processing, while an interest is a broader stake or benefit that a controller might have in the processing.[557] In this regard, the WP29 provides an example related to occupational safety and health (OSH), which I can connect with a previous example from this book: a company might prioritise the well-being and safety of its employees on the shop floor by installing AI-powered cameras such as *Intenseye*.[558] While the company is legally required to uphold OSH standards – and therefore to collect employee data for that purpose under Article 6(1)(c) GDPR – it may implement AI and IoT-enabled technologies to deliver a more detailed and proactive approach to accident prevention, thus going beyond its minimum duties. In this latter case, the purpose of processing is accident prevention, while the broader interest justifying the processing under Article 6(1)(f) GDPR is the employer's legitimate interest in improving employee well-being and maintaining a safe work environment.[559] This interest must be balanced against the fundamental

552. Article 6 Directive 89/391/EEC.
553. European Agency for Safety and Health at Work (n 8).
554. Article 29 Data Protection Working Party, 'Opinion 06/2014 on the Notion of Legitimate Interests of the Data Controller under Article 7 of Directive 95/46/EC' (n 544) 9.
555. *Ibid.*
556. *Ibid.*, 10.
557. *Ibid.*, 24.
558. *See* Chapter 4, section 3.1.1.
559. *Ibid.*

rights and freedoms of the data subjects, such as their right to privacy, in line with the requirements of Article 6(1)(f) GDPR.

How to balance employers' legitimate interests with employees' rights? The WP29 provides for four main factors coming from Member States' laws and DPAs' guidelines: assessing the controller's legitimate interest, the impact on data subjects, provisional balance, and additional safeguards to be taken by the controller.[560]

The need for monitoring may in fact be dictated by the protection of a fundamental right, such as the right to protect one's property or to conduct an economic activity.[561] In some circumstances, the WP29 has found that employee monitoring by employers may represent a public interest, as guaranteeing legitimate business interests may be a broad and protectable interest in society.[562]

The following criterion to be weighed up is the impact on employees (being the data subjects). Here, the WP29 stresses the importance of considering both positive and negative repercussions for data subjects. 'Negative repercussions' is a concept narrowly described in Opinion 6/2014: it includes potential discrimination, defamation, or damage to the reputation, negotiating power, or loss of agency and autonomy of the data subject. Emotional impacts, such as fear or distress resulting from a loss of control over personal information, are also relevant. Furthermore, the potential chilling effect on employees' fundamental rights and freedoms, such as freedom of expression, due to continuous monitoring must be taken into account.[563] According to the WP29, the presence of these 'repercussions', together with any asymmetries of power between the data controller and data subject, indicates the absence of legitimate interest. In Opinion 6/2014, the WP29 stresses the relevance of the statuses of both the data controller and the data subject in determining whether the processing has a legitimate basis. For example, a large multinational corporation may wield more influence and resources than an individual employee, potentially imposing its interests on the employee. If this power dynamic is left unchecked, it could disadvantage the individual data subject.[564]

The absence of legitimate interest can also be inferred from the lack of safeguarding measures in favour of data subjects. According to the WP29's four-part test, once a legitimate interest has been identified and the necessity of processing established, the balancing exercise must take into account whether appropriate safeguards are in place. These may include limiting the amount of data collected, promptly deleting data after use, or applying anonymisation and aggregation techniques. The absence of such

560. Article 29 Data Protection Working Party, 'Opinion 06/2014 on the Notion of Legitimate Interests of the Data Controller under Article 7 of Directive 95/46/EC' (n 544) 33. *See also* in Chapter 3, section 6.1, the case law pertaining to Article 8 ECHR and the employer's right to a smooth running of the company.
561. *Ibid.*, 34.
562. *Ibid.*, 35. In Chapter 3, section 6.1, I refer to some cases where intrusive monitoring by employers, even in violation of national laws (e.g., Lopez Ribalda, Florindo), was justified by the ECtHR because it was conducted to protect a higher social interest value: the protection of employers' property from misuse or theft.
563. *Ibid.*, 37.
564. *Ibid.*, 40.

safeguards may undermine the lawfulness of processing under Article 6(1)(f) GDPR.[565] As I will analyse more precisely in section 3.5.3, to counterbalance an illegitimate balancing carried out by the data controller, employees-data subjects should exercise the right to object the processing of their personal data (Article 21 GDPR).

3.4 Processing of Special Categories of Personal Data (Article 9 GDPR)

Alongside the principles applicable to processing (Article 5 GDPR) and the legal bases (Article 6 GDPR), Article 9 GDPR bans the processing of special categories of data: i.e., sensitive data. The collection of sensitive data is unlawful when concerning:

> personal data revealing racial or ethnic origin, political opinions, religious or philosophical beliefs, or trade union membership, and the processing of genetic data, biometric data for the purpose of uniquely identifying a natural person, data concerning health or data concerning a natural person's sex life or sexual orientation (...).

The EU legislator chose to protect *ex ante* certain categories of data, source of possible discrimination or violations of other fundamental rights. Since the 1989 CoE Recommendation, 'Particular Categories of Data' are established, which in turn are referred to in Article 6 of Convention 108 (1981).[566] Data relating to racial origins, political affiliations and religion, sexual life or criminal records could then only be collected when expressly provided for by national laws or with the explicit and particular consent of the employee. The GDPR, building on the DPD, upholds the general prohibition on processing sensitive data, with the addition of genetic data and biometric data for the purpose of uniquely identifying a natural person. In response to advancements in technology, including profiling and surveillance technologies such as AI and IoT-enabled ones, the European legislator shields data subjects from potentially intrusive processing.[567]

However, the data controller may rely on one of the exceptions outlined in Article 9(2) GDPR. This provision allows processing of sensitive data for certain purposes when specific conditions are met. In employment contexts, relevant exceptions include explicit consent from the data subject (Article 9(2)(a) GDPR) or when national law or collective agreements grant the employer the right or obligation to process this data for specific, identified purposes (Article 9(2)(b) GDPR).

Article 9(2)(a) GDPR falls within the debate about employers' use of consent given by employees. It is broadly accepted that consent should not be a legal basis for data processing at work, yet in some circumstances, an employer might have a strong

565. Article 29 Data Protection Working Party, 'Opinion 05/2014 on Anonymisation Techniques' (2014) 7 https://ec.europa.eu/justice/article-29/documentation/opinion-recommendation/files/2014/wp216_en.pdf accessed 22 October 2025.
566. Council of Europe (n 440).
567. Catherine Jasserand, 'Legal Nature of Biometric Data: From "Generic" Personal Data to Sensitive Data – Which Changes Does the New Data Protection Framework Introduce? Special Issue: The General Data Protection Regulation' (2016) 2 European Data Protection Law Review (EDPL) 297 https://doi.org/10.21552/edpl/2016/3/6 accessed 22 October 2025.

interest in implementing high standards of security (e.g., access to special areas restricted to selected personnel).[568] In that case, according to the Guidelines on consent, Article 9(2)(a) requires not just the 'statement or clear affirmative action' required by Article 4(11) GDPR and Article 7 GDPR for regular consent but also extra efforts for an data controller in collecting an express statement of consent, possibly with a written and signed statement.[569]

Article 9(2)(b) GDPR provides that where labour or social security law (or collective bargaining) allows employers to process sensitive data, the prohibition set in Article 9(1) GDPR does not apply. An example would be the obligation to monitor the health of employees when required by law under special conditions (e.g., toxic substances).[570] Or when collective bargaining allows for well-being programmes and monitoring tools such as *Fitbit*, which allows the employer to give advice on how to maintain a balanced lifestyle.[571] The exception related to labour law or social security law allows the processing of sensitive data only when specific legal provisions or collective agreements clearly define the circumstances in which employers are permitted to process these data. This ensures that the processing is justified within the context of labour and social security regulations.

With this subsection, I conclude the analysis of the principles governing data processing and the legal bases for data collection. I now turn to another central part of the GDPR: data subjects' rights.

3.5 Data Subjects' Rights as Employees' Rights (Articles 12-22 GDPR)

Chapter III of the GDPR contains the so-called rights of data subjects. The underlying rationale of the GDPR here is well reflected: data subjects in the EU single market shall have control over their own data and the way the data is read and used by the controllers.[572] This is further reflected in Recital 39, which states that 'it should be transparent to natural persons that personal data concerning them are collected, used, consulted or otherwise processed' and that they 'should be made aware of risks, rules, safeguards and rights in relation to the processing of personal data and how to exercise their rights'.

The GDPR, once the principles and obligations of data controllers have been introduced, empowers data subjects to supervise how the data controller acts. The idea

568. *See*, for instance, the Guidelines from the Italian DPA on the collection of biometric data for exceptional security reasons at work: *Linee guida sul trattamento di dati personali dei lavoratori privati – 23 novembre 2006 [1364939]*, https://www.garanteprivacy.it/web/guest/home/docweb/-/docweb-display/docweb/1364939 accessed 22 October 2025.
569. European Data Protection Board, 'Guidelines 05/2020 on Consent under Regulation 2016/679' (n 534) 21-22.
570. Directive 2004/37/EC of the European Parliament and of the Council of 29 April 2004 on the protection of workers from the risks related to exposure to carcinogens or mutagens at work.
571. *See* Chapter 4 (section 3.3) and Chapter 5 (section 2.3).
572. *See* the Charter of Fundamental Rights of the European Union, Articles 7-8 and comments on the data subject in command approach in the EU data governance by Salome Viljoen, 'Democratic Data: A Relational Theory For Data Governance' (2021) 2 The Yale Law Journal 573, 625-626.

of the EU legislator – coherently with the legal bases and principles applicable to the processing – is to enhance data subjects' knowledge and influence over the processing through transparency, along with further accountability on data controllers to communicate certain information.[573] Since the adoption of the new regulation, labour law literature has examined whether this framework of employee empowerment could effectively mitigate an illegitimate exercise of the employer's monitoring power.[574]

In section 3.5, I examine the role of data subjects' rights through three subsections. In section 3.5.1, I analyse the supervisory role of data subjects through their individual rights to receive information when their data is collected (Articles 12-14 GDPR) and their right to access information when the data processing is already underway (Article 15 GDPR). In section 3.5.2, I discuss the right of data subjects to restrict processing when necessary (Articles 16-19 GDPR). Finally, in section 3.5.3, I explore how data subjects can prevent or halt data processing (Articles 21-22 GDPR).

3.5.1 Transparency, Information and Access to Personal Data (Articles 12-15 GDPR)

Articles 12-14 GDPR provide transparency, information and access for data subjects to be exercised towards the data controller. Read together, these three articles act as the main channel for a symmetry of information and power between employers and employees in a datafied workplace.[575] Article 12 GDPR ('Transparent information, communication and modalities for the exercise of the rights of the data subject') mandates the employer implementing any surveillance technology to provide employees with information in a concise, transparent, intelligible, and easily accessible manner. This, according to the EDPB, means that the right amount of information has to be shared since providing extensive tables with large amounts of information would not produce awareness and understanding on the part of the employee.[576] Information should be understandable to the intended audience, using clear language tailored to their level of comprehension. The scope and consequences of data processing (required by Articles 5 and 6 GDPR) shall be communicated alongside the possible significant consequences of processing.[577] Information should be concrete and definite,

573. Gloria González Fuster, 'How Uninformed Is the Average Data Subject? A Quest for Benchmarks in EU Personal Data Protection' [2014] IDP Revista de Internet, Derecho y Política 92 https://doi.org/10.7238/idp.v0i19.2424 accessed 22 October 2025.
574. Aloisi and Gramano (n 360); Eddie Keane, 'The GDPR and Employee's Privacy: Much Ado but Nothing New' (2018) 29 King's Law Journal 354 https://doi.org/10.1080/09615768.2018.1555065 accessed 22 October 2025; Hendrickx, Mangan and Gramano (n 36).
575. Aloisi and Gramano (n 360) 111; Gabriela Zanfir-Fortuna, 'Article 15 Right of Access by the Data Subject' in Christopher Kuner et al. (eds), *The EU General Data Protection Regulation (GDPR)* (Oxford University Press, New York 2020) https://academic.oup.com/book/41324/chapter/352297801 accessed 22 October 2025.
576. Article 29 Data Protection Working Party, 'Guidelines on Transparency under Regulation 2016/679' (n 500) 7.
577. Article 29 Data Protection Working Party, 'Guidelines on Transparency under Regulation 2016/679' (n 500); Margot E Kaminski and Gianclaudio Malgieri, 'Algorithmic Impact Assessments under the GDPR: Producing Multi-Layered Explanations' (2021) 11 International Data Privacy Law 125 https://doi.org/10.1093/idpl/ipaa020 accessed 22 October 2025.

avoiding abstract or ambivalent wording.[578] Ultimately, when an employer implements software such as *Cogito* that monitors the tone of voice of call centre employees, s(he) will have to clearly communicate the purpose, how the technology works, and most importantly, what use s(he) intends to make of it. If it is not explicitly mentioned that it is used as an evaluation tool, it cannot be used as such unless it is clearly and correctly communicated to the employees. The installation of an AI camera on trucks to warn the driver of the risks of driving should be communicated as such and should not then be used as a disciplinary tool to evaluate the driver's performance. In this sense, Article 12 GDPR, through transparency duties, strengthens the principle of purpose limitation towards the employee.

Articles 13, 14 and 15 GDPR have a similar structure, restating the same duties of transparency on data controllers in three different rights: a right to receive information when personal data are collected from the data subject (Article 13 GDPR); a right to receive information when personal data have not been obtained from the data subject (Article 14 GDPR); a general right of access by the data subject (Article 15 GDPR).[579]

These norms provide for an employer's duty to inform the employee of detailed information when collecting personal data. This includes the data controller's (and, if any, the processor) identity, purpose(s) of processing, recipients of the data, and rights of the data subject (Articles 15-22 GDPR). Additional information must be provided regarding data storage, rights to access (Article 15) and rectify data (Article 16), withdrawal of consent (Article 7), and the existence of automated decision-making (Article 22). According to Article 13 GDPR, this information shall be communicated at the time of data collection from the employee. If the data collection is obtained from an external data set – i.e., the data are not collected from the employee – Article 14 GDPR specifies that the maximum timeframe for providing information is one month, yet data controllers are encouraged to provide it well in advance to uphold fairness and accountability principles.[580]

Article 15 GDPR provides for the right of access, i.e., when processing is already under way the data subject must have access to all the information mentioned above and receive information about his or her rights. The EDPB guidelines define the right of access as consisting of three components: confirmation that certain data are being processed or not, access in a meaningful way (*see* Article 12 GDPR on meaningful information) and information on the processing itself.[581] According to the ECJ's jurisprudence, this right gives access to data generated subsequently,[582] as in the

578. Article 29 Data Protection Working Party, 'Guidelines on Transparency under Regulation 2016/679' (n 500) 9-10.
579. Zanfir-Fortuna (n 575).
580. Article 29 Data Protection Working Party, 'Guidelines on Transparency under Regulation 2016/679' (n 500) 17-18.
581. European Data Protection Board, 'Guidelines 01/2022 on Data Subject Rights: Right of Access' (2022) 8 https://www.edpb.europa.eu/system/files/2023-04/edpb_guidelines_202201_data_subject_rights_access_v2_en.pdf accessed 22 October 2025.
582. Case C-434/16, *Novak v. Data Protection Commissioner*, ECLI:EU:C:2017:994.

example of employee performance evaluation data generated by any software processing employee data.[583] Article 15(1)(h) GDPR provides that the existence of automated decision-making, including profiling, shall be communicated through meaningful information about the logic involved, as well as the significance and the envisaged consequences of such a processing for the data subject. There is no specification about the exact meaning of 'meaningful information about the logic involved'. In this regard, however, the Dutch DPA in 2024 sanctioned Uber for complicating procedures relating to the right of access and discouraging employees from exercising this right: making the 'right of access accessible', in an employment relationship with power imbalances, puts the employee in a position to make use of it.[584] Similarly, in 2023, the District Court of Amsterdam ruled that Uber and Ola Cabs must provide transparency about the automated decision-making process used to dismiss drivers.[585] Uber and Ola Cabs, under Article 15(1)(h) GDPR, shall disclose information about the logic, significance, and consequences of the automated decision. Without an accessible right to access, Articles 21 and 22 GDPR ('Right to object and right not to be subject to automated decision making, including profiling') are precluded, as the employee-data subject cannot access any information or output of data processing and challenge it effectively.[586]

3.5.2 *Rectification and Erasure (Articles 16-18 GDPR)*

Articles 16-18 GDPR grant data subjects the right to rectify inaccurate data (Article 16), together with an obligation for the data controller to delete personal data when requested (upon certain conditions) by the data subject (Article 17 GDPR, 'right to be forgotten'), and the right to request a restriction of data processing (Article 18 GDPR) if the data controller fails to comply with GDPR principles and obligations.

Article 16 GDPR ('Right to rectification') allows data subjects to request that certain data be corrected from inaccuracies; this is often the case with data generated by automated profiling systems that generate predictions. The input data may be inaccurate or irrelevant, or taken out of context. The WP29 gives an example: a data subject, such as an employee, may be profiled by a system in a category that says something about his or her ability to perform a task. However, his or her correct information is placed in an incorrect category: the employee will have an interest in rectifying the category applied to him or her, and s(he) can exercise his or her right to rectification.[587]

583. Article 29 Data Protection Working Party, 'Recommendation 1/2001 on Employee Evaluation Data' (n 452).
584. Reuters, 'Dutch Watchdog Fines Uber 10 Mln Euros over Privacy Regulations Infringement' (31 January 2024) https://www.reuters.com/technology/dutch-watchdog-fines-uber-10-mln-euros-over-privacy-regulations-infringement-2024-01-31/ accessed 22 October 2025.
585. Gerechtshof Amsterdam 4 April 2023, ECLI:NL:GHAMS:2023:796, ECLI:NL:GHAMS:2023:793, and ECLI:NL:GHAMS:2023:804.
586. Calacci and Stein (n 38) 255-257.
587. Article 29 Data Protection Working Party, 'Guidelines on Automated Individual Decision-Making and Profiling for the Purposes of Regulation 2016/679' (n 494) 17-18.

Article 17(1) GDPR ('Right to erasure') grants any data subject the right to request the deletion of their personal data by the controller under certain conditions and without undue delay. In particular, Article 17(1)(a) GDPR provides that data must be erased when they are no longer necessary in relation to the purposes for which they were originally collected or otherwise processed. In the employment context, this might apply where an employer continues to retain performance-related data long after the evaluation or decision for which the data were collected has taken place. Once the purpose – such as performance appraisal or promotion decision – is fulfilled, continued storage of that data may no longer be justified.[588] In such cases, the employee has the right to request erasure, ensuring that his or her personal data remain proportionate, relevant, and not retained beyond what is strictly necessary.[589]

Under Article 17(1)(b) GDPR, a data subject may request deletion of his or her personal data if s(he) has withdrawn his or her consent and no other legal basis justifies the continued processing. Additionally, Article 17(1)(c) GDPR connects the right to erasure with the right to object under Article 21 GDPR: if an employee objects to the processing and the employer cannot demonstrate a compelling legitimate interest that overrides the employee's rights and freedoms, the controller is obliged to erase the data. These provisions reinforce the principle that data must not be retained or processed longer than necessary and must remain subject to the employee's control, particularly in cases where the original legal basis for processing no longer applies.[590]

Article 18 GDPR ('Right to Restriction of Processing') allows data subjects to request that their personal data be processed only in ways that comply with the principles of the GDPR, such as purpose limitation. For example, if an AI camera installed in a truck collects data to monitor driving safety but the employer uses this data for other purposes, like evaluating performance or tracking physiological breaks, employees could activate their right to restrict the data processing. In this case, the employee could request that the data be used exclusively for monitoring road safety, in line with the original, lawful purpose for which it was collected.

3.5.3 *Right to Object and Not to Be Subject to Automated Decision-Making (Articles 21-22 GDPR)*

Article 21 GDPR grants data subjects, including employees, the right to object at any time to the processing of their personal data when the legal ground is Article 6(1)(f) GDPR ('legitimate interest'). Once this right is invoked, the controller must cease

588. Cf. with Article 5 GDPR principles, in particular data minimisation and storage limitation, Articles 5(1)(c) and Article 5(1)(e) GDPR.

589. Cf. with the WP29 guidelines: 'The rights to rectification and erasure apply to both the "input personal data" (the personal data used to create the profile) and the "output data" (the profile itself or "score" assigned to the person).' Article 29 Data Protection Working Party, 'Guidelines on Automated Individual Decision-Making and Profiling for the Purposes of Regulation 2016/679' (n 494) 17-18.

590. Article 17(1)(c) GDPR: '[the controller shall have the obligation to erase personal data without undue delay where one of the following grounds applies:] the data subject objects to the processing pursuant to Article 21(1) and there are no overriding legitimate grounds for the processing, or the data subject objects to the processing pursuant to Article 21(2)'.

processing the data unless s(he) can demonstrate compelling legitimate grounds for the processing that override the interests, rights, and freedoms of the data subject. Thus, if, for example, the data controller, such as an employer, has based the data processing on a legitimate interest in monitoring employees' movements to streamline the work process in a warehouse, the employer will have to prove that the processing does not infringe the allegedly breached rights claimed by employees. Once the employee exercises this right, the controller must interrupt the profiling process,[591] unless it can demonstrate compelling legitimate grounds that override the rights of the employees.[592] Defining what is a compelling legitimate ground is not so straightforward, as I have discussed in section 3.3.4 of this chapter on the notion of legitimate interest. I refer to the notion elaborated there.[593]

Employees may also resort to the right not to be subjected to decisions based solely on automated processing, including profiling, according to Article 22 GDPR. Abraha stresses how this provision recognises that humans - employers - not algorithms, should make high-risk decisions, by banning fully automated decision-making with significant effects, such as in job recruitment or AI and IoT-enabled technologies producing performance assessments or disciplinary sanctions.[594]

The applicability of this right in employment contexts is based on a necessary precondition outlined in Article 22(1) GDPR: the processing must produce legal effects on the individual and must result in a final decision made without human involvement in its formulation. Thus, the decision must have legal effects or at least significantly affect the employee. While the article does not precisely define what constitutes legal or significant effects, the EDPB includes greater impacts on individuals' circumstances, behaviour, or choices, potentially leading to prolonged or permanent consequences, or even exclusion or discrimination. As mentioned earlier, any form of performance assessment will fall within the scope of Article 22(1) GDPR if generated by AI and IoT-enabled technologies.[595]

Article 22(2) GDPR outlines three exceptions that limit the protection granted in Article 22(1) GDPR. This right does not apply if: (a) the profiling or monitoring system

591. This is specifically provided by Article 18(1)(d) GDPR: '[the employer has to interrupt the processing if] the data subject has objected to processing pursuant to Article 21(1) pending the verification whether the legitimate grounds of the controller override those of the data subject'.

592. Article 29 Data Protection Working Party, 'Guidelines on Automated Individual Decision-Making and Profiling for the Purposes of Regulation 2016/679' (n 494) 18; Gabriela Zanfir-Fortuna, 'Article 21 Right to Object' in Christopher Kuner et al. (eds), *The EU General Data Protection Regulation (GDPR)* (Oxford University Press, New York 2020) https://academic.oup.com/book/41324/chapter/352298408 accessed 22 October 2025.

593. I refer to the discussion of how to 'detect' legitimate interest here: Article 29 Data Protection Working Party, 'Opinion 06/2014 on the Notion of Legitimate Interests of the Data Controller under Article 7 of Directive 95/46/EC' (n 544).

594. Abraha, 'Regulating Algorithmic Employment Decisions Through Data Protection Law' (n 26) 180.

595. Article 29 Data Protection Working Party, 'Guidelines on Automated Individual Decision-Making and Profiling for the Purposes of Regulation 2016/679' (n 494); Sandra Wachter, Brent Mittelstadt and Luciano Floridi, 'Why a Right to Explanation of Automated Decision-Making Does Not Exist in the General Data Protection Regulation' (2017) 7 International Data Privacy Law 76 https://doi.org/10.1093/idpl/ipx005 accessed 22 October 2025.

is necessary for performing a contract; (b) it is authorised by Union or Member State law to which the controller is subject and which also lays down suitable measures to safeguard the data subject's rights and freedoms and legitimate interests; or (c) the employer secures the employee's explicit consent.[596] As seen, according to the WP29, consent is generally invalid in employment contexts. The main applicable exception therefore is the performance of a contract. This exception is especially pertinent in discussions on the legitimate exercise of the employer's monitoring power via AI and IoT-enabled technologies. Increasingly, these technologies are integral to the viability of certain business models, where employee performance has to be continually monitored for shift planning or optimisation of workflow processes. This might pose some interpretative challenges which I will discuss later in Chapter 8 (section 2.1). Additionally, under Article 22(2)(b) GDPR, if these technologies serve purposes explicitly authorised by law, such as OSH compliance, this could justify the denial of the right provided by Article 22(1) GDPR. This means that monitoring systems implemented to uphold legally mandated workplace safety standards could override the general prohibition against fully automated decision-making.[597]

The European legislator, perhaps mindful of the broad exceptions given and of the risk of hollowing out the applicability of Article 22(1) GDPR, introduces a further guarantee in paragraph 3. If the employer uses one of the three exceptions, s(he) must at least give employees the opportunity to express their views to a human, to contest the decision and obtain explanations, i.e., the so-called human intervention. However, the practical application of this safeguard is unclear.[598] Many AI and IoT-enabled technologies are complex and opaque, making it challenging to understand their functioning. Moreover, most technologies are controlled by third parties – processors – leaving employers with limited understanding or control. This raises the question: what qualifies as genuine human intervention, and what responsibilities do employers have in ensuring it? For intervention to be meaningful, it must be more than just an approval of machine-generated results.[599] The GDPR does not specify answers to these challenges.[600] A review of EU case law conducted by the Future of Privacy Forum on automated decision-making shows that courts and DPAs assess the organisational context, examining factors such as organisational structure, reporting hierarchies, staff training, and whether supervisors have the authority to understand, modify, or

596. Abraha, 'Regulating Algorithmic Employment Decisions Through Data Protection Law' (n 26) 180.
597. Molè, 'The Internet of Things and Artificial Intelligence as Workplace Supervisors' (n 401) 90; Molè, 'Minimised Work Surveillance Exists under the GDPR: Amazon France and the DPA Sanction' (n 421).
598. Abraha, 'Regulating Algorithmic Employment Decisions Through Data Protection Law' (n 26) 181; Wachter, Mittelstadt and Floridi (n 595).
599. Michael Veale and Lilian Edwards, 'Clarity, Surprises, and Further Questions in the Article 29 Working Party Draft Guidance on Automated Decision-Making and Profiling' (2018) 34 Computer Law & Security Review 398 https://doi.org/10.31219/osf.io/y25ag_v1 accessed 22 October 2025.
600. Abraha, 'Regulating Algorithmic Employment Decisions Through Data Protection Law' (n 26) 181; Wachter, Mittelstadt and Floridi (n 595).

override the algorithmic decisions.[601] From these indicators, Courts and DPAs usually draw conclusions on whether the human intervention is actually meaningful and not a simple validation of systems' outputs.

3.6 Data Protection Impact Assessment and the Data Protection Officer (Articles 35-39 GDPR)

The GDPR imposes additional obligations on data controllers, such as employers, in Chapter IV. These include conducting a Data Protection Impact Assessment (DPIA) and, where required, Prior Consultation with a supervisory authority (Articles 35-36 GDPR). Data controllers are also required to appoint a Data Protection Officer (DPO) to oversee compliance with the Regulation (Articles 37-39 GDPR).

Article 35(1) GDPR provides that if the data controller is to establish a type of processing of personal data that poses a 'high-risk' to the rights and freedoms of data subjects, such as employees, a DPIA is required prior to its implementation. What poses a high-risk to employees' fundamental rights can be found in Article 35(3)(a) GDPR: 'a systematic and extensive evaluation of personal aspects relating to natural persons which is based on automated processing, including profiling, and on which decisions are based that produce legal effects concerning the natural person or similarly significantly affect the natural person'. This clearly overlaps with many forms of employee monitoring, where automated systems assess performance or behaviour and inform employment-related decisions. Ultimately, compliance with the DPIA requirement plays a crucial role in assessing whether the employer's monitoring practices constitute a legitimate exercise of his or her monitoring power.

Moreover, the WP29 guidelines on the DPIA expressly point to 'a company systematically monitoring its employees' activities, including the monitoring of the employees' work station, internet activity' as a high-risk processing involving 'vulnerable data subjects', which requires a DPIA under Article 35(3)(a) GDPR.[602] Recital 75 GDPR further refers to the evaluation of personal traits, including analysis or prediction of aspects related to work performance as a potential risk to the freedoms and rights of data subjects. The Recital also includes data subjects' behaviours, locations, or movements, with the intention of generating or employing personal profiles. Drafting a DPIA is thus required for employers who implement AI and IoT-enabled technologies processing employees' data.

Article 35(7) GDPR provides for several elements to be fulfilled while drafting the DPIA. First, a comprehensive examination of the foreseen monitoring activities shall be carried out, taking into account the means deployed and the purposes pursued by the employer (Article 35(7)(a) GDPR). This involves a systematic description detailing

601. Sebastião Barros Vale and Gabriela Zanfir-Fortuna, 'Automated Decision-Making Under the GDPR: Practical Cases from Courts and Data Protection Authorities' (Future of Privacy Form 2022) 28 https://fpf.org/wp-content/uploads/2022/05/FPF-ADM-Report-R2-singles.pdf accessed 22 October 2025.

602. Article 29 Data Protection Working Party, 'Guidelines on Data Protection Impact Assessment (DPIA)' (Article 29 Working Party 2017) 11.

how data will be processed, along with the specific objectives. Additionally, the data controller must outline the legitimate interests s(he) may have in carrying out these operations (according to the criteria seen in section 3.3.4. of this chapter). Then, Article 35(7)(b) GDPR demands an evaluation of the necessity and proportionality of the processing operations, with specific reference to their intended purposes. In other words, (a) and (b) require the employer, as data controller, to describe in detail his or her monitoring purposes (security, safety, performance of behaviour monitoring) and confront them with employees' rights. This requires that the employer contextualises the exercise of his or her monitoring power with the business model and checks whether the particular surveillance technology is strictly necessary to reach the intended aims (e.g., optimise the labour process, enhance cybersecurity standards).[603] Employees' rights and interests find a solid ground in Article 35(7)(c) GDPR since the data controller must provide an assessment of the risks to the rights and freedoms of data subjects' rights. The DPIA therefore must address if and how the AI and IoT-enabled technology will impact any of the fundamental rights of the data subjects. The last requirement for a DPIA is laid down in Article 35(7)(d) GDPR. The assessment should outline the measures intended to mitigate the identified risks. This encompasses implementing safeguards, security measures, and mechanisms to protect personal data effectively, such as more data aggregation, anonymisation when possible, shorter data retention and so on.

The GDPR details further the actors to be involved in the DPIA's drafting: (1) the 'data subjects or their representatives' (Article 35(9) GDPR), (2) the Data Protection Officer (DPO, Article 35(2) GDPR), and (3) (if any) the processor (Article 28(3)(f) GDPR).

Starting with Article 35(9) GDPR, which requires data controllers to seek the views of 'data subjects or their representatives', the prevailing interpretation in the literature is that this provision mandates the involvement of trade unions or works councils in the DPIA drafting.[604] Although Article 35(9) formally requires such consultation only 'where appropriate',[605] the consensus in the literature is that this involvement is always appropriate, and therefore required, in the employment context. I argue that this interpretation is further reinforced, as of 2024, by the explicit consultation obligations introduced in both the AI Act and the Platform Work Directive (PWD).[606] Specifically, Article 26(7) AI Act and Recital 92 AI Act require employers to comply with the applicable Union and national rules and practices governing the

603. On the criteria to distinguish legitimate from illegitimate interest: Article 29 Data Protection Working Party, 'Opinion 06/2014 on the Notion of Legitimate Interests of the Data Controller under Article 7 of Directive 95/46/EC' (n 544) 24-26.

604. *See,* among others: Aloisi (n 26); Giovanni Gaudio, 'Litigating the Algorithmic Boss in the EU: A (Legally) Feasible and (Strategically) Attractive Option for Trade Unions?' (2024) 40 International Journal of Comparative Labour Law and Industrial Relations 91 https://doi.org/10.54648/ijcl2024002 accessed 22 October 2025.

605. Article 35(9) GDPR: 'Where appropriate, the controller shall seek the views of data subjects or their representatives on the intended processing, without prejudice to the protection of commercial or public interests or the security of processing operations.'

606. Directive (EU) 2024/2831 of the European Parliament and of the Council of 23 October 2024 on improving working conditions in platform work.

information of employees and their representatives. Article 8 of the PWD goes even further by expressly addressing consultation in the context of the DPIA.[607] Under Article 8(1) PWD, digital labour platforms acting as data controllers, as defined in Article 4(7) GDPR, must actively seek the views of platform workers and their representatives during the drafting of the DPIA. Taken together, the GDPR, the AI Act, and the PWD form a coherent body of EU law that supports the view that, in the context of AI and IoT-enabled technologies used for employee monitoring, it is indeed 'appropriate', and thus required under Article 35(9) GDPR, to seek the views of data subjects or their representatives.

Moving on to the second actor to be involved in the DPIA, i.e., the Data Protection Officer (DPO, Article 35(2) GDPR), it can be either an employer's staff member or an external contractor. The appointment of a DPO is mandatory under Article 37(1) GDPR if the organisation is a public authority, engages in large-scale systematic monitoring of individuals, or processes sensitive data on a large scale. The DPO acts as an internal supervisor and monitors the drafting of the DPIA pursuant to Article 39(1)(c) GDPR[608] and verifies that the data controller is compliant with the GDPR, ensuring that data subjects have access to their rights. Pursuant to Article 38(3) GDPR, the DPO acts without any instructions from the data controller. This provision is specifically intended to enhance the DPO's independence from the employer, ensuring that his or her oversight and advice remain impartial and free from internal influence. The DPO cannot be in fact dismissed or penalised for fulfilling their GDPR-mandated responsibilities, reinforcing their protection and ability to act impartially.[609] The DPO under Article 39(1)(e) GDPR also notifies the DPA pursuant to Article 36 GDPR when the DPIA results in serious risks to, for instance, employees' fundamental rights who undergo the data processing designed by the data controller. The ECJ in the *Leistritz AG c. LH* case further confirmed that the DPO should act independently from employers'

607. Article 8 PWD ('Data Protection Impact Assessment'): 'The processing of personal data by a digital labour platform by means of automated monitoring systems or automated decision-making systems is a type of processing which is likely to result in a high risk to the rights and freedoms of natural persons within the meaning of Article 35(1) of Regulation (EU) 2016/679. When carrying out, pursuant to that provision, the assessment of the impact of the processing of personal data by automated monitoring systems or automated decision-making systems on the protection of personal data of persons performing platform work, including on the limitations of processing pursuant to Article 7 of this Directive, digital labour platforms, acting as controllers as defined in Article 4, point (7), of Regulation (EU) 2016/679, shall seek the views of persons performing platform work and their representatives. Digital labour platforms shall provide the assessment as referred to in paragraph 1 to workers' representatives.'

608. The Working Party suggests that controllers consult their Data Protection Officer (DPO) on various matters, including whether to conduct a Data Protection Impact Assessment (DPIA), the methodology for conducting it, whether to carry it out internally or externally, what safeguards to implement, and verifying the correctness of the DPIA and its compliance with GDPR. If the controller disagrees with the DPO's advice, they must document in writing the reasons for disregarding it. Article 29 Data Protection Working Party, 'Guidelines on Data Protection Officers ("DPOs")' (2017) 17 https://ec.europa.eu/newsroom/article29/items/612048/en accessed 22 October 2025.

609. Cecilia Alvarez Rigaudias and Alessandro Spina, 'Article 38 Position of the Data Protection Officer' in Christopher Kuner et al. (eds), *The EU General Data Protection Regulation (GDPR)* (Oxford University Press, New York 2020) https://academic.oup.com/book/41324/chapter/352300413 accessed 22 October 2025.

instructions and as a further guarantee that the employer makes data subject's rights effective for employees.[610] Under Article 37(6) GDPR, the role of DPO may be outsourced to an external certified expert who is not employed by the company. While this raises questions about the ability of an external DPO, especially one operating outside the company's structure, to effectively fulfil their duties as a point of contact between management and employees seeking guidance or wishing to exercise their rights, it also presents a potential advantage. Namely, the independence of the DPO from the employer may be more robustly guaranteed when the function is performed externally. Empirical research is needed to assess whether external DPOs can provide the same level of accessibility, oversight, and trust as their in-house counterparts, while potentially offering a higher degree of impartiality.[611]

Finally, Article 28(3)(f) GDPR requires the processor, i.e., the provider, to assist the controller in ensuring compliance with the obligations pursuant to Articles 32 to 36 GDPR, including the DPIA. In practice, this means the technology provider must enable the employer to assess and understand the potential risks posed by the AI and IoT-enabled technologies to employees. To support this, the processor must provide intelligible and accessible information about the technology's functioning, so that the employer, employee representatives (such as trade unions), and the DPO can carry out a well-informed DPIA that reflects the actual operation of the surveillance technologies.[612] However, as clarified by the European Data Protection Board (EDPB), this duty to assist does not shift responsibility for GDPR compliance from the controller to the processor. The ultimate responsibility remains with the controller, as clearly stated in Articles 24 and 25 GDPR. The processor's role is supportive and reactive, meaning that it is required to cooperate only 'where necessary and upon request', as set out in Recital 95.[613]

3.7 Employment as Special Category of Data Processing (Article 88 GDPR)

Chapter IX of the Regulation also includes 'Processing in the context of employment' under 'Provisions relating to specific processing situations'. According to Article 88(1) GDPR, Member States may, by law or by collective agreements, provide for more specific rules to ensure the protection of the rights and freedoms in respect of the processing of personal data in the employment context. The provision covers, by

610. Michele Molè, 'La Corte Di Giustizia Sul Responsabile Della Protezione Dei Dati: Primi Chiarimenti Sulle Tutele Speciali Di Un Protagonista Della Digitalizzazione al Lavoro' (2023) 33 Diritto delle Relazioni Industriali 215.
611. Article 29 Data Protection Working Party, 'Guidelines on Data Protection Officers ("DPOs")' (n 608) 12.
612. European Data Protection Board, 'Guidelines 07/2020 on the Concepts of Controller and Processor in the GDPR' (2020) 39 https://www.edpb.europa.eu/our-work-tools/our-documents/guidelines/guidelines-072020-concepts-controller-and-processor-gdpr_en accessed 22 October 2025.
613. *Ibid.* Consequently, it is the controller's responsibility to initiate and oversee the data protection impact assessment, not the processor.

means of a non-exhaustive list, the entire cycle of an employment relationship, from recruitment, through management and supervision, to termination of the contract.[614]

In EU law, this regulatory technique is often referred to as 'opening clause'.[615] These optional and open clauses allow Member States to enact further domestic legislation in specific domains, including data processing in the workplace. While the GDPR aims for harmonisation, these clauses paradoxically foster divergence among Member States' laws. I have already mentioned in section 2 of this chapter the reasons that led to Article 88 GDPR.[616] Since the only feasible regulatory path on data protection was towards a general legislation, Member States were left with the flexibility to adapt the GDPR to their domestic legal frameworks, whether through national legislation or collective bargaining.[617]

Article 88 GDPR can also be seen as the development that the WP29 has been hoping for since 2001: not all problems that arise in the employment context and involve the processing of personal data are exclusively data protection ones. Labour regulation must have a role in data processing at work.[618] By means of Article 88 GDPR, Member States may already today adopt (and notify to the European Commission under Article 88(3) GDPR) laws or collective agreements in this regard. Collective bargaining in many Member States has a primary role in regulating labour relations and the introduction of new technologies, be it at national, sectoral or company level.[619] Examples are Article 4 of the Italian Workers' Statute (Law 300/1970), which requires a trade union agreement for the introduction of any monitoring technology.[620] Spain's Organic Law 3/2018 provides for the possibility of regulating the right to disconnect through collective bargaining.[621] Finally, I refer to Article 26(4) of the German Federal

614. Article 88(1) mentions as areas of intervention covered by the provision: 'recruitment, the performance of the contract of employment, including discharge of obligations laid down by law or by collective agreements, management, planning and organisation of work, equality and diversity in the workplace, health and safety at work, protection of employer's or customer's property and for the purposes of the exercise and enjoyment, on an individual or collective basis, of rights and benefits related to employment, and for the purpose of the termination of the employment relationship'.
615. Emilia Mišćenić and Anna-Lena Hoffmann, 'The Role of Opening Clauses in Harmonization of EU Law: Example of the EU's General Data Protection Regulation (GDPR)', *EU 2020 – lessons from the past and solutions for the future* (2020) 45-46 https://hrcak.srce.hr/ojs/index.php/eclic/article/view/11895 accessed 22 October 2025. The authors report sixty-nine 'opening clauses' in the GDPR.
616. *See* sections 2.3 and 2.4 of this chapter.
617. Abraha, 'A Pragmatic Compromise?' (n 467).
618. Article 29 Data Protection Working Party, 'Opinion 8/2001 on the Processing of Personal Data in the Employment Context' (n 453) 14.
619. For an overview of the EU Member States' industrial relations systems: Beryl Ter Haar and Attila Kun (eds), *EU Collective Labour Law* (Edward Elgar Publishing 2021) https://china.elgaronline.com/view/edcoll/9781788116381/9781788116381.xml accessed 22 October 2025. *See also*: Mia Rönnmar et al., '7. Trade Union Participation and Influence in Decentralised Collective Bargaining' in Frank Tros (ed.), *Pathways in Decentralised Collective Bargaining in Europe* (Amsterdam University Press 2023) https://www.degruyter.com/document/doi/10.1515/9789048560240-007/html accessed 22 October 2025.
620. Ingrao (n 492).
621. Riso (n 2) 9.

Data Protection Act, which provides that the processing of employees' personal data shall only be permitted under the conditions laid down by collective bargaining.[622]

Although this provision preserves Member States' regulatory diversity, however, Article 88(2) GDPR places conditions on the activation of this 'opening clause'. The Member State's discretion is subject to substantive guidelines on how to exercise it: 'those rules shall include suitable and specific measures to safeguard the data subject's human dignity, legitimate interests and fundamental rights, with particular regard to the transparency of processing, (...) and monitoring systems at the workplace'. In the absence of further specific guidelines, some interpretative doubts arise: should such 'suitable and specific measures' necessarily be more stringent than those of the GDPR? What do these 'suitable and specific measures' actually entail for a Member State regulating data processing at work?[623] The ECJ in 2023 provided with the *Hauptpersonalrat der Lehrerinnen und Lehrer beim Hessischen Kultusministerium* case some initial response to these interpretative issues.[624] Suitable and specific rules must comply with the minimum requirements of the Regulation and not undermine its objectives.[625] Since one of the main objectives of the GDPR is precisely the harmonisation of personal data regulation in the European market, the ECJ provides further guidance on how Member States can diversify and contextualise their regulatory approaches. The Court specifies that:

> The conditions imposed by Article 88(2) of that regulation reflect the limits of the differentiation accepted by that regulation, in that that lack of harmonisation may be accepted only where the differences that remain are accompanied by specific and suitable safeguards intended to protect employees' rights and freedoms with regard to the processing of their personal data in the employment context.[626]

According to the ECJ, a dis-harmonisation of data regulation is legitimate when it meets the criteria listed in Article 88(2) GDPR. Specifically, these rules must incorporate appropriate and precise measures to protect the human dignity, legitimate interests, and fundamental rights of employees.[627] In addition, the Court found that national rules must adhere to the regulated area (labour law) and therefore differ from the general approach of the GDPR. The failure of Germany's national rules to qualify as 'more specific rules', in that case, stems indeed from their mere repetition of the GDPR's general requirements. Ultimately, the ECJ's ruling makes it clear that Member States aiming to establish 'more specific rules' under Article 88 must not simply

622. *Ibid.*, 16.
623. Abraha, 'A Pragmatic Compromise?' (n 467) 290.
624. Case C-34/21, *Hauptpersonalrat der Lehrerinnen und Lehrer beim Hessischen Kultusministerium*, 30 March 2023, ECLI:EU:C:2023:270.
625. *Ibid.*, para. 59 'when the Member States exercise the option granted to them by the opening clause of the GDPR, they must use their discretion under the conditions and within the limits laid down by the provisions of that regulation and must therefore legislate in such a way as not to undermine the content and objectives of that regulation'.
626. *Ibid.*, para. 73.
627. *Ibid.*, para. 74.

duplicate existing GDPR conditions and principles.[628] A positive example in this respect comes from France, where the DPA recently applied a provision of the French Labour Code (notified to the Commission) as a more specific and protective rule in the case of Amazon warehouses.[629]

As of March 2025, twenty-three Member States have notified more specific rules to protect employees' data under Article 88(3) GDPR.[630] Measuring the effects of this 'opening clause' is surely complicated, given the fragmentation it produces.[631] Positive effects are observed in Member States with labour and industrial relations regulations attentive to new technologies and codetermination.[632] However, it is difficult to draw a direct causal link between these national regulations and Article 88 GDPR. For instance, Germany's robust codetermination model for workplace technology adoption, along with Italy and Spain's specific rules on workplace monitoring, largely evolved independently of Article 88.[633] Article 88 GDPR, I suggest, seems to support Member States already inclined towards legislative initiatives in this area, potentially leaving behind those four Member States that have yet to focus on regulating data protection in the workplace. In Member States that have not adopted specific rules under Article 88 GDPR, this provision risks remaining a 'dead letter', as it merely offers the possibility – rather than imposing an obligation – for States to provide additional protections. As a result, it does not ensure that domestic labour laws will fill potential gaps in employee protection.

4 ANALYSIS OF THE GDPR IN EMPLOYMENT CONTEXTS: EMPLOYERS' OBLIGATIONS, EMPLOYEES' RIGHTS AND AI AND IOT-ENABLED TECHNOLOGIES

The analysis I have conducted thus far highlights that the GDPR adopts a general, rather than employment-specific, approach to data protection. It relies on general categories – namely, the data controller and the data subject – which are applicable across all data processing contexts. In the employment setting, these roles correspond

628. Halefom H Abraha, '*Hauptpersonalrat Der Lehrerinnen*: Article 88 GDPR and the Interplay between EU and Member State Employee Data Protection Rules' (2024) 87 The Modern Law Review 484, 495-496 https://doi.org/10.1111/1468-2230.12849 accessed 22 October 2025.
629. Molè, 'Minimised Work Surveillance Exists under the GDPR: Amazon France and the DPA Sanction' (n 421).
630. European Commission, 'EU Member States Notifications to the European Commission under the GDPR' https://commission.europa.eu/law/law-topic/data-protection/data-protection-eu/eu-member-states-notifications-european-commission-under-gdpr_en accessed 22 October 2025.
631. Abraha, 'A Pragmatic Compromise?' (n 467) 276.
632. Cf. Doellgast, Wagner and O'Brady (n 167).
633. Cf. with Martin Krzywdzinski, Detlef Gerst and Florian Butollo, 'Promoting Human-Centred AI in the Workplace. Trade Unions and Their Strategies for Regulating the Use of AI in Germany' (2023) 29 Transfer: European Review of Labour and Research 53 https://doi.org/10.1177/10242589221142273 accessed 22 October 2025; Ingrao (n 492); María Luz Rodríguez Fernández, 'Collective Bargaining and AI in Spain' in Aida Ponce Del Castillo (ed.), *Artificial Intelligence, Labour and Society* (European Trade Union Institute (ETUI) 2024) https://www.etui.org/publications/artificial-intelligence-labour-and-society accessed 22 October 2025.

respectively to the employer and the employee. While the Regulation is framed in these general terms, it nonetheless recognises that certain contexts – such as the employment one – may require additional safeguards. This is evident, for example, in the obligation to carry out a Data Protection Impact Assessment (DPIA) for high-risk processing under Article 35 GDPR, and in the opening clause present in Article 88 GDPR allowing for more specific national rules for data processing in employment contexts.

Therefore, employers must comply with the GDPR's principles by implementing appropriate measures under Articles 5, 24 and 25 GDPR, ensuring a valid legal basis for processing, and conducting a DPIA to prevent harm to employees' fundamental rights. The DPIA plays a key role in the deployment of AI and IoT-enabled technologies by requiring employers to anticipate and mitigate risks for employees' fundamental rights. Employees, meanwhile, hold individual rights under Articles 12-22 GDPR. However, their ability to exercise these rights largely depends on their initiative to proactively inform themselves, in particular through their right of access to personal data, and to raise issues of non-compliance with their employer.[634] In this sense, the GDPR's individualistic regulatory approach could be insufficiently responsive to the systemic effects of an AI and IoT-enabled monitoring power. I will discuss this issue in Chapter 8 (section 3).

The GDPR, in determining obligations and rights, establishes a framework in which both controllers and data subjects are assumed to have different forms of agency. Employers, as controllers, are endowed with responsibilities: they must ensure that data processing is lawful, necessary, and proportionate, and that data protection is integrated by design and by default. They shall also identify and justify the recourse to at least one of the legal grounds provided for by Article 6 GDPR. Articles 9 and 22 GDPR include exceptions that employers can interpret broadly, especially when processing sensitive data (Article 9 GDPR) or making decisions based on automated processing (Article 22 GDPR).[635] This implies that, under the GDPR, employers are expected not only to correctly interpret Articles 6, 9, and 22 GDPR but also to have the capacity to anticipate and mitigate risks through compliance, technical measures, and *ex ante* assessments, such as the DPIA. In Chapter 8 (section 4), I will further analyse the interpretative leeway for employers in applying the GDPR and the gaps in the regulation of the data controller-processor relationship.

Overall, the GDPR imposes a layered set of requirements on the employer's exercise of monitoring power through AI and IoT-enabled technologies. These include: proactive design obligations (Articles 24-25 GDPR), adherence to data processing principles (Article 5 GDPR), a valid legal basis for processing (Article 6 GDPR), the safeguarding of data subject's rights (Articles 12-22 GDPR), and the completion of a DPIA for high-risk processing activities (Article 35 GDPR), potentially supplemented by national labour law standards (Article 88 GDPR).

634. European Data Protection Board, 'Guidelines 01/2022 on Data Subject Rights: Right of Access' (n 581) 29.
635. *See also* on this: Abraha, 'Regulating Algorithmic Employment Decisions Through Data Protection Law' (n 26).

5 CONCLUSIONS

In this chapter, I answered research sub-question 5: *What requirements does the GDPR impose on the legitimate exercise of the employer's monitoring power via AI and IoT-enabled technologies?*

In the absence of a dedicated Directive on data processing at work (*see* section 2 of this Chapter), the GDPR is the main legal framework for the processing of employees' personal data by employers' AI and IoT-enabled technologies.

As data controllers, employers must comply with Articles 24 and 25 GDPR by implementing appropriate technical and organisational measures. They are required to embed the principles of data protection by design and by default into the functioning of AI and IoT-enabled technologies, ensuring that processing complies with the principles established by Article 5 GDPR. Prior to processing, employers must identify a valid legal basis under Article 6 GDPR. While the legal bases for processing – such as necessity for the performance of a contract, compliance with a legal obligation, or the pursuit of a legitimate interest – may be invoked, consent is generally not considered valid in the employment context due to the imbalance of power, as emphasised by the WP29. Employers must also conduct a DPIA under Article 35 GDPR when deploying technologies likely to pose high-risks to employees' rights, such as those involving AI and IoT-enabled technologies. DPIAs must include mitigating measures, and employees and their representatives must be involved in the assessment. National labour laws notified under Article 88(3) GDPR may impose further obligations.

Employees, as data subjects, are granted specific individual rights under Chapter III GDPR. These rights include the rights to be informed, to access their personal data and details of its processing, to correct inaccurate information, and to halt unlawful data processing (Articles 12-21). Additionally, employees have the right not to be subject to solely automated decision-making, and they are entitled to human intervention when such decisions affect them in the context of employment (Article 22). These rights impose clear obligations on employers: they must put in place effective structures and procedures to ensure that employees can exercise these rights in practice. Doing so is essential not only to enable scrutiny of the lawfulness of monitoring practices but also to maintain a fair balance of power in the workplace.

However, as suggested in section 4, AI and IoT-enabled technologies introduce a level of opacity, adaptiveness, and dependency from processors that may hinder both employers' compliance efforts and employees' understanding of the monitoring to which they are subject. Employers may not have full access to the necessary information about how these technologies operate, making it difficult for them to conduct thorough and meaningful DPIAs. As a result, it remains uncertain whether the GDPR alone provides sufficient protection for employees in workplaces shaped by these complex and opaque technologies. Hence, Chapter 7 will turn to the analysis of the AI Act, which introduces targeted obligations for both AI providers and AI deployers, including employers, potentially offering a more structured approach to safeguarding fundamental rights in the workplace.

CHAPTER 7

Applying the AI Act to the Employment Context: Requirements for a Legitimate Exercise of the Employer's Monitoring Power via AI and IoT-Enabled Technologies

1 INTRODUCTION

This chapter examines the Artificial Intelligence Act's (which I refer to as the 'AI Act') relevant provisions in relation to the employer's monitoring power. It aims to address the research sub-question 6: *What requirements does the AI Act impose on the legitimate exercise of the employer's monitoring power via AI and IoT-enabled technologies?*

In April 2021, the European Commission proposed a new and dedicated regulation on Artificial Intelligence.[636] The 2021 proposal was a first output of the EC's 'Coordinated Plan on Artificial Intelligence', initiated in 2018, which aimed to foster Europe's competitiveness.[637] In the proposal, the EU Commission took on the guidelines

636. European Commission, 'Communication on Fostering a European Approach to Artificial Intelligence' https://digital-strategy.ec.europa.eu/en/library/communication-fostering-european-approach-artificial-intelligence accessed 22 October 2025; European Commission, 'Proposal for a Regulation Laying Down Harmonised Rules on Artificial Intelligence' https://digital-strategy.ec.europa.eu/en/library/proposal-regulation-laying-down-harmonised-rules-artificial-intelligence accessed 22 October 2025.
637. European Commission, 'Coordinated Plan on Artificial Intelligence' https://digital-strategy.ec.europa.eu/en/policies/plan-ai accessed 22 October 2025.

issued by the Council,[638] Parliament,[639] the Commission's White Paper on AI[640] and Industry 5.0 EU strategy,[641] in ensuring robust safeguards for fundamental rights and Union values, legal clarity, governance and enforcement mechanisms and, overall, a unified market for lawful, safe, and trustworthy AI applications.[642]

Three years later, on 12 July 2024, following the approval by the Parliament, the Council and the Commission, the Regulation 2024/1689 of the European Parliament and of the Council of 13 June 2024 laying down harmonised rules on artificial intelligence was published on the Official Journal of the European Union.[643] This Regulation introduces new obligations and requirements for providers and deployers of AI systems, including those used in employment contexts, particularly for monitoring employees. As a result, employers using AI and IoT-enabled technologies must comply not only with the GDPR but also with the AI Act. The Regulation establishes a framework for prohibited AI practices (Article 5 AI Act), including bans on certain AI applications that conflict with fundamental rights, some of which pertain to employment. Moreover, AI systems used for employee monitoring and management are classified as 'high-risk' deployment (Article 6 AI Act, Annex III) and must meet specific requirements before being placed on the EU market.

This chapter opens by outlining the overarching objectives of the AI Act (section 2). It then defines and examines the roles and responsibilities of the main actors – namely, AI providers and AI deployers (employers) – in the context of employment-related AI systems applications (section 3). Section 4 introduces the AI Act's risk-based regulatory approach, followed by an analysis of the prohibited AI practices set out in Article 5 AI Act (section 5). Section 6 focuses on the specific obligations imposed on providers and deployers of high-risk AI systems. Section 7 focuses on the lack of individual rights for employees in the AI Act, and section 8 presents two tables summarising the overall prohibitions, obligations for employers and the corresponding protections afforded to employees under the AI Act. Finally, section 9 addresses the research sub-question 6 by examining the requirements for a legitimate exercise of an AI and IoT-enabled employer's monitoring power.

638. European Council, 'European Council Meeting (19 October 2017): Conclusion, EUCO 14/17' 8 https://www.consilium.europa.eu/media/21620/19-euco-final-conclusions-en.pdf accessed 22 October 2025.
639. European Parliament, 'Resolution of 20 October 2020 with Recommendations to the Commission on a Framework of Ethical Aspects of Artificial Intelligence, Robotics and Related Technologies, 2020/2012(INL)'.
640. European Commission, 'White Paper on Artificial Intelligence: A European Approach to Excellence and Trust, COM(2020) 65 Final' https://commission.europa.eu/publications/white-paper-artificial-intelligence-european-approach-excellence-and-trust_en accessed 22 October 2025.
641. Maija Breque, Lars De Nul and Athanasios Petridis, *Industry 5.0: Towards a Sustainable, Human-Centric and Resilient European Industry* (Publications Office of the European Union 2021).
642. European Commission, 'Coordinated Plan on Artificial Intelligence' (n 637).
643. 'Regulation (EU) 2024/1689 of the European Parliament and of the Council of 13 June 2024 Laying down Harmonised Rules on Artificial Intelligence and Amending Regulations (EC) No 300/2008, (EU) No 167/2013, (EU) No 168/2013, (EU) 2018/858, (EU) 2018/1139 and (EU) 2019/2144 and Directives 2014/90/EU, (EU) 2016/797 and (EU) 2020/1828 (Artificial Intelligence Act)' https://eur-lex.europa.eu/eli/reg/2024/1689/oj accessed 22 October 2025.

2 AI ACT: SCOPE, LEGAL BASES, AND AIM

Article 1(2)(a) of the AI Act states that it harmonises the rules for:

> The placing on the market, the putting into service and the use of AI systems in the Union.

In other words, the AI Act aims to regulate the entire life cycle of AI systems in the EU.[644] In its first Recital, the Regulation states that a consistent legal framework specifically for the development, market introduction, implementation, and use of AI systems is needed.[645] Article 2 AI Act limits the scope of the Regulation by excluding AI systems used for military, security, law enforcement, and scientific research purposes.[646] Beyond these exceptions, Article 1(1) emphasises that the AI Act, guided by the EU fundamental rights framework, aims to ensure the adoption of 'human-centric and trustworthy' AI systems, safeguarding health, safety, democracy, the rule of law, and fundamental rights from potential adverse impacts in the EU.

According to Recital 6 AI Act, human-centric AI is a technological approach designed to prioritise human dignity, well-being, and fundamental rights. Given the profound impact that AI can have on society, the Recital emphasises the need to align its development and deployment (its 'life cycle') with the core values of the European Union as outlined in Article 2 of the Treaty on European Union (TEU). These values include respect for human dignity, freedom, democracy, equality, and the rule of law. Additionally, the Recital draws on the fundamental rights enshrined in the EU Treaties and the Charter of Fundamental Rights of the European Union under Article 6 TEU.[647]

Recital 6 AI Act outlines human-centric AI as a technology that has the potential to enhance human well-being rather than replace or undermine human autonomy. It reflects the principle that technological advancement should serve societal interests, empowering individuals while safeguarding their rights and freedoms. This approach, according to the following Recital 7, involves embedding protections for privacy, non-discrimination, and transparency within AI systems, ensuring that decisions influenced by these systems remain fair, accountable, and subject to human oversight.

644. Article 3(1) AI Act defines 'AI system' as a machine-based system that is designed to operate with varying levels of autonomy and that may exhibit adaptiveness after deployment, and that, for explicit or implicit objectives, infers, from the input it receives, how to generate outputs such as predictions, content, recommendations, or decisions that can influence physical or virtual environments. *See also* section 2.1. of Chapter 4 on the definition of AI system.
645. Recital 1, AI Act.
646. According to Article 2, the AI Act does not apply to AI systems used for military, defence, or national security purposes, nor to those used by foreign authorities for law enforcement and judicial cooperation if fundamental rights are upheld. It also excludes AI systems for scientific research, those not yet on the market, and does not override existing EU laws on data protection, privacy, or confidentiality. Personal, non-professional AI use is likewise exempt. Patrick Van Eecke and Bartholomäus Regenhardt, 'Article 2 Scope' in Ceyhun Necati Pehlivan, Nikolaus Forgó and Valcke Peggy (eds), *The EU Artificial Intelligence (AI) Act: A Commentary* (Wolters Kluwer 2024).
647. Guillaume Couneson, 'Article 6 Classification Rules for High-Risk AI Systems' in Ceyhun Necati Pehlivan, Nikolaus Forgó and Valcke Peggy (eds), *The EU Artificial Intelligence (AI) Act: A Commentary* (Wolters Kluwer 2024).

The ultimate aim of the Regulation thus is to make the development, deployment and operation of AI system respectful of human values and EU fundamental rights, while contributing positively to societal progress.[648]

To promote human-centric AI, the AI Act establishes uniform obligations for AI systems providers and deployers with the aim of protecting public interests and individual rights throughout the Union. The Regulation is in fact grounded in Article 114 of the Treaty on the Functioning of the European Union (TFEU), which provides the legal basis for harmonising laws across Member States to ensure the functioning of the internal market. The AI Act's provisions that address personal data processing are rooted instead in Article 16 TFEU. Article 16 TFEU establishes the right to personal data protection within the EU, providing a legal basis that balances technological innovation with privacy rights, particularly in relation to AI-driven data processing and law enforcement applications.[649]

By imposing prohibitions and requirements from the design phase onwards (Articles 5-49 AI Act), the Regulation seeks to prevent harmful or opaque AI applications from entering the EU market. Its life-cycle regulatory approach ensures that AI systems remain compliant and human-centric even after deployment. As stated in Recital 12 AI Act, AI systems must be monitored during their operation as they do not operate as 'simpler traditional software systems or programming approaches (...) that are based on the rules defined solely by natural persons to automatically execute operations'.[650] AI systems have the capability to produce 'outputs, such as predictions, content, recommendations, or decisions, which can influence physical and virtual environments'.[651] Given its adaptive nature, the AI Act mandates continuous monitoring throughout an AI system's operational life to ensure ongoing compliance with legal standards. Accordingly, the Regulation incorporates post-market monitoring measures, including monitoring obligations, incident reporting, and corrective mechanisms to address emerging risks and unintended consequences (Articles 57-94 AI Act).[652]

In the following sections, I introduce the AI Act definitions of 'provider' and 'deployer' and contextualise them in employment contexts. I then examine how the AI Act regulates the entire life cycle of AI systems through a risk-based approach. This includes an analysis of its requirements for AI development by providers, obligations imposed on AI deployers, and the mechanisms established for post-market monitoring.

3 DEPLOYERS AND PROVIDERS

Before analysing the requirements for developing, deploying, and monitoring AI systems, I first introduce the key actors around whom the AI Act's principles and

648. Van Eecke and Regenhardt (n 646).
649. Recital 3, AI Act.
650. Recital 12, AI Act.
651. *Ibid.*
652. Cf. Article 1(2)(f), AI Act.

obligations revolve: AI system providers and deployers. The Regulation places obligations on providers, shaping the development of AI systems both before and during their implementation. The Regulation defines in Article 3(3) AI Act 'provider' as a:

> Natural or legal person, public authority, agency or other body that develops an AI system or a general-purpose AI model or that has an AI system or a general-purpose AI model developed and places it on the market or puts the AI system into service under its own name or trademark, whether for payment or free of charge.

In practice, any company that develops, sells, or operates AI systems falls under this definition. Providers of high-risk AI systems must register both themselves and their systems[653] in the European Commission's database, as required by Article 49 AI Act ('Registration') and Article 71 AI Act ('EU database for high-risk AI systems listed in Annex III').

Article 3(4) defines 'deployer' as a:

> Natural or legal person, public authority, agency or other body using an AI system under its authority (...).

In other words, deployers are the customers of AI providers. They purchase licences to use AI systems developed by providers. Employers who license AI systems for workplace use, therefore, qualify as deployers under the AI Act. As I discussed in Chapter 4, employers frequently deploy AI-enabled technologies for exercising their monitoring power.[654] Recital 13 further clarifies the role of deployers, emphasising that they professionally use AI systems, often affecting individuals beyond themselves. The extent of this impact, continues the Recital, depends on the nature of the AI system. In employment contexts, for instance, AI-enabled technologies might directly influence employees, shaping their working conditions and daily interactions.[655] In the latter case, the deployer uses an AI system in his or her business affecting other individuals.

I focus on providers and deployers because they are the central actors responsible for the development and use of AI systems in the employment context. While the AI Act defines other actors in Article 3 AI Act – such as importers, distributors, authorised representatives, and others – these actors play more peripheral roles in this investigation on how AI reshape the exercise of the employer's monitoring power.[656] Providers define the technical capabilities of AI systems, while deployers, particularly employers, make critical decisions about their application in ways that directly impact employees' rights and working conditions. Understanding their obligations is therefore essential to what requirements this Regulation imposes on the legitimate exercise of an AI and IoT-enabled employer's monitoring power.

In the following sections, I analyse the obligations imposed on both providers and deployers, with a particular focus on the deployment of AI systems in employment contexts.

---

653. *See* next section on AI systems risk classification.
654. *See* Chapter 4, sections 3 and 4.
655. Recital 13, AI Act. Cf. with Recital 57 on 'AI systems used in employment'.
656. Article 3(5) AI Act, Article 3(6) AI Act, Article 3(7) AI Act.

4 A RISK-BASED APPROACH TO AI SYSTEMS: PROHIBITIONS AND REQUIREMENTS FOR PROVIDERS

AI systems, according to the AI Act, hold significant potential for positive implications, offering benefits in various domains such as, among others, healthcare, education, food safety, and agriculture.[657] However, alongside these opportunities, AI systems also pose potential risks to public interests and fundamental rights. These risks can manifest in various ways – they may be physical, psychological, societal, or economic – and can threaten the fundamental rights and values protected by Union law.[658] To manage both the benefits and risks, the AI Act adopts a *risk-based approach*. This approach evaluates the risks posed by AI systems applications from the perspective of EU fundamental values and rights.[659] Through this framework, the Regulation seeks to maximise the benefits of AI systems while minimising potential harm to European citizens.

This risk-based approach classifies AI systems into four risk categories based on the intensity and scope of their potential impact on EU fundamental rights and values. This tiered framework ensures that regulatory obligations are proportionate to the level of risk posed by an AI system. The categories are as follows:

- *Unacceptable risk, Article 5 AI Act*: AI systems that pose a clear threat to fundamental rights are prohibited. Examples include social scoring by governments and real-time biometric surveillance in public spaces (with limited exceptions).[660]
- *High-risk, Article 6 AI Act*: AI systems that significantly affect people's fundamental rights or safety are subject to strict requirements before they can be placed on the market (Articles 8-49 AI Act). This includes AI used in critical sectors such as employment, education, law enforcement, and healthcare. These systems must undergo risk assessments, transparency obligations, human oversight, and data governance measures.

657. Recital 4, AI Act: 'AI is a fast evolving family of technologies that contributes to a wide array of economic, environmental and societal benefits across the entire spectrum of industries and social activities. By improving prediction, optimising operations and resource allocation, and personalising digital solutions available for individuals and organisations, the use of AI can provide key competitive advantages to undertakings and support socially and environmentally beneficial outcomes, for example in healthcare, agriculture, food safety, education and training, media, sports, culture, infrastructure management, energy, transport and logistics, public services, security, justice, resource and energy efficiency, environmental monitoring, the conservation and restoration of biodiversity and ecosystems and climate change mitigation and adaptation.'
658. Recitals 28 and 29 AI Act highlight how certain AI implementations can be misused, leading to manipulation, exploitation, or forms of social control that conflict with the EU's core values of human dignity, freedom, equality, democracy, and the rule of law, as well as essential rights like non-discrimination, data protection, and privacy. Due to their particularly harmful nature, Recital 28 deems that certain AI system implementations shall be prohibited as they pose unacceptable risks to the fundamental values and rights protected by Union law.
659. Cf. with Recital 27 AI Act.
660. Cf. with Recitals 28 and 29. *See* below section 5.

- *Limited risk, Article 50 AI Act*: AI systems that require transparency obligations, such as chatbots and deepfake generators.[661] Users, for instance, must be informed that they are interacting with AI or viewing AI-generated content.
- *Minimal or no risk*: AI systems that do not pose significant risks (e.g., spam filters, AI-powered video games) are not regulated by the AI Act, though voluntary codes of conduct may apply.[662]

In the following sections, I analyse the prohibitions and requirements set out in Articles 5 and 6 AI Act, as they are particularly relevant to the discussion on the legitimate exercise of an AI and IoT-enabled employer's monitoring power.

5 PROHIBITED ARTIFICIAL INTELLIGENCE PRACTICES (ARTICLE 5 AI ACT)

Article 5 AI Act prohibits certain applications of AI systems, classifying the risks posed by these uses to certain EU fundamental rights and values as unacceptable. A large part of the prohibitions concerns the use of AI in public places or in criminal justice. However, as I shall explore in the following subsections, there are four paragraphs of a more general scope that might find an application in employment contexts.

5.1 Article 5(1)(b): AI Systems Exploiting Social and Economic Circumstances

In the first place, I refer to Article 5(1)(b) AI Act. There, the Regulation bans AI systems exploiting vulnerabilities associated with a person's age, disability, or particular social or economic circumstances, with the intent or effect of significantly altering that individual's behaviour or the behaviour of a person in their group, resulting in or potentially causing substantial harm to that individual or others. In light of the analysis conducted in Chapters 4 and 5, it is worth stressing that certain AI systems allow employers to minutely modify the behaviours of employees – modulation of tone of voice[663] or AI cameras on drivers[664] – leveraging their economic and social dependence. Employees, in fact, have no choice as to how to perform their work except through the employer's means,[665] which may impose certain behaviours that, in some instances, could infringe upon fundamental rights.[666]

The reference to 'particular social or economic circumstances', I suggest, encompasses certain aspects of the economic and social dependence inherent in an employment contract. However, there is no express reference to employment contexts. The

661. Chatbots are AI-driven programs that simulate human conversation, while deepfakes are AI-generated media that manipulate images, videos, or audio to create realistic but deceptive content.
662. Cf. with Article 95 AI Act.
663. 'Cogito: Real-Time AI Coaching & Guidance for Contact Centers' (n 281).
664. Netradyne, 'Driveri' https://www.netradyne.com/ accessed 22 October 2025.
665. *See* sections 3 and 4, Chapter 4.
666. *See* section 2, Chapter 5.

wording of Article 5(1)(b) AI Act is vague and difficult to interpret. This is to some extent confirmed in Article 96(1)(b) AI Act, which mandates the Commission to develop guidelines for the specific interpretation and enforcement of Article 5 AI Act. In February 2025, the European Commission released its draft guidelines on the interpretation of Article 5 AI Act, clarifying the scope of the prohibition of AI systems that exploit specific socio-economic vulnerabilities. The guidelines do not explicitly extend this protection to employment-related AI systems.[667] The guidelines however make the case of 'other people in unique social contexts (...), for instance, migrants or refugees, who often lack stable legal status and socio-economic stability and may be particularly susceptible to exploitation by AI systems'.[668] Whether this reasoning could be extended to a broader category of 'vulnerable employees' remains an open question and warrants further investigation on whether the guidelines should be revised on this point. I will analyse further this issue in Chapter 8 (section 5) on the limitations of the AI Act.

5.2 Article 5(1)(c): Social Scoring

The second paragraph that might find an application in workplace contexts is Article 5(1)(c) AI Act. In this paragraph, the Regulation prohibits any 'use of AI systems for the evaluation or classification of natural persons or groups of persons over a certain period of time based on their social behaviour or known, inferred or predicted personal or personality characteristics'. This assessment is defined in Article 5(1)(c) AI Act as a 'social score' and might lead to 'detrimental or unfavourable treatment of certain natural persons or groups of persons' either in 'social contexts that are unrelated to the contexts in which the data was originally generated or collected' or generating 'unjustified or disproportionate [treatment] to their social behaviour or its gravity'. Beyond these broad formulations, the Regulation does not define the precise scope of this prohibition of 'social scoring' in the employment context. Yet, Recital 31 AI Act refers to them as AI systems that can be used by either 'public or private actors', thus including public or private employers, and potentially lead to discrimination and exclusion, unless they are compliant with other applicable Union law.

The Commission, in its draft guidelines, likewise, is non-specific as regards the application of Article 5(1)(c) AI Act in the employment context. The guidelines only specify that AI-enabled social scoring is permissible for specific, lawful purposes, such as fraud detection, provided they comply with Union and national laws. Moreover, among the lawful purposes, the guidelines include social scoring 'to perform specific employee evaluations'.[669] Hence, when these systems aggregate personal or behavioural data to create a broader and non-specific 'social score' that impacts natural

667. These guidelines are not binding. European Commission, 'Commission Guidelines on Prohibited Artificial Intelligence Practices Established by Regulation (EU) 2024/1689 (AI Act)' (2025) 37 https://digital-strategy.ec.europa.eu/en/library/commission-publishes-guidelines-prohibited-artificial-intelligence-ai-practices-defined-ai-act accessed 22 October 2025.
668. *Ibid.*, 38.
669. *Ibid.*, 61.

persons (such as employees) in ways that are unjustified or disproportionate, they could fall under Article 5(1)(c) AI Act.[670] For instance, AI and IoT-enabled technologies such as *Perceptyx* or *WorkTango* which aggregate personal or behavioural data beyond job-relevant metrics – for instance, by analysing employees' social media activity or private workplace chats[671] – could generate insights that influence employment decisions based on irrelevant factors. If AI systems aggregate personal data unrelated to job performance, up to including their private social life, they could fall under the prohibition. However, the guidelines do not provide employment-specific criteria to determine when social scoring at work is based on relevant, job-related criteria and not on irrelevant personal characteristics. In Chapter 8, I will discuss how the guidelines from the Commission could be more specific on this issue.

5.3 Article 5(1)(f): Infer Emotions at Work

Article 5(1)(f) AI Act, instead, makes an explicit reference to the workplace. It prohibits the 'use of AI systems to infer emotions of a natural person in the areas of workplace and education institutions, except where the use of the AI system is intended to be put in place or into the market for medical or safety reasons'. Recital 44 AI Act explicitly acknowledges the power imbalance in employment and education contexts, recognising that individuals in these settings are particularly vulnerable to intrusive AI systems.[672] The legislator makes this recognition clear by stating: 'Considering the imbalance of power in the context of work or education ...' and then directly linking this imbalance to the prohibition set out in Article 5(1)(f) AI Act. The power asymmetry in employment contexts jointly with AI systems inferring emotions, according to Recital 44 AI Act, 'Could lead to detrimental or unfavourable treatment of certain natural persons or whole groups thereof.'[673]

Article 3(39) AI Act defines 'emotion recognition system' as an AI system for the purpose of identifying or inferring emotions or intentions of natural persons on the basis of their biometric data. Recital 18 AI Act provides a nuanced clarification of what constitutes the inference of emotions or intentions based on biometric data. This Recital refers to emotions and intentions such as happiness, sadness, anger, surprise,

670. *Ibid.*, 61-62.
671. On private social life, *see* section 6.1, Chapter 3 on the right to private life.
672. *See also*: Kate Crawford, 'Time to Regulate AI That Interprets Human Emotions' (2021) 592 Nature 167 https://doi.org/10.1038/d41586-021-00868-5 accessed 22 October 2025.
673. Recital 44 AI Act: 'There are serious concerns about the scientific basis of AI systems aiming to identify or infer emotions, particularly as expression of emotions vary considerably across cultures and situations, and even within a single individual. Among the key shortcomings of such systems are the limited reliability, the lack of specificity and the limited generalisability. Therefore, AI systems identifying or inferring emotions or intentions of natural persons on the basis of their biometric data may lead to discriminatory outcomes and can be intrusive to the rights and freedoms of the concerned persons. Considering the imbalance of power in the context of work or education, combined with the intrusive nature of these systems, such systems could lead to detrimental or unfavourable treatment of certain natural persons or whole groups thereof (...).'

and others,[674] while recognising that physical states, such as pain or fatigue, may be detected where safety or medical attention constitutes a critical concern, such as monitoring professional drivers or pilots to prevent accidents.[675] This suggests that AI systems designed to assess fatigue, presumably through biometric markers such as blinking frequency, head nodding, or gaze tracking, fall outside the regulatory scope concerning emotion inference.[676] Hence, according to the EU Commission draft guidelines, 'Using AI recognition systems to infer a professional pilot's or driver's fatigue to alert them and suggest when to take brakes to avoid accidents is not "emotion recognition".'[677] For instance, *Driveri*, an AI-powered camera that uses real-time video analytics and machine learning to detect risky actions such as distraction or fatigue, is allowed under Article 5(1)(f) AI Act.

The guidelines also specify that this exception does not cover systems used for general well-being monitoring, such as tracking stress levels in the workplace. Therefore, the use of AI systems to detect conditions like burnout or depression among employees is prohibited, even under the guise of health or safety.[678] Another important point in Recital 18 is its exclusion from the prohibitions of systems that merely detect 'readily apparent expressions, gestures or movements' unless they are used specifically to infer emotions. This means that basic facial expressions (like a smile or frown), physical gestures (such as hand or head movements), and vocal characteristics (such as whispering or raising one's voice) do not fall within the scope of inferred emotions unless an AI system explicitly processes them to draw conclusions about an individual's emotional state. Hence, *Cogito*, which assesses employees' emotional states (e.g., anger, apathy) during phone calls with customers, is prohibited under Article 5(1)(f) AI Act.[679]

674. Recital 18 AI Act: 'The notion of "emotion recognition system" referred to in this Regulation should be defined as an AI system for the purpose of identifying or inferring emotions or intentions of natural persons on the basis of their biometric data. The notion refers to emotions or intentions such as happiness, sadness, anger, surprise, disgust, embarrassment, excitement, shame, contempt, satisfaction and amusement (...).'
675. Recital 18 AI Act: 'It does not include physical states, such as pain or fatigue, including, for example, systems used in detecting the state of fatigue of professional pilots or drivers for the purpose of preventing accidents. This does also not include the mere detection of readily apparent expressions, gestures or movements, unless they are used for identifying or inferring emotions. Those expressions can be basic facial expressions, such as a frown or a smile, or gestures such as the movement of hands, arms or head, or characteristics of a person's voice, such as a raised voice or whispering.'
676. *See*, for instance, AI-enabled cameras monitoring driving behaviours: Netradyne and Amazon, 'Driveri – The Power of Vision' https://www.amazon.com/stores/Netradyne/Netradyne/page/3304DF88-2CA0-4498-96B3-28F7F9F1A57C accessed 22 October 2025. *See also*: Wood (n 15) 6.
677. European Commission, 'Commission Guidelines on Prohibited Artificial Intelligence Practices Established by Regulation (EU) 2024/1689 (AI Act)' (n 667) 83.
678. *Ibid.*, 87.
679. 'Cogito: Real-Time AI Coaching & Guidance for Contact Centers' (n 281). The guidelines explicitly state that 'Using webcams and voice recognition systems by a call centre to track their employee's emotions, such as anger, is prohibited', unless the data is used for training and has no impact on the work relationship (performance assessment, promotion). European Commission, 'Commission Guidelines on Prohibited Artificial Intelligence Practices Established by Regulation (EU) 2024/1689 (AI Act)' (n 667) 85.

Ultimately, according to the EU Commission, the exception for safety reasons should be narrowly applied, focusing solely on the protection of life and health, not on safeguarding other interests like property.[680] Any use of emotion recognition systems in the workplace for medical or safety reasons must be strictly necessary and proportionate, and any detection of expressions, gestures or movements is allowed provided they are not processed to infer forbidden emotional states. This includes ensuring that the use is limited in scope, duration, and application. The EU Commission's guidelines stress the need for additional safeguards, such as obtaining an expert opinion before implementing allowed systems: the necessary recourse to the AI system must be assessed objectively, rather than based solely on the employer's needs. The evaluation should also consider whether less intrusive alternatives could achieve the same objective.[681] I will further analyse the scope of Article 5(1)(f) and its exceptions in Chapter 8 on the limitations of the AI Act.

5.4 Article 5(1)(g): Categorising Natural Persons Through Biometric Data to Deduce or Infer Beliefs and Trade Union Membership

Article 5(1)(g) AI Act bans the use of biometric categorisation AI systems to deduce and categorise sensitive characteristics of employees, such as race, political opinions, religious beliefs, sexual orientation, or trade union membership. This prohibition directly impacts the use of AI for biometric categorisation based on attributes or characteristics that could lead to discriminatory practices in hiring, employee performance assessment, or other job-related aspects.

For example, AI systems that attempt to infer an employee's race or political views through biometric data (like facial recognition or voice analysis) would be prohibited. These systems, according to the Commission's guidelines on Article 5 AI Act, could contribute to discrimination by making decisions about promotions, terminations, or hiring based on characteristics unrelated to job performance, potentially violating fundamental rights of employees. Similarly, the use of *Perceptyx* by employers to predict unionisation patterns of employees falls also under this prohibition.[682] The guidelines specify that if the biometric data is collected and processed in compliance with the GDPR and pursuing legitimate purposes, such as ensuring unbiased algorithm training, the AI system could be legitimately used to prevent discrimination by ensuring that hiring algorithms do not unfairly disadvantage certain demographic groups.[683]

680. 'The notion of safety reasons within this exception should be understood to apply only in relation to the protection of life and health and not to protect other interests, for example property against theft or fraud.' *See*: European Commission, 'Commission Guidelines on Prohibited Artificial Intelligence Practices Established by Regulation (EU) 2024/1689 (AI Act)' (n 667) 87.
681. *Ibid.*
682. 'Perceptyx' (n 417).
683. European Commission, 'Commission Guidelines on Prohibited Artificial Intelligence Practices Established by Regulation (EU) 2024/1689 (AI Act)' (n 667) 93-94.

6 'HIGH-RISK' AI SYSTEMS AND EMPLOYMENT CONTEXTS (ARTICLES 6, 7 AI ACT)

In addition to the prohibitions laid down in Article 5, the AI Act establishes a distinct regulatory regime for high-risk AI systems under Chapter III (Articles 6-49 AI Act). These AI systems are not banned per se, but they are considered to pose significant risks to health, safety, or EU fundamental rights, particularly when used in sensitive domains such as law enforcement, education, or employment.[684]

This regulatory regime requires that high-risk AI systems meet requirements regarding transparency, accountability, and human oversight before being put into the EU single market. These systems must be designed by providers and implemented by deployers in ways that ensure they prevent and mitigate the potential harms associated with high-risk AI applications, ensuring that their use is compliant with EU fundamental rights and values. This is clarified by Recital 48 AI Act, which states that the AI Act classifies AI system as high-risk when 'the extent of the adverse impact caused by the AI system on the fundamental rights protected by the Charter is of particular relevance', with particular attention on fundamental right such as 'the right to human dignity, respect for private and family life, protection of personal data, freedom of expression and information, freedom of assembly and of association, the right to non-discrimination, the right to education, consumer protection, workers' rights, the rights of persons with disabilities, gender equality (...)'.[685]

Notably, Article 6(2) AI Act, by referring to Annex III, includes certain AI systems used in employment contexts as high-risk AI systems. The fourth paragraph of Annex III reads as follows:

> Employment, workers management and access to self-employment:
>
> (a) AI systems intended to be used for recruitment or selection of natural persons, in particular to place targeted job advertisements, to analyse and filter job applications, and to evaluate candidates;
>
> (b) AI systems intended to be used to make decisions affecting terms of the work-related relationships, the promotion and termination of work-related contractual relationships, to allocate tasks based on individual behaviour or personal traits or characteristics or to monitor and evaluate performance and behaviour of persons in such relationships.

Therefore, any AI system that can have a legal effect on employees (e.g., recruitment/promotion, performance assessment, monitoring behaviours) is to be considered as a high-risk AI system. These systems, according to Recital 57 AI Act,

684. Couneson (n 647).

685. Recital 48 AI Act: 'The extent of the adverse impact caused by the AI system on the fundamental rights protected by the Charter is of particular relevance when classifying an AI system as high risk. Those rights include the right to human dignity, respect for private and family life, protection of personal data, freedom of expression and information, freedom of assembly and of association, the right to non-discrimination, the right to education, consumer protection, workers' rights, the rights of persons with disabilities, gender equality, intellectual property rights, the right to an effective remedy and to a fair trial, the right of defence and the presumption of innocence, and the right to good administration.' *See also* Recital 57 AI Act.

'may have an appreciable impact on future career prospects, livelihoods of those persons and workers' rights'. They may perpetuate discriminatory practices, affecting various groups based on gender, age, disability, race, ethnicity, or sexual orientation. Additionally, AI monitoring systems may infringe upon individuals' fundamental rights to data protection and privacy.[686]

The AI systems I analysed in Chapters 4 and 5, if not falling within the prohibitions of Article 5, will be classifiable as high-risk systems under Article 6(2) and Annex III. While Article 6(3) sets out specific exceptions for AI systems that, despite falling within Annex III, do not actually pose significant risks and are therefore exempt from the requirements in Articles 8-15 AI Act, these exceptions do not apply in employment contexts when the AI system is implemented to exercise the employer's monitoring power. According to Article 6(3) AI Act, 'an AI system shall always be considered high-risk if the AI system performs profiling of natural persons'. Monitoring by employers invariably entails profiling: it involves the processing of employees' personal data for purposes such as performance evaluation, behaviour monitoring, OSH, or security (*see* Chapter 3). Profiling is not incidental but structural to how employers exercise their monitoring power. As such, AI systems used in employment for monitoring purposes fall within the high-risk category, and providers developing these tools cannot invoke the exemptions under Article 6(3) to avoid compliance.[687] Therefore, AI and IoT-enabled technologies such as *Controlio, Interguard*, and *FlexiSpy*, which monitor employees' digital activities and process biometric or behavioural data for authentication or fraud detection, are classified as high-risk under Annex III. Similarly, tools such as *Genome, RescueTime, HubStaff*, and *Occupeye*, used for performance evaluation and productivity tracking, fall under the high-risk category when they inform significant employment decisions like hiring, promotion, or dismissal. Lastly, AI-enabled wellness tools like *Fitbit Care*, which monitor physical

686. Recital 57 AI Act: 'AI systems used in employment, workers management and access to self-employment, in particular for the recruitment and selection of persons, for making decisions affecting terms of the work-related relationship, promotion and termination of work-related contractual relationships, for allocating tasks on the basis of individual behaviour, personal traits or characteristics and for monitoring or evaluation of persons in work-related contractual relationships, should also be classified as high-risk, since those systems may have an appreciable impact on future career prospects, livelihoods of those persons and workers' rights. (...) Throughout the recruitment process and in the evaluation, promotion, or retention of persons in work-related contractual relationships, such systems may perpetuate historical patterns of discrimination, for example against women, certain age groups, persons with disabilities, or persons of certain racial or ethnic origins or sexual orientation. AI systems used to monitor the performance and behaviour of such persons may also undermine their fundamental rights to data protection and privacy.'

687. According to Article 3(52), 'profiling' means any form of automated processing of personal data as defined in point (4) of Article 4 of Regulation (EU) 2016/679. Article 4(4) GDPR reads as follows: '"profiling" means any form of automated processing of personal data consisting of the use of personal data to evaluate certain personal aspects relating to a natural person, in particular to analyse or predict aspects concerning that natural person's performance at work, economic situation, health, personal preferences, interests, reliability, behaviour, location or movements'.

activity and health indicators, may also be high-risk if they influence employees' working conditions or access to benefits.[688]

Finally, the AI Act acknowledges in Article 7 ('Amendments to Annex III') that defining all AI systems uses in law risks rapid obsolescence due to the fast-evolving technology market. To address this, Articles 7(1) and 97 AI Act grant the EU Commission authority to amend Annex III by 'adding or modifying use-cases of high-risk AI systems'. However, this mandate is limited. Under Article 7(2), any amendment to Annex III must consider specific criteria. This article requires that updating the list of high-risk AI systems in Annex III shall take into account the purpose of the systems and their diffusion in the EU market; the nature and amount of the data processed; the extent of the already caused harms to EU's fundamental rights; and also 'the extent to which there is an imbalance of power, or the persons who are potentially harmed or suffer an adverse impact are in a vulnerable position in relation to the deployer of an AI system',[689] such as is the case for the employment relationship.

High-risk systems, as defined by Article 6 and Annex III AI Act, are subject to rigorous requirements, and their providers must comply with the requirements set in Articles 8-15 AI Act ('Requirements for High-Risk AI systems'). Articles 16-27, 72, 86 AI Act introduce further obligations for providers, deployers and other parties involved. In the following section 6.1, I analyse the obligations for providers of high-risk AI systems. In section 6.2, I will focus on the obligations for deployers.

6.1 Obligations for Providers of High-Risk AI Systems

To ensure the safe and trustworthy deployment of high-risk AI systems, Articles 8-20 AI Act set out a comprehensive compliance framework for providers, structured around core categories: risk management, data governance, technical robustness, transparency and information sharing, and human oversight. These obligations must be implemented in accordance with the system's intended purpose and the current state of the art, embedding both procedural and substantive safeguards throughout the system's life cycle.[690] Providers are expected to comply with these requirements through the latest and most widely accepted standards, methodologies, and best practices in AI technology.[691] Additionally, Article 8 requires providers to integrate a risk management system (as detailed further in Articles 9 and 17 AI Act) into the compliance process.

688. Cf. with the classification developed in Chapter 4, section 3.
689. Article 7(2)(h) AI Act.
690. Moreover, Article 16 provides that providers of high-risk AI systems must ensure compliance with high-risk requirements (Articles 8-15), display their contact information on the system or its packaging, maintain a quality management system per Article 17, retain documentation as per Article 18, and store automatically generated logs under their control as per Article 19. Additionally, they must ensure that the AI system undergoes the relevant conformity assessment procedure before market placement or service deployment and draw up an EU declaration of conformity in accordance with Article 47.
691. Article 8(1) AI Act.

6.1.1 *Risk Management and Training Duties for High-Risk AI Systems*

Article 9 AI Act provides that any AI provider shall thus establish a 'Risk management system'.[692] According to this requirement, the risk management system shall operate throughout the AI system's life cycle, involving continuous review and updating. Among its aims are identifying and analysing potential risks to health, safety, and fundamental rights, estimating risks during use and misuse, and evaluating emerging risks, especially in the post-market monitoring phase (i.e., when deployers deploy it). Risk management measures shall be tailored to minimise risks, through strategies such as designing the AI system to eliminate or reduce risks, implementing mitigation measures, providing essential information and training, and conducting thorough testing. Under Article 60(1) and (2) AI Act, it is possible to conduct pre-emptive testing of high-risk AI systems in real-world conditions.[693] However, Article 60(4) AI Act also stipulates that humans involved in the testing must provide informed consent, which is generally considered invalid in employment contexts.[694] Article 17 AI Act ('Quality Management System') further obliges providers to implement a quality management system covering areas such as risk management, data governance, post-market monitoring, and internal accountability, tailored to the size and nature of the organisation.

Risk management, in fact, must be supported by adequate AI systems' training to prevent harms to the fundamental rights of European citizens/employees. That is why Article 10 AI Act ('Data and data governance') provides for training, validation, and testing data sets tailored to the system's intended purpose. Therefore, relevant design choices, data collection processes, and the original purpose of data collection, especially regarding personal data, shall be taken into account by the provider. Additionally, further standards provide for data preparation operations like annotation,[695] cleaning,[696] and aggregation, to develop representative and contextualised assumptions about the data used to train the AI system (e.g., I can refer to the case made in this research: that in employment contexts, asymmetries of power, social and economic

692. Not to be confused with the 'Quality management system' provided for by Article 17. The latter mandates providers of high-risk AI systems to establish a documented quality management system ensuring compliance with the Regulation. This system should include strategies for regulatory compliance, design, development, testing, validation procedures, technical specifications, data management, risk management, post-market monitoring, incident reporting, communication protocols, record-keeping, resource management, and accountability frameworks. Implementation must be proportionate to the provider's organisation size while maintaining the necessary level of protection.
693. Article 60(2) AI Act: 'Providers or prospective providers may conduct testing of high-risk AI systems referred to in Annex III in real world conditions at any time before the placing on the market or the putting into service of the AI system on their own or in partnership with one or more deployers or prospective deployers.'
694. *See* section 3.3.1, Chapter 6.
695. Data annotation consists in adding meaningful and informative tags to a dataset, making it easier for machine learning algorithms to understand and process the data. In other words, it allows to better contextualise certain information which would otherwise not be meaningful for a machine learning algorithm.
696. Similarly to data annotation, data cleaning means fixing or rectifying incorrect, corrupted, incorrectly formatted, duplicate, or incomplete data within a dataset.

dependency of employees shall be considered and thus shape the design of the tool). Article 10(4) AI Act, in this regard, provides that data sets (i.e., the data to train AI systems) should reflect the specific characteristics of the geographical, contextual, behavioural, or functional setting in which the high-risk AI system will be deployed, as required by its intended purpose. Article 10 requirements are echoed in Article 15 AI Act principles ('Accuracy, robustness and cybersecurity') which provide for accuracy, robustness, and cybersecurity in high-risk AI systems. These systems should maintain an appropriate level of accuracy and robustness throughout their life cycle, with declared accuracy metrics in accompanying instructions. Technical and organisational measures shall further enhance resilience against errors or faults. Jointly with Article 10 AI Act, I find it useful to mention that Article 20 AI Act ('Corrective Actions and Duty of Information') introduces a duty of corrective action: if a provider becomes aware of non-compliance or risk, it must immediately take remedial steps, notify deployers and distributors, and inform competent authorities. In employment settings, these obligations provide a basis to counteract the risks of opacity, discrimination, or error inherent in algorithmic decision-making that can significantly impact individuals' livelihoods.

All the above-mentioned requirements shall be reported in 'technical documentation'. Article 11 mandates the creation and maintenance of technical documentation for high-risk AI systems before they are placed on the market or put into service. This documentation must demonstrate compliance with the Regulation to provide necessary information for national competent Authorities. This documentation shall prove that the high-risk AI systems have logging capabilities to automatically record events throughout their lifetime.[697] These logs should facilitate identifying risks,[698] monitoring the system operation and allow for post-market monitoring. Articles 18 ('Documentation Keeping') and 19 ('Automatically Generated Logs') AI Act further impose long-term documentation and logging storage duties to support regulatory oversight, requiring providers to retain technical documentation and automatically generated logs for up to ten years and at least six months, respectively.

6.1.2 Transparency and Human Oversight

Articles 13 and 14 AI Act similarly provide guidance to providers on how to design these systems and in relation to who will be using them (i.e., deployers). Article 13 AI Act ('Transparency and provision of information to deployers') emphasises transparency and the provision of information to deployers. It requires these systems to be designed transparently so that deployers can interpret their output effectively. Instructions for use must be provided in a clear and accessible format, containing information

697. Article 12(3) AI Act provides the elements to be recorded in the log: (a) recording of the period of each use of the system (start date and time and end date and time of each use); (b) the reference database against which input data has been checked by the system; (c) the input data for which the search has led to a match; (d) the identification of the natural persons involved in the verification of the results, as referred to in Article 14(5).
698. Record-keeping of AI logs, as required by Article 12, allows for the identification of further risks according to Article 79 ('Procedure for dealing with AI systems presenting a risk at national level').

such as the provider's identity and contact details, system characteristics, intended purpose, accuracy metrics, potential risks, and human oversight measures. Additionally, the instructions should include details on system changes, computational requirements, expected lifetime, maintenance needs, and mechanisms for collecting and interpreting system logs.[699]

Article 14 AI Act ('Human oversight') states that providers must design AI systems to put natural persons at the centre of their operation, so as to oversee their operation effectively and prevent risks to health, safety, or fundamental rights. Article 14(3)(b) AI Act specifies that the deployer must be able to implement/use these oversight measures. Deployers, under Article 14(4)(a) AI Act, must be able to understand the system's capabilities and limitations, monitor its operation, interpret its output, and intervene or override decisions when necessary. Thus, an AI camera system on drivers should have an interface that allows the deployer to access the evaluations for each employee. That interface must provide sufficient elements to allow the employer to learn how the assessment was made and, if necessary, to change it. In this regard, Article 14(4)(d) AI Act provides that the human oversight principle shall allow the deployer to decide, in any particular situation, to disregard, override or reverse the output of the high-risk AI system. This can happen, according to Article 14(4)(e) AI Act, through a 'stop button' or a similar procedure that allows the system to come to a halt in a safe state.[700]

6.1.3 Post-market Monitoring

Finally, providers under Article 72 AI Act must create and cooperate to the 'Post-market monitoring by providers and post-market monitoring plan for high-risk AI systems'. According to Article 72(1), providers shall establish and document a post-market monitoring system in a manner that is proportionate to the nature of AI technologies and the risks of the high-risk AI system. Article 3(25) AI Act further defines 'post-market monitoring system' as any activity carried out by providers to collect and review experience gained from the use of AI systems they place on the market for the purpose of identifying any necessary corrective or preventive action. The provider must actively gather, document, and analyse relevant data throughout the AI system's life cycle to ensure ongoing compliance with regulatory requirements. This information is obtained from several sources: the AI system's integrated risk management system (Article 9(2)(c) AI Act), log record-keeping (Article 12(2) AI Act), and reports from deployers using the AI systems (Article 26(5) AI Act).

---

699. Transparency of AI developers towards employers enforces the several warnings coming from the legal scholarship on empowering employers in understanding the functioning of their AI tools: Molè, 'The Internet of Things and Artificial Intelligence as Workplace Supervisors' (n 401); Giovanni Gaudio, 'Algorithmic Bosses Can't Lie! How to Foster Transparency and Limit Abuses of the New Algorithmic Managers' (2022) 42 Comparative Labor Law & Policy Journal 707.

700. This procedural and technical requirements shall allow the human-worker centric operation of AIs as outlined by the Industry 5.0 EU Commission strategy: Breque, De Nul and Petridis (n 641) 15.

This post-market monitoring system, according to Recital 155 AI Act, is key to timely address the possible risks emerging from AI systems which continue to 'learn' after being placed on the market or put into service. Providers, therefore, should be able to report to the relevant authorities (market surveillance authorities,[701] DPAs, Labour Inspectorates) any serious harm resulting from the deployment in workplaces of their AI systems, which can imply any 'infringement of obligations under Union law intended to protect fundamental rights',[702] among which, obviously, labour rights. Post-market monitoring can even lead to the consequences outlined in Article 79(5) AI Act, i.e., the withdrawal of the AI system from the market, or recalling it within a period prescribed by the relevant Authority under Article 79(2) AI Act.

Taken together, these provisions serve a preventive and corrective function. They seek to ensure that high-risk AI systems do not merely function accurately but do so legally, especially when individuals' rights, freedoms, and economic security are at stake. They not only protect employees as rights holders but also protect employers as deployers, by clarifying responsibilities and setting a regulatory framework that reduces legal uncertainty. Ultimately, these compliance obligations reflect the regulatory approach of the AI Act I outlined in the introductory section 2: that AI innovation must be human-centred and that technological development must align with the Union's values also during the operation of the system, not only during the design phase.

Providers are not the only entities subject to obligations. Deployers also have specific obligations when using these AI systems. I will discuss them in the next section.

6.2 Obligations for Deployers of High-Risk AI Systems

6.2.1 Responsible Use and Oversight from Deployers

Article 26 AI Act ('Obligations of Deployers of High-Risk AI Systems') provides that deployers must deploy AI systems according to the instructions for use, taking appropriate technical and organisational measures outlined by the provider according to Articles 8-15 AI Act. In other words, once deployers have received information and instructions according to Articles 13 and 14 AI Act, they will be accountable to the extent they exert control over the system and shall ensure that input data is relevant and sufficiently representative in view of the intended purpose of the high-risk AI system (Article 26(4) AI Act).[703] Deployers must ensure, in particular, that their staff overseeing the AI system have the necessary competence, training, authority, and

701. Recital 156 AI Act specifies that 'In order to ensure an appropriate and effective enforcement of the requirements and obligations set out by this Regulation, which is Union harmonisation legislation, the system of market surveillance and compliance of products established by Regulation (EU) 2019/1020.'
702. Article 3(49)(c) AI Act.
703. Daniel Gallagher, 'Article 26 Obligations of Deployers of High-Risk AI Systems' in Ceyhun Necati Pehlivan, Nikolaus Forgó and Valcke Peggy (eds), *The EU Artificial Intelligence (AI) Act: A Commentary* (Wolters Kluwer 2024).

support to do so (Article 26(2) AI Act). If deployers suspect that following the instructions could pose a risk under Article 79(1) AI Act, they must promptly inform the provider pursuant to Article 72 AI Act and the relevant market surveillance authority and suspend the use of that AI system (Article 26(5) AI Act).[704] Deployers are in fact a source of information for the post-marketing monitoring duties of providers.[705] Article 79(1) explicitly refers to Article 3, point 19 of EU Reg. 2019/1020[706] which states that:

> 'Product presenting a risk' means a product having the potential to affect adversely health and safety of persons in general, health and safety in the workplace, (...) protected by the applicable Union harmonisation legislation, to a degree which goes beyond that considered reasonable and acceptable in relation to its intended purpose or under the normal or reasonably foreseeable conditions of use of the product concerned, including the duration of use and, where applicable, its putting into service, installation and maintenance requirements.

Article 26(5) AI Act and its referral to Article 72 AI Act ultimately establishes a proactive role for deployers in monitoring and ensuring the safe and compliant use of high-risk AI, creating an ongoing exchange of information with providers to manage potential risks.[707]

6.2.2 Information and Consultation Duties for Employers

Article 26(7) AI Act introduces a key obligation for a central category of actors in this research: employers. This article provides that:

> Before putting into service or using a high-risk AI system at the workplace, deployers who are employers shall inform workers' representatives and the affected workers that they will be subject to the use of the high-risk AI system. This information shall be provided, where applicable, in accordance with the rules and procedures laid down in Union and national law and practice on information of workers and their representatives.

The AI Act expressly refers to the fact that employees must be consulted and informed in line with national laws and practices. Once employers acquire AI and

704. According to Article 79(1) AI Act: 'AI systems presenting a risk shall be understood as a product presenting a risk defined in Article 3, point 19 of Regulation (EU) 2019/1020 insofar as risks to the health or safety or to fundamental rights of persons are concerned.'
705. According to Article 72(2) AI Act: 'The post-market monitoring system shall actively and systematically collect, document and analyse relevant data which may be provided by deployers or which may be collected through other sources on the performance of high-risk AI systems throughout their lifetime, and which allow the provider to evaluate the continuous compliance of AI systems with the requirements set out in Chapter III, Section 2.'
706. Regulation (EU) 2019/1020 of the European Parliament and of the Council of 20 June 2019 on market surveillance and compliance of products and amending Directive 2004/42/EC and Regulations (EC) No 765/2008 and (EU) No 305/2011.
707. Ayça Atabey, Lachlan Urquhart and Burkhard Schafer, 'Article 72 Post-Market Monitoring by Providers and Post-Market Monitoring Plan for High-Risk AI Systems' in Ceyhun Necati Pehlivan, Nikolaus Forgó and Valcke Peggy (eds), *The EU Artificial Intelligence (AI) Act: A Commentary* (Wolters Kluwer 2024).

IoT-enabled technologies to exercise their monitoring powers, they must comply with national rules on information and consultation before implementing the system. Recital 92 AI Act further underscores the connection to the employee information and consultation framework established under Directive 2002/14/EC. There, the Recital states that 'This Regulation is without prejudice to obligations for employers to inform or to inform and consult workers or their representatives under Union or national law and practice, including Directive 2002/14/EC of the European Parliament and of the Council, on decisions to put into service or use AI systems.'[708]

The information to be provided must include the purpose of the AI system, its functioning, the data it processes, and any potential consequences for workers. This obligation enhances procedural safeguards and ensures that AI systems are not introduced unilaterally, but within a framework that respects collective labour rights and enables contestation or negotiation. Enforcement of this provision may fall within the remit of national labour inspectorates or data protection authorities, depending on the system's scope and risks.[709]

6.2.3 *Connections with the DPIA and (Limited) Obligation to Conduct an FRIA*

Article 26(9) AI Act provides for another relevant obligation for deployers. They must use the information provided under Article 13 AI Act ('Transparency and provision of information to deployers') to comply with their obligation to carry out a DPIA under Article 35 GDPR. Article 26(9) AI Act reflects the European legislator's intent to harmonise the AI regulatory framework with the GDPR's personal data protections. Article 27 AI Act further reinforces this alignment by introducing a new instrument resembling the DPIA, specifically tailored for high-risk AI systems.[710] According to Article 27(1) AI Act, deployers such as employers must conduct a 'Fundamental Rights Impact Assessment' (FRIA). This requirement, however, applies only to deployers that are bodies governed by public law or are private entities providing public services. Hence, the scope of the FRIA is limited to public or private employers involved in public services according to national laws. Article 27(1) AI Act details the elements that must be included in the FRIA, ensuring a comprehensive assessment of the potential impact on fundamental rights before the deployment of high-risk AI systems.[711] The

708. Gallagher (n 703).
709. *Ibid.*
710. Article 2(7) AI Act states that 'Union law on the protection of personal data, privacy and the confidentiality of communications applies to personal data processed in connection with the rights and obligations laid down in this Regulation. This Regulation shall not affect Regulation (EU) 2016/679.'
711. Article 27(1) AI Act lists six requirements for an FRIA: (1) a description of the deployer's processes in which the high-risk AI system will be used in line with its intended purpose; (2) a description of the period of time within which, and the frequency with which, each high-risk AI system is intended to be used; (3) the categories of natural persons and groups likely to be affected by its use in the specific context; (4) the specific risks of harm likely to have an impact on the categories of natural persons or groups of persons identified pursuant to point (c) of this paragraph, taking into account the information given by the provider pursuant to Article 13; (5)

Regulation demands deployers to conduct an FRIA because they possess specific knowledge of usage contexts and potential risks, often unforeseen during development (Recital 57 AI Act). The employer when implementing an AI system for employee monitoring specifies on which work process it will be implemented (e.g., logistics: monitoring of drivers; productivity: monitoring of desk attendance times); for how long; which employees it will involve (e.g., delivery workers who deliver goods on vans); what fundamental rights are at risk (e.g., privacy); and what measures will be taken to prevent these rights from being violated (e.g., minimisation of collected data, purpose limitation preventing the use of collected data for further purposes). In short, the process of carrying out an FRIA aims to identify and mitigate risks to individuals or groups, considering factors such as affected categories and potential harms.[712] Deployers who are employers must collaborate with relevant stakeholders – including providers, affected employees and their representatives – pursuant to Article 26(7) AI Act. They must also notify market surveillance authorities after completing the assessments, as required by Articles 26(4) and 27(3) of the AI Act.[713]

7 EMPLOYEES' INDIVIDUAL RIGHTS UNDER THE AI ACT

The AI Act provides only limited rights to individuals, such as employees, who are affected by AI systems. Unlike the GDPR, which sets out a comprehensive framework of data subject's rights (*see* Chapter 6, section 3.5), the AI Act's focus is predominantly on obligations for AI providers and AI deployers. This marks an important difference in approach and reflects the AI Act's regulatory focus on governing the market for AI systems and the relationship between their developers/vendors and deployers, rather than establishing a rights-based framework for affected individuals.[714]

The only individual right for employees in the AI Act is found in Article 86 ('Right to explanation of individual decision-making'), which introduces a right to an explanation where decisions are based on the output of a high-risk AI system.[715] Affected

a description of the implementation of human oversight measures, according to the instructions for use; (6) the measures to be taken in the case of the materialisation of those risks, including the arrangements for internal governance and complaint mechanisms.

712. Tünde Fülöp and Philipp Poindl, 'Article 27 Fundamental Rights Impact Assessment for High-Risk AI Systems' in Ceyhun Necati Pehlivan, Nikolaus Forgó and Valcke Peggy (eds), *The EU Artificial Intelligence (AI) Act: A Commentary* (Wolters Kluwer 2024).
713. For a first discussion of the FRIA in the context of AI use and development: Alessandro Mantelero, *Beyond Data Human Rights, Ethical and Social Impact Assessment in AI* (TMC Asser Press 2022).
714. On the overall aims of the AI Act, *see* section 2 in this chapter. Cf. also with: Patrick Van Eecke and Bartholomäus Regenhardt, 'Article 1 Subject Matter' in Ceyhun Necati Pehlivan, Nikolaus Forgó and Valcke Peggy (eds), *The EU Artificial Intelligence (AI) Act: A Commentary* (Wolters Kluwer 2024); Van Eecke and Regenhardt (n 646).
715. Article 86(1) AI Act: 'Any affected person subject to a decision which is taken by the deployer on the basis of the output from a high-risk AI system listed in Annex III, with the exception of systems listed under point 2 thereof, and which produces legal effects or similarly significantly affects that person in a way that they consider to have an adverse impact on their health, safety or fundamental rights shall have the right to obtain from the deployer clear and meaningful explanations of the role of the AI system in the decision-making procedure and the main elements of the decision taken.' According to Article 85 AI Act ('Right to Lodge a Complaint

individuals are entitled to request a meaningful explanation of how the system contributed to the outcome and what key factors shaped the decision. In employment contexts, this right is particularly relevant where AI systems inform decisions about hiring, promotions, performance evaluations, or dismissals.[716]

However, this right is narrowly framed and does not allow employees to challenge decisions made by AI systems. Moreover, neither Article 86 nor Recital 171 AI Act specifies how deployers, such as employers, should obtain or provide such explanations, particularly when using third-party AI systems.[717] This raises concerns about whether the provision offers substantive protection or merely a formalistic guarantee, as Kaminski and Malgieri have noted.[718] Employers are thus not required to revise the decision, and the AI Act provides no guidance on how they should technically comply with this obligation. Employers may in fact lack the technical capacity or contractual leverage to deliver meaningful insights into the AI system's logic, especially when compared to the AI provider.[719]

Beyond Article 86, the AI Act does not establish other specific rights for individuals. For example, there is no right to object to the AI decision, nor is there a right to human intervention. In effect, the Act does not grant employees any new rights beyond Article 86 AI Act.

Where AI systems process employees' personal data, individuals must thus continue to rely on the GDPR's data subjects' rights framework (Articles 12-22 GDPR), which includes rights of access, rectification, objection, and the right not to be subject to automated decision-making, including profiling. While these rights may help fill some of the gaps left by the AI Act, it remains an open question whether they are designed to effectively address the specific risks posed by AI systems. These rights may be difficult for employees to exercise in practice, particularly in opaque or highly technical environments.[720]

In this sense, the AI Act should be understood as a complementary, but not sufficient, regime to the GDPR from the perspective of employees' individual rights. While the Act imposes important obligations on AI providers and AI deployers, it contributes

with a Market Surveillance Authority'), natural persons, such as employees, can also 'submit complaints to the relevant market surveillance authority'.

716. Maja Brkan and Hana Palčič Vilfan, 'Article 86 Right to Explanation of Individual Decision-Making' in Ceyhun Necati Pehlivan, Nikolaus Forgó and Valcke Peggy (eds), *The EU Artificial Intelligence (AI) Act: A Commentary* (Wolters Kluwer 2024).

717. Recital 171 AI Act: 'Affected persons should have the right to obtain an explanation where a deployer's decision is based mainly upon the output from certain high-risk AI systems that fall within the scope of this Regulation and where that decision produces legal effects or similarly significantly affects those persons in a way that they consider to have an adverse impact on their health, safety or fundamental rights. That explanation should be clear and meaningful and should provide a basis on which the affected persons are able to exercise their rights. The right to obtain an explanation should not apply to the use of AI systems for which exceptions or restrictions follow from Union or national law and should apply only to the extent this right is not already provided for under Union law.'

718. Margot E Kaminski and Gianclaudio Malgieri, 'The Right to Explanation in the AI Act' (2025) 25-29 University of Colorado Law School Legal Studies Research Paper Series 1.

719. *Ibid.*

720. *Ibid.*

little to strengthening employees' ability to receive a meaningful explanation or to challenge decisions made by AI systems. Whether the GDPR's data subject's rights provide effective safeguards in this regard is a question I will explore in Chapter 8, section 3.

8 ANALYSIS OF THE AI ACT IN THE EMPLOYMENT CONTEXT: EMPLOYERS' OBLIGATIONS, EMPLOYEES' RIGHTS AND AI AND IOT-ENABLED TECHNOLOGIES

The AI Act, despite the missing focus on individual rights, with its risk-based approach, provides for several requirements for the legitimate exercise of an AI and IoT-enabled employer's monitoring power.

First, the prohibitions on 'unacceptable risks' outlined in Article 5 AI Act establish some 'red lines' that AI providers cannot cross in developing and selling to employers AI systems for monitoring employees. For example, in Article 5, the Act prohibits the use of AI systems to infer employees' emotions and intentions,[721] to apply disproportionate social scoring,[722] or to use biometric categorisation to infer union membership or other personal characteristics of employees.[723] These prohibitions mean that certain systems, such as *Cogito* and *Perceptyx*, are not to be developed and deployed within the European Union, thereby addressing the protection needs I outlined in Chapter 5 as regards employees' fundamental rights to privacy, trade union rights, and non-discrimination.[724] Article 5 AI Act, in these instances, effectively prevents the development of potentially harmful AI systems in the EU single market. In Table 7.1, I outline the relevant prohibitions for the employment context.

Table 7.1 Article 5 AI Act, Prohibited AI Practices Relevant to Employment Contexts

Article AI Act	*Prohibited AI Practice*	*Potential Employment Application*	*Comments/Scope*
5(1)(b)	**Exploiting vulnerabilities due to age, disability, or social/economic circumstances**	AI systems that manipulate employee behaviour (e.g., tone modulation, driver monitoring via cameras)	May apply to employees due to their subordinate position and economic dependence, but no explicit reference to employment; scope remains vague. Draft guidelines mention other vulnerable groups (e.g., migrants), not employees explicitly.

721. Article 5(1)(f) AI Act.
722. Article 5(1)(c) AI Act.
723. Article 5(1)(g) AI Act.
724. Cf. with section 2, Chapter 5.

Article AI Act	*Prohibited AI Practice*	*Potential Employment Application*	*Comments/Scope*
5(1)(c)	**Social scoring based on behaviour or inferred characteristics leading to unjustified/disproportionate treatment**	Systems like *Perceptyx* or *WorkTango* that generate workplace profiles by analysing irrelevant data (e.g., social media, chat logs)	No employment-specific criteria in the AI Act or guidelines. Could apply if AI systems generate unjustified scoring unrelated to job performance. Recital 31 includes public and private actors (e.g., employers).
5(1)(f)	**Emotion recognition in the workplace (unless for safety or medical reasons)**	AI systems assessing employee emotions (e.g., *Cogito* assessing anger/apathy in customer calls; stress monitoring apps)	Explicitly prohibits emotion inference in employment settings, with exceptions (e.g., fatigue detection in drivers). Exceptions must meet necessity and proportionality standards.
5(1)(g)	**Biometric categorisation to deduce sensitive characteristics (e.g., race, political views, trade union membership)**	AI predicting unionisation trends (e.g., *Perceptyx*), or using facial/voice data to infer religion, sexuality, political views.	Explicitly prohibits use for inferring protected characteristics unless compliant with GDPR and used to promote fairness (e.g., anti-bias training datasets).

To be legitimate, AI and IoT-enabled employee monitoring by employers must not fall within the above prohibitions set out in Article 5 AI Act. Article 5 AI Act, however, still raises important interpretative challenges, as I briefly noted in the analysis of these prohibitions.[725] I will discuss in more detail the latter challenges in Chapter 8 (section 5).

Beyond the prohibitions in Article 5, AI systems used for monitoring employees are classified as high-risk under Article 6 and Annex III AI Act. This classification introduces a framework of obligations for both AI providers and AI deployers. Providers of AI systems are responsible for ensuring transparency, accuracy, and human oversight. Employers have additional duties grounded not only in their role as

725. European Commission, 'Commission Guidelines on Prohibited Artificial Intelligence Practices Established by Regulation (EU) 2024/1689 (AI Act)' (n 667).

deployers but also in their specific position of authority within the employment relationship. These include, for instance, obligations to inform and consult employees under European and national labour laws.[726]

Table 7.2 below summarises the obligations of providers and deployers, as analysed in sections 6.1 and 6.2 in this chapter. While the AI Act distinguishes between the roles of providers and deployers, their responsibilities often intersect in practice, particularly where employers influence how systems are implemented and how their outputs affect workers. Table 7.2 highlights key compliance areas, illustrating where responsibilities lie, where they overlap, and where coordination is required to ensure that AI and IoT-enabled monitoring is compliant with the AI Act.

Table 7.2 Obligations for AI Providers and AI Deployers/Employers

Compliance Category	*Providers' Obligations*	*Deployers'/Employers' Obligations*
Risk Management System	*Must implement a life cycle-wide risk management system (Article 9), identifying, analysing, and mitigating risks to health, safety, and fundamental rights.*	*Must monitor the system during use and report to provider/authorities if risks arise (Article 26(5)). Required to ensure input data is relevant and representative (Article 26(4)).*
Data Governance & Training	*Must ensure training, validation, and testing datasets reflect intended purpose and deployment context (Article 10). Power asymmetries in employment must be considered.*	*Must ensure competent, trained staff oversee the system (Article 26(2)). Obliged to follow provider instructions and ensure appropriate data input.*
Technical Robustness & Logging	*Must ensure robustness, accuracy, and cybersecurity (Article 15). Must create technical documentation (Article 11) and maintain logs (Article 19) for traceability and accountability.*	*Must manage input conditions and cooperate in post-market monitoring (Article 26(5)). Must make use of transparency and oversight tools provided by the provider during deployment.*
Transparency	*Must provide clear, accessible instructions for deployers regarding, among others, system purpose, risks, accuracy, oversight mechanisms (Article 13).*	*Must follow these instructions and ensure the system is used as intended. Must inform employees and their representatives before use (Article 26(7)).*
Human Oversight	*Must design systems with oversight features: override functions, explainability, halt options (Article 14).*	*Must understand system limitations, interpret outputs, override decisions where necessary (Article 14(4)).*

726. Article 26(7) AI Act. *See also* Recital 92 AI Act.

Compliance Category	*Providers' Obligations*	*Deployers'/Employers' Obligations*
Quality Management System (QMS)	*Must maintain a QMS (Article 17) to ensure compliance, including risk, data, monitoring, and internal accountability.*	*No direct QMS obligation but must align internal use with the system's design and reported risks.*
Post-market Monitoring	*Must implement a post-market monitoring plan (Article 72), collecting feedback from deployers and system logs. Must act on emerging risks.*	*Must report anomalies or risks to provider and competent authority (Article 26(5)). Active role in continuous feedback and safety assurance.*
Corrective Action & Information	*Must take action and inform authorities and users if non-compliance or risk is discovered (Article 20).*	*Must suspend use and report issues to provider and authorities if risks materialise (Article 26(5)).*
Information & Consultation	*N/A*	*Must inform and consult employees before use of high-risk AI (Article 26(7)), in line with national law and Directive 2002/14/EC. Covers purpose, functioning, data use, and consequences.*
Fundamental Rights Impact Assessment	*N/A*	*Conduct a DPIA under GDPR (if applicable) with info received according to Article 13 AI Act (Article 26(9) AI Act).* *Conduct a Fundamental Rights Impact Assessment (FRIA) (Article 27 AI Act) – this applies only to public employers/employers providing public services.*
Explanation of AI systems' decisions	*N/A*	*Must provide clear, meaningful explanations of AI's role and main elements of the decision to affected persons (Article 86 AI Act).*

Together, these obligations require employers to detect and respond to risks from AI and IoT-enabled monitoring based on the information provided by AI providers, to intervene when harms arise, to inform and consult employees' representatives, and to explain outcomes to affected employees. These obligations operate within the AI Act's broader framework of duties imposed on providers of high-risk systems, which aim to align the design, and subsequent use by deployers, of AI systems with the EU's foundational values, as set out in Article 1(1) AI Act. These obligations may also help employers fulfil their responsibilities under the GDPR when they deploy AI systems that process employees' personal data (*see* Chapter 6, section 4). In this regard, the AI

Act offers a promising structure to support employers' compliance with the GDPR by addressing information asymmetries between AI providers and deployers. However, as several key provisions remain open to interpretation in the employment context, the extent to which this combined regime ensures a legitimate exercise of the employer's monitoring power remains uncertain. I return to this question in Chapter 8.

9 CONCLUSIONS

This chapter answered the research sub-question 6: *What requirements does the AI Act impose on the legitimate exercise of the employer's monitoring power via AI and IoT-enabled technologies?*

The AI Act introduces a risk-based regulatory framework that governs both the development and deployment of AI systems in the EU, with direct implications for the exercise of an AI and IoT-enabled employer's monitoring power. Although its primary focus is on regulating what AI providers may develop and the obligations they must meet, the AI Act also imposes specific requirements on AI deployers, including employers, when using such systems in the workplace. Overall, these requirements aim to ensure that AI use aligns with the core values of the European Union as set out in Article 2 TEU, including respect for human dignity, freedom, equality, and the rule of law.

The AI Act sets out outright prohibitions under Article 5. These include certain practices that are especially relevant in the employment context, such as the use of AI systems for emotion recognition in the workplace and biometric categorisation that infers sensitive characteristics like trade union membership. Other prohibited practices, such as social scoring and AI systems that exploit individuals' vulnerabilities, may also apply to the workplace and warrant further investigation (to be discussed in Chapter 8, section 5). These bans establish red lines against uses of AI systems that are structurally incompatible with employees' fundamental rights, such as privacy, non-discrimination, and freedom of association.

Beyond prohibited practices, the AI Act designates certain AI systems as 'high-risk', including those used for monitoring employees where monitoring produces legal or similarly significant effects. In these cases, employers become subject to a range of obligations intended to safeguard employee rights. High-risk classification triggers duties for both AI providers (Articles 8-49 AI Act) and deployers (Articles 26, 72, 86 AI Act), reinforcing the shared responsibility for fundamental rights protection. For AI providers, this includes duties around data governance, documentation, accuracy, transparency, and the incorporation of human oversight into system design. Employers, however, are required to:

- exercise effective and meaningful human oversight over the system's outputs (Article 26(1)-(3) AI Act);
- inform and consult affected employees prior to deployment (Article 26(7) AI Act and Recital 92 AI Act);
- offer clear and meaningful explanations to employees upon request when decisions or actions are taken based on AI system outputs (Article 86 AI Act);

- report serious incidents and malfunctions to both providers and national competent authorities (Articles 26(5), 79 AI Act);
- cooperate with AI providers and regulators to ensure compliance during deployment (Article 72 AI Act).

Through these requirements, the AI Act requires that the deployment of AI systems is transparent, accountable, subject to prior consultation, and continuously monitored for risk. The Act operationalises the idea that employers, as deployers, must not passively use AI systems but must actively ensure that such tools are used in ways compatible with employees' rights and dignity. This dual responsibility, split between providers and employers, ensures that legitimacy does not rest solely on the technical design of AI systems but also on how they are embedded into workplace practices. It positions the employer not merely as a recipient of technology but as a legally accountable actor responsible for the deployment of AI and IoT-enabled monitoring technologies. This regulatory architecture is anchored in the AI Act's aim to establish a human-centred approach to AI, as articulated in Article 1 and Recitals 6 and 7 AI Act. It reflects the view that AI systems should enhance human well-being and be designed and deployed in ways that respect fundamental rights, particularly in sensitive domains like employment. Together, these obligations establish a framework of procedural and substantive safeguards that define a legitimate exercise of an AI and IoT-enabled employer's monitoring power.

However, as this chapter has hinted, the AI Act is not without limitations when applied to the employment context. In particular, vague wording in Article 5 AI Act and limitations in employers' actual capacity to oversee inherently complex AI systems raise concerns about the effectiveness of the safeguards in practice. These challenges are explored in greater detail in the next chapter, which critically assesses the gaps in the EU's regulatory framework, under the GDPR and AI Act.

CHAPTER 8

The Limitations of the GDPR and AI Act in the Employment Context

1 INTRODUCTION

This chapter addresses the research sub-question 7: *Can the GDPR and AI Act ensure the legitimate exercise of the AI and IoT-enabled employer's monitoring power?*

Building on the analyses of the GDPR and the AI Act in Chapters 6 and 7, this chapter explores whether these Regulations, taken separately or together, can ensure the legitimate exercise of the employer's monitoring power. In the previous two chapters, I hinted several potential limitations of each regulation when considered in isolation. This chapter examines those limitations in greater depth by assessing how the two regimes interact and whether, together, they provide a coherent and effective framework for safeguarding employees' rights.

In section 2, I examine the uncertain scope of two legal bases for lawful processing under Article 6 GDPR, focusing on how Article 6(1)(b) and (f) (performance of a contract and legitimate interest) grants employers' significant interpretative leeway to process employees' data using AI and IoT-enabled technologies in ways that may not respect fundamental rights. The AI Act does not address this issue directly, as its requirements for deployers focus on other aspects than the lawfulness of data processing. Similarly, the obligation to inform and consult employees under Article 26(7) AI Act, I argue, only requires employers to inform employee representatives about the implementation of AI systems, without granting participatory rights in the determination of the legal bases for lawful processing. Section 3 addresses instead the limited effectiveness of data subject's rights (Articles 12-22 GDPR) in employment contexts, especially when AI and IoT-enabled technologies are deployed, where power imbalances may discourage employees from exercising them. This creates a significant gap in protection, considering that the AI Act, except for Article 86 AI Act, does not provide individual rights to individuals affected by AI systems.[727] Section 4 explores how employers, as data controllers, are held accountable for designing GDPR-compliant data processing despite lacking sufficient transparency and information from third-party technology providers under Article 28 GDPR, a gap the AI Act addresses by imposing specific duties on providers of high-risk AI systems. Section 5 turns to the uncertain scope of Article 5 AI Act prohibitions and the challenges of ensuring effective human oversight under Article 14 AI Act. Section 6 concludes and answers the research question.

2 PERFORMANCE OF A CONTRACT AND LEGITIMATE INTERESTS: INTERPRETATIVE LEEWAY OF GDPR'S LEGAL GROUNDS IN THE CONTEXT OF AI AND IOT-ENABLED TECHNOLOGIES

The GDPR balances data subjects' fundamental rights while recognising the growing economic value of personal data in the EU single market.[728] In this section, I explore how this focus on protecting the economic sphere, particularly within employment contexts, might create significant room for employers to interpret certain legal grounds for lawful processing provided in Article 6 GDPR in such a way as to justify the implementation of AI and IoT-enabled technologies that do not respect employees' fundamental rights.[729] I also highlight that the AI Act does not address the lawfulness of data processing, leaving employers' discretion under Article 6 GDPR largely untouched and central to determining the legal basis for processing employees' data. The AI Act in fact focuses on the design, development, deployment, and monitoring of AI systems, without reference to how deployers should ground the processing of affected individuals' data, such as employees. Article 26(7) AI Act, for its part, only requires employers to inform and consult employees' representatives about the implementation of AI systems, without imposing any obligation to consider their views when determining the lawful basis for data processing. Hence, it is topical to understand the interpretative leeway employers retain under Article 6 GDPR in justifying employees' data processing in the age of AI and IoT-enabled technologies, which, as discussed in Chapters 4 and 5, involves intensive processing of personal data.

This section builds on the discussion of Article 6 GDPR developed in Chapter 6 (section 3.3). There, my focus was on identifying and analysing which legal bases employers may rely on (and how they apply) when processing employees' data. As I have already explained in Chapter 6 section 3.3.1, the WP29 has excluded consent as

727. In this regard cf. with section 7, Chapter 7.

728. Viljoen (n 572) 623. In the opening recitals (1-13) on the subject matter and objectives of the GDPR, there are two basic cores guiding the overall structure of the Regulation: the protection of data subjects' fundamental rights (Recitals 1-4, 11) and facilitating the data economy in the Union's single market (Recitals 5-13). *See also* section 3, Chapter 6.

729. *See* Chapter 5.

a valid basis due to the structural power imbalance in employment relationships, where employees may have little or no real bargaining power.[730]

In the following analysis, I set aside consent and examine whether relying on the performance of a contract (Article 6(1)(b) GDPR) and legitimate interests (Article 6(1)(f) GDPR) as legal bases for data processing in employment contexts enables an appropriate balancing act between employers' monitoring interests and employees' fundamental rights, particularly when AI and IoT-enabled technologies are used.

2.1 Necessity under Article 6(1)(b) GDPR: Performance of a Contract as a Gateway for AI and IoT-Enabled Technologies

While analysing Article 6(1)(b) GDPR ('Performance of a contract') as a legal ground (in Chapter 6, section 3.3.2),[731] I highlighted how the WP29 guidelines interpret it in a way that allows for genuinely necessary data processing for the performance of the employment contract.[732] Article 6(1)(b) GDPR provides that processing shall be lawful when:

> Processing is necessary for the performance of a contract to which the data subject is party or in order to take steps at the request of the data subject prior to entering into a contract.

The WP29 specifies that monitoring of employees' internet access, email, or telephone usage, as well as video surveillance, extends beyond what is strictly necessary to perform the contract.[733] The WP29 seems to include under this legal ground only the collection of those personal data necessary for the formal establishment of the contract itself, such as the employee's identification data or the bank number to pay wages.[734]

Concurrently and ambiguously, the WP29 further mentions that:

> What is necessary for the performance of an employment contract (...) may depend on the nature of the employment contract.[735]

730. Article 29 Data Protection Working Party, 'Opinion 02/2017 on Data Processing at Work' (n 21); Article 29 Data Protection Working Party, 'Opinion 8/2001 on the Processing of Personal Data in the Employment Context' (n 453).
731. Article 6(1)(b) GDPR: 'processing is necessary for the performance of a contract to which the data subject is party or in order to take steps at the request of the data subject prior to entering into a contract'.
732. Article 29 Data Protection Working Party, 'Opinion 06/2014 on the Notion of Legitimate Interests of the Data Controller under Article 7 of Directive 95/46/EC' (n 544) 16. *See also*: Kotschy (n 530) 330-331.
733. Article 29 Data Protection Working Party, 'Opinion 06/2014 on the Notion of Legitimate Interests of the Data Controller under Article 7 of Directive 95/46/EC' (n 544) 17.
734. Article 29 Data Protection Working Party, 'Opinion 02/2017 on Data Processing at Work' (n 21) 7; Article 29 Data Protection Working Party, 'Opinion 06/2014 on the Notion of Legitimate Interests of the Data Controller under Article 7 of Directive 95/46/EC' (n 544) 16.
735. Article 29 Data Protection Working Party, 'Opinion 06/2014 on the Notion of Legitimate Interests of the Data Controller under Article 7 of Directive 95/46/EC' (n 544) 17.

This statement opens the door to contextual justifications based on organisational design. It acknowledges that, for some (undefined) employment contracts, data processing might be a precondition to perform the work itself, suggesting a more flexible or context-dependent notion of necessity. In other words, according to the WP29, if a contract's nature inherently demands significant data processing, as is the case in Amazon warehouses,[736] this processing may fall under the legal ground of Article 6(1)(b) GDPR to fulfil contractual obligations.

I find that the WP29's ambivalent interpretation of Article 6(1)(b) GDPR creates a problematic interpretive leeway for employers in the context of AI and IoT-enabled technologies. If certain business models, like those of food delivery platforms or logistics warehouses, are structured in a way that AI and IoT-enabled technologies become an inherent part of performing work, the employer may claim that such data processing is necessary under Article 6(1)(b) GDPR. This allows organisational design, rather than a substantive test of necessity, to dictate the lawfulness of data processing. In such a scenario, the employer effectively defines what is 'necessary' by shaping the employment contract around certain data processing, including those carried out by AI and IoT-enabled technologies for employee monitoring.[737]

Some national Data Protection Authorities (DPAs) have objected to expansive interpretations of 'necessity' of intensive data processing in cases relating to the data minimisation principle (Article 5(1)(c) GDPR).[738] This underlines how the interpretation of necessity is left to individual decisions by employers without clear guidance on the part of WP29. In the *Amazon France* case, for instance, the company claimed that intensive employee monitoring was necessary for its warehouse logistics to function. The French DPA rejected this claim, stating that organisational efficiency alone could not justify such extensive data collection, and that a necessity test (not properly conducted by Amazon) would have shown that less intrusive alternatives were feasible.[739] Similarly, the Italian DPA has held that collecting biometric data (such as fingerprints) for monitoring employee attendance is unjustified unless it is strictly necessary, such as in high-security areas where an increased risk justifies stronger identification measures.[740] The DPA consistently found that, where less intrusive

736. Molè, 'Minimised Work Surveillance Exists under the GDPR: Amazon France and the DPA Sanction' (n 421).
737. On the role of contractual design and Article 6(1)(b) GDPR, *see*: Martin Nettesheim, *Data Protection in Contractual Relationships (Art. 6 (1) (b) GDPR)* (1st edn, Lexxion Verlagsgesellschaft mbH 2024).
738. Molè, 'Minimised Work Surveillance Exists under the GDPR: Amazon France and the DPA Sanction' (n 421). *See also* a similar case in Germany as illustrated by Abraha: Halefom H Abraha, 'Automated Monitoring in the Workplace and the Search for a New Legal Framework: Lessons from Germany and Beyond' (2024) available at SSRN https://dx.doi.org/10.2139/ssrn.4595760 accessed 22 October 2025.
739. *Délibération de la formation restreinte n°SAN-2023-021 du 27 décembre 2023 concernant la société AMAZON FRANCE LOGISTIQUE* (Commission Nationale de l'Informatique et des Libertés).
740. Article 9(2)(b) GDPR allows for the processing of special categories of personal data when necessary to carry out obligations or exercise specific rights in the field of employment, social

alternatives like badge-operated access gates are available, they must be used instead.[741] These DPA interventions point to the above seen systemic weakness: the WP29/EDPB should more clearly outline a structured *ex ante* assessment of necessity of data processing for employee monitoring.

In sum, the formulation of Article 6(1)(b) GDPR and the WP29 guidelines, in the employment context, leave a significant interpretative leeway to employers. This ambiguity allows for surveillance technologies infringing on employees' fundamental rights to find legal ground in Article 6(1)(b) GDPR under a broadly construed notion of necessity. Without a structured test to evaluate when such monitoring is truly indispensable to the contract's performance, the 'performance of a contract' ground risks becoming a backdoor for an illegitimate exercise of the employer's monitoring power.[742] I suggest that one way to operationalise a structured test for assessing the necessity of data processing for the performance of a (employment) contract, particularly when AI and IoT-enabled technologies are involved, is through the Data Protection Impact Assessment (DPIA) under Article 35 GDPR.[743] The DPIA requires a prior evaluation of several elements, including, among others, 'an assessment of the necessity and proportionality of the processing operations in relation to the purposes' and the measures envisaged to ensure the protection of personal data.[744] As such, it can serve as a safeguard against employers embedding surveillance technologies into contractual terms in a way that predefines necessity. The DPIA could provide the *ex ante* assessment necessary to reconcile contractual and business needs with the protection of employees' fundamental rights when AI and IoT-enabled technologies are deployed in the employment context. This would ensure that the legal ground of Article 6(1)(b) is not used to normalise an illegitimate exercise of the employer's monitoring power under the guise of contractual and operational necessity.[745] I will focus with greater detail on the role the DPIA could play, as complemented by the AI Act, in Chapter 9.

---

security, or social protection law. Where such processing is based on Union/Member State law or a collective agreement, the provision explicitly requires that they provide 'appropriate safeguards for the fundamental rights and the interests of the data subject'.

741. Garante per la Protezione dei Dati Personali, 'Lavoro: No Del Garante Privacy All'uso Del Riconoscimento Facciale per Controllo Presenze. Sanzionate Cinque Società Che Trattavano Illecitamente Dati Biometrici' (28 March 2024) https://www.garanteprivacy.it/home/docweb/-/docweb-display/docweb/9997208#1 accessed 22 October 2025; Maria Teresa Carinci, Silvia Giudici and Pierluigi Perri, 'Obblighi Di Informazione e Sistemi Decisionali e Di Monitoraggio Automatizzati (Art. 1-Bis "Decreto Trasparenza"): Quali Forme Di Controllo per i Poteri Datoriali Algoritmici?' (2023) 8 Labor – il lavoro nel diritto 7; Ingrao (n 492).
742. In Chapter 3 (sections 7 and 8), I defined illegitimate exercise of the employer's monitoring power when the monitoring of employee activities does not respect employees' fundamental rights.
743. *See* section 3.6, Chapter 6.
744. Article 35(7)(b) GDPR.
745. I define an illegitimate exercise of the employer's monitoring power as one that is not respectful of employees' fundamental rights, *see* Chapter 3, sections 7 and 8.

2.2 Legitimate Interest and Employees' Fundamental Rights: Risks of Overreach in AI and IoT-Enabled Employer Monitoring under Article 6(1)(f) GDPR

If Article 6(1)(b) GDPR risks validating employer-defined necessity through contractual framing, Article 6(1)(f) GDPR, as I shall explore in this section, raises parallel concerns by enabling employers to self-assess their legitimate interests, often with insufficient regard for the rights asymmetry embedded in employment relations.

Article 6(1)(f) GDPR provides that data processing is lawful when:

> Processing is necessary for the purposes of the legitimate interests pursued by the controller or by a third party, except where such interests are overridden by the interests or fundamental rights and freedoms of the data subject which require protection of personal data, in particular where the data subject is a child.

While this provision offers a relevant legal basis for data processing in employment contexts,[746] it also grants a high degree of interpretative leeway to employers to establish a data processing, also when deploying AI and IoT-enabled technologies.

Under this provision, the responsibility for balancing is left to the employer's discretion. The WP29 has explicitly cautioned on this, stressing that legitimate interest must not become the 'weakest link' or serve as an 'open door to legitimise all data processing activities which do not fall under any of the other legal grounds'.[747] This warning highlights the risk that, without clear boundaries, legitimate interest could be used too broadly, potentially undermining the GDPR's protective aims. The WP29 in its Opinion on the notion of legitimate interest (Opinion 06/2014) highlights that the inherent power imbalance in employment contexts complicates the assessment of legitimate interests in data processing. This imbalance makes it challenging to ensure that the exercise of the employer's monitoring power does not harm the employee's rights and freedoms.[748] The WP29 clarifies that although the balancing test under

746. *See* section 3.3.4, Chapter 6.
747. Article 29 Data Protection Working Party, 'Opinion 06/2014 on the Notion of Legitimate Interests of the Data Controller under Article 7 of Directive 95/46/EC' (n 544) 10. *See also*: European Data Protection Board, 'Guidelines 1/2024 on Processing of Personal Data Based on Article 6(1)(f) GDPR' 5 https://www.edpb.europa.eu/system/files/2024-10/edpb_guidelines_202401_legitimateinterest_en.pdf accessed 22 October 2025. In the latest guidelines on legitimate interest (1/2024), the EDPB confirms that: 'Article 6(1)(f) GDPR cannot be considered as a legal basis "by default". On the contrary, before relying on such a legal basis, the controller should perform a careful assessment of the planned processing and follow a specific methodology. The open-ended nature of Article 6(1)(f) GDPR does not necessarily mean that this legal basis should be seen as one that can only be used as a "last resort" in rare and unforeseen situations, or that Article 6(1)(f) should be seen as a last option if no other legal bases apply. Nor should Article 6(1)(f) be seen as a preferred option by controllers and its use should not be unduly extended to circumvent specific legal requirements or because it would be considered as less constraining than the other legal bases in Article 6(1) GDPR. In other words, Article 6(1)(f) should not be considered as an "open door" to legitimise all data processing activities which do not fall under any of the other legal bases in Article 6(1) GDPR.'
748. Article 29 Data Protection Working Party, 'Opinion 06/2014 on the Notion of Legitimate Interests of the Data Controller under Article 7 of Directive 95/46/EC' (n 544) 63.

Article 6(1)(f) GDPR is generally to be conducted with reference to an average data subject, certain contexts, such as employment, necessitate a more nuanced approach.[749] Considerations such as whether the data subject as employee experiences an imbalanced relationship with the employer-data controller is something that the latter must take into account when providing a legitimate interest for monitoring.[750] In its Opinion on data processing at work, the WP29 identifies some concrete restrictions to prevent structural overreach of employers' interests over employees' fundamental rights. These include geographical limitations (e.g., excluding monitoring in sensitive areas like religious sites, sanitary zones, or break rooms), data-related restrictions (e.g., avoiding access to personal files or communications), and time-based constraints (e.g., relying on sampling instead of continuous surveillance).[751] However, the WP29 guidelines do not elaborate a structured test for assessing whether an employer's claimed legitimate interest requires the monitoring in question, particularly in light of the necessary balance with employees' fundamental rights and freedoms required by Article 6(1)(f) GDPR.

On the contrary, the WP29's Opinion 06/2014 on the notion of legitimate interest acknowledges that, in certain cases, a company's private business interest may partially coincide with a broader public interest. For example, efforts to combat financial fraud or protect property may serve both the company's economic interests and the legitimate concerns of customers, taxpayers, or the wider public.[752] In these situations, the WP29 notes that when a data controller acts not solely for its own benefit but also in the interest of the wider community, this dual purpose can lend additional weight to the legitimacy of the processing. Also in this instance, the Opinion leaves substantial interpretative leeway in defining both business and public interests. This flexibility allows employers to justify data processing by invoking overlapping interests, such as monitoring employee performance or securing company assets, as partially aligned with broader societal concerns. As a result, the threshold for establishing the necessity and legitimacy of monitoring may be lowered, increasing the risk of overly broad interpretations of interests.[753]

This approach falls short in addressing the power and information imbalances introduced by AI and IoT-enabled technologies. These technologies enable employers to monitor employees in ways that were not previously possible, further increasing the existing asymmetries in the employment context. As a result, it becomes essential to assess not only whether such monitoring is necessary for a legitimate interest but also whether less intrusive means are available and whether the enjoyment of employees' fundamental rights is not disproportionately restricted. Exemplary in this regard are the

749. *Ibid.*, 35.
750. *Ibid.*, 55.
751. Article 29 Data Protection Working Party, 'Opinion 02/2017 on Data Processing at Work' (n 21) 8.
752. Article 29 Data Protection Working Party, 'Opinion 06/2014 on the Notion of Legitimate Interests of the Data Controller under Article 7 of Directive 95/46/EC' (n 544) 35.
753. *Ibid.*

cases before the French[754] and German[755] DPAs: Amazon had justified using surveillance technology on employees as a legitimate interest in maintaining sustainable and operational warehouses' logistics, which was based on a second-by-second monitoring of employees' actions.[756] Both DPAs went into detail about the warehouses' organisation, concluding that building a legitimate interest must take into account those negative repercussions on the rights of warehouse employees.[757] Organising a business does not by itself automatically justify the existence of a legitimate interest in monitoring at any intensity, and, where applicable, must take into account more specific national measures according to Article 88 GDPR.[758] Both DPAs concluded that Amazon failed to demonstrate a legitimate interest in deploying the surveillance technologies at issue. These DPAs' decisions underscore that the legitimate interest ground under Article 6(1)(f) GDPR cannot be reduced to a mere economic interest to run a business efficiently. Rather, it requires a careful balancing of the data controller's interests against the rights and freedoms of the data subject. In the employment context, this means that even if an employer can demonstrate a business rationale, that interest must not impose disproportionate consequences on employees' rights. The DPAs' reasoning highlights that legitimate interest must integrate both economic and social considerations, and that monitoring measures must be designed to minimise adverse impacts on employees' rights.[759]

In conclusion, while Article 6(1)(f) GDPR offers a legal basis for data processing in the employment context, its reliance on the employer's self-assessment creates a risk of interpretative leeway that may undermine employees' fundamental rights, particularly in light of the power and information asymmetries intensified by AI and

754. There the DPA established through the French Labour Code, which mandates that restrictions on individual or collective rights must be necessary and proportionate to the task, shall not disproportionately infringe with data subject-employee interests. The DPA in the particular case of Amazon warehouses directly connects these principles to the negative repercussions experienced by Amazon employees under intense surveillance. Molè, 'Minimised Work Surveillance Exists under the GDPR: Amazon France and the DPA Sanction' (n 421).
755. Amazon's Winsen logistics was found by the DPA with a lack of legitimate interest (Article 6(1)(f)) in processing workers' data. Amazon claimed that it was necessary for logistics and performance assessment. The Hanover Court disagreed with the DPA, allowing Amazon's practices. Critics argue that the court prioritised Amazon's economic interests over employee privacy, underestimated monitoring's negative impact, and over trusted Amazon's algorithmic systems. This case highlights how pliable to technological development are businesses organisation and related legitimate interests to monitor. Abraha, 'Automated Monitoring in the Workplace and the Search for a New Legal Framework: Lessons from Germany and Beyond' (n 738).
756. Sam Gruet, 'Amazon Fined for "Excessive" Surveillance of Workers' (*BBC*, 23 January 2024) https://www.bbc.com/news/business-68067022 accessed 22 October 2025.
757. Article 29 Data Protection Working Party, 'Opinion 06/2014 on the Notion of Legitimate Interests of the Data Controller under Article 7 of Directive 95/46/EC' (n 544) 37.
758. In both cases, the DPAs referred to more specific and suitable laws to protect the employees: i.e., the labour laws notified by the Member State to the EU Commission pursuant to Article 88(3) GDPR.
759. For an overview of such a discussion on legitimate interest in monitoring employees: Molè, 'Minimised Work Surveillance Exists under the GDPR: Amazon France and the DPA Sanction' (n 421); Abraha, 'Automated Monitoring in the Workplace and the Search for a New Legal Framework: Lessons from Germany and Beyond' (n 738); Hießl (n 409).

IoT-enabled monitoring. National DPA decisions, such as those concerning Amazon, demonstrate that such discretion can lead to unnecessary and disproportionate monitoring practices. I suggest that the GDPR's requirement to carry out a DPIA under Article 35, also in this case (cf. with the previous section 2.1), offers a more structured and *ex ante* assessment to evaluate necessity, proportionality, and to balance the potential risks to employees' rights with employers' interests. In Chapter 9, I will focus on the role of the DPIA in imposing a documented, transparent, and preventive evaluation that limits employers' interpretative leeway and ensures that data processing respects the fundamental rights of employees, thus allowing for a legitimate exercise of the employer's monitoring power.

3 THE LIMITS OF DATA SUBJECT RIGHTS: ASSUMPTIONS OF AUTONOMY AND AGENCY AND THEIR IMPACT ON THE EMPLOYMENT RELATIONSHIP

The GDPR, alongside legal grounds, principles, and obligations imposed on data controllers, provides for data subject's rights in Chapter III (Articles 12-22 GDPR). These rights, which I have discussed in Chapter 6 (section 3.5), allow individuals in the EU single market to exercise control over their personal data and ensure transparency and accountability in data processing. Labour law literature has examined whether this framework of individual rights is sufficient to address the power asymmetries present in employment relationships.[760] As I highlighted in section 7 of Chapter 7, the AI Act offers only limited individual rights, primarily a narrow right to explanation under Article 86, which makes the GDPR's data subject's rights still central in guaranteeing individual protections when AI systems process employees' personal data. However, in this section, I note how the data subject's rights under the GDPR face important limitations in the employment context. In the following analysis, I will examine what I consider to be a relevant aspect that has been overlooked in the existing literature, i.e., how these rights are designed around a particular conception of the data subject/individual: one who is presumed to act as an autonomous agent capable of defending his or her own interests.

In this section, I will critically assess the underlying assumptions of the GDPR's data subject's rights and argue that these rights are built on a regulatory framework that presumes individuals possess the autonomy and agency to protect their interests, an assumption that does not always align with the realities of employment relationships. I will therefore analyse the design of these rights and their limitations in mitigating the structural power imbalance between employer and employee in the context of AI and IoT-enabled monitoring.

760. Cf. with sections 3.5.1, 3.5.2, 3.5.3, Chapter 6. *See also*: Abraha, 'Regulating Algorithmic Employment Decisions Through Data Protection Law' (n 26); Aloisi and Gramano (n 360); Dagnino (n 36).

3.1 Who Is the Data Subject in the GDPR

Each field of law is shaped by the context in which it operates and the assumptions it makes about the actors involved. The GDPR, like any legislation, refers to a context and its surrounding assumptions. Labour law refers to employment relationships and assumes the potentially harmful economic and social dependence of employees on their employers. Environmental law refers to the ecosystem and assumes that it is a universal good to be protected from harmful human actions.[761] The GDPR, with particular reference to the data subjects' rights (Articles 12-22 GDPR), assumes that natural persons in the European single market enjoy autonomy and agency to protect their interests. These rights therefore empower data subjects with sufficient legal guarantees and information, so that they are able to control, choose and withdraw which information to give to a data controller.[762]

According to Cohen, the regulatory approach adopted by the GDPR assumes a rational person – or, 'the liberal self' – critically independent from relational ties.[763] This approach is particularly evident in how the rights of data subjects are designed. The assumption behind these rights is that the 'liberal self' can act in several directions, e.g.:

- 'To be aware of, and verify, the lawfulness of the processing':[764] the right of access (Article 15 GDPR) allows data subjects to meaningfully understand how their personal data are being processed as well as the consequences of such processing, or to verify the accuracy of the processing without stating their reasons for asking this information, as clarified by the EDPB.[765] The data subject shall build such awareness also on the clear and simple explanations on the data processing provided *ex ante* by the data controller (Articles 13-14 GDPR).[766]
- To rectify inaccuracies concerning him/her in the data processing (Article 16 GDPR). Or to request that his or her data is deleted pursuant to the conditions laid down in Article 17 GDPR, or that processing is restricted pursuant to Article 18 GDPR. The ECJ emphasised how the implementation of these rights

761. Richard J Lazarus, *The Making of Environmental Law* (2nd edn, The University of Chicago Press 2023) 1-9.
762. Jef Ausloos, Michael Veale and René Mahieu, 'Getting Data Subject Rights Right' (JIPITEC 283 para. 1 2019) https://www.jipitec.eu/jipitec/article/view/262 accessed 22 October 2025 https://doi.org/10.31228/osf.io/e2thg accessed 22 October 2025; Margot E Kaminski, 'The Right to Explanation, Explained' (2019) 34 Berkeley Technology Law Journal https://www.ssrn.com/abstract=3196985 accessed 22 October 2025.
763. Julie E Cohen, 'What Is Privacy For' (2013) 126 Harvard Law Review 1904, 1910.
764. European Data Protection Board, 'Guidelines 01/2022 on Data Subject Rights: Right of Access' (n 581) 10.
765. *Ibid.*, 10-11.
766. Article 29 Data Protection Working Party, 'Guidelines on Automated Individual Decision-Making and Profiling for the Purposes of Regulation 2016/679' (n 494) 16.

hinges on the right of access: if the data subject can develop awareness through access, s(he) will be better able to activate Articles 16-18 GDPR.[767]

- To object to the data processing on grounds relating to the data subject's situation according to the conditions set in Article 21 GDPR. The data controller must interrupt the processing unless s(he) can demonstrate the existence of a compelling interest to process the data subject's personal data.
- To avoid being subjected to automated decision-making according to Article 22 GDPR. The data subject can 'opt out' from automated decision-making having legal or significant effects on him or her. If in certain circumstances this right is not available to the data subject, (s)he retains the right to have a human intervention to express his or her point of view and to challenge the decision.[768]

These rights assume the existence of an informed and actively interested individual to determine his or her own representation in the personal data processed, or to stop the processing itself – the liberal self. These are general rights that can be activated by any data subject in any context. The problem here is that the 'liberal self' may have little room in employment contexts. Employees might, paradoxically, have an interest in *not* using those rights. They conflict with the fundamental assumptions of labour law: the individual employee does not have sufficient bargaining power to counteract employer choices.[769] Regardless of whether the latter are fair or not, agreeing to working conditions does not necessarily mean consent, as silence may stem from fear of repercussions. Often, employees accept conditions due to the natural degree of economic (and thus social) coercion stemming from subordination, jointly with individual needs that may be related to poverty, limited choices, debt, or other vulnerabilities.[770]

In developing rights and obligations, and defining roles such as data subjects and data controllers, the EU legislator – while recognising the unique needs and vulnerabilities of certain groups – primarily refers to a context distinct from the workplace: the European single market.[771] Recital 7 GDPR emphasises the necessity for a robust and cohesive data protection framework in the Union for fostering the trust necessary for the digital economy to flourish across the internal market. In such a 'digital economy to develop' the GDPR sets, in other words, these bilateral relationships[772]

767. Case C-434/16, *Novak v. Data Protection Commissioner*, ECLI:EU:C:2017:994.
768. Recital 71, EU Reg. 2016/679. *See also*: Article 29 Data Protection Working Party, 'Guidelines on Automated Individual Decision-Making and Profiling for the Purposes of Regulation 2016/679' (n 494) 21.
769. Davidov (n 149) 54.
770. Maayan Niezna, 'Consent to Labour Exploitation' (2024) 53 Industrial Law Journal 3 https://doi.org/10.1093/indlaw/dwad036 accessed 22 October 2025; Virginia Mantouvalou, 'The Right to Non-Exploitative Work' in Virginia Mantouvalou (ed.), *The Right to Work: Legal and Philosophical Perspectives* (Hart Publishing 2015).
771. Viljoen (n 572) 623-628.
772. As I have discussed, the role of processors is largely secondary. They have a duty to cooperate in certain circumstances, but data controllership remains predominantly in the hands of the employer as the exerciser of monitoring power. In section 4 of the present chapter, I further develop on the relationship between the data controller and processor.

where one party (the data controller) holds and uses information from another party, who without adequate (and from time to time tailored) protections, could be denied the right to the protection of his or her personal data and other fundamental rights (the data subject).[773]

Data subjects' rights, in this context, outline the EU data subject as an informed, rational and proactive individual exercising his or her individual rights. Yet, the employee exists and relies upon a hierarchical structure where the employer wields significant control over his or her livelihood and working conditions. Unlike, for instance, a consumer who can switch vendors, an employee cannot easily 'opt out' of an employment relationship without serious consequences, such as losing income or career stability.[774] The employer influences not just the employee's economic situation but also his or her social and professional life:[775] receiving sanctions, being fired or resigning from work is not tantamount to choosing a different vendor or being deceived by misleading information from an e-commerce seller.[776]

Data subject's rights are instead based on the expectation that the data subject exercises them autonomously. This concept of autonomy and agency of the data subject, I argue, is further confirmed by Article 80 GDPR ('Representation of data subjects'), which excludes the representative of the data subjects (for instance, a trade union) from exercising on their behalf the rights provided in Articles 12-22 GDPR. According to Article 80, the representatives of the data subjects are only allowed to exercise on their behalf the rights provided by Articles 77-79 and 82 GDPR (i.e., to lodge complaints to DPAs),[777] and make no reference to Articles 12-22 GDPR. I therefore do not agree with the argument developed in labour law scholarship that Article 80 GDPR directly provides trade unions with a legal basis to exercise data subjects' rights.[778] The

773. Recital 4, GDPR: 'This Regulation respects all fundamental rights and observes the freedoms and principles recognised in the Charter as enshrined in the Treaties, in particular the respect for private and family life, home and communications, the protection of personal data, freedom of thought, conscience and religion, freedom of expression and information, freedom to conduct a business, the right to an effective remedy and to a fair trial, and cultural, religious and linguistic diversity.' *See also*: Viljoen (n 572) 623-628.

774. Phoebe V Moore, 'Problems in Protections for Working Data Subjects: The Social Relations of Data Production' (2022) 1 Global Political Economy 257 https://doi.org/10.1332/ukge7444 accessed 22 October 2025.

775. On the impact on social, economic and professional life, *see* the next subsection on the implications for labour law protection.

776. Michele Molè, 'Lost in Translation: Is Data Protection Labour Law Protection?' (2025) 45 Comparative Labor Law & Policy Journal 553; Moore (n 774).

777. Respectively: Right to lodge a complaint with a supervisory authority (Article 77), Right to an effective judicial remedy against a supervisory authority (Article 78), Right to an effective judicial remedy against a controller or processor (Article 79), and Right to compensation and liability (Article 82).

778. *See* in this regard Hießl (n 409) 20; Aloisi (n 26); Gaudio (n 604). Part of the labour law scholarship argues that recent cases before the Amsterdam Court have led to a favourable interpretation for a right of access to allow unions to have clear information on algorithmic systems and to defend workers. This right of access, according to the Court, must be enforced with respect to the data subject and not with respect to the trade union. The latter, unless national law provides differently, has no entitlement in the GDPR to exercise the right directly and can only lodge complaints to the DPA on the basis of information provided by the worker

right to lodge a complaint with the DPA (*see* Articles 77 and 80 GDPR) is not equivalent to the right to access or rectify one's personal data. Unions may only do so once the rights in Articles 12-22 GDPR have been exercised individually by the employee, who then later might (or not) turn to a trade union.[779] The EDPB guidelines on the right of access (01/2022) state that, although the right of access – as a data subject's right – is generally exercised by data subjects themselves, it is possible for a third party to make a request on their behalf. This may apply to proxies, legal guardians for minors, or even trade unions, but these provisions are ultimately governed by national (private) laws on mandate or agency.[780] As the EDPB highlights, unauthorised exercises of data subject's rights – such as requests made by third parties or proxies – could constitute a personal data breach under Article 4(12).[781] Therefore, I conclude that Article 80 does not permit trade unions to exercise individual data subjects' rights, as doing so could constitute a personal data breach, unless specific national provisions exist that explicitly allow trade unions to exercise these essentially personal and individual rights.[782] Clearly outlining this narrow interpretation of Article 80 GDPR helps me to illustrate the central and underlying assumption present in the GDPR: the data subject is an actor who reads the information policies and notices (from the data controller) and is able to consciously choose and act, whether alone or through representatives.[783] Hence, the GDPR does, in the rights of the data subject, not adequately account for contexts of structural (economic and social) dependence, such as employment, where the data subject's autonomy and free will are significantly constrained. This lack of recognition of structural dependency is further compounded by the limited individual protections in the AI Act. Beyond the narrow right to explanation under Article 86 AI Act, individuals affected by AI systems – including employees – do not have specific rights to object to AI system data processing or to be protected from AI system

himself/herself once he/she has exercised his/her rights. Gerechtshof Amsterdam 4 April 2023, ECLI:NL:GHAMS:2023:796, ECLI:NL:GHAMS:2023:793, and ECLI:NL:GHAMS:2023:804.

779. This is further discussed by Adams and Wenckebach (n 38) 222.

780. European Data Protection Board, 'Guidelines 01/2022 on Data Subject Rights: Right of Access' (n 581) 29.

781. According to Article 4(12) GDPR: 'personal data breach' means a breach of security leading to the accidental or unlawful destruction, loss, alteration, unauthorised disclosure of, or access to, personal data transmitted, stored or otherwise processed. A personal data breach activates other obligations for the data controller, i.e., Article 33 ('Notification of a personal data breach to the supervisory authority') and Article 34 ('Communication of a personal data breach to the data subject'). *See also*: *ibid.*, 29-30.

782. Article 80(2) GDPR: 'Member States may provide that any body, organisation or association referred to in paragraph 1 of this Article, independently of a data subject's mandate, has the right to lodge, in that Member State, a complaint with the supervisory authority which is competent pursuant to Article 77 and to exercise the rights referred to in Articles 78 and 79 if it considers that the rights of a data subject under this Regulation have been infringed as a result of the processing.'

783. This is further supported by the report on collective bargaining and AI published by UNI Europa. UNI Europa, 'Collective Bargaining Practices on AI and Algorithmic Management in European Services Sectors' (Friedrich Ebert Stiftung 2024) 7 https://www.uni-europa.org/wp-content/uploads/sites/3/2024/03/CollectiveBargainingPracticesOnAI_final.pdf accessed 22 October 2025.

decisions, thereby leaving the GDPR's data subject's rights framework central to determining individual protections (*see* section 7, Chapter 7).

I shall now turn to the implications for employee protection in the light of these limitations in the GDPR's data subject's rights.

3.2 The Implications for Labour Law Protection

The GDPR's model of the data subject presumes an informed and autonomous individual, capable of asserting his or her rights regarding personal data. Once this assumption is transposed to the employment context it becomes problematic. Employment relationships are characterised by subordination and economic dependency, which may hinder employees from meaningfully exercising these rights. As a result, the level of protection the GDPR affords in theory may fall short in practice when applied to employment contexts.

Although subordinate employment is rooted in a contractual relationship, the autonomy and agency of the employee, as a data subject, are significantly shaped and constrained by the employer, who acts as the data controller.[784] The employer holds the power to unilaterally determine working conditions and issue directives, including monitoring and disciplinary measures. Both domestic and EU labour law recognise this structural imbalance and seek to mitigate it by limiting the employee's exposure to unfair terms that fall below the minimum standards set by labour protections.[785] In this context, the principles of private autonomy and contractual freedom take on a different meaning.[786] Employment relationships operate within a framework of asymmetry that

784. Niezna and Davidov (n 153) 2.
785. The EU social acquis reflects this regulatory approach inherent in domestic laws. *See* in general: Juliane Bir, 'The European Social Dialogue' in Peter Scherrer et al. (eds), *The Future of Europe* (European Trade Union Institute (ETUI) 2019). Directives such as 2000/78/EC, 2000/43/EC, and 2006/54/EC protect against discrimination and uphold workers' health and safety, curbing the employer bargaining power. Additionally, directives like 2002/14/EC on information and consultation of workers, 2009/38/EC on European Works Councils, mandates firms with fifty + employees to inform and consult workers and their representatives on organisational changes; Directive 2019/1152 ensures workers receive clear information on employment status, working conditions, and pay, protecting them from exploitation and promoting fairness and transparency. They all balance employers' freedom to run a business with employees' rights and promote shared governance in the workplace. Bartłomiej Bednarowicz, 'The Tale of Transparent and Predictable Working Conditions Intertwined with Work-Life Balance: Assessing the Impact of the New Social Policy Directives on Decent Working Conditions and Social Protection' (2020) 22 European Journal of Social Security 421 https://doi.org/10.1177/1388262720968575 accessed 22 October 2025. Furthermore, the directive on Platform Work explicitly addresses employer data collection practices. It prohibits platforms from collecting unnecessary data, mandates human oversight of automated systems, and emphasises transparency and accountability in decision-making processes. This directive underscores the EU's efforts to mitigate growing power imbalances due to digitalisation. It also fills gaps in the GDPR by restricting the use of sensitive data and automated processing solely based on consent or contract performance. Potocka-Sionek and Aloisi (n 41).
786. Davidov (n 149) 34-54.

affects aspects such as human dignity,[787] essential social inclusion,[788] human and decent working conditions,[789] and an economic livelihood.[790]

It follows that while the data subject in Articles 12-22 GDPR can be identified as an informed and autonomous individual, capable of asserting his or her rights regarding personal data, in employment contexts, this cannot be assumed. The assumption on the average employee by labour law is that his or her subordination to the employer shall be shielded from hierarchical abuses.[791] For the same reason, the WP29/EDPB treat employee consent with caution. Consent assumes a negotiation between equal parties, disregarding the social and economic dependencies inherent in the employment relationship. Labour law assumes that a symmetry of powers is to be re-established through non-waivable labour rights against market/contractual logics that might offset human dignity, social inclusion, emancipation, and economic livelihood.[792]

The subordination of the data subject to the data controller – jointly with the social and economic significance that employment has for employees – makes the employee what Malgieri (and the WP29)[793] defines as a structurally 'vulnerable' data subject, which cannot be protected solely through the data subjects' rights.[794] The disharmony between the autonomy and agency of the employee compared to those of the data subject therefore leads me to conclude that, under Articles 12-22 GDPR, the employer and the employee are not equivalent in substance to a data controller and a data subject. The protections linked to the data subject's rights presume an interest in activating them which, by contrast, must be presumed to be lacking. The employee, in fact, contrary to the assumption of the GDPR (and of Article 86 AI Act), may, in some instances, have an interest in *not* exercising his or her data subject's rights against the

787. Colin Fenwick and Tonia Novitz, *Human Rights at Work: Perspectives on Law and Regulation* (Hart Publishing 2010); De Schutter, 'Human Rights in Employment Relationships: Contracts as Powers' (n 171).
788. Hugh Collins writes that one of the main goals of labour law is to reduce or minimise social exclusion. Work usually has a social importance for the individual. It means being part of a community; laws therefore are designed to counter the social exclusion that results from not having a job, balancing and allowing family life. Hugh Collins, *Employment Law* (2nd edn, Oxford University Press 2010) 22. *See also*: MR Freedland and Nicola Countouris, *The Legal Construction of Personal Work Relations* (New York: Oxford University Press 2011) 374-375; Adelle Blackett, 'Emancipation in the Idea of Labour Law' in Guy Davidov and Brian Langille (eds), *The Idea of Labour Law* (Oxford University Press 2011) 420.
789. Refer to Chapter 3, section 6.
790. One of the main vulnerabilities that characterise employment is the economic dependence of employees on their employment contract. The employee relies on the employer and its solvency of the continued payment of wages. A job loss implies a set of personal and social repercussions, like poverty, debts and so on. Davidov (n 149) 45-46.
791. *Ibid.*, 54.
792. Vladimir Bogoeski, 'Nonwaivability of Labour Rights, Individual Waivers and the Emancipatory Function of Labour Law' (2023) 52 Industrial Law Journal 179 https://doi.org/10.1093/indlaw/dwac020 accessed 22 October 2025; Guy Davidov, 'Non-Waivability in Labour Law' (2020) 40 Oxford Journal of Legal Studies 482 https://doi.org/10.1093/ojls/gqaa016 accessed 22 October 2025.
793. Article 29 Data Protection Working Party, 'Guidelines on Data Protection Impact Assessment (DPIA)' (n 602) 11.
794. Gianclaudio Malgieri, *Vulnerability and Data Protection Law* (Oxford University Press 2023) 77-100.

exercise of an employer's monitoring power for the fear of any job-related repercussions. That interest lies in not (running the risk of) losing his or her position in society (personal and family sustenance, prestige, or whatever meaning s(he) entrusts to it),[795] and in the remuneration and the development opportunities provided by the data controller.[796] The employee's social and economic dependence on his or her job and the employer's hierarchical superiority have thus a direct impact on how the data subject-employee behaves. This analysis helps to clarify why rights-based protections under Articles 12-22 GDPR are ill-suited to address the layered vulnerabilities present in employment contexts. In the following Chapter 9, I build on this critique by analysing alternative regulatory approaches - specifically, the role of DPIAs, the AI Act's obligations for high-risk systems, and sector-specific interventions such as the Platform Work Directive – as more appropriate mechanisms for safeguarding employee rights in digitally mediated work environments.

The challenges of effective data protection in employment do not arise solely from the imbalances inherent in the employment relationship. They are reinforced by the dependencies employers themselves develop when relying on third-party technology providers who often design, implement, and manage AI and IoT-enabled technologies. This introduces a second asymmetry to be further explored: between data controllers who must ensure lawful processing, and processors who hold key technical knowledge but bear limited transparency obligations under the GDPR.

4 THE ROLE OF GDPR PROCESSORS AND AI ACT PROVIDERS: EMPLOYERS DEPLOYING AI AND IOT-ENABLED TECHNOLOGIES AND INFORMATIONAL ASYMMETRIES

As I discussed in Chapter 4 (section 4.1), companies providing AI and IoT-enabled technologies play a key role in shaping employee monitoring. By turning to the market, employers expand their monitoring capabilities or discover new ones. Employers often act like consumers in a marketplace, purchasing or licensing AI systems developed by external providers to meet existing needs or to introduce new capabilities. In this sense, these companies create and influence employers' choices as to what purposes, tools and possible risks arise from processing.[797] What employer alone would have had access to a sensor capable of constantly listening to the voice of all employees in a call centre?[798] Or to be able to index unionisation probability for each employee?[799] Or to

795. Davidov (n 149) 43. Research on the social and economic meaning of work is vast. For a useful overview: Donald E Super, Branimir Šverko and Charles M Super (eds), *Life Roles, Values, and Careers: International Findings of the Work Importance Study* (1st edn, Jossey-Bass Publishers 1995).
796. Moore (n 774).
797. On the role of technology developers in shaping employers' needs and powers over employees: Molè, 'Commodified, Outsourced Authority: A Research Agenda for Algorithmic Management at Work' (n 339).
798. 'Cogito: Real-Time AI Coaching & Guidance for Contact Centers' (n 281).
799. 'Perceptyx' (n 417).

have smart cameras on drivers to monitor their behaviour?[800] These rhetorical questions serve to stress how these companies have a strong influence on employers' monitoring activities. Employers, as costumers, purchase products generating new forms of monitoring they could not otherwise access.

In Chapter 6 (sections 3.1 and 3.2), I discussed how the GDPR assigns accountability for data protection-compliant processing to data controllers. However, the GDPR does not provide for comprehensive transparency obligations for processors towards data controllers. This is a significant gap considering that data controllers bear the responsibility for designing a lawful processing. In this section, I examine another assumption embedded in the GDPR; namely, that employers, as data controllers under Articles 24 and 25 GDPR, always possess the necessary information and expertise to manage the AI and IoT-enabled technologies they acquire (and deploy over employees), and to ensure that the resulting data processing complies with the GDPR. I then discuss how the obligations for high-risk AI systems under the AI Act (such as transparency, documentation, and post-market monitoring) go beyond what is required of processors in the GDPR framework.[801] The interplay between these regulations, I will argue, potentially enhances employers' capacity to fulfil their data protection obligations in complex digital ecosystems.

4.1 The Role and Duties of Processors Towards Data Controllers

The GDPR establishes, in Article 4(8), that data controllers, including employers, may rely on processors to handle personal data on their behalf.[802] More specifically, processors have the following connotations:

- They are *a separate entity* (i.e., a company developing and selling the AI and IoT-enabled technology) in relation to the data controller. The employer-data controller delegates all or part of the processing activities to the processor.[803]
- They process personal data *on the controller's behalf*. According to the EDPB, acting 'on behalf of' means serving someone else's interest and recalls the legal concept of delegation. The processor receives instructions from the controller on the purpose and means of processing.[804]

Under Article 28(1) GDPR, it is the data controller who bears the duty to select only processors that provide sufficient guarantees for implementing appropriate technical and organisational measures in compliance with the GDPR.[805] The EDPB further clarifies that the data controller must assess whether a prospective processor

800. Netradyne and Amazon (n 676).
801. Cf. with sections 8 and 9, Chapter 7, on the application of the AI Act in the employment context.
802. Article 4(8) GDPR: '"processor" means a natural or legal person, public authority, agency or other body which processes personal data on behalf of the controller'.
803. European Data Protection Board, 'Guidelines 07/2020 on the Concepts of Controller and Processor in the GDPR' (n 612) 25-26.
804. *Ibid.*, 26.
805. Recital 81, GDPR: 'To ensure compliance with the requirements of this Regulation (...) the controller should use only processors providing sufficient guarantees, in particular in terms of

allows for a sufficient degree of control and whether any risks to data subjects can be adequately managed.[806] In contrast, the GDPR imposes limited obligations on processors to proactively provide data controllers with all the information they may need to fulfil their own GDPR responsibilities.

For example, Article 28(3)(e) GDPR requires processors to assist the data controller in responding to data subjects' rights requests. Under Article 28(3)(h) GDPR, processors must make available to data controllers – only upon request – all information necessary to demonstrate compliance with the processor's obligations under the Regulation.[807] To prove GDPR compliance, processors may adhere to codes of conduct[808] or certification mechanisms[809] under Article 28(5), thereby assisting data controllers in verifying compliance. However, these mechanisms are optional for processors and do not absolve data controllers from their obligation to conduct due diligence.[810]

In essence, while processors are not directly bound by the full scope of GDPR obligations, data controllers remain responsible for ensuring that their processors comply. This has been further confirmed by DPAs. The Italian DPA fined the company *Wind Tre* (as a data controller) for unauthorised marketing practices with customers' data due to a lack of control over its processors, who conducted campaigns on its behalf without proper oversight. *Wind Tre* was found accountable for not addressing its processors' illicit practices, failing to implement adequate control measures over them. Similarly, the Spanish DPA fined *Vodafone* for not ensuring its processor maintained GDPR compliance.[811]

These DPA decisions confirm that it is the data controller who remains responsible for ensuring that data processing complies with GDPR standards, even when the processing is carried out by a third-party processor. In other words, while an employer may rely on a processor to perform the actual processing, the employer, as the data controller, retains full accountability for ensuring that the design and execution of the processing meet the GDPR's data protection requirements.[812] The processor under Article 28(10) GDPR is not authorised to process on its own, i.e., outside the instructions received from the data controller. By going beyond the instructions, the

expert knowledge, reliability and resources, to implement technical and organisational measures which will meet the requirements of this Regulation.' This allows then the data controller to demonstrate compliance with the GDPR as required by Article 24 ('Responsibility of the controller').

806. European Data Protection Board, 'Guidelines 07/2020 on the Concepts of Controller and Processor in the GDPR' (n 612) 27-28.
807. *Ibid.*, 40.
808. Article 40, GDPR.
809. Article 42, GDPR.
810. Efstratios Koulierakis, 'Certification as Guidance for Data Protection by Design' [2023] International Review of Law, Computers & Technology 1 https://doi.org/10.1080/13600869.2023.2269498 accessed 22 October 2025.
811. Monique Kalsi, 'Still Losing the Race with Technology? Understanding the Scope of Data Controllers' Responsibility to Implement Data Protection by Design and by Default' (2024) 38 International Review of Law, Computers & Technology 346, 357 https://doi.org/10.1080/13600869.2024.2324546 accessed 22 October 2025.
812. European Data Protection Board, 'Guidelines 07/2020 on the Concepts of Controller and Processor in the GDPR' (n 612) 28.

processor becomes the data controller of independently established processing. The EDPB defines controllership and processorship as functional concepts: they shall be determined by the actual activities undertaken in a specific situation.[813] Hence, if the fictitious processor instead determines the purposes of processing and the means, it shall be regarded as data controller. This allows, also according to the ECJ case law, to materially identify who the data controller is, so as to entrust it with the accountability envisaged in the GDPR.[814]

While it is the responsibility of the data controller to have responsible processors, s(he) may lack the information and technical expertise to determine exactly what information to request from processors. This is particularly true in complex data processing involving AI or IoT-enabled technologies. As a result, data controllers often depend on processors to disclose relevant details, creating an asymmetry where data controllers are not always fully equipped to assess compliance risks. In this regard, Kalsi noted how Article 25 GDPR (on data protection by design and by default), by targeting only data controllers, assumes they can influence others involved in data processing, thus resulting in a vague catch-all provision, undermining robust data protection through technology design as envisioned by privacy by design and by default principles.[815]

Further illustrative in this regard is the processor's role in carrying out the DPIA under Article 35 GDPR.[816] According to the EDPB, the processor shall retain only a duty of assistance towards the data controller, which does not entail a transfer of responsibility.[817] The responsibility remains firmly with the data controller as mandated by Articles 5, 6, 24 and 25 GDPR.[818] Although a processor may be in a better situation to conduct the DPIA, the data controller is ultimately responsible for ensuring its completion.[819] Hence, the DPIA drafting suffers from a critical flaw: it overly relies on the employer's ability to account for information that is available to the processor. Yet, under Article 28(3)(f) and Recital 95 GDPR, the processor's obligation to assist the controller with a DPIA is restricted to situations deemed 'necessary' and only when explicitly requested. This effectively limits the flow of critical technical information unless the controller is aware of what to ask for – a problematic expectation when

813. European Data Protection Board, 'Guidelines 07/2020 on the Concepts of Controller and Processor in the GDPR' (n 612). *See also* the previous guidelines: Article 29 Data Protection Working Party, 'Opinion 1/2010 on the Concepts of "Controller" and "Processor"' (2010) 9 https://ec.europa.eu/justice/article-29/documentation/opinion-recommendation/files/2010/wp169_en.pdf accessed 22 October 2025.
814. Case C-131/12, *Google Spain SL and Google Inc. v. Agencia Española de Protección de Datos (AEPD) and Mario Costeja González*, judgment of 13 May 2014, para. 34; Case C-210/16, *Wirtschaftsakademie Schleswig-Holstein*, judgment of 5 June 2018, para. 28; ECJ, Case C-40/17, *Fashion ID GmbH & Co.KG v. Verbraucherzentrale NRW eV*, judgment of 29 July 2019, para. 66.
815. Kalsi (n 811) 351-352.
816. *See* section 3.6, Chapter 6.
817. European Data Protection Board, 'Guidelines 07/2020 on the Concepts of Controller and Processor in the GDPR' (n 612) 39.
818. Kalsi (n 811) 347-348.
819. *Ibid.*, 7.

dealing with opaque or adaptive AI-enabled technologies.[820] Articles 24, 25 and 35 GDPR, moreover, provide insufficient safeguards against the interpretative leeway employers may exercise in grounding intrusive data processing on the basis of the performance of a contract or legitimate interests under Article 6(1)(b) and (f) GDPR.[821] While the employer (as controller) is formally responsible for assessing data protection risks, in practice, this assessment depends on his or her own interpretation of the GDPR's legal grounds for a lawful processing and on technical details and operational parameters of the system that are known primarily to the provider – often acting as a processor under the GDPR. This approach assumes that the employer is always informed enough to navigate the complexities of AI and IoT-enabled technologies, able to interpret correctly the GDPR's provisions, and request the right information from processors.

4.2 Bridging the Information Gap: The AI Act's Provider Obligations

While the GDPR offers limited mechanisms requiring processors to share information with data controllers, the AI Act introduces a different model of responsibility for providers of high-risk AI systems. As discussed in Chapter 7, where an AI-enabled monitoring technology qualifies as 'high-risk' (e.g., systems used to assess or monitor employees), the AI provider is subject to a distinct set of obligations under the AI Act, including among others risk management, providing technical documentation, transparency, and human oversight (Articles 8-15 AI Act).[822]

This means that even if the AI provider encounters few obligations as a processor under the GDPR, the AI Act still imposes independent responsibilities on it as an AI provider of a high-risk AI system. The regulatory approach there adopted recognises the increasing influence of AI developers in shaping how AI-enabled technologies function and the risks they pose, particularly in employment contexts where employers, although formally accountable under the GDPR, may lack the knowledge to fully understand the implications of these systems. For instance, Article 13 AI Act requires providers to ensure that high-risk AI systems are accompanied by clear and concise instructions for use, including information on the system's intended purpose, performance limitations, and conditions under which it can be used safely. Article 14 AI Act further mandates that such systems be designed and developed to enable appropriate human oversight, with a view to preventing or minimising risks to fundamental rights and safety.[823] The AI Act thus complements the GDPR by helping to close the accountability gap between data controllers and increasingly powerful processors, reinforcing the principle of shared responsibility when deploying high-risk AI and

820. Consequently, it is the controller's responsibility to initiate and oversee the data protection impact assessment, not the processor.
821. Cf. with section 2, Chapter 8.
822. Cf. section 6, Chapter 7.
823. *See* my discussion of Articles 8-27 AI Act, including Articles 13 and 14 AI Act, section 6, Chapter 7.

IoT-enabled technologies at work.[824] This could enhance employers' ability to comply with the GDPR's data protection standards, by giving them greater access to relevant documentation, risk assessments, and oversight tools. I will return to this point in Chapter 9, where I explore how the AI Act's requirements can support the drafting of the Data Protection Impact Assessment (DPIA) under Article 35 GDPR in a way that strengthens compliance with data protection and fundamental rights in AI and IoT-enabled monitoring.

5 ARTICLE 5 AI ACT AND ITS UNCERTAIN SCOPE IN EMPLOYMENT CONTEXTS

While the AI Act offers a promising framework to enhance employer compliance with the GDPR, particularly by addressing information asymmetries between AI providers and AI deployers, the interpretation of some of the AI Act provisions in the employment context is still uncertain. As I briefly discussed in Chapter 7, sections 5 and 8, the scope and interpretation of Article 5 AI Act ('Prohibited AI Practices') raise important interpretative questions. In the following subsections, I address two key areas of ambiguity within the AI Act. First, I analyse Article 5(1)(b) and 5(1)(c) AI Act, which provisions prohibit certain uses of AI systems that exploit social and economic vulnerabilities and apply social scoring. These provisions leave questions open regarding what qualifies as exploitation of vulnerabilities and what counts as social scoring in the context of AI systems at work. Second, I examine some issues in the concept of human oversight outlined by Article 14 AI Act, particularly in light of the exception outlined in Article 5(1)(f) AI Act for AI systems used to detect, prevent, or respond to health and safety risks in the workplace.

5.1 The Vague Wording of Article 5(1)(b) and 5(1)(c) AI Act and of the Draft EU Commissions Guidelines

In Chapter 7 (section 5.1), I discussed how Article 5(1)(b) AI Act prohibits AI systems that exploit vulnerabilities associated with a person's age, disability, or socio-economic circumstances to significantly alter behaviour; I found that this provision does not mention employment contexts. The provision's vague language, combined with the Commission's draft guidelines, does not explicitly address how AI systems might exploit socio-economic vulnerabilities in employees, particularly in precarious employment situations.[825] Although the guidelines acknowledge AI-driven exploitation risks in areas like financial services and targeted advertising, they overlook how these systems might exploit employees in precarious conditions, particularly those in low-wage, insecure, or highly monitored jobs.[826] Given that the draft guidelines for Article 5(1)(b) already recognise the vulnerability of certain groups, such as migrants

824. *See* below section 5.1.
825. European Commission, 'Commission Guidelines on Prohibited Artificial Intelligence Practices Established by Regulation (EU) 2024/1689 (AI Act)' (n 667) 33-50.
826. *Ibid.*, 41.

and refugees, due to their unstable socio-economic conditions, this reasoning should in my view be explicitly extended in the guidelines to employees or workers who, by virtue of their employment conditions, face similar vulnerabilities.[827] This includes workers in the gig-economy, those on zero-hour contracts, or in highly monitored environments, such as warehouse or delivery jobs. In these contexts, AI systems may exploit employees' dependence on precarious work by dynamically assigning shifts or workloads and imposing penalties, such as automatic pay deductions for short breaks or minor deviations from algorithmic benchmarks.[828] These forms of monitoring, as argued already in both legal and sociological scholarship, exploit the power imbalance inherent in the employment relationship, particularly when workers and employees have limited alternatives or bargaining power.[829] I argue that such groups of vulnerable workers should fall within the protective scope of Article 5(1)(b), and that the Commission's guidelines should be revised by expanding this vulnerability category where there is evidence that intensive monitoring can foster forms of AI-driven exploitation. As I will further discuss in Chapter 9, the prohibitions set in the Platform Work Directive (PWD) could complement and steer the interpretation of Article 5(1)(b) AI Act and may lead to a potential update in the current draft guidelines.

Article 5(1)(c) AI Act prohibits the use of AI systems for social scoring, specifically when the AI systems evaluate or classify individuals based on their social behaviour, socio-economic status, or personal characteristics in ways that lead to unjust or disproportionate treatment. As I noted in Chapter 7 (section 5.2), the Commission's guidelines on this provision do not provide clear distinctions between what job-related and non-job-related information can be used by an AI system producing a social score at work, leaving room for overly broad interpretations of what constitutes permissible social scoring in the workplace. The guidelines, I noted in Chapter 7, only specify that social scores that lead to detrimental or unfavourable treatment in unrelated social contexts and/or unjustified or disproportionate treatment in relation to the gravity of the social behaviour are prohibited.[830] To enhance legal clarity and prevent misuse of social scoring systems in the workplace, the guidelines should explicitly exclude non-work-related data from the scope of relevant information. Examples of non-work-related data are personal social media activity, lifestyle choices, political opinions inferred from online activity, or algorithmically generated personality scores based on browsing history, none of which bear a direct connection to the employee's work performance.[831]

827. *Ibid.*, 38.
828. Seonok Lee, 'The "AI Mode": How Food Delivery Riders in the Netherlands and South Korea Experience Algorithmic Management' (2024) 17 Italian Labour Law e-Journal 67.
829. *Ibid.*; Heiland (n 402); Delfanti (n 337); Niels Van Doorn, 'Platform Labor: On the Gendered and Racialized Exploitation of Low-Income Service Work in the "On-Demand" Economy' (2017) 20 Information, Communication & Society 898 https://doi.org/10.1080/1369118x.2017.1294194 accessed 22 October 2025.
830. European Commission, 'Commission Guidelines on Prohibited Artificial Intelligence Practices Established by Regulation (EU) 2024/1689 (AI Act)' (n 667) 54-55.
831. On the relevance and effectiveness of performance metrics and how the law should take this into account in outlining safeguards and protections: Gould (n 14); Gould (n 339).

For example, an employer using an AI system that lowers an employee's rating or restricts shift allocation based on his or her participation in online forums or spending habits inferred from transaction data would be engaging in a form of social scoring that is not job-related and risks reinforcing socio-economic biases. These practices could result in unfair treatment and undermine employees' autonomy, especially when no clear link exists between the data used and the tasks performed. A more targeted and employment-specific interpretation in the guidelines would help clarify that AI-based evaluations must be strictly prescribed by the law, pursue a legitimate aim and be necessary and proportionate. The guidelines should therefore explicitly prohibit the use of AI systems that score employees based on inferred characteristics or aggregated behavioural profiles unrelated to the core duties of their job. This would better align the interpretation of Article 5(1)(c) with the AI Act's core objectives, as well as with the protection of employees' fundamental rights.

5.2 Employers' Capacity to Oversee Complex AI Systems: The Case of Article 5(1)(f) AI Act Exception

Further contributing to the uncertainties surrounding the AI Act, several labour law scholars question both the scope and practical effectiveness of some of the requirements imposed on high-risk AI systems.[832] In this subsection, I focus specifically on the human oversight obligation. Article 14 AI Act requires providers to design systems in a way that allows a natural person to interpret the system's outputs and to intervene, by halting the system, for example, when a risk or harm occurs. This conception of deployer control is reinforced in Article 26(5) AI Act, which enables deployers to participate in the post-market monitoring of AI systems.[833] However, as I briefly hinted in Chapter 4 (section 4) and Chapter 6 (section 4), employers may often lack the technical knowledge and information necessary to understand how these systems function. This structural information asymmetry may significantly impair their ability to exercise effective human oversight. Indeed, some AI systems, by design, can facilitate an illegitimate exercise of monitoring power in subtle ways that are not readily detectable by the employer. This raises critical concerns about whether the current oversight framework under the AI Act is sufficient in employment contexts

832. Mario Guglielmetti, 'Automated Work and Workers' Rights: Platform Work and AI Work Management Systems' in Aida Ponce Del Castillo (ed.), *Artificial Intelligence, Labour and Society* (European Trade Union Institute 2024) https://www.etui.org/publications/artificial-intelligence-labour-and-society accessed 22 October 2025; Aloisi and De Stefano, 'Between Risk Mitigation and Labour Rights Enforcement' (n 37); Aude Cefaliello and Miriam Kullmann, 'Offering False Security: How the Draft Artificial Intelligence Act Undermines Fundamental Workers Rights' (2022) 13 European Labour Law Journal 542 https://doi.org/10.1177/20319525221114474 accessed 22 October 2025; Jeremias Adams-Prassl, 'Regulating Algorithms at Work: Lessons for a "European Approach to Artificial Intelligence"' (2022) 13 European Labour Law Journal 30 https://doi.org/10.1177/20319525211062558 accessed 22 October 2025; Aida Ponce Del Castillo, 'The AI Regulation: Entering an AI Regulatory Winter?' (European Trade Union Institute 2021) https://www.etui.org/sites/default/files/2021-06/The%20AI%20Regulation.%20Entering%20an%20AI%20regulatory%20winter_2021.pdf accessed 22 October 2025.

833. Cf. with section 6.1.3, Chapter 7.

where the deployer is typically not the system developer and lacks meaningful access to its inner design and operation.

To illustrate these concerns, consider the case of *Driveri*,[834] an AI-powered camera used by companies such as Amazon to monitor the driving behaviour of employees.[835] This system can infer emotional or cognitive states (such as stress, distraction, or fatigue) through facial analysis and body language. Under Article 5(1)(f) AI Act, AI systems that infer emotions are generally prohibited when used to assess individuals in the workplace, educational institutions, or law enforcement. However, as I discussed in Chapter 7 (section 5.3), Article 5(1)(f) AI Act provides for an exception to the prohibition by allowing the use of these systems when necessary for health or safety purposes. In the case of *Driveri*, its purpose is to prevent accidents and improve driving performance, which may allow it to fall under this exception.[836]

Nevertheless, *Driveri* still qualifies as a high-risk system under Article 6 and Annex III of the AI Act, which include as high-risk 'AI systems intended to be used to make decisions affecting terms of work-related relationships, the promotion or termination of work-related contractual relationships, to allocate tasks based on individual behaviour or personal traits or characteristics or to monitor and evaluate the performance and behaviour of persons in such relationships' (Annex III, 4(b) AI Act). Once the system is deployed, among the other requirements,[837] Article 14 AI Act requires the deployer to be capable of recognising when the system poses risks or causes harm and to intervene, what Article 14(4)(e) AI Act describes as the ability to 'interrupt the system through a "stop" button or similar procedure that allows the system to come to a halt in a safe state'.

This requirement raises a critical question in relation to the *Driveri* case: does the AI system create clear and observable conditions that would enable the deployer, the employer, to recognise when employees are being harmed or when the system poses a disproportionate risk, thereby triggering the obligation to intervene under Article 14(4)(e) AI Act? Without such identifiable thresholds and without guidance on how to detect harm, the obligation to exercise human oversight may remain largely theoretical in practice.

I argue that a deployer will not always have a sufficient understanding to recognise a harm, simply because AI systems like *Driveri* introduce systematic monitoring that quietly over time instils in employees a feeling of insidious and secret control. *Driveri*, in fact, sends acoustic signals to the driver who takes a bottle of water from the beverage holder. Or sounds in case the driver's gaze is not exactly focused on the road according to the system's standards. It also signals if the road turned is not exactly the one indicated by the system. Systems such as *Driveri*, which are 'high-risk' according to the AI Act, propose a structurally rigid safety model.[838]

834. Netradyne (n 664).
835. Wood (n 15) 4.
836. Recital 18 AI Act further specifies that the ban on emotion is not applicable to 'physical states, such as pain or fatigue. It does not refer for example to systems used in detecting the state of fatigue of professional pilots or drivers for the purpose of preventing accidents'.
837. *See* section 6, Chapter 7, on the requirements of high-risk AI systems in employment contexts.
838. Wood (n 15) 4.

Over the years, numerous reports emerged that drivers were carrying out 'physiological needs' in bottles while driving.[839] They feared repercussions in the metrics generated by AI systems like *Driveri*. Therefore, they preferred to keep driving and deny themselves breaks. This phenomenon was not generated in an instant but rather by a layering over time. It became normalised as a practice over a long period of time. Employment contracts, being relational contracts,[840] concern a hierarchical collaboration between natural persons. When an AI system is introduced in such a hierarchical setting, it could put employees in a state of subjection.[841] In other words, the employee experiences this state of subjection as a permanent and necessary condition for the work itself. So, in a way, s(he) decides to cooperate with the surveillance technology.[842]

When a high-risk system is in use, it is difficult for the deployer to determine when it is time to hit the 'stop button'. It is also unclear how the provider of *Driveri* could materially verify the working conditions generated by the system after activation. Both will be very difficult in practice. Article 86 AI Act, which grants individuals the right to a meaningful explanation of the role played by high-risk AI systems in decisions that substantially impact their health, safety, or rights, will not address these practical difficulties and uncertainties.[843] In practice, many employers, such as small and medium-sized enterprises, lack the technical means, or contractual leverage, to meaningfully access or scrutinise complex AI systems developed by third-party providers.[844] Moreover, no third-party audits or employee representative consultations are required in the Regulation to verify how this human oversight is exercised by deployers once the system is deployed. As a result, accountability might become abstract and delayed, especially in dynamic work environments where harms build incrementally over time.

Building on my reflection in the previous section 5.1 regarding the need to update the Commission's guidelines on Article 5(1)(b) AI Act, I suggest that these forms of

839. BBC News, 'Amazon Apologises for Wrongly Denying Drivers Need to Urinate in Bottles' (4 April 2021) https://www.bbc.com/news/world-us-canada-56628745 accessed 22 October 2025; Palmer (n 308); UNI Global Union, 'Life in the Amazon Panopticon: An International Survey of Amazon Workers' (2023) https://uniglobalunion.org/report/amazon-panopticon-survey/ accessed 22 October 2025.

840. *See* discussion on employment contracts in Chapter 3, sections 2, 3, 4.

841. Delfanti (n 337); Phoebe V Moore, Martin Upchurch and Xanthe Whittaker (eds), *Humans and Machines at Work: Monitoring, Surveillance and Automation in Contemporary Capitalism* (1st edn, 2018, Springer International Publishing: Imprint: Palgrave Macmillan 2018); Maša Galič, Tjerk Timan and Bert-Jaap Koops, 'Bentham, Deleuze and Beyond: An Overview of Surveillance Theories from the Panopticon to Participation' (2017) 30 Philosophy & Technology 9 https://doi.org/10.1007/s13347-016-0219-1 accessed 22 October 2025; Lupton (n 291).

842. Cf. with the concept of 'self-quantification' developed by Deborah Lupton, 'The Diverse Domains of Quantified Selves: Self-Tracking Modes and Dataveillance' (2016) 45 Economy and Society 101 https://doi.org/10.1080/03085147.2016.1143726 accessed 22 October 2025.

843. Cf. with section 7, Chapter 7 on Article 86 AI Act.

844. Maria Da Conceição Freitas and Miguel Mira Da Silva, 'GDPR Compliance in SMEs: There Is Much to Be Done' (2018) 3 Journal of Information Systems Engineering & Management https://pdfs.semanticscholar.org/5976/4bd60d47803b6b2c9c6d0adc4a53550b539b.pdf accessed 22 October 2025.

intense AI and IoT-enabled monitoring could also be considered exploitative, particularly when they leverage the structural dependency of employees in precarious working conditions. The EU Commission's guidelines on Article 5(1)(f) AI Act state that, before implementing these systems, employers must consider whether less intrusive alternatives could achieve the same objectives. While this guideline offers a potential safeguard, the focus on alternatives does not fully address the systemic pressures that can evolve over time under an AI and IoT-enabled employer's monitoring power. Merely considering less intrusive alternatives overlooks the deeper issue: the profound power imbalance created by the pervasive nature of these systems. It fails to ensure adequate accountability for the impacts on employees' rights, dignity, and well-being. The Commission's approach may not go far enough and overlooks potential structural reforms that are necessary to protect employees against such an exercise of the employer's monitoring power.

In short, applying the risk-based approach provided for by the AI Act already poses important challenges. The AI Act lacks specific provisions that require employers, as deployers, to assess the systemic effects of AI and IoT-enabled technologies on employees. Without such a requirement, deployers are not explicitly obligated nor empowered to evaluate the implications of these technologies on employees' fundamental rights.

6 CONCLUSIONS

This chapter answered the research sub-question 7: *Can the GDPR and AI Act ensure the legitimate exercise of the AI and IoT-enabled employer's monitoring power?*

The analysis conducted in this chapter shows that the GDPR and the AI Act can, in principle, complement each other in certain areas. For instance, the AI Act introduces specific obligations for high-risk AI system providers (Articles 6, 8-27), including design, transparency, and human oversight requirements. These obligations could support employers in meeting their duties as data controllers under the GDPR, particularly in cases where AI and IoT-enabled technologies are integrated into workplace infrastructure by AI providers. In this sense, the AI Act may help fill some of the accountability and transparency gaps left by the GDPR, especially under Article 28(3) GDPR, which imposes only minimal obligations on processors. This creates a potential pathway for complementarity where processors' (lack of) responsibilities under the GDPR intersect with (stronger) providers' obligations under the AI Act (*see* next Chapter 9).

However, there are also areas where both the GDPR and AI Act are individually weak, and their combined application does little to strengthen employees' protection. A central example in this regard is the framework of individual rights. As shown in my analysis, data subject's rights under the GDPR (Articles 12-22) presuppose an autonomous and informed data subject, which does not reflect the structural dependencies and asymmetries in the employment context. Employees often lack the practical means or incentives to assert their rights, especially in environments where they fear job-related repercussions due to their subordination to the employer. Meanwhile, the

AI Act does not introduce any comparable rights for individuals subject to AI-based decision-making. Article 86 AI Act provides only a minimal transparency obligation and does not grant data subjects the right to object to AI system data processing or to avoid AI decisions altogether.[845] As a result, the protection of employees' individual rights remains weak under both frameworks, and their combination does not remedy this limitation.

Finally, there are further provisions where the weaknesses of both the GDPR and AI Act remain unresolved. Article 6 GDPR allows broad interpretations of lawful bases for processing, particularly when employers rely on the performance of a contract or legitimate interests to ground their processing of employees' data with AI and IoT-enabled technologies. These grounds could be stretched to cover practices that should require a stricter necessity and proportionality assessment. The AI Act, in this regard, does not provide any reference to the lawfulness of data processing with AI systems. On the AI Act side, Article 5(1) lists prohibited AI practices, but its vague wording - especially in points (b), (c), and (f) and related EC guidelines - offers limited clarity as to their scope. I noted how the EC guidelines should incorporate more specific elements for clarifying the scope of such prohibitions in the employment context.

Nevertheless, as noted several times throughout this chapter, the Data Protection Impact Assessment (DPIA) under Article 35 GDPR could be a promising tool to address these limitations in employee protection and uphold a legitimate exercise of the employer's monitoring power. This *ex ante* assessment explicitly requires a forward-looking, contextual, and risk-based assessment of data processing operations. It could facilitate, jointly with the AI Act requirements for high-risk AI systems, data controllers' compliance by requiring them to mitigate risks on employees' fundamental rights before deployment, thereby acting as a preventive tool that reduces the burden on individual employees to assert their rights after harm has occurred. In the next chapter, I will further explore the potential of this mechanism by examining how the DPIA, and other provisions in the current EU legal framework, could offer pathways to prevent an illegitimate exercise of an AI and IoT-enabled employer's monitoring power.

845. Cf. with section 7, Chapter 7.

CHAPTER 9

Existing Avenues Within the Current EU Legal Framework to Address an Illegitimate Exercise of the AI and IoT-Enabled Employer's Monitoring Power

1 INTRODUCTION

The aim of this chapter is to answer the research sub-question 8: *What pathways exist within the current EU legal framework to address an illegitimate exercise of the AI and IoT-enabled employer's monitoring power?* By illegitimate, I refer to forms of employer monitoring that fail to respect employees' fundamental rights, as defined in Chapter 3 (section 7).

The chapter is structured as follows. Section 2 examines the DPIA under Article 35 GDPR and its application alongside the requirements for high-risk AI systems to determine whether it can better equip employers in assessing and preventing risks in collaboration with AI providers. I focus on the DPIA and not the FRIA (Article 27 AI Act) since the latter has a limited scope, as it applies only to 'deployers that are bodies governed by public law, or are private entities providing public services' and certain high-risk systems, not including those for employee monitoring.[846] The DPIA, by contrast, is always applicable in this context because, as discussed in Chapter 6 (section 3.6), it is explicitly required when data processing is 'likely to result in a high

846. Article 27(1) AI Act: 'Prior to deploying a high-risk AI system referred to in Article 6(2), with the exception of high-risk AI systems intended to be used in the area listed in point 2 of Annex III, *deployers that are bodies governed by public law, or are private entities providing public services, and deployers of high-risk AI systems referred to in points 5 (b) and (c) of Annex III,* shall perform an assessment of the impact on fundamental rights that the use of such system may produce.' Emphasis added. *See also* the discussion relating to the FRIA in section 6.2.3, Chapter 7.

risk to the rights and freedoms of natural persons',[847] a requirement met by AI and IoT-enabled technologies monitoring employees. I will explore whether this combined framework offers a more structured approach to preventing an illegitimate exercise of employers' monitoring power.

In section 3, I explore a further possible pathway in the current EU legal framework. I examine the potential for national labour laws, specifically those adopted under Article 88 GDPR, to function as an additional legal avenue for addressing an illegitimate exercise of the AI and IoT-enabled employer's monitoring power. I focus on a decision from the French DPA in 2023, where Article 88(3) GDPR was interpreted in conjunction with national labour law to restrict illegitimate employee monitoring practices.[848] This case study illustrates how the interaction between the GDPR and specific labour law protections can strengthen safeguards for employees' fundamental rights.

In section 4, I consider the recent adoption of the Platform Work Directive (2024) and reflect on how certain provisions offer valuable reference points for developing more tailored regulation of employee monitoring at the EU level. Finally, section 5 concludes the chapter by answering the research sub-question 8.

2 PREVENTING AN ILLEGITIMATE EXERCISE OF THE EMPLOYER'S MONITORING POWER: STRENGTHENING THE DPIA THROUGH THE AI ACT AND THE ROLE FOR EMPLOYEES' REPRESENTATIVES

In this section, I build on the analysis from Chapter 8, section 4, by examining whether and how certain provisions of the GDPR, when integrated with the AI Act's obligations for high-risk AI systems,[849] can help address the challenges previously identified in ensuring the legitimate exercise of the employer's monitoring power. More specifically, the AI Act requirements for high-risk AI systems (*see* section 6, Chapter 7) could enhance the DPIA's process (Article 35 GDPR, *see* section 3.6, Chapter 6) by introducing additional transparency and documentation duties for AI providers towards employers. I analyse whether such an enhanced DPIA can prevent an illegitimate exercise of the employer's monitoring power. Moreover, the DPIA's involvement of employees' representatives under Article 35(9) GDPR gains further significance when these representatives are empowered to scrutinise the risk assessments and documentation produced under the AI Act. Their involvement may be reinforced through Articles 77 and 80 GDPR, which enable data subjects and their representatives to lodge complaints with supervisory authorities and act on their behalf.

847. Article 35(1) GDPR. *See also* Recital 75 GDPR.
848. *Délibération de la formation restreinte n°SAN-2023-021 du 27 décembre 2023 concernant la société AMAZON FRANCE LOGISTIQUE*; Molè, 'Minimised Work Surveillance Exists under the GDPR: Amazon France and the DPA Sanction' (n 421).
849. Cf. with section 6, Chapter 7, on the requirements for high-risk AI systems in the AI Act.

2.1 How the AI Act Enhances the GDPR's DPIA

The AI Act reduces the informational asymmetry that typically exists between employers (as deployers) and technology providers (as processors) by requiring providers of high-risk AI systems to document and disclose key information. This includes details about the system's intended purpose, technical capabilities, risk management processes, and performance metrics (Articles 6, 9-15 AI Act).

Article 26(9) AI Act reinforces the connection between these requirements and the DPIA process by providing that deployers of high-risk AI systems shall use the information provided under Article 13 AI Act to comply with their obligation to carry out a DPIA under Article 35 GDPR.[850] While the AI Act itself mandates a Fundamental Rights Impact Assessment (FRIA, Article 27 AI Act), this applies only to public law entities or private companies providing public services. This leaves a substantial portion of private companies outside the FRIA's scope, whereas the DPIA would be applicable in most employment contexts when AI and IoT-enabled technologies are deployed to monitor employees.[851]

An employer implementing AI and IoT-enabled technologies and conducting a DPIA benefits from Article 11 AI Act ('Technical Documentation'), which requires providers to prepare comprehensive technical documentation detailing how the AI system complies with the relevant EU legal frameworks, including the AI Act, GDPR, and EU Regulation 2019/1020 on product safety. This documentation must explain the functionality of the logging system, with Article 12(3) AI Act ('Record-keeping') specifying the required content of logs. These logs must record the duration of each system use (start and end times), the reference database employed, the specific input data that triggered a match, and, crucially, the identification of individuals affected by the AI output. Furthermore, Article 13 AI Act ('Transparency and provision of information to deployers') obliges processor-providers to deliver this information to employer-deployers in an intelligible format. This includes clear instructions for system use, its intended purpose, accuracy metrics, potential risks, and human oversight measures, as outlined in Article 14 AI Act ('Human oversight'). Consequently, employers can base their DPIA on clearly defined, detailed, and reliable information that providers are mandated to share under the AI Act.

The transfer of information from the provider to the deployer can ensure that the employer's *ex ante* assessment is grounded in detailed data from the provider.[852]

850. Article 26(9) AI Act: 'Where applicable, deployers of high-risk AI systems shall use the information provided under Article 13 of this Regulation to comply with their obligation to carry out a data protection impact assessment under Article 35 of Regulation (EU) 2016/679 or Article 27 of Directive (EU) 2016/680.' *See also*: Gallagher (n 703).

851. Article 27(1) AI Act: ' Prior to deploying a high-risk AI system referred to in Article 6(2), with the exception of high-risk AI systems intended to be used in the area listed in point 2 of Annex III, deployers that are bodies governed by public law, or are private entities providing public services, and deployers of high-risk AI systems referred to in points 5 (b) and (c) of Annex III, shall perform an assessment of the impact on fundamental rights that the use of such system may produce.' *See also* section 1 of this chapter and section 6.2.3 of Chapter 7.

852. Joanna Mazur, 'Artificial Intelligence vs Data Protection: How the GDPR Can Help to Develop a Precautionary Regulatory Approach to AI?' in Angelos Kornilakis et al. (eds), *Artificial*

Through the combined application of Articles 11-14 AI Act and Article 35 GDPR, employers are better equipped to conduct an impact assessment of the 'high-risk' processing activities they implement and to outline the necessary measures to prevent any harm to employees. This improved access to information creates the conditions under which such an assessment can be meaningfully conducted.

Furthermore, the involvement of employees' representatives and DPOs in the DPIA introduces a co-monitored process. This fosters an environment in which different and potentially conflicting interests are brought to the table. Such a participatory framework can mitigate the risk that the DPIA becomes a check-box exercise and can serve as an ongoing mechanism for employees' representatives and DPOs to determine and later monitor whether the measures envisaged in the DPIA are properly implemented; and to scrutinise how employers interpret the legal bases such as Article 6(1)(b) and (f) GDPR, i.e., when the processing is necessary for the performance of a contract or for the purposes of the legitimate interests pursued by the controller.[853] This creates a meaningful opportunity to represent the interests of data subjects and potentially challenge the employer's reliance on legal grounds where they are considered to have been incorrectly interpreted in relation to the specific data processing pursued by the employer.

In section 2.3, I will expand on how this co-monitoring process is strengthened through the involvement of employees' representatives. In the next section (2.2), I focus specifically on how the employer's legitimate interests and employees' fundamental rights should be balanced under Article 35(7) GDPR.

2.2 Impact Assessments: Relevant Normative Framework

In this analysis of the DPIA as a tool enhanced by the AI Act, it is appropriate to examine what normative framework employers must draw from in assessing the legitimacy of the exercise of their AI and IoT-enabled monitoring power. The DPIA Article 35(7)(c) GDPR provides that the data controller shall take into account 'the rights and legitimate interests of data subjects'. By referring to any right and legitimate interest pertaining to data subjects, I suggest that the DPIA mandates the employer to consider any domestic labour law and the EU social acquis relating to employees' fundamental rights.

Intelligence and Normative Challenges, vol 59 (Springer International Publishing 2023) https://link.springer.com/10.1007/978-3-031-41081-9_12 accessed 22 October 2025.

853. For instance, the Italian DPA, in November 2024, found that the company Foodinho had incorrectly assessed in DPIA the legal basis for processing biometric data, such as facial recognition, in the context of employment. Although the company claimed contractual necessity and compliance with labour obligations under Article 9(2)(b) of the GDPR, these justifications were deemed insufficient. Neither collective agreements nor informal protocols can replace the requirement for a specific legal basis under national or EU law, especially when processing sensitive data like biometrics. As a result, the data processing was found unlawful, and the impact assessment failed to properly evaluate the lawfulness of the processing activities. Garante per la Protezione dei Dati Personali, 'Provvedimento Del 13 Novembre 2024 [10074601]' (13 November 2024) https://www.garanteprivacy.it/web/guest/home/docweb/-/docweb-display/docweb/10074601 accessed 22 October 2025.

The impact assessment serves as a reflective instrument that enables data controllers to evaluate and document the risks that data processing poses to fundamental rights at work, as well as to labour law protections (*see* the DPIA requirements in section 3.6, Chapter 6). These include rights enshrined in the ECHR and the CFREU,[854] along with those set out in EU Directives and corresponding national laws on working conditions, equal treatment, information and consultation, platform work, and OSH.[855] Under this interpretation, employers must consider not only the European fundamental rights framework but also employees' rights under domestic labour laws, collective agreements, and other relevant EU social legislation when deploying AI and IoT-enabled technologies in the workplace. This obligation reflects a comprehensive approach, requiring employers to integrate both data protection and labour law considerations into the DPIA process.

Article 35(7)(b) further requires the data controller to assess 'the necessity and proportionality of the processing operations in relation to the purposes'. Provided that the DPIA, complemented with the AI Act requirements, enables the data controller to gain a deeper understanding of a surveillance technology, (s)he is able to conduct a detailed balancing of the impact of the processing on employees' rights versus the employer's legitimate interests. In this regard, the adoption of an AI and IoT-enabled technology for employee monitoring should lead to a systematic consideration of fundamental rights at work and other applicable standards.

Conducting a DPIA must therefore substantiate that the enjoyment of fundamental rights is not compromised, particularly in an environment where the use of surveillance technologies is increasingly normalised. Opinion 01/2014 of the WP29 supports this view by stressing the need for a harmonious and comprehensive look at fundamental rights,[856] being:

> Necessary to assess how the new measure would add to the existing ones and whether all of them taken together would still proportionately limit the fundamental rights of data protection and privacy.[857]

This suggests that an individual DPIA for each adopted AI and IoT-enabled technology might be insufficient on its own. Instead, the DPIA should adopt a holistic approach, considering all technologies and measures in use together. By doing so, the cumulative impact of these technologies on employees' rights (such as privacy, non-discrimination, freedom of assembly and association, and freedom of expression)

---

854. Michele Molè, 'The Quest For Effective Fundamental Labour Rights in the European Post-Pandemic Scenario: Introducing Principles of Explainability and Understanding for Surveillance Through AI Algorithms and IoT Devices' [2022] University of Groningen Faculty of Law Research Paper No 26/2022 https://www.ssrn.com/abstract=4099663 accessed 22 October 2025.
855. I further discuss this idea in: Molè, 'The Internet of Things and Artificial Intelligence as Workplace Supervisors' (n 401).
856. A Belden Fields and Wolf-Dieter Narr, 'Human Rights as a Holistic Concept' (1992) 14 Human Rights Quarterly 1, 3 https://doi.org/10.2307/762549 accessed 22 October 2025.
857. Article 29 Data Protection Working Party, 'Opinion 01/2014 on the Application of Necessity and Proportionality Concepts and Data Protection within the Law Enforcement Sector' (2014) 21 https://ec.europa.eu/justice/article-29/documentation/opinion-recommendation/files/2014/wp211_en.pdf accessed 22 October 2025.

can be fully evaluated. Even if each individual technology deployed appears justified and proportionate when assessed in isolation, their combined effect may nonetheless lead to a gradual erosion of fundamental rights, potentially undermining the essence of those rights in practice. This concern has been increasingly recognised in the literature on mass surveillance, which warns against a fragmented legal approach that fails to account for systemic risks arising from the totality of intrusive measures.[858]

If the combination of these technologies undermines these rights, the DPIA should reflect these risks and outline measures to mitigate them. To ensure that this proper balancing is carried out by employers, I suggest that employees' representatives and Data Protection Authorities should – with different roles – actively check the drafting and outputs of the DPIAs. I explore these aspects in the next sections.

2.3 Empowering Employees' Representatives: Using Articles 77 and 80(1) GDPR to Address Violations in the DPIA Process

In section 3.1 of Chapter 8 ('Who is the data subject in the GDPR'), I argued that the GDPR does not allow employees' representatives to exercise data subject's rights (Articles 12-22 GDPR), unless explicitly provided for by Member States' laws (Article 80(2) GDPR). The Regulation consistently centres on safeguarding individual rights and interests. Besides this limitation, which weakens collective actions under the GDPR, I contend that Article 80(1) GDPR ('Representation of data subjects')[859] offers a valuable tool for employees' representatives to lodge complaints to the DPA under Article 77 GDPR ('Right to lodge a complaint with a supervisory authority') after the completion (or missed completion) of a DPIA.[860] This approach, together with Article 35(9) GDPR, enables employees' representatives to oversee and act on the implementation of the mitigating measures identified in the DPIA.

More specifically, I argue that while Article 77 GDPR applies to complaints concerning ongoing data processing, a failure to carry out or properly implement a DPIA before processing begins – especially when required, such as for the case of

858. Carolin Kaiser, 'Privacy and Identity Issues in Financial Transactions: The Proportionality of the European Anti-money Laundering Legislation' (University of Grioningen 2018) 577 https://research.rug.nl/en/publications/privacy-and-identity-issues-in-financial-transactions-the-proport accessed 22 October 2025.

859. Article 80(1) GDPR: 'The data subject shall have the right to mandate a not-for-profit body, organisation or association which has been properly constituted in accordance with the law of a Member State, has statutory objectives which are in the public interest, and is active in the field of the protection of data subjects' rights and freedoms with regard to the protection of their personal data to lodge the complaint on his or her behalf, to exercise the rights referred to in Articles 77, 78 and 79 on his or her behalf, and to exercise the right to receive compensation referred to in Article 82 on his or her behalf where provided for by Member State law.'

860. Article 77 GDPR: 'Without prejudice to any other administrative or judicial remedy, every data subject shall have the right to lodge a complaint with a supervisory authority, in particular in the Member State of his or her habitual residence, place of work or place of the alleged infringement if the data subject considers that the processing of personal data relating to him or her infringes this Regulation. The supervisory authority with which the complaint has been lodged shall inform the complainant on the progress and the outcome of the complaint including the possibility of a judicial remedy pursuant to Article 78.'

employee monitoring – can still justify a complaint under Article 77 GDPR, as it constitutes a procedural violation with substantive consequences. If the DPIA process is not adequately conducted, or if employees' representatives are not consulted as required under Article 35(9) GDPR, this undermines the ability to assess and mitigate risks in advance, thus compromising the lawfulness and legitimacy of the subsequent processing. The employer, accountable also under Articles 24 and 25 GDPR, is required to ensure both proactive compliance and the implementation of appropriate safeguards prior to processing. When the mitigating measures identified through the DPIA are not adopted beforehand, this omission can directly expose employees to risks or infringements on their fundamental rights – risks the DPIA is specifically intended to prevent.[861]

Thus, although Article 77 is concerned with violations arising in the course of data processing, procedural breaches that occur prior to processing – such as failing to complete a DPIA or disregarding its prescribed safeguards once the processing starts – can still fall within its scope due to their downstream effects on rights and freedoms of employees.[862] In such cases, employees' representatives may invoke Article 80(1) GDPR to act on behalf of the data subjects, demanding that the employer fulfils its pre-processing obligations. This empowers representatives to ensure that the necessary mitigating measures identified in the DPIA are not only formalised but also effectively implemented before data processing begins.

Ultimately, under Articles 77 and 80 GDPR, employees' representatives could file complaints against employers for failing to properly conduct the DPIA or failing to adopt the mitigating measures, or for failing to comply with other obligations, such as those outlined in Articles 6, 24, and 25 GDPR. They could also challenge risks they believe are inadequately mitigated by employers in the light of the information received through Articles 8-15 AI Act. These collective complaints could hold employers accountable for breaches of their duties as data controllers, reinforced by the AI Act's obligations. This approach not only ensures compliance but also allows for an ongoing monitoring of AI and IoT-enabled technologies during their operation. By monitoring these systems over time in relation to the DPIA findings, employee representatives can

861. Waltraut Kotschy, 'Article 77 Right to Lodge a Complaint with a Supervisory Authority' in Christopher Kuner et al. (eds), *The EU General Data Protection Regulation (GDPR)* (Oxford University Press, New York 2020) https://academic.oup.com/book/41324/chapter/352304824 accessed 22 October 2025.

862. The Italian DPA in its decision of 13 November 2024 fined the company *Foodinho* EUR 5,000,000 for being non-compliant with Article 35 of the GDPR (among others, GDPR's obligations and principles). The DPA found that the DPIA failed to properly assess the lawfulness of processing biometric data within the employment context and wrongly relied on inappropriate legal bases such as contractual necessity. Moreover, the DPIA did not sufficiently address the high-risks posed by automated decision-making systems and profiling used to manage a large number of vulnerable data subjects (riders). The DPA also noted that an updated DPIA submitted during the proceedings did not cover key risks, such as disconnection from the platform and order allocation, thus falling short of the regulatory requirements. For the full-text of the DPA decision: Garante per la Protezione dei Dati Personali, 'Provvedimento Del 13 Novembre 2024 [10074601]' (n 853).

actively oversee whether these systems comply with applicable standards/mitigating measures also during the data processing. These actors are thus able to identify if new measures are necessary or if infringements have occurred.[863]

2.4 Connecting DPIA, AI Act, and Employees' Representatives Within the Framework Agreement on Digitalisation

This joint application of the GDPR and AI Act in the DPIA context, I suggest, aligns with the objectives of the 2020 European Framework Agreement on Digitalisation by the European Social Partners, which underscores the need for transparency, accountability, and the active involvement of employees' representatives in the governance of digital transformation processes.[864]

This framework agreement is binding for the EU social partners who have signed it, and provides for a supervisory role for employees' representatives in the introduction of new technologies in the workplace. It advocates for technology development in the workplace that benefits all stakeholders, emphasising an employee-centric approach rather than solely focusing on business needs.[865] In addition to these principles, the European social partners have launched various initiatives to equip their representatives for negotiating the implementation of AI in the workplace.[866] These include, for instance, public databases of collective agreements regulating the introduction of digital tools for employees' management and monitoring in order to share best practices among representatives of employees across Europe.[867] I suggest that the DPIA and AI Act reinforce the principles laid down in the Agreement. The latter, in fact, envisions strategies to ensure equitable participation and awareness-raising measures that empower employees and their representatives to engage in bargaining over how employers exercise their AI and IoT-enabled monitoring power.[868]

By embedding these commitments into the DPIA process, employers not only fulfil their legal obligations under GDPR and the AI Act but also foster a collaborative approach to digital transformation as sought by the Agreement. The DPIA, in this way, not only protects employees' rights and supports employers' compliance but also

863. In the case of *Foodinho*, the DPA highlighted the need for ongoing oversight to ensure that employee monitoring systems comply with applicable data protection standards and that new measures, thus new DPIA, are introduced if risks evolve or infringements are identified. *ibid.*
864. 'European Social Partners Framework Agreement on Digitalisation' (European Social Partners (ETUC, BusinessEurope, SMEunited, CEEP)) 2020) https://www.businesseurope.eu/publications/european-social-partners-framework-agreement-digitalisation accessed 22 October 2025.
865. Iacopo Senatori, 'The European Framework Agreement on Digitalisation: A Whiter Shade of Pale?' (2020) 13 Italian Labour Law e-Journal 159.
866. Guidelines for negotiators: UNI Europa, 'AI and Algorithmic Management in European Services Sectors' (Friedrich Ebert Stiftung 2024) https://www.uni-europa.org/wp-content/uploads/sites/3/2024/03/CollectiveBargainingPracticesOnAI_final.pdf accessed 22 October 2025. *See*, among others, the English Trade Unions Congress on AI at work: Trade Union Congress (n 73).
867. De Stefano (n 38); De Stefano and Taes (n 38).
868. Senatori (n 865).

fosters collaborative governance over the digital transition in the workplace.[869] By requiring consultation and transparency, it encourages joint deliberation over how monitoring technologies are introduced and used. This approach can help balance potentially conflicting interests by promoting monitoring measures that respect employees' rights and by fostering cooperation between staff and management.[870] A stronger involvement of employees' representatives in the DPIA also has the potential to establish a common practice at the EU level regarding collective bargaining on the introduction of new technologies in the workplace.

3 THE ADDED VALUE OF NATIONAL LABOUR LAWS IN CONJUNCTION WITH ARTICLE 88 GDPR: ANOTHER AVENUE FOR ADDRESSING AN ILLEGITIMATE EXERCISE OF THE EMPLOYER'S MONITORING POWER

In this section, I explore an additional avenue – complementary to the one discussed in section 2 – for addressing an illegitimate exercise of an AI and IoT-enabled employer's monitoring power. Specifically, I focus on the integration of national labour law standards through Article 88 GDPR, which I discussed in Chapter 6 (section 3.7). This integration enhances the interpretation and application of the GDPR alongside labour law protection provisions present in EU Member States. I illustrate the potential strength of this interaction using the December 2023 case involving Amazon France and the French DPA. This case highlights the value of Member States notifying to the EU Commission their more specific legislation or collective agreements under Article 88(3) GDPR to enable such integration.[871]

From 2019 onwards, the French DPA conducted inspections at Amazon facilities to verify the company's claim of a legitimate interest in monitoring the performance of warehouse employees.[872] The DPA inspected Amazon's warehouses under a French law on data processing, files, and freedoms[873] and Article 58(1)(f) GDPR, which grants DPAs the power to access all premises of the data controller and processor, including all data processing tools and means, in accordance with Union law or Member State

869. Silvia Rainone and Antonio Aloisi, 'Time to Deliver? Assessing the Action Plan on the European Pillar of Social Rights' (European Trade Union Institute (ETUI) 2021) https://www.etui.org/publications/time-deliver accessed 22 October 2025.
870. On the trade union's role in improving businesses organisations and competitiveness, *see*: Richard B Freeman and James L Medoff, *What Do Unions Do?* (Basic Books 1992). *See also*: Niels Jansen, '2. Decentralised Bargaining and the Role of Law' in Frank Tros (ed.), *Pathways in Decentralised Collective Bargaining in Europe* (Amsterdam University Press 2023) 55 https://www.degruyter.com/document/doi/10.1515/9789048560240-002/html accessed 22 October 2025.
871. Article 88(3) GDPR: 'Member State shall notify to the Commission those provisions of its law which it adopts pursuant to paragraph 1, by 25 May 2018 and, without delay, any subsequent amendment affecting them.'
872. *See* as overview: Molè, 'Minimised Work Surveillance Exists under the GDPR: Amazon France and the DPA Sanction' (n 421); Abraha, 'Automated Monitoring in the Workplace and the Search for a New Legal Framework: Lessons from Germany and Beyond' (n 738).
873. Articles 19-23 of Law No 78-17 of 6 January 1978, relating to data processing, files, and freedoms.

procedural law. Following the administrative procedure, concluded on 27 December 2023, the DPA fined Amazon France EUR 32 million for violations of Articles 5, 6, 12, 13, and 32 GDPR.[874] The DPA found that the surveillance technologies used by Amazon France placed excessive pressure on warehouse employees by continuously tracking detailed performance metrics, such as idle time between tasks or scanning speed, at an unnecessarily granular level. This form of monitoring went beyond what was strictly necessary for the stated purpose of performance evaluation, thereby violating the data minimisation principle under Article 5(1)(c) GDPR. According to this principle, employers must ensure that the personal data collected are adequate, relevant, and limited to what is necessary in relation to the purposes for which they are processed. The DPA also found that Amazon had failed to demonstrate a legitimate interest under Article 6(1)(f) GDPR that could justify such an intrusive level of monitoring.[875]

In reaching these conclusions, the DPA relied both on its inspection powers under Article 58 GDPR and on the application of more specific national provisions governing data processing in the employment context, as envisaged by Article 88 GDPR. The DPA analysed the absence of legitimate interest under Article 6(1)(f) GDPR in conjunction with the French *Code du travail* (Article L1121-1) and the case law of the *Cour de Cassation*, which states that the restriction of individual or collective rights can only be justified in proportion to the nature of the tasks performed.[876] The reference by the DPA to Article L1121-1 *Code du travail* is not coincidental: this very article was notified to the European Commission in 2018 as a more specific and suitable law applicable to personal data processing in employment relationships, under Article 88(3) GDPR. Thus, the DPA, although not explicitly referring to it in the decision, relied on Article 88 GDPR as a useful provision to promote integration between the Regulation and French labour law.[877]

This case illustrates how the interaction between the GDPR and national labour law standards can strengthen the safeguards against illegitimate exercises of the employer's monitoring power. Rather than relying solely on the GDPR, this integrated approach enhances the effectiveness of its provisions by grounding them in labour law principles that are better attuned to the specificities of the employment context. By inspecting workplaces and referring to labour law regulations, the French DPA checked the data processing and organisational model (Article 58 GDPR) and applied data protection and labour law standards accordingly (thus, in this case, Articles 5, 6 GDPR, Article L1121-1 *Code du travail* via Article 88(3) GDPR). This shows the importance, I conclude, of having EU Member States notifying relevant labour law norms under Article 88(3) GDPR to improve the protection of labour rights.

874. Gruet (n 756).
875. *Délibération de la formation restreinte n°SAN-2023-021 du 27 décembre 2023 concernant la société AMAZON FRANCE LOGISTIQUE* (n 848) para. 168.
876. *Ibid.*, 58. *See also* the French *Cour de Cassation* case mentioned in the DPA decision: Cass. Soc., 23 June 2021, n. 19-13.856. Available at: https://www.legifrance.gouv.fr/juri/id/JURITEXT000043711120, accessed 22 October 2025.
877. Michele Molè, 'Surveiller et Punir: Amazon Francia e La Sanzione Del Garante Dei Dati per La Sorveglianza "Intrusiva e Pressante" Dei Suoi Magazzinieri' (2024) 34 Diritto delle Relazioni Industriali 553.

4 LOOKING AHEAD: THE PLATFORM WORK DIRECTIVE AS A BLUEPRINT FOR TAILORED EU LEGISLATION ON EMPLOYEE MONITORING

Before concluding this chapter, I examine the Platform Work Directive (PWD) as a valuable legislative precedent – one that could inspire future tailored EU legislation on employee monitoring.[878] As I noted in Chapter 1, section 5.3, the scope of the PWD is limited to digital labour platforms and those engaged in platform work, as defined in Article 1 PWD. Therefore, it does not apply to employees in standard employment relationships. While currently limited to platform workers, the PWD offers useful insights for the regulation of employee monitoring. In force since 1 December 2024, the PWD grants specific rights to platform workers affected by, among others, 'automated monitoring systems'.[879] In fact, in Chapter III 'Algorithmic Management' (Articles 7-15), the Directive regulates the use of automated monitoring systems and 'automated decision-making systems'[880] in the specific domain of platform work.

A central provision in the PWD is Article 7, which sets out targeted limitations on the types of personal data that digital labour platforms may process through automated monitoring systems or automated decision-making systems. This provision reflects a strong normative stance against intrusive data processing, which addresses many of the issues highlighted in Chapters 5 and 8 of this book. More specifically, Article 7(1)(a) PWD prohibits platforms from processing personal data related to a worker's emotional or psychological state,[881] therefore providing for a ban on emotion recognition systems without problematic exceptions as it is the case for Article 5(1)(f) AI Act.[882] It also prohibits monitoring of private communications in Article 7(1)(b) PWD,[883] including exchanges with other workers or their representatives, thereby safeguarding not only privacy but also the possibility of organising and mutual support. If applied to standard employment relationships, this provision could potentially

878. Directive (EU) 2024/2831 of the European Parliament and of the Council of 23 October 2024 on improving working conditions in platform work.

879. Article 2(1)(h) PWD ('Definitions'): '"automated monitoring systems" means systems which are used for or which support monitoring, supervising or evaluating, by electronic means, the work performance of persons performing platform work or the activities carried out within the work environment, including by collecting personal data'.

880. Article 2(1)(i) PWD ('Definitions'): '"automated decision-making systems" means systems which are used to take or support, by electronic means, decisions that significantly affect persons performing platform work, including the working conditions of platform workers, in particular decisions affecting their recruitment, their access to and the organisation of work assignments, their earnings, including the pricing of individual assignments, their safety and health, their working time, their access to training, their promotion or its equivalent, and their contractual status including the restriction, suspension or termination of their account'.

881. Article 7(1)(a) PWD: 'Digital labour platforms shall not, by means of automated monitoring systems or automated decision-making systems (...) process any personal data on the emotional or psychological state of a person performing platform work.'

882. Cf. with section 5.2 in Chapter 8 and section 5.3 in Chapter 7 on Article 5(1)(f) AI Act concerning the prohibition of AI systems for emotion recognition in employment contexts.

883. Article 7(1)(b): 'Digital labour platforms shall not, by means of automated monitoring systems or automated decision-making systems (...) process any personal data in relation to private conversations, including exchanges with other persons performing platform work and the representatives of persons performing platform work.'

prevent the violation of the freedom of expression, assembly and association by AI and IoT-enabled technologies, as I found in Chapter 5.[884] Furthermore, Article 7(1)(c) PWD establishes that digital labour platforms may not collect personal data when a worker is not actively offering or performing platform work.[885] This provision introduces a clear temporal boundary for lawful monitoring, limiting data collection to periods of actual work activity. Transposed to the standard employment context, this restriction could serve as a valuable safeguard against an illegitimate exercise of an AI and IoT-enabled employer's monitoring power, particularly in remote or hybrid working arrangements.[886] While exceptions may be necessary – such as when monitoring outside working hours is essential for specific security or compliance purposes, or in results-oriented roles not tied to fixed schedules – the underlying principle of such a provision could be that employers should not use AI or IoT-enabled technologies to intrude into employees' private lives. By clearly delimiting the timeframe during which monitoring may occur, such a rule would strengthen the protection of employees' fundamental right to privacy.[887]

In terms of predictive analytics,[888] Article 7(1)(d) PWD bans the processing of data to forecast whether a worker will exercise fundamental rights – such as joining a trade union, engaging in collective bargaining, or participating in workplace consultations.[889] This article, jointly with Article 7(1)(b) PWD, could be particularly significant also in standard employment, as it addresses the risk that AI-driven profiling could be used to deter or penalise employees for engaging in collective action. Finally, Article 7(1)(e) PWD explicitly bans the inference or use of particularly sensitive attributes – such as racial or ethnic origin, political or religious beliefs, health conditions, or sexual orientation[890] – as well as, in Article 7(1)(f) PWD, the use of biometric data for identity verification via comparison with existing biometric databases.[891] In doing so, the

884. More specifically, in sections 2.1.1 and 2.3.2 of Chapter 5.
885. Article 7(1)(c) PWD: 'Digital labour platforms shall not, by means of automated monitoring systems or automated decision-making systems (...) collect any personal data of a person performing platform work while that person is not offering or performing platform work.'
886. Aloisi and De Stefano, 'Essential Jobs, Remote Work and Digital Surveillance' (n 11); Ben Laker et al., 'How to Monitor Remote Workers: Ethically' (*MIT Sloan Management Review*, 20 November 2020).
887. Cf. with sections 2.1.1, 2.2.1, 2.3.1 of Chapter 5.
888. This is one of the main features of AI systems. *See* in this regard sections 2.1 and 4.2 of Chapter 4.
889. Article 7(1)(d) PWD: 'Digital labour platforms shall not, by means of automated monitoring systems or automated decision-making systems (...) process personal data to predict the exercise of fundamental rights, including the freedom of association, the right of collective bargaining and action or the right to information and consultation as laid down in the Charter.'
890. Article 7(1)(e) PWD: 'Digital labour platforms shall not, by means of automated monitoring systems or automated decision-making systems (...) process any personal data to infer the racial or ethnic origin, migration status, political opinions, religious or philosophical beliefs, disability, state of health, including chronic disease or HIV status, emotional or psychological state, trade union membership, sex life or sexual orientation.'
891. Article 7(1)(f) PWD: 'Digital labour platforms shall not, by means of automated monitoring systems or automated decision-making systems (...) process any biometric data, as defined in Article 4, point (14), of Regulation (EU) 2016/679, of a person performing platform work to establish that person's identity by comparing that data to stored biometric data of natural persons in a database.'

Directive offers a model of sector-specific data protection tailored to the vulnerabilities of platform workers, which however could be of benefit also for standard employment relationships.

I argue that this set of prohibitions addresses employees' fundamental rights violations in standard employment contexts when AI and IoT-enabled technologies for employee monitoring are deployed; hence, this approach could be instructive for a broader legislative initiative on employee monitoring across the EU, as already proposed by Adam-Prassl and others in a Blueprint for the regulation of algorithmic management in the EU.[892]

These restrictions apply from the beginning of the recruitment or selection procedure and extend beyond automated monitoring or decision-making systems to all automated systems that take or support decisions affecting workers.[893] Article 8 PWD reinforces these safeguards by requiring digital labour platforms to carry out a DPIA, as mandated under Article 35 GDPR. This assessment must identify, evaluate, and mitigate risks linked to the use of automated systems, ensuring that workers' rights and interests are properly considered before such systems are deployed.[894] The explicit requirement to conduct a DPIA for digital labour platforms, I suggest, further supports my stance (which could be explicitly adopted in future legislation applicable to subordinate employment) for a more central role in the DPIA for preventing and monitoring compliance with data protection and fundamental rights standards.[895]

Article 9 PWD builds on this by establishing strong transparency obligations: platforms must clearly inform workers and their representatives about the operation of automated systems, including the logic involved, the significance of decisions taken or supported by these systems, and the potential consequences for workers.[896] Articles 10 and 11 PWD require respectively meaningful human oversight and human review over the operation of automated monitoring systems. Therefore, platforms are obliged to regularly review the effects of automated decisions, particularly in relation to working conditions and rights. They must also provide workers with timely explanations and accessible channels to contest and seek redress for decisions that negatively affect them.[897] Finally, Articles 12 to 14 PWD broaden the regulatory focus to include OSH and participatory governance. These provisions require platforms to assess how algorithmic management may pose risks to workers' physical and mental health, to engage workers' representatives in decision-making processes concerning the use of such technologies (by referring to the EU Directives on information and consultation), and to ensure workers are kept informed about any relevant changes or risks in their working environment.[898]

892. Adams-Prassl et al. (n 39).
893. Article 7(2) and (3) PWD.
894. Article 8 PWD ('Data-protection impact assessment').
895. *See* section 2 of this chapter.
896. Article 9 PWD ('Transparency with regard to automated monitoring systems and automated decision-making systems').
897. Article 10 PWD ('Human oversight of automated monitoring systems and automated decision-making systems'); Article 11 PWD ('Human review').
898. Article 12 PWD ('Safety and health'); Article 13 PWD ('Information and consultation'); Article 14 PWD ('Provision of information to workers').

Taken together, these provisions amount to a coherent and context-specific regulatory framework that addresses the challenges of automated monitoring systems in platform work. However, employees in standard employment relationships – who may be subject to equivalent monitoring with AI and IoT-enabled technologies – are not covered by this specialised framework. Instead, they must rely on the general protections afforded by the GDPR and the AI Act, which, while relevant, do not offer the same sector-sensitive and rights-oriented approach. This divergence creates a potential disparity in treatment: platform workers are explicitly protected against certain risks brought by AI and IoT-enabled monitoring, while standard employees are left without comparable safeguards. Given the growing prevalence of AI and IoT-enabled technologies across all sectors and employment forms, I argue that this model should be extended beyond platform work. The provisions in Chapter III of the PWD offer a promising blueprint for a more comprehensive EU legislative initiative that addresses the legitimate exercise of the employer's monitoring power across all forms of employment, including subordinate employment.[899]

5 CONCLUSIONS

This chapter answered the research sub-question 8: *What pathways exist within the current EU legal framework to address an illegitimate exercise of the AI and IoT-enabled employer's monitoring power?*

I identified two coexisting and complementary pathways, both rooted in the GDPR. The first is the Data Protection Impact Assessment (DPIA) under Article 35 GDPR, and the second is the integration of national labour standards through Article 88 GDPR. Together, these mechanisms offer a partial but structured framework for both preventive and corrective oversight of AI and IoT-enabled monitoring during its deployment by employers. However, for these pathways to be viable, certain conditions must be met.

First, a more functional integration of the AI Act and the GDPR is necessary. Although the AI Act enhances transparency by imposing documentation and disclosure obligations on AI providers (Articles 8-15 AI Act), these obligations must be meaningfully operationalised in DPIAs. Employers, as deployers, must use this information to assess risks comprehensively under Article 35(7) GDPR and involve employees' representatives, as supported by Article 35(9) GDPR and Article 26(7) AI Act. The DPIA, therefore, must evolve from a formal assessment prior to data processing to a structured, participatory governance tool capable of preventing fundamental rights infringements by AI and IoT-enabled technologies.

Second, such an enhanced DPIA could constitute a co-monitoring process through the involvement of employees' representatives, who can already lodge complaints under Articles 77 and 80(1) GDPR when DPIAs are incomplete, outdated, or

899. On this point, *see* the research of Potocka-Sionek and Aloisi: Potocka-Sionek and Aloisi (n 41); Nastazja Potocka-Sionek, 'Gestión de Algoritmos. El Caso Del Trabajo En Plataformas' (2024) 5 LABOS Revista de Derecho del Trabajo y Protección Social 47 https://doi.org/10.20318/labos.2024.9031 accessed 22 October 2025; Potocka-Sionek and Aloisi (n 41).

improperly implemented once the data processing starts. This includes also recognising when adaptive AI or IoT-enabled technologies trigger the need for updated DPIAs or revised legal bases under Article 6 GDPR. Hence, employees' representatives must take a more active role in overseeing the DPIA process and lodging complaints, while Data Protection Authorities, in turn, must respond to such complaints and support the joint application of the AI Act and the GDPR to prevent the illegitimate exercise of the employer's monitoring power.

Third, the role of national labour law standards under Article 88 GDPR must be fully realised by EU Member States. These standards allow DPAs to base their decisions on broader and labour law-contextual compliance assessments, thus providing essential protections not available under data protection law alone. The example of the French DPA's reliance on the Code du travail in the *Amazon France* case illustrates the value of such integration.

Furthermore, while the Platform Work Directive (PWD) remains limited to platform workers, it already presents a promising pathway for a future legislative initiative applicable also to subordinate employment. Chapter III PWD provides for important standards needed also for employee monitoring, and particularly Article 7 PWD explicitly prohibits certain monitoring practices and mandates detailed information sharing, thereby addressing employees' fundamental rights protection more directly than the GDPR or AI Act. These principles could guide future EU legislation to extend similar safeguards to all employees exposed to AI and IoT-enabled monitoring technologies.

In conclusion, the current EU legal framework offers a few pathways for addressing the illegitimate exercise of the employer's monitoring power, but only if certain conditions are met. It requires a more integrated and functional relationship between the GDPR and the AI Act; innovative, employee rights-oriented interpretations of existing legal obligations; greater engagement from data protection and labour Authorities, as well as employees' representatives. Without these further steps, the existing legal framework risks remaining fragmented and insufficient to prevent the illegitimate use of AI and IoT-enabled monitoring in the workplace.

CHAPTER 10

Conclusion

1 INTRODUCTION

Whether it is the waiters in any (past or present) restaurant[900] or the mill workers at Crossley's Dean Clough Mill in 19th-century Halifax (UK),[901] they all share a condition that is typical of the employment relationship, namely: being *monitored at work*. From the simple mirror installed above the factory floor to today's deployment of AI and IoT-enabled technologies that track, assess, and predict employee behaviour, the employer's monitoring power has remained a defining feature of subordinate employment since its emergence during the Industrial Revolutions.

At the heart of this investigation on the employer's monitoring power lies the recent surge in monitoring technologies in European workplaces, driven by the proliferation of AI and IoT-enabled technologies designed to assist employers in monitoring employees.

More specifically, the main research question answered by this book is:

> What are the effects of the use of AI and IoT-enabled technologies on the exercise of the employer's monitoring power and can the existing EU legal framework ensure the legitimacy of this exercise?

To answer this question, I examined how AI and IoT-enabled technologies reshape employee monitoring by expanding its reach, enabling real-time, predictive control, and deepening the employer's dependency on third-party technology providers. These technologies, while enhancing monitoring capabilities, reduce employers' understanding of how these complex monitoring technologies function, making it harder to meet legal standards and raising concerns about whether such monitoring remains legitimate (*Finding 1*).

900. Cf. with the opening example of section 1, Chapter 1.
901. Cf. with the opening example of section 1, Chapter 2.

To assess this legitimacy, I defined a legitimate exercise of monitoring power as one that complies with EU fundamental rights under the ECHR and CFREU – specifically the rights to privacy and data protection, freedom of expression and assembly, collective bargaining and action, and non-discrimination. While these rights can be lawfully restricted if respecting certain criteria, my analysis shows that the implementation of AI and IoT-enabled monitoring can lead to violations of these criteria and, ultimately, of employee protections (*Finding 2*).

In evaluating the EU legal framework, I found that the GDPR alone is insufficient to ensure a legitimate exercise of the employer's monitoring power, particularly due to challenges in defining lawful bases, the enjoyment of data subject's rights in a subordinate relationship, and addressing the controller–processor relationship. The AI Act, however, helps to fill the latter gap by imposing obligations on both AI providers and employers, particularly for high-risk AI systems (*Finding 3*). I found that the intersection of the GDPR and AI Act enhances the DPIA process, making risk assessment more robust and collaborative by involving providers, DPOs, and employee representatives. These representatives may also rely on Articles 77 and 80 GDPR to challenge or improve DPIAs where needed. Together, if put in practice, these measures enable a more structured approach to prevent and correct an illegitimate exercise of an AI and IoT-enabled employer's monitoring power (*Finding 4*).

I further develop on these four findings in the following sections.

2 FINDING 1: THE EMPLOYER'S MONITORING POWER REMAINS CONSTANT IN PURPOSES, BUT ITS METHODS AND IMPACT OVER EMPLOYEES EVOLVE OVER TIME

In Chapters 2 and 4, I addressed research sub-questions 1 ('What are the origins of the employer's monitoring power?') and 3 ('How do AI and IoT-enabled technologies reshape the exercise of the employer's monitoring power?') and found that while the purposes of the employer's monitoring power have remained largely constant over time, its methods have evolved significantly – particularly with the introduction of AI and IoT-enabled technologies.

By tracing the origins of this power from the 18th-century textile industries through Taylorism and Fordism to today's AI and IoT-enabled technologies, I illustrated that while the employer's monitoring power is continuously shaped by technological and regulatory changes, its main purposes remain constant. Historically, monitoring has served three main functions: to monitor employers' properties and workers' access; to monitor workers' performance; to monitor workers' personal characteristics.

Today, the employer's monitoring power remains an open-ended, flexible authority embedded in employment contracts and regulated by labour law. It continues to encompass the observation of employees' personal characteristics, behaviours, and performance, as well as the protection of company assets (Chapter 3, research sub-question 2). However, AI and IoT-enabled technologies are reshaping how this monitoring is carried out, through the use of advanced data analytics from AI systems and IoT networks. As discussed in Chapter 4 (research sub-question 3), these technologies enable descriptive, diagnostic, predictive, and prescriptive analytics, allowing employers to monitor employees with unprecedented depth. Monitoring thus shifts from passive observation to active and anticipatory intervention, influencing employee behaviour in real time. The impact of such data analysis is not merely quantitative – expanding the volume and granularity of data collected – but also qualitative. Descriptive and diagnostic analytics enable employers to visualise and interpret past and present employees' behaviours, while predictive and prescriptive analytics allow them to anticipate risks, forecast performance issues, and recommend or automatically implement interventions. For example, AI-enabled cameras may be used to infer a driver's emotional state and alertness levels; AI models can analyse behavioural patterns during employee interactions with customers or colleagues, and they can also flag potential non-compliance with OSH measures; or productivity dashboards based on keystroke and application usage data can monitor individual performance in real time.

Furthermore, while answering research sub-question 3, I found that employers often purchase and deploy AI and IoT-enabled monitoring technologies from third-party technology providers, whose systems they may not fully understand or control. This outsourcing creates a structural opacity and dependency that weakens employers' ability to oversee how these technologies function and assess their compliance with data protection and fundamental rights obligations. From this, I conclude that regulation must not place the full burden of legitimacy on the employer alone. Instead, it must ensure shared accountability by imposing clear, enforceable obligations on both AI providers, particularly in relation to design transparency, documentation, and cooperation, and on employers, who must exercise due diligence and responsible deployment.

3 FINDING 2: AI AND IOT-ENABLED MONITORING TECHNOLOGIES FAIL TO MEET THE CRITERIA FOR A LEGITIMATE EXERCISE OF THE EMPLOYER'S MONITORING POWER AND VIOLATE EMPLOYEES' FUNDAMENTAL RIGHTS

In Chapters 2 and 3, I also traced how the developments of employer monitoring practices have been shaped by both early and modern forms of international and domestic labour regulation. My aim was to determine what constitutes a legitimate exercise of the employer's monitoring power.

While answering the research sub-question 1 ('What are the origins of the employer's monitoring power?'), I found that with the advance of industrialisation, employment relationships – including the employer's power to monitor – gradually came under the scope of regulation by States. This shift, described by Simitis as the 'juridification of labor relations', marked a transition from informal, private arrangements to legal norms governing the employment relationship.[902] This development was

902. Simitis, 'The Juridification of Labor Relations' (n 122).

reinforced by international initiatives, notably the founding of the International Labour Organization (ILO) and the adoption of Convention C001, which introduced the first international labour standards and further constrained employer discretion.

In the current regulatory landscape, although the EU legal framework does not explicitly define the employer's monitoring power, I argue that its legitimate exercise must be assessed in light of the European fundamental rights framework. I answered the research sub-question 2 ('What is a legitimate exercise of the employer's monitoring power in the European fundamental rights framework?') by defining legitimate exercise as compliance with employees' rights to privacy and data protection, freedom of expression, freedom of assembly and association, the right to collective bargaining and action, and the right to non-discrimination. Monitoring practices that fail to respect these rights cannot be considered legitimate. Any restriction on their enjoyment must meet the *general criteria* set out in the ECHR and the CFREU, as interpreted by the ECtHR and the ECJ. These criteria require that the interference be *prescribed by law, pursue a legitimate aim, be necessary in a democratic society, be proportionate to that aim, and respect the essence of the right or freedom concerned.*

In Chapter 5, while answering the research sub-question 4 ('What is a legitimate exercise of the AI and IoT-enabled employer's monitoring power in the European fundamental rights framework?'), I found that the deployment of AI and IoT-enabled technologies in employment contexts often restricts the enjoyment of fundamental rights in ways that fail to meet these general criteria.

In relation to the rights to privacy and data protection, these technologies are frequently justified on grounds such as occupational safety, cybersecurity, or performance management. However, where their implementation does not meet the structured criteria established by the ECtHR in *Bărbulescu v. Romania*, their use constitutes an illegitimate interference with these rights. In paragraph 121, the Court established that proportionality and the presence of adequate procedural safeguards against arbitrariness are essential to ensure that employee monitoring complies with Article 8 ECHR. The judgment introduced a six-factor test to assess whether such safeguards are in place and whether the interference is justified: (1) *ex ante* notification, (2) extent of monitoring, (3) legitimate reasons, (4) less invasive methods, (5) impact on the employee, and (6) provision of adequate safeguards. Failure to meet these requirements renders the interference with Article 8 ECHR and Articles 7 and 8 CFREU unlawful.

Privacy infringements frequently overlap with violations of freedom of expression and freedom of assembly and association, particularly when monitoring deters workplace communication, suppresses dissent, or targets collective action. AI and IoT-enabled technologies that analyse tone, language, or behavioural patterns – such as tools like *Perceptyx's* 'union vulnerability index' or AI-moderated chat platforms – may create chilling effects that inhibit employees from expressing dissatisfaction or engaging in union-related discussions. According to the jurisprudence of the ECtHR and ECJ, any interference with Article 10 ECHR and Article 11 CFREU must be clearly defined by law and must not undermine the essence of the right. I found that these technologies violate the essence of these freedoms by deterring trade union activities. The WP29 has further confirmed that such a monitoring exacerbates chilling effects and undermines the legitimacy of monitoring where it targets or discourages unionisation or collective action, either directly or indirectly.

Moreover, where AI and IoT-enabled technologies infer or act upon sensitive or protected characteristics, they give rise to discrimination. Technologies that monitor behavioural or emotional traits, such as *Cogito*, may disproportionately affect individuals based on health status, gendered behavioural expectations, or socio-cultural expression. In these instances, legitimacy hinges on whether the monitoring can meet an objective justification test: it must be clearly prescribed by law, pursue a legitimate aim, be strictly necessary and proportionate, and respect the essence of the right. Where these conditions are not met, particularly in the absence of a legal ground or where the system disproportionately affects protected groups or individuals engaged in protected activities, the monitoring constitutes a violation of Article 14 ECHR and Article 21 CFREU.

In conclusion, I found that the deployment of AI and IoT-enabled technologies for employee monitoring frequently fails to meet the *general criteria* established by the ECHR, the CFREU, and case law. Their opacity, adaptiveness, and predictive capabilities present substantial compliance challenges. This underscores the need for the EU legal framework to provide specific and robust safeguards to ensure that employer monitoring practices remain legitimate under the European fundamental rights framework.

4 FINDING 3: THE GDPR AND AI ACT IMPOSE REQUIREMENTS FOR THE LEGITIMATE EXERCISE OF THE EMPLOYER'S MONITORING POWER, BUT FALL SHORT OF PROVIDING PROTECTION SUITABLE TO SUBORDINATE EMPLOYMENT

To assess whether these safeguards exist in the EU legal framework, I turned to the analysis of the General Data Protection Regulation (GDPR) and the Artificial Intelligence Act (AI Act). Through the sub-questions 5, 6 and 7 explored in Chapters 6, 7, and 8, I examined whether these Regulations and their requirements ensure a legitimate exercise of the employer's monitoring power, thus addressing the risks to employees' fundamental rights posed by AI and IoT-enabled technologies.

While answering the research sub-question 5 in Chapter 6 ('What requirements does the GDPR impose on the legitimate exercise of the employer's monitoring power via AI and IoT-enabled technologies?'), I have found that under the GDPR, employers qualify as data controllers responsible for ensuring that processing of employees' data through AI and IoT-enabled technologies aligns with their principles and obligations (Articles 5, 6, 24, 25 GDPR). Employers must demonstrate compliance, facilitate employees' exercise of data subjects' rights (Articles 12-22 GDPR), conduct DPIAs (Article 35 GDPR), and comply with more specific national rules (Article 88 GDPR). This framework requires employers to possess the resources and expertise to manage data processing responsibly by complying with obligations intended to balance data controllers' interests with data subjects' rights and interests.

The AI Act instead, as seen in Chapter 7, introduces a risk-based regulatory framework for AI systems, categorising them according to their impact on EU fundamental rights and values into unacceptable, high-risk, limited-risk, and minimal or no-risk systems. Its aim is to promote a human-centric approach to AI development that respects EU fundamental rights. Article 5 AI Act prohibits certain AI practices deemed to pose unacceptable risks, including systems designed to infer employees' emotional states. For high-risk AI systems (which, under Annex III, include those used for employee monitoring), the Act imposes, among other obligations, transparency and human oversight requirements on AI providers (Articles 13-14 AI Act, and more broadly Chapter III 'High-Risk AI Systems', Articles 8-49 AI Act). It also requires employers, as deployers of AI systems (Article 3(4) AI Act), to monitor how these systems operate, to inform and consult employees about their use, and to notify both providers and competent authorities in case risks or harms occur (Article 26 AI Act). These requirements outlined my answer to the research sub-question 6 ('What requirements does the AI Act impose on the legitimate exercise of the employer's monitoring power via AI and IoT-enabled technologies?').

Both the GDPR and AI Act, however, when applied individually or jointly, present limitations in the employment context. In answering the research sub-question 7 in Chapter 8 ('Can the GDPR and AI Act ensure the legitimate exercise of the AI and IoT-enabled employer's monitoring power?'), I illustrated how both the GDPR and the AI Act are based on assumptions about the information and expertise available to employers and employees, as well as their ability to comply with obligations or exercise their rights – assumptions that do not reflect the realities of employment contexts. Moreover, the prohibitions in Article 5 of the AI Act and certain requirements for high-risk AI systems raise several interpretative challenges that remain unresolved. As a result, the protective aims of this dual framework may be difficult to achieve.

The following subsections present the main limitations of this framework in more detail.

4.1 Problem 1: Employers' Interpretative Leeway in Basing Data Processing on Necessity for Performance of a Contract and Legitimate Interest under Article 6(1)(b) and (f) GDPR

In Chapter 8, section 2, I have found that the legal bases for a lawful processing of personal data under the GDPR – particularly the performance of a contract (Article 6(1)(b) GDPR) and legitimate interest (Article 6(1)(f) GDPR) – leave significant interpretative leeway to employers in light of technological developments. While the AI Act introduces requirements for high-risk AI systems, it does not provide independent legal bases for the processing of personal data. As a result, the legal bases under Article 6 GDPR remain central to determining the lawfulness of data processing. As AI and IoT-enabled technologies become increasingly embedded in business operations, employers are better positioned to justify their monitoring interests. The deeper these technologies are integrated in the business organisation, the more such a monitoring is presented as essential to organisational functioning, creating a feedback loop that risks normalising what may, in fact, be an illegitimate exercise of the employer's monitoring power. I argued that this interpretative leeway calls for a more structured and rigorous test of necessity. Such a test should critically assess whether data processing is necessary for the performance of the employment contract or the pursuit of legitimate interests, and whether the resulting interference with employees' rights is proportionate to the aim pursued. This approach is essential to distinguish truly necessary data processing from those that undermine employees' fundamental rights.

4.2 Problem 2: Employees as Data Subjects, Employers as Data Controllers: Power Imbalances and Regulatory Challenges in the GDPR

In Chapter 8, section 3, I analysed the GDPR's data subject's rights (Articles 12-22 GDPR). I showed how the Regulation constructs data subjects as autonomous individuals capable of asserting their rights through access, rectification, objection, and opting out of automated decision-making. The GDPR's data subjects' rights framework, I argued, is premised on the notion of the 'liberal self'[903] - one who, when adequately informed, can act freely and independently to protect their privacy and personal data. Furthermore, the AI Act does not provide for individual rights to natural persons affected by AI systems, except for a narrowly scoped transparency obligation under Article 86 AI Act (Cf. section 7, Chapter 7).

I found that the GDPR's model of agency and autonomy of the individual is poorly suited to the employment context. It presumes an equality of bargaining power and overlooks the structural asymmetries between employers and employees. Employees operate within a hierarchical relationship of dependency and subordination, which often constrains their ability to exercise data protection rights. Fear of retaliation or job-related consequences may discourage employees from asserting their rights, effectively rendering the GDPR's protections hollow in practice.

In the employment context, the very individuals the GDPR seeks to empower (data subjects) may choose not to invoke their rights due to the economic and social pressures they face. This reveals a gap between the GDPR's normative framework – grounded in the 'liberal self' concept of an autonomous subject – and the lived realities of data subjects within employment relations. This underscores the need for a different regulatory logic in the employment context – still lacking also after the introduction of the AI Act – one that moves beyond self-determination and includes targeted prohibitions and tailored safeguards that recognise these structural constraints.

A parallel problem arises in the GDPR's treatment of employers as data controllers under Articles 24, 25 and 35 GDPR. In Chapter 8, section 4, I noted how the Regulation assumes that data controllers are autonomous and technically capable actors, fully responsible for designing and implementing GDPR-compliant data processing. Yet, in practice, employers often act as customers of complex AI and IoT-enabled technologies developed by third-party technology providers. This creates

903. Cohen (n 763).

significant information asymmetries: employers may lack the technical expertise to fully understand these technologies, let alone verify that they comply with the GDPR's obligations.

Despite being accountable for compliance, under the GDPR, employers are not guaranteed access to sufficient information from their technology providers. Article 28 GDPR – which regulates the processor–controller relationship – imposes only vague obligations on processors to support controllers with the necessary information. The burden falls on employers to investigate how the data processing operates and to evaluate its risks, particularly in conducting DPIAs. This model presumes that employers have the capacity to obtain, interpret, and act on complex technical information – a presumption that often does not hold true in practice. In this instance, the AI Act, however, addresses this regulatory blind spot of the GDPR, with particular reference to AI systems processing employees' data. Its prohibitions and obligations on high-risk AI systems (Articles 6 and 8-15 AI Act) introduce stronger transparency and human oversight requirements (e.g., Articles 13 and 14 AI Act). These provisions enhance employers' capacity to assess and manage the risks of AI deployment, for example, by requiring AI providers to provide clear documentation, risk analyses, and human oversight tools. In doing so, the AI Act complements the GDPR by helping employers meet their data protection obligations.

4.3 Problem 3: Uncertain Scope of Article 5 AI Act and Human Oversight in Employment Contexts

In Chapter 8, while answering the research sub-question 7, I examined the uncertain scope of Article 5(1)(b) and 5(1)(c) AI Act in the context of employment. I found that the European Commission's February 2025 draft guidelines on Article 5 AI Act fail to adequately define how these prohibitions apply within the employment setting. As regards Article 5(1)(b) AI Act, which prohibits AI systems from exploiting individuals' social or economic vulnerabilities, the guidelines acknowledge the risk of AI-driven exploitation in sectors such as financial services and advertising. However, they overlook the employment context; employees in precarious, low-wage, or heavily monitored roles may be particularly vulnerable to such an exploitation. I argued that the Commission's recognition that socio-economic vulnerability increases the risk of AI-driven exploitation, especially for migrants and refugees, should also apply to workers in gig-economy roles, zero-hour contracts, and other insecure employment situations. These workers are especially exposed to exploitative uses of AI systems that automatically assign tasks, monitor performance, and enforce penalties.

Additionally, I found the guidance on Article 5(1)(c) AI Act, which prohibits AI systems used for social scoring, to be vague – particularly in how it distinguishes between job-related and non-job-related information. They fail to clarify what qualifies as relevant workplace data. I interpreted this to mean that performance metrics directly linked to job-related inputs and outputs may be permissible, whereas data concerning an employee's private life – such as non-professional social media activity or lifestyle choices – should be excluded from social scoring conducted at the workplace. This lack of clarity leaves room for overly broad interpretations and highlights the need for more employment-specific guidance to prevent misuse.

In discussing the limitations of the AI Act, I pointed to the challenges arising from Article 14 AI Act ('Human oversight') and the exception under Article 5(1)(f) AI Act, which permits the use of emotion recognition systems in the workplace for medical or safety purposes. I questioned the practicality of real-time oversight required from deployers, especially when AI-related harms are often opaque and systemic. I used the example of *Driveri*, an AI-enabled camera system used to monitor drivers in real time, to illustrate this problem. Despite *Driveri* potentially falling under the exception in Article 5(1)(f) AI Act due to its safety purpose, I showed how its constant monitoring reshapes driver behaviour, creating environments where employees, driven by fear of penalties, deny themselves basic needs. I concluded that such harms are incremental and difficult to recognise, which undermines the assumption that deployers can intervene effectively under Article 14 AI Act. I argued that employers may lack the technical expertise or contractual power to properly oversee third-party systems, making oversight obligations largely symbolic. The European Commission's draft guidelines, which require employers to consider less intrusive alternatives before deployment, offer limited protection. I contended that this approach does not address deeper systemic power imbalances created by AI and IoT-enabled technologies for employee monitoring.

Overall, I concluded that while the AI Act's risk-based approach holds promise in theory, it struggles to address the practical realities of employment relationships. It relies too heavily on assumptions of deployer autonomy and fails to recognise how harms can accumulate over time. These findings prompted a return to similar issues in the GDPR, setting the stage for broader conclusions in Chapter 9 regarding the regulatory gaps in both the GDPR and the AI Act in protecting employees' fundamental rights.

5 FINDING 4: WHEN THE GDPR AND AI ACT WORK (WELL) TOGETHER: DPIA, HIGH-RISK AI SYSTEMS REQUIREMENTS AND EMPLOYEES' REPRESENTATIVES FOR A LEGITIMATE EXERCISE OF THE EMPLOYER'S MONITORING POWER

The challenges I outlined above led me to conclude that preventing the illegitimate exercise of AI and IoT-enabled employer monitoring power requires a stricter regulatory approach, with clearly defined responsibilities for both providers and employers. Throughout Chapter 9, in addressing research sub-question 8, 'What pathways exist within the current EU legal framework to address an illegitimate exercise of the AI and IoT-enabled employer's monitoring power?', I explored an interpretative solution rooted in the GDPR and the AI Act.

A key pathway is the integration of the Data Protection Impact Assessment (DPIA) under Article 35 GDPR with the transparency and documentation obligations imposed on AI providers by the AI Act (Articles 8-15). This combination better equips employers to assess and mitigate risks to employees' fundamental rights before and during the deployment of AI and IoT-enabled technologies. Unlike the more limited Fundamental Rights Impact Assessment (FRIA) in the AI Act (Article 27), which applies only to public service providers, the DPIA has broader applicability across all employers processing employees' data for monitoring purposes (Recital 75 GDPR).

Under the AI Act, the employer, as AI deployer, will receive specific information and guarantees from the AI and IoT-enabled technology provider under Articles 8-15 AI Act. Additionally, Article 26(9) AI Act requires deployers, such as employers, to use the information they receive under Article 13 AI Act to fulfil their obligation to carry out a DPIA according to Article 35 GDPR. The AI Act's requirements include technical documentation that explains the risks and potential of the instrument, a design that allows for sufficient control over the system, and measures to stop and report any malfunctions or risks to employees, as well as to the provider and competent authorities. While this may not amount to full human oversight (*see* above Finding 3, Problem 3), it nonetheless offers essential input for conducting a DPIA with detailed information from AI providers. Moreover, I argued that recent EU legislative developments, including the AI Act and the PWD, have clarified the 'appropriateness' requirement under Article 35(9) GDPR, thus clarifying that employees' representatives must always be informed and consulted during the DPIA process.

Hence, the DPIA process established under the GDPR and complemented by the AI Act involves multiple stakeholders (employers, data protection officers, AI providers, and employees' representatives) whose collaboration ensures that the legal framework is applied correctly and that the balance of interests is maintained when deploying AI and IoT-enabled technologies. Employees' representatives play a critical role in this process: if the employer fails to initiate a DPIA or does not implement the mitigating measures agreed upon with employees' representatives, they may lodge a complaint with the Data Protection Authority (DPA) under Articles 77 and 80 GDPR. For example, employees' representatives may raise complaints about inadequately mitigated risks, particularly in relation to high-risk AI systems. These collective complaint mechanisms enhance accountability by enabling ongoing oversight of AI and IoT-enabled technologies throughout their deployment. By continuously monitoring these systems in light of the DPIA findings, they can assess whether the technologies comply with applicable standards during data processing.

In this context, Article 88(3) GDPR emerges as a further and complementary pathway within the current EU legal framework for addressing the illegitimate exercise of AI and IoT-enabled employer monitoring power. It allows Member States to adopt more specific provisions to safeguard employees' rights in the employment context, thereby reinforcing the GDPR's general principles through alignment with national labour law standards. However, for this pathway to function effectively and consistently across the EU, it is essential that Member States notify such national provisions to the European Commission. This notification process enables the integration of data protection law with domestic rules, ensuring that employer monitoring practices are not only lawful under the GDPR but also legitimate in light of national labour law protections.

6 CONCLUSION

Returning to the main research question of this book:

> What are the effects of the use of AI and IoT-enabled technologies on the exercise of the employer's monitoring power and can the existing EU legal framework ensure the legitimacy of this exercise?

This research has established that the use of AI and IoT-enabled technologies enhances the reach and effectiveness of the employer's monitoring power, but may result in violations of employees' fundamental rights and freedoms. In light of these possible fundamental rights violations, I conclude that the existing EU legal framework, namely the GDPR and the AI Act, can support the legitimate exercise of such a reshaped monitoring power, despite their many limitations, which are largely linked to the fact that they were not specifically designed for the employment context. If applied as established in the present research, this framework provides for a solid foundation for preventing rights violations before and during the deployment of AI and IoT-enabled technologies for employee monitoring. However, this protective potential must be fully operationalised through certain further steps.

A more integrated and functional relationship between the GDPR and the AI Act must be developed by competent bodies and put in practice by employees' representatives to ensure these Regulations reinforce one another. Consequently, the interpretation and implementation of this framework must be grounded in active oversight by Courts, DPAs and competent bodies and meaningful involvement of employees' representatives. I also conclude that if the GDPR and the AI Act are not operationalised through such a coordinated and participatory interpretation and implementation, there will remain gaps in protection. In light of this, future legislative initiatives may be necessary. In the following and final section, I note how future research should explore whether the regulatory approach adopted in the Platform Work Directive[904] offers a more promising model that could be extended to standard employment relationships.

7 FURTHER RESEARCH

In addressing the last research sub-question (8) – which investigates what pathways exist within the current EU legal framework to prevent an illegitimate exercise of the AI and IoT-enabled employer's monitoring power – I noted that, although only applicable to digital labour platforms (*see* section 5.3, Chapter 1), there is currently in force a relevant EU legislation that could serve as a reference point for future regulatory initiatives. That legislation is the Platform Work Directive (PWD), which offers a valuable legislative precedent for regulating AI and IoT-enabled technologies in employment contexts. Although limited in scope to digital labour platforms, the Directive introduces a series of targeted prohibitions and safeguards, particularly in Chapter III on algorithmic management, that could inform broader EU legislation (*see*

904. *See* section 5.3, Chapter 1 and section 4, Chapter 9.

section 4, Chapter 9). I found that these measures together form a coherent framework tailored to the vulnerabilities of platform workers – a framework that is currently unavailable to standard employees.

While the GDPR and the AI Act jointly offer protections, they lack the contextual specificity needed to address the vulnerabilities created by the use of AI and IoT-enabled technologies in the employment context. It is thus relevant for future research to explore whether and how the PWD rights-based and sector-sensitive approach could be extended beyond platform work. In this regard, the existing proposal by Jeremias Adams-Prassl and others – A Blueprint for the Regulation of Algorithmic Management in the EU[905] – already outlines a concrete policy model that EU legislators could adopt. It could also be explored whether the recently established European Labour Authority could play a role in enforcing any future EU legislation on the matter.[906]

905. Adams-Prassl et al. (n 39).
906. Regulation (EU) 2019/1149 of the European Parliament and of the Council of 20 June 2019 establishing a European Labour Authority, amending Regulations (EC) No 883/2004, (EU) No 492/2011, and (EU) 2016/589 and repealing Decision (EU) 2016/344.

Bibliography

Abraha HH, 'Regulating Algorithmic Employment Decisions Through Data Protection Law' (2023) 14 European Labour Law Journal 117.

Abraha HH, 'A Pragmatic Compromise? The Role of Article 88 GDPR in Upholding Privacy in the Workplace' (2022) 12 International Data Privacy Law 276.

Abraha HH, 'Automated Monitoring in the Workplace and the Search for a New Legal Framework: Lessons from Germany and Beyond' (2024) available at SSRN, https://dx.doi.org/10.2139/ssrn.4595760 accessed 22 October 2025.

Abraha HH, '*Hauptpersonalrat Der Lehrerinnen*: Article 88 GDPR and the Interplay between EU and Member State Employee Data Protection Rules' (2024) 87 The Modern Law Review 484.

Adams Z and Wenckebach J, 'Collective Regulation of Algorithmic Management' (2023) 14 European Labour Law Journal 211.

Adams-Prassl J, 'What If Your Boss Was an Algorithm? Economic Incentives, Legal Challenges, and the Rise of Artificial Intelligence at Work' (2019) 41 Comparative Labor Law & Policy Journal 123.

Adams-Prassl J, 'Regulating Algorithms at Work: Lessons for a "European Approach to Artificial Intelligence"' (2022) 13 European Labour Law Journal 30.

Adams-Prassl J, 'Regulating Algorithmic Management: A Blueprint' (2023) 14 European Labour Law Journal 124.

Aitken HGJ, *Taylorism at Watertown Arsenal: Scientific Management in Action 1908-1915* (Harvard University Press 1960).

Ajunwa I, *The Quantified Worker: Law and Technology in the Modern Workplace* (Cambridge University Press 2023).

Ajunwa I, Crawford K and Schultz J, 'Limitless Worker Surveillance' (2017) 735 California Law Review 101.

Alavi HS, Lalanne D and Rogers Y, 'The Five Strands of Living Lab: A Literature Study of the Evolution of Living Lab Concepts in HCI' (2020) 27 ACM Transactions on Computer-Human Interaction 1.

Albin E, 'Channelling Technologies to Benefit Employees via Labour Law' in Nicolas Bueno, Beryl Ter Haar and Nuna Zekic (eds), *Labour Law Utopias* (1st edn,

Oxford University Press Oxford 2024) https://academic.oup.com/book/58011/chapter/477420515 accessed 22 October 2025.

Aloisi A, 'Regulating Algorithmic Management at Work in the European Union: Data Protection, Non-discrimination and Collective Rights' (2024) 40 International Journal of Comparative Labour Law and Industrial Relations 37.

Aloisi A and De Stefano V, *Your Boss Is an Algorithm: Artificial Intelligence, Platform Work and Labour* (Hart Publishing, an imprint of Bloomsbury Publishing 2022).

Aloisi A and De Stefano V, 'Essential Jobs, Remote Work and Digital Surveillance: Addressing the COVID-19 Pandemic Panopticon' (2022) 161 International Labour Review 289.

Aloisi A and De Stefano V, 'Between Risk Mitigation and Labour Rights Enforcement: Assessing the Transatlantic Race to Govern AI-Driven Decision-Making Through a Comparative Lens' (2023) 14 European Labour Law Journal 283.

Aloisi A and Gramano E, 'Artificial Intelligence Is Watching You at Work. Digital Surveillance, Employee Monitoring, and Regulatory Issues in the EU Context' (2019) 41 Comparative Labor Law & Policy Journal 95.

Aloisi A and Potocka-Sionek N, 'De-Gigging the Labour Market? An Analysis of the "Algorithmic Management" Provisions in the Proposed Platform Work Directive' (2022) 15 Italian Labour Law e-Journal 29.

Aloisi A and Stefano V, 'Regulation and the Future of Work: The Employment Relationship as an Innovation Facilitator' (2020) 159 International Labour Review 47.

Alonso DA, 'Social Media in the Employment Relationship Context: A Typology of Emerging Conflicts' (2018) 39 Comparative Labor Law & Policy Journal 287.

'Amazon Web Services Marketplace' https://aws.amazon.com/marketplace accessed 22 October 2025.

Anderson E and Macedo S, *Private Government: How Employers Rule Our Lives (and Why We Don't Talk about It)* (Princeton University Press 2017).

Article 29 Data Protection Working Party, 'Opinion 8/2001 on the Processing of Personal Data in the Employment Context' (2001) https://ec.europa.eu/justice/article-29/documentation/opinion-recommendation/files/2001/wp48_en.pdf accessed 22 October 2025.

Article 29 Data Protection Working Party, 'Recommendation 1/2001 on Employee Evaluation Data' (2001) https://ec.europa.eu/justice/article-29/documentation/opinion-recommendation/files/2001/wp42_en.pdf accessed 22 October 2025.

Article 29 Data Protection Working Party, 'Working Document on the Surveillance and Monitoring of Electronic Communications in the Workplace' (2002) https://ec.europa.eu/justice/article-29/documentation/opinion-recommendation/files/2002/wp55_en.pdf accessed 22 October 2025.

Article 29 Data Protection Working Party, 'Opinion 1/2010 on the Concepts of "Controller" and "Processor"' (2010) https://ec.europa.eu/justice/article-29/documentation/opinion-recommendation/files/2010/wp169_en.pdf accessed 22 October 2025.

Article 29 Data Protection Working Party, 'Opinion 3/2013 on Purpose Limitation' (2013) https://ec.europa.eu/justice/article-29/documentation/opinion-recommendation/files/2013/wp203_en.pdf accessed 22 October 2025.

Article 29 Data Protection Working Party, 'Opinion 05/2014 on Anonymisation Techniques' (2014) https://ec.europa.eu/justice/article-29/documentation/opinion-recommendation/files/2014/wp216_en.pdf accessed 22 October 2025.

Article 29 Data Protection Working Party, 'Opinion 06/2014 on the Notion of Legitimate Interests of the Data Controller under Article 7 of Directive 95/46/EC' (2014) https://ec.europa.eu/justice/article-29/documentation/opinion-recommendation/files/2014/wp217_en.pdf accessed 25 February 2025.

Article 29 Data Protection Working Party, 'Opinion 01/2014 on the Application of Necessity and Proportionality Concepts and Data Protection within the Law Enforcement Sector' (2014) https://ec.europa.eu/justice/article-29/documentation/opinion-recommendation/files/2014/wp211_en.pdf accessed 22 October 2025.

Article 29 Data Protection Working Party, 'Guidelines on Data Protection Officers ("DPOs")' (2017) https://ec.europa.eu/newsroom/article29/items/612048/en accessed 22 October 2025.

Article 29 Data Protection Working Party, 'Guidelines on Data Protection Impact Assessment (DPIA)' (Article 29 Working Party 2017).

Article 29 Data Protection Working Party, 'Opinion 02/2017 on Data Processing at Work' https://ec.europa.eu/newsroom/article29/items/610169/en accessed 22 October 2025.

Article 29 Data Protection Working Party, 'Guidelines on Automated Individual Decision-Making and Profiling for the Purposes of Regulation 2016/679' (2018) https://ec.europa.eu/newsroom/article29/items/612053 accessed 22 October 2025.

Article 29 Data Protection Working Party, 'Guidelines on Transparency under Regulation 2016/679' (2018) https://ec.europa.eu/newsroom/article29/items/622227 accessed 22 October 2025.

Article 29 Data Protection Working Party, 'Opinion 15/2011 on the Definition of Consent' https://ec.europa.eu/justice/article-29/documentation/opinion-recommendation/files/2011/wp187_en.pdf accessed 22 October 2025.

Ashton TS, *The Industrial Revolution, 1760-1830* (1997 ed., Oxford University Press 1997).

Atabey A, Urquhart L and Schafer B, 'Article 72 Post-Market Monitoring by Providers and Post-Market Monitoring Plan for High-Risk AI Systems' in Ceyhun Necati Pehlivan, Nikolaus Forgó and Valcke Peggy (eds), *The EU Artificial Intelligence (AI) Act: A Commentary* (Wolters Kluwer 2024).

Ausloos J, Veale M and Mahieu R, 'Getting Data Subject Rights Right' (JIPITEC 283 para. 1 2019) https://www.jipitec.eu/jipitec/article/view/262 accessed 22 October 2025.

'AWS Search for "Workforce Management" (426 Results)' https://aws.amazon.com/marketplace/search/results?searchTerms=workforce+management accessed 22 October 2025.

Baiocco S et al., 'The Algorithmic Management of Work and Its Implications in Different Contexts' (European Commission 2022) https://publications.jrc.ec.europa.eu/repository/handle/JRC129749 accessed 22 October 2025.

Ball K, 'Workplace Surveillance: An Overview' (2010) 51 Labor History 87.

Ball K, 'Electronic Monitoring and Surveillance in the Workplace: Literature Review and Policy Recommendations.' (European Union Publications Office 2021) https://data.europa.eu/doi/10.2760/451453 accessed 22 October 2025.

Barnard C, *EU Employment Law* (4th edn, Oxford University Press 2012).

Barros Vale S and Zanfir-Fortuna G, 'Automated Decision-Making Under the GDPR: Practical Cases from Courts and Data Protection Authorities' (Future of Privacy Form 2022) https://fpf.org/wp-content/uploads/2022/05/FPF-ADM-Report-R2-singles.pdf accessed 22 October 2025.

BBC News, 'Amazon Apologises for Wrongly Denying Drivers Need to Urinate in Bottles' (4 April 2021) https://www.bbc.com/news/world-us-canada-56628745 accessed 22 October 2025.

Bednarowicz B, 'The Tale of Transparent and Predictable Working Conditions Intertwined with Work-Life Balance: Assessing the Impact of the New Social Policy Directives on Decent Working Conditions and Social Protection' (2020) 22 European Journal of Social Security 421.

Behn O, Leyer M and Iren D, 'Employees' Acceptance of AI-Based Emotion Analytics from Speech on a Group Level in Virtual Meetings' (2024) 76 Technology in Society 102466.

Bell M and Numhauser-Henning A, 'Equal Treatment' in Teun Jaspers, Frans Pennings and Saskia Peters (eds), *European Labour Law* (2nd edn, Intersentia 2024).

Biernacki R, *Fabrication of Labor: Germany and Britain, 1640-1914* (University of California Press 2018).

Bir J, 'The European Social Dialogue' in Peter Scherrer et al. (eds), *The future of Europe* (European Trade Union Institute (ETUI) 2019).

Blackett A, 'Emancipation in the Idea of Labour Law' in Guy Davidov and Brian Langille (eds), *The Idea of Labour Law* (Oxford University Press 2011).

Bloodworth J, *Hired: Six Months Undercover in Low-Wage Britain* (Revised and updated edition, Atlantic Books 2019).

Bodie MT et al., 'The Law and Policy of People Analytics' (2016) 88 University of Colorado Law Review 961 https://ssrn.com/abstract=2769980 accessed 22 October 2025.

Bogg A and Estlund C, 'Between Authority and Domination: Taming the Managerial Prerogative' (2024) 44 Comparative Labor Law & Policy Journal 237.

Bogoeski V, 'Nonwaivability of Labour Rights, Individual Waivers and the Emancipatory Function of Labour Law' (2023) 52 Industrial Law Journal 179.

Bonnici JPM, 'Exploring the Non-absolute Nature of the Right to Data Protection' (2014) 28 International Review of Law, Computers & Technology 131.

Braverman H, *Labor and Monopoly Capital: The Degradation of Work in the Twentieth Century* (25th anniversary ed., Monthly Review Press 1998).

Breque M, De Nul L and Petridis A, *Industry 5.0: Towards a Sustainable, Human-Centric and Resilient European Industry* (Publications Office of the European Union 2021).

Brkan M, 'In Search of the Concept of Essence of EU Fundamental Rights Through the Prism of Data Privacy' [2017] SSRN Electronic Journal http://www.ssrn.com/abstract=2900281 accessed 22 October 2025.

Brkan M and Palčič Vilfan H, 'Article 86 Right to Explanation of Individual Decision-Making' in Ceyhun Necati Pehlivan, Nikolaus Forgó and Valcke Peggy (eds), *The EU Artificial Intelligence (AI) Act: A Commentary* (Wolters Kluwer 2024).

Brodie D, 'How Relational Is the Employment Contract?' (2011) 40 Industrial Law Journal 232.

Bruun N, 'Prohibition of Discrimination under Article 14 European Convention on Human Rights' in Filip Dorssemont, Klaus Lörcher and Isabelle Schömann (eds), *European Convention on Human Rights and the Employment Relation* (Hart Publishing 2013).

Bruun N, 'Articles 20 and 21: Equality and Non-discrimination' in Filip Dorssemont et al. (eds), *The Charter of Fundamental Rights of the European Union and the Employment Relation* (Hart 2019).

Brynjolfsson E and Mitchell T, 'What Can Machine Learning Do? Workforce Implications' (2017) 358 Science 1530.

Buder S, *Pullman: An Experiment in Industrial Order and Community Planning, 1880-1930* (Oxford University Press 1980).

Bygrave LA, 'Article 25 Data Protection by Design and by Default' in Christopher Kuner et al. (eds), *The EU General Data Protection Regulation (GDPR)* (Oxford University Press, New York 2020) https://academic.oup.com/book/41324/chapter/352299028 accessed 22 October 2025.

Calacci D and Stein J, 'From Access to Understanding: Collective Data Governance for Workers' (2023) 14 European Labour Law Journal 253.

Carby–Hall J, 'The Contractual Nature of Social Law' (2003) 45 Managerial Law 23.

Carinci MT, Giudici S and Perri P, 'Obblighi Di Informazione e Sistemi Decisionali e Di Monitoraggio Automatizzati (Art. 1-Bis "Decreto Trasparenza"): Quali Forme Di Controllo per i Poteri Datoriali Algoritmici?' (2023) 8 Labor – il lavoro nel diritto 7.

Carlson L, *Company Towns of the Pacific Northwest* (University of Washington Press 2003).

Cefaliello A and Kullmann M, 'Offering False Security: How the Draft Artificial Intelligence Act Undermines Fundamental Workers Rights' (2022) 13 European Labour Law Journal 542.

Cefaliello A, Moore PV and Donoghue R, 'Making Algorithmic Management Safe and Healthy for Workers: Addressing Psychosocial Risks in New Legal Provisions' (2023) 14 European Labour Law Journal 192 https://doi.org/10.1177/20319525231167476 accessed 22 October 2025.

Christen M et al., 'A Review of Value-Conflicts in Cybersecurity' (2017) 1 The ORBIT Journal 1.

Christoffersen J, *Fair Balance: Proportionality, Subsidiarity and Primarity in the European Convention on Human Rights* (Martinus Nijhoff Publishers 2009).

Clifford D and Ausloos J, 'Data Protection and the Role of Fairness' (2018) 37 Yearbook of European Law 130.

Coase RH, 'The Nature of the Firm' (1937) 4 Economica 386.

Cobbaut E, 'Article 11: Freedom of Expression and Information' in Filip Dorssemont et al. (eds), *The Charter of Fundamental Rights of the European Union and the Employment Relation* (Hart 2019).

'Cogito: Real-Time AI Coaching & Guidance for Contact Centers' https://cogitocorp.com accessed 22 October 2025.

Cohen JE, 'What Is Privacy For' (2013) 126 Harvard Law Review 1904.

Collins H, 'Market Power, Bureaucratic Power, and the Contract of Employment' (1986) 15 Industrial Law Journal 1.

Collins H, *Employment Law* (2nd edn, Oxford University Press 2010).

Collins H, 'Employment as a Relational Contract' (2021) 137 Law Quarterly Review 426.

Collins PM, *Putting Human Rights to Work: Labour Law, the ECHR, and the Employment Relation* (1st edn, Oxford University Press 2022).

Corradini I, *Building a Cybersecurity Culture in Organizations* (Springer 2020).

Council of Europe, 'Recommendation No. R(89)2 of the Committee of Ministers to Member States on the Protection of Personal Data Used for Employment Purposes' (1989) https://rm.coe.int/1680500b15 accessed 22 October 2025.

Council of Europe, 'Recommendation No. CM/Rec(2015)5 of the Committee of Ministers to Member States on the Processing of Personal Data in the Context of Employment' (2015) https://rm.coe.int/cmrec-2015-5-on-the-processing-of-personal-data-in-the-context-of-empl/1680a43b68 accessed 22 October 2025.

Council of Europe, *Handbook on European Data Protection Law: 2018 Edition* (Publications Office 2019).

Couneson G, 'Article 6 Classification Rules for High-Risk AI Systems' in Ceyhun Necati Pehlivan, Nikolaus Forgó and Valcke Peggy (eds), *The EU Artificial Intelligence (AI) Act: A Commentary* (Wolters Kluwer 2024).

Countouris N, *The Changing Law of the Employment Relationship: Comparative Analyses in the European Context* (Routledge 2016) https://www.taylorfrancis.com/books/e/9781315614472 accessed 22 October 2025.

Countouris N, 'The Concept of "Worker" in European Labour Law: Fragmentation, Autonomy and Scope' (2018) 47 Industrial Law Journal 192.

Crawford K, 'Time to Regulate AI That Interprets Human Emotions' (2021) 592 Nature 167.

Crawford M, *Building the Workingman's Paradise: The Design of American Company Towns* (Verso 1995).

Cristofolini C, 'Navigating the Impact of AI Systems in the Workplace: Strengths and Loopholes of the EU AI Act from a Labour Perspective' (2024) 17 Italian Labour Law e-Journal 75.

Cross GS, 'The Quest for Leisure: Reassessing the Eight-Hour Day in France' (1984) 18 Journal of Social History 195.

Dagnino E, 'People Analytics: Work and Labour Protection in the Era of HRM Through Big Data' (2017) 3 Labour Law & Issues 1.

Dagnino E and Armaroli I, 'A Seat at the Table: Negotiating Data Processing in the Workplace. A National Case Study and Comparative Insights' (2019) 41 Comparative Labor Law & Policy Journal https://www.ssrn.com/abstract=3403729 accessed 22 October 2025.

Dai W and Zhu Z, 'Employee Resignation Prediction Model Based on Machine Learning' in Jemal H Abawajy et al. (eds), *2020 International Conference on Applications and Techniques in Cyber Intelligence*, vol 1244 (Springer International Publishing 2021) http://link.springer.com/10.1007/978-3-030-53980-1_55 accessed 22 October 2025.

Dale S, 'Gamification: Making Work Fun, or Making Fun of Work?' (2014) 31 Business Information Review 82.

Dandeker C, *Surveillance, Power and Modernity: Bureaucracy and Discipline from 1700 to the Present Day* (Polity 1990).

Darvall FO, *Popular Disturbances and Public Order in Regency England: Being an Account of the Luddite and Other Disorders in England During the Years 1811-1817 and of the Attitude and Activity of the Authorities* (Oxford University Press 1969).

Davidov G, *A Purposive Approach to Labour Law* (Oxford University Press 2016).

Davidov G, 'Non-waivability in Labour Law' (2020) 40 Oxford Journal of Legal Studies 482.

Davidov G, Freedland M and Countouris N, 'The Subjects of Labor Law: "Employees" and Other Workers' in Matthew Finkin and Guy Mundlak (eds), *Comparative Labor Law Handbook* (Edward Elgar Publishing 2015) http://www.elgaronline.com/view/9781781000120.xml accessed 22 October 2025.

De Hert P and Lammerant H, 'Protection of Personal Data in Work-Related Relations' (European Parliament's Committee on Civil Liberties, Justice and Home Affairs 2013) https://eur-lex.europa.eu/resource.html?uri=cellar:cce0203c-caf8-4a7b-a79d-69e279c677c0.0002.06/DOC_1&format=PDF accessed 22 October 2025.

De Lombaert T et al., 'Mass Collection of Workers' Data in Warehouse Facilities: Reflections on Privacy and Workforce Well-Being' (2024) 17 Italian Labour Law e-Journal 145.

De Schutter O, 'Human Rights in Employment Relationships: Contracts as Powers' in Filip Dorssemont, Klaus Lörcher and Isabelle Schömann (eds), *European Convention on Human Rights and the Employment Relation* (Hart Publishing 2013).

De Schutter O, 'The European Social Charter as the Social Constitution of Europe' in Niklas Bruun et al. (eds), *The European Social Charter and the Employment Relation* (Hart Publishing 2017).

De Schutter O, 'The CFREU and Its Specific Role to Protect Fundamental Social Rights' in Filip Dorssemont et al. (eds), *The Charter of Fundamental Rights of the European Union and the Employment Relation* (Hart 2019).

De Stefano V, 'Negotiating the Algorithm: Automation, Artificial Intelligence and Labour Protection' (2018) 41 Comparative Labor Law & Policy Journal https://www.ssrn.com/abstract=3178233 accessed 22 October 2025.

De Stefano V, 'Does Labour Law Trust Workers? Questioning Underlying Assumptions Behind Managerial Prerogatives' (2023) 53 Industrial Law Journal 206.

De Stefano V and Countouris N, '"Lifting the Private-Law Veil": Employer Authority and the "Contractual Coating" of Worker Subordination' (2024) 44 Comparative Labor Law & Policy Journal 274.

De Stefano V and Taes S, 'Algorithmic Management and Collective Bargaining' (2023) 29 Transfer: European Review of Labour and Research 21.

De Stefano V and Taes S, 'Algorithmic Management and Collective Bargaining' (European Trade Union Institute (ETUI)) 10 https://www.etui.org/publications/algorithmic-management-and-collective-bargaining accessed 22 October 2025.

De Stefano V and Wouters M, 'AI and Digital Tools in Workplace Management and Evaluation: An Assessment of the EU's Legal Framework' (European Parliament 2022) https://doi.org/10.2861/305539 accessed 22 October 2025.

Deakin SF and Wilkinson F, *The Law of the Labour Market: Industrialization, Employment, and Legal Evolution* (Oxford University Press 2005).

Delfanti A, 'Machinic Dispossession and Augmented Despotism: Digital Work in an Amazon Warehouse' (2021) 23 New Media & Society 39.

Délibération de la formation restreinte n°SAN-2023-021 du 27 décembre 2023 concernant la société Amazon France Logistique (Commission Nationale de l'Informatique et des Libertés).

Demetzou K, 'GDPR and the Concept of Risk: The Role of Risk, the Scope of Risk and the Technology Involved' in Eleni Kosta et al. (eds), *Privacy and Identity Management. Fairness, Accountability, and Transparency in the Age of Big Data*, vol 547 (Springer International Publishing 2019) https://link.springer.com/10.1007/978-3-030-16744-8_10 accessed 22 October 2025.

Deshpande PS, Sharma SC and Peddoju SK, 'Predictive and Prescriptive Analytics in Big-Data Era' in Prachi S Deshpande, Subhash C Sharma and Sateesh K Peddoju (eds), *Security and Data Storage Aspect in Cloud Computing* (Springer Singapore 2019) https://doi.org/10.1007/978-981-13-6089-3_5 accessed 22 October 2025.

Dick RP et al., 'Embedded Intelligence in the Internet-of-Things' (2020) 37 IEEE Design & Test 7.

Diefenbach H, Grosse EH and Glock CH, 'Human-and-Cost-Centric Storage Assignment Optimization in Picker-to-Parts Warehouses' (2024) 315 European Journal of Operational Research 1049.

Docksey C, 'Article 24 Responsibility of the Controller' in Christopher Kuner et al. (eds), *The EU General Data Protection Regulation (GDPR)* (Oxford University Press, New York 2020) https://academic.oup.com/book/41324/chapter/352298857 accessed 22 October 2025.

Dodd G, *Days at the Factories: Or, the Manufacturing Industry of Great Britain Described* (Charles Knight 1843) https://books.google.nl/books/about/Days_at_the_Factories.html?id=1hQLAQAAIAAJ&redir_esc=y accessed 22 October 2025.

Doellgast V, Wagner I and O'Brady S, 'Negotiating Limits on Algorithmic Management in Digitalised Services: Cases from Germany and Norway' (2023) 29 Transfer: European Review of Labour and Research 105.

Dorssemont F, 'The Right to Take Collective Action under Article 11 ECHR' in Filip Dorssemont, Klaus Lörcher and Isabelle Schömann (eds), *European Convention on Human Rights and the Employment Relation* (Hart Publishing 2013).

Dorssemont F et al. (eds), *The Charter of Fundamental Rights of the European Union and the Employment Relation* (Hart Publishing 2019).

Dorssemont F, Lörcher K and Schömann I (eds), *European Convention on Human Rights and the Employment Relation* (Hart Publishing 2013).

Dorssemont F and Rocca M, 'Article 28: Right to Collective Bargaining and Action' in Filip Dorssemont et al. (eds), *The Charter of Fundamental Rights of the European Union and the Employment Relation* (Hart 2019).

Edwards R, *Contested Terrain: The Transformation of the Workplace in the Twentieth Century* (Nachdr, Basic Books 1996).

Erhag T and Pennings F, 'European Union Law and the Protection of Precarious Workers' in Teun Jaspers, Frans Pennings and Saskia Peters (eds), *European Labour Law* (Intersentia 2024).

European Agency for Safety and Health at Work, 'Smart Digital Monitoring Systems for Occupational Safety and Health: Opportunities and Challenges' (2023) https://osha.europa.eu/en/publications/smart-digital-monitoring-systems-occupational-safety-and-health-opportunities-and-challenges accessed 22 October 2025.

European Commission, 'Second Stage Consultation of Social Partners on the Protection of Workers' Personal Data' https://www.eumonitor.nl/9353000/1/j9vvik7m1c3gyxp/vi7jgsu3tgzr accessed 22 October 2025.

European Commission, 'Commission Staff Working Paper SEC(2012) 72 Final' https://www.europarl.europa.eu/cmsdata/59702/att_20130508ATT65856-1873079025799224642.pdf accessed 22 October 2025.

European Commission, 'Coordinated Plan on Artificial Intelligence' https://digital-strategy.ec.europa.eu/en/policies/plan-ai accessed 22 October 2025.

European Commission, 'White Paper on Artificial Intelligence: A European Approach to Excellence and Trust, COM(2020) 65 Final' https://commission.europa.eu/publications/white-paper-artificial-intelligence-european-approach-excellence-and-trust_en accessed 22 October 2025.

European Commission, 'Communication on Fostering a European Approach to Artificial Intelligence' https://digital-strategy.ec.europa.eu/en/library/communication-fostering-european-approach-artificial-intelligence accessed 22 October 2025.

European Commission, 'Proposal for a Regulation Laying Down Harmonised Rules on Artificial Intelligence' https://digital-strategy.ec.europa.eu/en/library/proposal-regulation-laying-down-harmonised-rules-artificial-intelligence accessed 22 October 2025.

European Commission, 'Commission Guidelines on Prohibited Artificial Intelligence Practices Established by Regulation (EU) 2024/1689 (AI Act)' (2025) https://digital-strategy.ec.europa.eu/en/library/commission-publishes-guidelines-prohibited-artificial-intelligence-ai-practices-defined-ai-act accessed 22 October 2025.

European Commission, 'EU Member States Notifications to the European Commission under the GDPR' https://commission.europa.eu/law/law-topic/data-protection

/data-protection-eu/eu-member-states-notifications-european-commission-under-gdpr_en accessed 22 October 2025.

European Council, 'European Council Meeting (19 October 2017): Conclusion, EUCO 14/17' https://www.consilium.europa.eu/media/21620/19-euco-final-conclusions-en.pdf accessed 22 October 2025.

European Data Protection Board, 'Guidelines 07/2020 on the Concepts of Controller and Processor in the GDPR' (2020) https://www.edpb.europa.eu/our-work-tools/our-documents/guidelines/guidelines-072020-concepts-controller-and-processor-gdpr_en accessed 22 October 2025.

European Data Protection Board, 'Guidelines 05/2020 on Consent under Regulation 2016/679' https://edpb.europa.eu/sites/default/files/files/file1/edpb_guidelines_202005_consent_en.pdf accessed 22 October 2025.

European Data Protection Board, 'Guidelines 4/2019 on Article 25 Data Protection by Design and by Default' (2020) https://www.edpb.europa.eu/sites/default/files/files/file1/edpb_guidelines_201904_dataprotection_by_design_and_by_default_v2.0_en.pdf accessed 22 October 2025.

European Data Protection Board, 'Guidelines 01/2022 on Data Subject Rights: Right of Access' (2022) https://www.edpb.europa.eu/system/files/2023-04/edpb_guidelines_202201_data_subject_rights_access_v2_en.pdf accessed 22 October 2025.

European Data Protection Board, 'Guidelines 1/2024 on Processing of Personal Data Based on Article 6(1)(f) GDPR' https://www.edpb.europa.eu/system/files/2024-10/edpb_guidelines_202401_legitimateinterest_en.pdf accessed 22 October 2025.

European Foundation for the Improvement of Living and Working Conditions, *Employee Monitoring and Surveillance the Challenges of Digitalisation* (2020) https://doi.org/10.2806/424580 accessed 22 October 2025.

European Parliament, 'Resolution of 20 October 2020 with Recommendations to the Commission on a Framework of Ethical Aspects of Artificial Intelligence, Robotics and Related Technologies, 2020/2012(INL)'.

'European Social Partners Framework Agreement on Digitalisation' (European Social Partners (ETUC, BusinessEurope, SMEunited, CEEP) 2020) https://www.businesseurope.eu/publications/european-social-partners-framework-agreement-digitalisation accessed 22 October 2025.

European Union Agency for Cybersecurity, *ENISA Threat Landscape 2021: April 2020 to Mid July 2021* (Publications Office 2021) https://data.europa.eu/doi/10.2824/324797 accessed 22 October 2025.

'Factsheet: Surveillance at Workplace' (European Court of Human Rights 2023) https://www.echr.coe.int/Documents/FS_Workplace_surveillance_ENG.pdf accessed 25 February 2025.

Fan J, Han F and Liu H, 'Challenges of Big Data Analysis' (2014) 1 National Science Review 293.

Favaretto M et al., 'What Is Your Definition of Big Data? Researchers' Understanding of the Phenomenon of the Decade' (2020) 15 PLOS ONE e0228987.

Fenwick C and Novitz T, *Human Rights at Work: Perspectives on Law and Regulation* (Hart Publishing 2010).

Fields AB and Narr W-D, 'Human Rights as a Holistic Concept' (1992) 14 Human Rights Quarterly 1.

Finkin MW, *Privacy in Employment Law* (Bureau of National Affairs 1995).

Ford H, *My Philosophy of Industry* (Coward-McCann 1929) https://hdl.handle.net/2027/mdp.39015071144326 accessed 22 October 2025.

Ford H, *My Life and Work* (Open Road Integrated Media 2015) https://search.ebscohost.com/login.aspx?direct = true&scope = site&db = nlebk&db = nlabk&AN = 1058736 accessed 22 October 2025.

Foucault M, *Surveiller Et Punir: Naissance De La Prison* (Gallimard 1975).

Frazzetto D et al., 'Prescriptive Analytics: A Survey of Emerging Trends and Technologies' (2019) 28 The VLDB Journal 575.

Fredman S, *Discrimination Law* (3rd edn, Oxford University Press 2022).

Freedland M, 'Data Protection and Employment in the European Union: An Analytical Study of the Law and Practice of Data Protection and the Employment Relationship in the EU and Its Member States' (European Commission 1999).

Freedland M, *The Personal Employment Contract* (Oxford University Press 2005) https://academic.oup.com/book/10120 accessed 22 October 2025.

Freedland M et al., *Data Protection and Employment in the European Union: An Analytical Study of the Law and Practice of Data Protection and the Employment Relationship in the EU and Its Member States* (EC 1999) https://books.google.co.uk/books?id = v-VNtwAACAAJ accessed 22 October 2025.

Freedland MR and Countouris N, *The Legal Construction of Personal Work Relations* (New York: Oxford University Press 2011).

Freeman RB and Medoff JL, *What Do Unions Do?* (Basic Books 1992).

Freitas MDC and Mira Da Silva M, 'GDPR Compliance in SMEs: There Is Much to Be Done' (2018) 3 Journal of Information Systems Engineering & Management https://pdfs.semanticscholar.org/5976/4bd60d47803b6b2c9c6d0adc4a53550b539b.pdf accessed 22 October 2025.

Fudge J, 'Labour as a "Fictive Commodity": Radically Reconceptualizing Labour Law' in Guy Davidov and Brian Langille (eds), *The Idea of Labour Law* (Oxford University Press 2011) https://oxford.universitypressscholarship.com/view/10.1093/acprof:oso/9780199693610.001.0001/acprof-9780199693610-chapter-9 accessed 22 October 2025.

Fülöp T and Poindl P, 'Article 27 Fundamental Rights Impact Assessment for High-Risk AI Systems' in Ceyhun Necati Pehlivan, Nikolaus Forgó and Valcke Peggy (eds), *The EU Artificial Intelligence (AI) Act: A Commentary* (Wolters Kluwer 2024).

Fuster GG, 'How Uninformed Is the Average Data Subject? A Quest for Benchmarks in EU Personal Data Protection' [2014] IDP. Revista de Internet, Derecho y Política 92.

Galič M, Timan T and Koops B-J, 'Bentham, Deleuze and Beyond: An Overview of Surveillance Theories from the Panopticon to Participation' (2017) 30 Philosophy & Technology 9.

Gallagher D, 'Article 26 Obligations of Deployers of High-Risk AI Systems' in Ceyhun Necati Pehlivan, Nikolaus Forgó and Valcke Peggy (eds), *The EU Artificial Intelligence (AI) Act: A Commentary* (Wolters Kluwer 2024).

Garante per la Protezione dei Dati Personali, 'Riders: Italian SA Says No to Algorithms Causing Discrimination A Platform in the Glovo Group Fined EUR 2.6 Million' (2021) https://www.garanteprivacy.it/home/docweb/-/docweb-display/docweb/9677377#english accessed 22 October 2025.

Garante per la Protezione dei Dati Personali, 'Lavoro: No Del Garante Privacy All'uso Del Riconoscimento Facciale per Controllo Presenze. Sanzionate Cinque Società Che Trattavano Illecitamente Dati Biometrici' (28 March 2024) https://www.garanteprivacy.it/home/docweb/-/docweb-display/docweb/9997208#1 accessed 22 October 2025.

Garante per la Protezione dei Dati Personali, 'Provvedimento Del 13 Novembre 2024 [10074601]' (13 November 2024) https://www.garanteprivacy.it/web/guest/home/docweb/-/docweb-display/docweb/10074601 accessed 22 October 2025.

'Garante Privacy: Ordinanza Del 10.11.2022: Illegittimo Il Trattamento Di Dati Biometrici per La Rilevazione Delle Presenze' (*Lavorosì*, 11 January 2023) http://www.lavorosi.it/rapporti-di-lavoro/riservatezza/garante-privacy-ordinanza-del-10112022-illegittimo-il-trattamento-di-dati-biometrici-per-la-ri/ accessed 22 October 2025.

Gaudio G, 'Algorithmic Bosses Can't Lie! How to Foster Transparency and Limit Abuses of the New Algorithmic Managers' (2022) 42 Comparative Labor Law & Policy Journal 707.

Gaudio G, 'Litigating the Algorithmic Boss in the EU: A (Legally) Feasible and (Strategically) Attractive Option for Trade Unions?' (2024) 40 International Journal of Comparative Labour Law and Industrial Relations 91.

Gerards J, 'The Discrimination Grounds of Article 14 of the European Convention on Human Rights' (2013) 13 Human Rights Law Review 99.

Gerards J, 'How to Improve the Necessity Test of the European Court of Human Rights' (2013) 11 International Journal of Constitutional Law 466.

Gerasimova E and Sychenko E, 'Council of Europe: European Social Charter and European Convention on Human Rights' in Beryl Ter Haar and Attila Kun (eds), *EU Collective Labour Law* (Edward Elgar Publishing 2021) https://china.elgaronline.com/view/edcoll/9781788116381/9781788116381.00012.xml accessed 22 October 2025.

Godart J, 'Les clauses du travail dans le traité de Versailles (28 juin 1919) les décisions de la conférence de Washington (novembre 1919)' (Dunod 1920).

'Google Cloud Marketplace' https://cloud.google.com/ accessed 22 October 2025.

Gorz A, *Métamorphoses du travail: critique de la raison économique* (Gallimard 2004).

Gould SJJ, 'Measuring Work Is Hard. Subcontracting It Won't Help. Explainable AI Won't Help.' in Aida Ponce Del Castillo (ed.), *Artificial Intelligence, Labour and Society* (European Trade Union Institute (ETUI) 2024) https://www.etui.org/publications/artificial-intelligence-labour-and-society accessed 22 October 2025.

Gould SJJ, 'Stochastic Machine Witnesses at Work: Today's Critiques of Taylorism Are Inadequate for Workplace Surveillance Epistemologies of the Future' [2024] Proceedings of the CHI Conference on Human Factors in Computing Systems 1.

Gouldner AW, *Patterns of Industrial Bureaucracy: A Case Study of Modern Factory Administration* (1. Free Press Paberback ed., The Free Press 1964).

Gruet S, 'Amazon Fined for "Excessive" Surveillance of Workers' (*BBC*, 23 January 2024) https://www.bbc.com/news/business-68067022 accessed 22 October 2025.

Gstrein OJ and Beaulieu A, 'How to Protect Privacy in a Datafied Society? A Presentation of Multiple Legal and Conceptual Approaches' (2022) 35 Philosophy & Technology https://link.springer.com/10.1007/s13347-022-00497-4 accessed 22 October 2025.

Guglielmetti M, 'Automated Work and Workers' Rights: Platform Work and AI Work Management Systems' in Aida Ponce Del Castillo (ed.), *Artificial Intelligence, Labour and Society* (European Trade Union Institute 2024) https://www.etui.org/publications/artificial-intelligence-labour-and-society accessed 22 October 2025.

Heiland H, 'Controlling Space, Controlling Labour? Contested Space in Food Delivery Gig Work' (2021) 36 New Technology, Work and Employment 1.

Hendrickx F, 'Privacy 4.0 at Work: Regulating Employment, Technology and Automation, Artificial Intelligence, & Labor Law' (2019) 41 Comparative Labor Law & Policy Journal 147.

Hendrickx F, *Protection of Workers' Personal Data: General Principles* (International Labour Organization ed., ILO 2022).

Hendrickx F and Castro C (eds), *Employment Privacy Law in the European Union. Surveillance and Monitoring* (Intersentia 2002).

Hendrickx F, Mangan D and Gramano E (eds), *Privacy@Work* (Wolters Kluwer 2023).

Hendrickx F and Van Bever A, 'Article 8 ECHR: Judicial Patterns of Employment Privacy Protection' in Filip Dorssemont, Klaus Lörcher and Isabelle Schömann (eds), *European Convention on Human Rights and the Employment Relation* (Hart Publishing 2013).

Hepple B and Veneziani B (eds), *The Transformation of Labour Law in Europe: A Comparative Study of 15 Countries, 1945-2004* (Hart Publishing 2009).

Hießl C, 'Algorithmic Management in the Workplace: Taking Stock of Case Law and Litigation in Europe' [2022] Hungarian Labour Law eJournal https://hllj.hu/letolt/2022_2_a/01_ChHiessl_hllj_uj_2022_2.pdf accessed 22 October 2025.

Hobsbawm EJ, 'The Machine Breakers' (1952) 1 Past and Present 57.

Hobsbawm EJ, *The Age of Revolution: Europe 1789-1848* (Repr, Abacus 2007).

Hounshell DA, 'Ford Automates: Technology and Organization in Theory and Practice' (1995) 24 Business and Economic History 59.

'IBM Cloud Catalog' https://www.ibm.com/consulting/cloud accessed 22 October 2025.

Ingrao A, *Il Controllo a Distanza Sui Lavoratori e La Nuova Disciplina Privacy: Una Lettura Integrata* (Cacucci 2018).

'Intenseye' https://www.intenseye.com accessed 22 October 2025.

Intenseye; Koçtaş Case Study (*Intenseye: Transforming Workplace Safety with computer Vision AI*) https://www.intenseye.com/case-studies/koctas-managing-missing-ppe-and-work-at-height-risks-with-ai accessed 22 October 2025.

International Labour Conference and Internationales Arbeitsamt (eds), *The Employment Relationship: La Relation de Travail: International Labour Conference, 95th Session 2006* (International Labour Organization 2006).

International Labour Organization, '"Declaration Concerning the Aims and Purposes of the International Labour Organisation"' https://www.ilo.org/static/english/inwork/cb-policy-guide/declarationofPhiladelphia1944.pdf accessed 22 October 2025.

International Labour Organization, 'Code of Practice: Protection of Workers' Personal Data' https://www.ilo.org/global/topics/safety-and-health-at-work/normative-instruments/code-of-practice/WCMS_107797/lang--en/index.htm accessed 22 October 2025.

Jacobs A, 'Article 11 ECHR: The Right to Bargain Collectively under Article 11 ECHR' in Filip Dorssemont, Klaus Lörcher and Isabelle Schömann (eds), *European Convention on Human Rights and the Employment Relation* (Hart Publishing 2013).

Jacobs A, 'Article 12: Freedom of Assembly and of Association' in Filip Dorssemont et al. (eds), *The Charter of Fundamental Rights of the European Union and the Employment Relation* (Hart 2019).

Jacobs A, 'The Future of the Charter on Fundamental Rights of the European Union' in Filip Dorssemont et al. (eds), *The Charter of Fundamental Rights of the European Union and the Employment Relation* (Hart 2019).

Jacobs ATJM, *Labour Law in the Netherlands* (3rd edn, Kluwer Law International BV 2020).

Jansen N, '2. Decentralised Bargaining and the Role of Law' in Frank Tros (ed.), *Pathways in Decentralised Collective Bargaining in Europe* (Amsterdam University Press 2023) https://www.degruyter.com/document/doi/10.1515/9789048560240-002/html accessed 22 October 2025.

Jaribion A, Khajavi SH and Holmstrom J, 'IoT-Enabled Workplaces: A Case Study of Energy Management and Data Analytics', *IECON 2019 – 45th Annual Conference of the IEEE Industrial Electronics Society* (IEEE 2019) https://ieeexplore.ieee.org/document/8927003/ accessed 22 October 2025.

Jarrahi MH et al., 'Algorithmic Management in a Work Context' (2021) 8 Big Data & Society http://journals.sagepub.com/doi/10.1177/20539517211020332 accessed 22 October 2025.

Jasserand C, 'Legal Nature of Biometric Data: From "Generic" Personal Data to Sensitive Data – Which Changes Does the New Data Protection Framework Introduce? Special Issue: The General Data Protection Regulation' (2016) 2 European Data Protection Law Review (EDPL) 297.

Jeffery M, 'Information Technology and Workers' Privacy: Introduction' (2002) 23 Comparative Labor Law & Policy Journal 251.

Joerges C and Rödl F, 'Informal Politics, Formalised Law and the "Social Deficit" of European Integration: Reflections after the Judgments of the ECJ in *Viking* and *Laval*' (2009) 15 European Law Journal 1.

Jones ML and Kaminski ME, 'An American's Guide to the GDPR' (2020) 98 Denver Law Review 93.

Kaiser C, 'Privacy and Identity Issues in Financial Transactions: The Proportionality of the European Anti-money Laundering Legislation' (University of Grioningen 2018) https://research.rug.nl/en/publications/privacy-and-identity-issues-in-financial-transactions-the-proport accessed 22 October 2025.

Kalsi M, 'Still Losing the Race with Technology? Understanding the Scope of Data Controllers' Responsibility to Implement Data Protection by Design and by Default' (2024) 38 International Review of Law, Computers & Technology 346.

Kamarinou D, Millard C and Singh J, 'Machine Learning with Personal Data', *Data Protection and Privacy. The Age of Intelligent Machines* (Hart Publishing 2017) https://www-bloomsburycollections-com.proxy-ub.rug.nl/book/data-protection-and-privacy-the-age-of-intelligent-machines/ch4-machine-learning-with-personal-data-this-paper-has-been-produced-by-members-of-the-microsoft-cloud-computing-research-centre-a-collaboration-betwe?from=search accessed 22 October 2025.

Kaminski ME, 'The Right to Explanation, Explained' (2019) 34 Berkeley Technology Law Journal https://www.ssrn.com/abstract=3196985 accessed 22 October 2025.

Kaminski ME and Malgieri G, 'Algorithmic Impact Assessments under the GDPR: Producing Multi-Layered Explanations' (2021) 11 International Data Privacy Law 125.

Kaminski ME and Malgieri G, 'The Right to Explanation in the AI Act' (2025) 25-29 University of Colorado Law School Legal Studies Research Paper Series 1.

Kanigel R, 'Taylor-Made: How the World's First Efficiency Expert Refashioned Modern Life in His Image' (1997) 37 The Science http://www.ams.sunysb.edu/~weinig/Taylor-made.pdf accessed 22 October 2025.

Katznelson I and Zolberg AR (eds), *Working-Class Formation: Nineteenth-Century Patterns in Western Europe and the United States* (Princeton University Press 1986).

Keane E, 'The GDPR and Employee's Privacy: Much Ado but Nothing New' (2018) 29 King's Law Journal 354.

Kilic L et al., 'Smart Digital Monitoring Systems for Occupational Safety and Health: Uses and Challenges' (European Agency for Safety and Health at Work 2023) https://osha.europa.eu/en/publications/smart-digital-monitoring-systems-occupational-safety-and-health-uses-and-challenges accessed 22 October 2025.

Kim PT, 'Data-Driven Discrimination at Work' (2017) 58 William and Mary Law Review 857 https://scholarship.law.wm.edu/wmlr/vol58/iss3/4 accessed 22 October 2025.

Kim PT and Bodie MT, 'Artificial Intelligence and the Challenges of Workplace Discrimination and Privacy' (2021) 35 Journal of Labor and Employment Law 289.

Klippenstein K, 'Leaked: New Amazon Worker Chat App Would Ban Words Like "Union," "Restrooms," "Pay Raise," And "Plantation"' (*The Intercept*, 4 April 2022) https://theintercept.com/2022/04/04/amazon-union-living-wage-restrooms-chat-app/ accessed 22 October 2025.

Knoop D and Jones GP, *The Medieval Mason* (Barnes and Noble 1967) https://historyofeconomicthought.mcmaster.ca/knoop/MediaevalMason.pdf accessed 22 October 2025.

Köchling A and Wehner MC, 'Discriminated by an Algorithm: A Systematic Review of Discrimination and Fairness by Algorithmic Decision-Making in the Context of HR Recruitment and HR Development' (2020) 13 Business Research 795.

Koops B-J, 'The Concept of Function Creep' (2021) 13 Law, Innovation and Technology 29.

Kotschy W, 'Article 6 Lawfulness of Processing' in Christopher Kuner et al. (eds), *The EU General Data Protection Regulation (GDPR)* (Oxford University Press, New York 2020) https://academic.oup.com/book/41324/chapter/352296511 accessed 22 October 2025.

Kotschy W, 'Article 77 Right to Lodge a Complaint with a Supervisory Authority' in Christopher Kuner et al. (eds), *The EU General Data Protection Regulation (GDPR)* (Oxford University Press, New York 2020) https://academic.oup.com/book/41324/chapter/352304824 accessed 22 October 2025.

Koulierakis E, 'The Challenge of Incorporating Legal Rules into Digital Applications: A Theoretical Exploration of Article 25 GDPR' (2022) 18 Illyrius – International Scientific Review 35.

Koulierakis E, 'Certification as Guidance for Data Protection by Design' [2023] International Review of Law, Computers & Technology 1.

Krzywdzinski M, Gerst D and Butollo F, 'Promoting Human-Centred AI in the Workplace. Trade Unions and Their Strategies for Regulating the Use of AI in Germany' (2023) 29 Transfer: European Review of Labour and Research 53.

Laker B et al., 'How to Monitor Remote Workers: Ethically' (*MIT Sloan Management Review*, 20 November 2020).

Lazarus RJ, *The Making of Environmental Law* (2nd edn, The University of Chicago Press 2023).

Lee S, 'The "AI Mode": How Food Delivery Riders in the Netherlands and South Korea Experience Algorithmic Management' (2024) 17 Italian Labour Law e-Journal 67.

Leicht-Deobald U et al., 'The Challenges of Algorithm-Based HR Decision-Making for Personal Integrity' (2019) 160 Journal of Business Ethics 377.

Leonardi P and Contractor N, 'Better People Analytics Measure Who They Know, Not Just Who They Are' [2018] Harvard Business Review 70.

Lepri B et al., 'Fair, Transparent, and Accountable Algorithmic Decision-Making Processes: The Premise, the Proposed Solutions, and the Open Challenges' (2018) 31 Philosophy & Technology 611.

Linhart D, *La commedia umana del lavoro: dal taylorismo al management neoliberale* (Mimesis Edizioni 2021).

Liu J, Sun J and Wang S, 'Pattern Recognition: An Overview' (2006) 6 International Journal of Computer Science and Network Security 57.

Lix K et al., 'Expressly Different: Discursive Diversity and Team Performance' [2019] Research Papers 3773, Stanford University, Graduate School of Business https://ideas-repec-org.proxy-ub.rug.nl/p/ecl/stabus/3773.html accessed 22 October 2025.

Lörcher K, 'The New Social Dimension of the Jurisprudence of the European Court of Human Rights (ECtHR): The Demir and Baykara Judgement, Its Methodology and Follow-Up' in Filip Dorssemont, Klaus Lörcher and Isabelle Schömann (eds), *European Convention on Human Rights and the Employment Relation* (Hart Publishing 2013).

Lörcher K, 'Article 31: Fair and Just Working Conditions' in Filip Dorssemont et al. (eds), *The Charter of Fundamental Rights of the European Union and the Employment Relation* (Hart 2019).

Lucassen J, *The Story of Work: A New History of Humankind* (Yale University Press 2021).

Lupton D, *The Quantified Self: A Sociology of Self–Tracking* (Polity 2016).

Lupton D, 'The Diverse Domains of Quantified Selves: Self-Tracking Modes and Dataveillance' (2016) 45 Economy and Society 101.

'Major Progress on the Path to EU Accession to the ECHR: Negotiations Concluded at Technical Level in Strasbourg' *Delegation of the European Union to the Council of Europe* (31 March 2023) https://www.eeas.europa.eu/delegations/council-europe/major-progress-path-eu-accession-echr-negotiations-concluded-technic al-level-strasbourg_en?s=51 accessed 22 October 2025.

Makortoff K, 'Barclays Using "Big Brother" Tactics to Spy on Staff, Says TUC' (*The Guardian,* 20 February 2020) https://www.theguardian.com/business/2020/feb /20/barlays-using-dytopian-big-brother-tactics-to-spy-on-staff-says-tuc accessed 22 October 2025.

Malgieri G, 'The Concept of Fairness in the GDPR: A Linguistic and Contextual Interpretation', *Proceedings of the 2020 Conference on Fairness, Accountability, and Transparency* (ACM 2020) https://dl.acm.org/doi/10.1145/3351095.337 2868 accessed 22 October 2025.

Malgieri G, *Vulnerability and Data Protection Law* (Oxford University Press 2023).

Mallafi H and Widyantoro DH, 'Prediction Modelling in Career Management', *2016 International Conference on Computational Intelligence and Cybernetics* (2016).

Mangan D, 'Beyond Procedural Protection: Information Technology, Privacy and the Workplace' [2019] European Law Review 559.

Mangan D, 'From Monitoring of the Workplace to Surveillance of the Workforce' in Tamas Gyulavári and Emanuele Menegatti (eds), *Decent Work in the Digital Age* (Hart Publishing 2022).

Mantelero A, *Beyond Data Human Rights, Ethical and Social Impact Assessment in AI* (TMC Asser Press 2022).

Mantouvalou V, 'The Right to Non-Exploitative Work' in Virginia Mantouvalou (ed.), *The Right to Work: Legal and Philosophical Perspectives* (Hart Publishing 2015).

Mantouvalou V, 'I Lost My Job over a Facebook Post: Was That Fair? Discipline and Dismissal for Social Media Activity' (2019) 35 International Journal of Comparative Labour Law and Industrial Relations 101.

Marassi S and Bolte J, 'Leveraging Data Protection Law for Protecting Workers' Fundamental Right to Health and Safety in the Workplace: The Amazon Case' (2024) 10 International Labor Rights Case Law 263.

Marassi S and Földes MÉ, 'From Healthcare to Employment: Tackling the Regulatory Challenges of in-Body Wearable Devices at Work in the European Union' (2025) 16 European Labour Law Journal 195.

Mateescu A and Nguyen A, 'Explainer: Workplace Monitoring & Surveillance' (Data & Society Research Institute 2019) https://datasociety.net/library/explainer-workplace-monitoring-surveillance/ accessed 22 October 2025.

Mazur J, 'Artificial Intelligence vs Data Protection: How the GDPR Can Help to Develop a Precautionary Regulatory Approach to AI?' in Angelos Kornilakis et al. (eds), *Artificial Intelligence and Normative Challenges*, vol 59 (Springer International Publishing 2023) https://link.springer.com/10.1007/978-3-031-41081-9_12 accessed 22 October 2025.

McGoldrick D, 'The Development and Status of Sexual Orientation Discrimination under International Human Rights Law' (2016) 16 Human Rights Law Review 613.

'Microsoft Azure Marketplace' https://azure.microsoft.com/en-us/ accessed 22 October 2025.

Milaj J, 'Privacy, Surveillance, and the Proportionality Principle: The Need for a Method of Assessing Privacy Implications of Technologies Used for Surveillance' (2016) 30 International Review of Law, Computers & Technology 115.

Millard C and Kamarinou D, 'Article 26 Joint Controllers' in Christopher Kuner et al. (eds), *The EU General Data Protection Regulation (GDPR)* (Oxford University Press, New York 2020) https://academic.oup.com/book/41324/chapter/352299120 accessed 22 October 2025.

Mišćenić E and Hoffmann A-L, 'The Role of Opening Clauses in Harmonization of EU Law: Example of the EU's General Data Protection Regulation (GDPR)', *EU 2020 – lessons from the past and solutions for the future* (2020) https://hrcak.srce.hr/ojs/index.php/eclic/article/view/11895 accessed 22 October 2025.

Mitrou L and Karyda M, 'Employees' Privacy vs. Employers' Security: Can They Be Balanced?' (2006) 23 Telematics and Informatics 164.

Molè M, 'The Quest For Effective Fundamental Labour Rights in the European Post-Pandemic Scenario: Introducing Principles of Explainability and Understanding for Surveillance Through AI Algorithms and IoT Devices' [2022] University of Groningen Faculty of Law Research Paper No 26/2022 https://www.ssrn.com/abstract=4099663 accessed 22 October 2025.

Molè M, 'The Internet of Things and Artificial Intelligence as Workplace Supervisors: Explaining and Understanding the New Surveillance to Employees Beyond Art. 8 ECHR' (2022) 15 Italian Labour Law e-Journal 87.

Molè M, 'La Corte Di Giustizia Sul Responsabile Della Protezione Dei Dati: Primi Chiarimenti Sulle Tutele Speciali Di Un Protagonista Della Digitalizzazione al Lavoro' (2023) 33 Diritto delle Relazioni Industriali 215.

Molè M, 'Commodified, Outsourced Authority: A Research Agenda for Algorithmic Management at Work' (2024) 17 Italian Labour Law e-Journal 169.

Molè M, 'Surveiller et Punir: Amazon Francia e La Sanzione Del Garante Dei Dati per La Sorveglianza "Intrusiva e Pressante" Dei Suoi Magazzinieri' (2024) 34 Diritto delle Relazioni Industriali 553.

Molè M, 'Minimised Work Surveillance Exists under the GDPR: Amazon France and the DPA Sanction' (*Global Workplace Law & Policy*, 4 March 2024) https://global-workplace-law-and-policy.kluwerlawonline.com/2024/03/04/minimised-work-surveillance-exists-under-the-gdpr-amazon-france-and-the-dpa-sanction/ accessed 22 October 2025.

Molè M, 'Lost in Translation: Is Data Protection Labour Law Protection?' (2025) 45 Comparative Labor Law & Policy Journal 553.

Molè M and Mangan D, '"Just More Surveillance": The ECtHR and Workplace Monitoring' (2023) 14 European Labour Law Journal 694.

Moore PV, 'Artificial Intelligence: What Everyone Needs to Know' (2019) 40 Organization Studies 466.

Moore PV, 'Problems in Protections for Working Data Subjects: The Social Relations of Data Production' (2022) 1 Global Political Economy 257.

Moore PV, Upchurch M and Whittaker X (eds), *Humans and Machines at Work: Monitoring, Surveillance and Automation in Contemporary Capitalism* (1st edn, 2018, Springer International Publishing: Imprint: Palgrave Macmillan 2018).

Naidu S and Yuchtman N, 'Coercive Contract Enforcement: Law and the Labor Market in Nineteenth Century Industrial Britain' (2013) 103 American Economic Review 107.

Negrón W, 'Bossware and Employment Tech Database' (2021) https://home.coworker.org/worktech/ accessed 22 October 2025.

Negrón W, 'Little Tech Is Coming for Workers: A Framework for Reclaiming and Building Worker Power.' (*CoWorker.org*, 2021) https://home.coworker.org/wp-content/uploads/2021/11/Little-Tech-Is-Coming-for-Workers.pdf accessed 22 October 2025.

Netradyne, 'Driveri' https://www.netradyne.com/ accessed 22 October 2025.

Netradyne and Amazon, 'Driveri: The Power of Vision' https://www.amazon.com/stores/Netradyne/Netradyne/page/3304DF88-2CA0-4498-96B3-28F7F9F1A57C accessed 22 October 2025.

Nettesheim M, *Data Protection in Contractual Relationships (Art. 6 (1) (b) GDPR)* (1st edn, Lexxion Verlagsgesellschaft mbH 2024).

Neurospot.tech, 'Neurospot: Restaurant Solutions' https://neurospot.tech/en/solutions/restaurant/ accessed 22 October 2025.

Nguyen A, 'The Constant Boss: Labor under Digital Surveillance' (Data & Society Research Institute 2021) https://datasociety.net/library/the-constant-boss/ accessed 22 October 2025.

Niezna M, 'Consent to Labour Exploitation' (2024) 53 Industrial Law Journal 3 https://doi.org/10.1093/indlaw/dwad036 accessed 13 December 2025.

Niezna M and Davidov G, 'Consent in Contracts of Employment' (2023) 86 The Modern Law Review 1134 https://doi.org/10.1111/1468-2230.12802 accessed 13 December 2025.

OECD, 'Algorithms and Collusion: Competition Policy in the Digital Age' (2017) https://www.oecd.org/content/dam/oecd/en/publications/reports/2017/05/algorithms-and-collusion-competition-policy-in-the-digital-age_02371a73/258dcb14-en.pdf accessed 22 October 2025.

Otto M, *The Right to Privacy in Employment: A Comparative Analysis* (Hart Publishing 2016).

Otto M, 'Workforce Analytics v Fundamental Rights Protection in the EU in the Age of Big Data' (2019) 40 Comparative Labor Law and Policy Journals https://cllpj.law.illinois.edu/ accessed 22 October 2025.

Otto M, Pennings F and Peters S, 'Fundamental Social Rights in European Union Law' in Teun Jaspers, Frans Pennings and Saskia Peters (eds), *European Labour Law* (2nd edn, Intersentia 2024).

Palmer A, 'Amazon Is Rolling out Cameras That Can Detect If Warehouse Workers Are Following Social Distancing Rules' (*CNBC*, 16 June 2020) https://www.cnbc.com/2020/06/16/amazon-using-cameras-to-enforce-social-distancing-rules-at-warehouses.html accessed 22 October 2025.

Palmer A, 'Amazon Is Using AI-Equipped Cameras in Delivery Vans and Some Drivers Are Concerned about Privacy' (*CNBC*, 3 February 2021) https://www.cnbc.com/2021/02/03/amazon-using-ai-equipped-cameras-in-delivery-vans.html accessed 22 October 2025.

Parodi E, 'Discrimination in the Automated Targeting of Job Advertising: The Role of the General Data Protection Regulation' (2024) 16 European Labour Law Journal 109 https://doi.org/10.1177/20319525241285424 accessed 22 October 2025.

Parsons KC, 'The Model Company Town: Urban Design Through Private Enterprise in Nineteenth-Century New England by John S. Garner' (1985) 58 The New England Quarterly 639.

Peppet SR, 'Regulating the Internet of Things: First Steps Toward Managing Discrimination, Privacy, Security & Consent' [2014] University of Colorado Law School Legal Studies Research Paper Series.

'Perceptyx' https://www.perceptyx.com accessed 22 October 2025.

Pietrogiovanni V, 'Collective Bargaining: (Not Just) a Fundamental Right' in Beryl Ter Haar and Attila Kun (eds), *EU Collective Labour Law* (Edward Elgar Publishing 2021) https://china.elgaronline.com/view/edcoll/9781788116381/9781788116381.00010.xml accessed 22 October 2025.

Plumb JH, *England in the Eighteenth Century* (Reprinted, Penguin Books 1986).

Podgórski D (ed.), *New Opportunities and Challenges in Occupational Safety and Health Management* (7th edn, CRC Press 2020).

Ponce Del Castillo A, 'The AI Regulation: Entering an AI Regulatory Winter?' (European Trade Union Institute 2021) https://www.etui.org/sites/default/files/2021-06/The%20AI%20Regulation.%20Entering%20an%20AI%20regulatory%20winter_2021.pdf accessed 22 October 2025.

Ponce Del Castillo A (ed.), *Artificial Intelligence, Labour and Society* (European Trade Union Institute (ETUI) 2024) https://www.etui.org/publications/artificial-intelligence-labour-and-society accessed 22 October 2025.

Posey C and Shoss M, 'Research: Why Employees Violate Cybersecurity Policies' (*Harvard Business Review*, 20 January 2022) https://hbr.org/2022/01/research-why-employees-violate-cybersecurity-policies accessed 22 October 2025.

Potocka-Sionek N, 'Gestión de Algoritmos. El Caso Del Trabajo En Plataformas' (2024) 5 LABOS Revista de Derecho del Trabajo y Protección Social 47.

Potocka-Sionek N and Aloisi A, 'The Spillover Effect of Algorithmic Management and How (Not) to Tame It', in Kurt Vandaele and Silvia Rainone (eds), *The Elgar Companion to Regulating Platform Work. Insights from the Food Delivery Sector* (Edward Elgar Publishing 2024) http://dx.doi.org/10.2139/ssrn.4738680 accessed 22 October 2025.

Rainone S and Aloisi A, 'Time to Deliver? Assessing the Action Plan on the European Pillar of Social Rights' (European Trade Union Institute (ETUI) 2021) https://www.etui.org/publications/time-deliver accessed 22 October 2025.

Razak MFA et al., 'The Rise of "Malware": Bibliometric Analysis of Malware Study' (2016) 75 Journal of Network and Computer Applications 58.

'RetailNext' https://retailnext.net accessed 22 October 2025.

Reuters, 'Dutch Watchdog Fines Uber 10 Mln Euros over Privacy Regulations Infringement' (31 January 2024) https://www.reuters.com/technology/dutch-watchdog-fines-uber-10-mln-euros-over-privacy-regulations-infringement-2024-01-31/ accessed 22 October 2025.

Rigaudias CA and Spina A, 'Article 38 Position of the Data Protection Officer' in Christopher Kuner et al. (eds), *The EU General Data Protection Regulation (GDPR)* (Oxford University Press, New York 2020) https://academic.oup.com/book/41324/chapter/352300413 accessed 22 October 2025.

Rišak ME, 'Employer Acquisition and Use of the Contents of Employee Social Media: An Overview' (2018) 39 Comparative Labor Law & Policy Journal 441.

Risak ME and Dullinger T, *The Concept of 'Worker' in EU Law: Status Quo and Potential for Change* (ETUI 2018).

Riso S, *Employee Monitoring and Surveillance: The Challenges of Digitalisation* (Publications Office of the European Union 2020).

Rodgers EC, *Discussion of Holidays in the Later Middle Ages* (AMS Press 1967) https://books.google.it/books/about/Discussion_of_Holidays_in_the_Later_Middd.html?id=bBQoAQAAMAAJ&redir_esc=y accessed 22 October 2025.

Rodríguez Fernández ML, 'Collective Bargaining and AI in Spain' in Aida Ponce Del Castillo (ed.), *Artificial intelligence, labour and society* (European Trade Union Institute (ETUI) 2024) https://www.etui.org/publications/artificial-intelligence-labour-and-society accessed 22 October 2025.

Rönnmar M et al., '7. Trade Union Participation and Influence in Decentralised Collective Bargaining' in Frank Tros (ed.), *Pathways in Decentralised Collective Bargaining in Europe* (Amsterdam University Press 2023) https://www.degruyter.com/document/doi/10.1515/9789048560240-007/html accessed 22 October 2025.

Rooksby E and Cica N, 'Personal Autonomy and Electronic Monitoring in the Workplace': in John Weckert (ed.), *Electronic Monitoring in the Workplace* (IGI Global 2005) https://www.igi-global.com/chapter/personal-autonomy-electronic-monitoring-workplace/10022 accessed 22 October 2025.

'Rules for the Observance of Feast-Days in Medieval England' (1961) 34 Historical Research 117 https://doi.org/10.1111/j.1468-2281.1961.tb02090.x accessed 22 October 2025.

Schäfer MT and Es, van K (eds), *The Datafied Society. Studying Culture Through Data* (Amsterdam University Press 2017) https://library.oapen.org/handle/20.500.12657/31843 accessed 22 October 2025.

Senatori I, 'The European Framework Agreement on Digitalisation: A Whiter Shade of Pale?' (2020) 13 Italian Labour Law e-Journal 159.

Shakuf V et al., 'Processing Emotional Prosody in a Foreign Language: The Case of German and Hebrew' (2022) 6 Journal of Cultural Cognitive Science 251.

Sharma AK et al., 'Analytics Techniques: Descriptive Analytics, Predictive Analytics, and Prescriptive Analytics' in P Mary Jeyanthi et al. (eds), *Decision Intelligence Analytics and the Implementation of Strategic Business Management* (Springer International Publishing 2022) https://doi.org/10.1007/978-3-030-82763-2_1 accessed 22 October 2025.

Sheila Blackburn, 'Ideology and Social Policy: The Origins of the Trade Boards Act' (1991) 34 The Historical Journal 43.

Simbeck K, 'HR Analytics and Ethics' (2019) 63 IBM Journal of Research and Development 9.

Simitis S, 'The Juridification of Labor Relations' (1986) 7 Comparative Labor Law & Policy Journal 93.

Simitis S, 'Reviewing Privacy in an Information Society' (1987) 135 University of Pennsylvania Law Review 707.

Simitis S, 'Reconsidering the Premises of Labour Law: Prolegomena to an EU Regulation on the Protection of Employees' Personal Data' (1999) 5 European Law Journal 45.

Singh A, Singh H and Singh A, 'People Analytics: Augmenting Horizon from Predictive Analytics to Prescriptive Analytics' in P Mary Jeyanthi et al. (eds), *Decision Intelligence Analytics and the Implementation of Strategic Business Management* (Springer International Publishing 2022) https://doi.org/10.1007/978-3-030-82763-2_13 accessed 22 October 2025.

Sprague RD, 'From Taylorism to the Omnipticon: Expanding Employee Surveillance Beyond the Workplace' (2007) 25 Journal of Computer & Information Law 1.

Super DE, Šverko B and Super CM (eds), *Life Roles, Values, and Careers: International Findings of the Work Importance Study* (1st edn, Jossey-Bass Publishers 1995).

Supiot A, *Critique du droit du travail* (Presses Universitaires de France 2015).

Tapiola K, 'What Happened to International Labour Standards and Human Rights at Work?' in Tarja Halonen and Ulla Liukkunen (eds), *International Labour Organization and Global Social Governance* (Springer International Publishing 2021) https://doi.org/10.1007/978-3-030-55400-2_3 accessed 22 October 2025.

Taylor FW, *The Principles of Scientific Management* (Harper & Brothers 1919) https://archive.org/details/principlesofscie00taylrich/page/n5/mode/2up?view=theater&q=rate accessed 22 October 2025.

Ter Haar B and Kun A (eds), *EU Collective Labour Law* (Edward Elgar Publishing 2021) https://china.elgaronline.com/view/edcoll/9781788116381/9781788116381.xml accessed 22 October 2025.

Thompson EP, 'Time, Work-Discipline, and Industrial Capitalism' [1967] Past & Present 56.

Trade Union Congress, 'Technology Managing People: The Worker Experience' (2020) https://www.tuc.org.uk/research-analysis/reports/technology-managing-people-worker-experience accessed 22 October 2025.

UNI Europa, 'AI and Algorithmic Management in European Services Sectors' (Friedrich Ebert Stiftung 2024) https://www.uni-europa.org/wp-content/uploads/sites/3/2024/03/CollectiveBargainingPracticesOnAI_final.pdf accessed 22 October 2025.

UNI Europa, 'Collective Bargaining Practices on AI and Algorithmic Management in European Services Sectors' (Friedrich Ebert Stiftung 2024) https://www.uni-europa.org/wp-content/uploads/sites/3/2024/03/CollectiveBargainingPracticesOnAI_final.pdf accessed 22 October 2025.

UNI Global Union, 'Life in the Amazon Panopticon: An International Survey of Amazon Workers' (2023) https://uniglobalunion.org/report/amazon-panopticon-survey/ accessed 22 October 2025.

UNICE, 'Commission's Second-Stage Consultation on the Protection of Workers' Personal Data – UNICE Reply' https://www.businesseurope.eu/publications/commissions-second-stage-consultation-on-the-protection-of-workers-personal-data-unices-reply/ accessed 22 October 2025.

Van Doorn N, 'Platform Labor: On the Gendered and Racialized Exploitation of Low-Income Service Work in the "On-Demand" Economy' (2017) 20 Information, Communication & Society 898.

Van Eecke P and Regenhardt B, 'Article 1 Subject Matter' in Ceyhun Necati Pehlivan, Nikolaus Forgó and Valcke Peggy (eds), *The EU Artificial Intelligence (AI) Act: A Commentary* (Wolters Kluwer 2024).

Van Eecke P and Regenhardt B, 'Article 2 Scope' in Ceyhun Necati Pehlivan, Nikolaus Forgó and Valcke Peggy (eds), *The EU Artificial Intelligence (AI) Act: A Commentary* (Wolters Kluwer 2024).

Varini V, 'Building an Industrial Society: Welfare Capitalism in the "City of Factories", Sesto San Giovanni, Italy' (2016) 23 European Review of History: Revue européenne d'histoire 724.

Veale M and Edwards L, 'Clarity, Surprises, and Further Questions in the Article 29 Working Party Draft Guidance on Automated Decision-Making and Profiling' (2018) 34 Computer Law & Security Review 398.

Veneziani B, 'The Evolution of the Employment Relationship' in Bob Hepple (ed.), *The Making of Labour Law in Europe: A Comparative Study of Nine Countries up to 1945* (Mansell 1986).

Vijai P and Muralidhara G, 'Inside Amazon: Chaotic Storage System' (IBS Center for Management Research 2016) https://www.thecasecentre.org/main/products/view?id = 138531 accessed 22 October 2025.

Viljoen S, 'Democratic Data: A Relational Theory For Data Governance' (2021) 2 The Yale Law Journal 573.

Waas B and Heerma van Voss G (eds), *Restatement of Labour Law in Europe: The Concept of the Employee*, vol 1 (Hart Publishing 2017).

Wachter S and Mittelstadt B, 'A Right to Reasonable Inferences: Re-Thinking Data Protection Law in the Age of Big Data and AI' (2019) Columbia Business Law

Review 494 https://doi.org/10.7916/cblr.v2019i2.3424 accessed 22 October 2025.

Wachter S, Mittelstadt B and Floridi L, 'Why a Right to Explanation of Automated Decision-Making Does Not Exist in the General Data Protection Regulation' (2017) 7 International Data Privacy Law 76.

Warren SD and Brandeis LD, 'The Right to Privacy' (1890) 4 Harvard Law Review 193.

Warter J, 'The Legitimacy of Modern Data Processing in the Workplace' (2025) 16 European Labour Law Journal 179.

Wedderburn L, 'The Italian Workers' Statute: Some British Reflections' (1990) 19 Industrial Law Journal 154.

Wellman B, *Networks in the Global Village: Life in Contemporary Communities* (Barry Wellman ed., 1st edn, Routledge 2018) https://www.taylorfrancis.com/books/9780429967269 accessed 22 October 2025.

West I, 'Industrializing Light: The Development and Deployment of Artificial Lighting in Early Factories' in Costas Papadopoulos and Holley Moyes (eds), Ian West, *The Oxford Handbook of Light in Archaeology* (Oxford University Press 2017) https://oxfordhandbooks.com/view/10.1093/oxfordhb/9780198788218.001.0001/oxfordhb-9780198788218-e-23 accessed 22 October 2025.

Wood AJ, 'Algorithmic Management. Consequences for Work and Organisation and Working Conditions' (European Commission 2021) https://publications.jrc.ec.europa.eu/repository/handle/JRC124874 accessed 22 October 2025.

Woodham JM, *Twentieth Century Design* (Oxford University Press 1997).

Woytinsky WS, 'Hours of Labour', *Encyclopedia of the Social Sciences* (Macmillan 1935).

Zanfir-Fortuna G, 'Article 15 Right of Access by the Data Subject' in Christopher Kuner et al. (eds), *The EU General Data Protection Regulation (GDPR)* (Oxford University Press, New York 2020) https://academic.oup.com/book/41324/chapter/352297801 accessed 22 October 2025.

Zanfir-Fortuna G, 'Article 21 Right to Object' in Christopher Kuner et al. (eds), *The EU General Data Protection Regulation (GDPR)* (Oxford University Press, New York 2020) https://academic.oup.com/book/41324/chapter/352298408 accessed 22 October 2025.

Zeisel JS, 'The Workweek in American Industry 1850-1956' (1958) 81 Monthly Labor Review 23.

Table of Cases

ECJ

C-66/85 *Deborah Lawrie-Blum v. Land Baden- Württemberg* [1986] ECR 2121, 12, 35
C-197/86 *Steven Malcolm Brown v. The Secretary of State for Scotland* [1988] ECR 03205, 35
C-344/87 *Bettray v. Staatssecretaris van Justitie*, [1989] ECR 01621, 35
C-256/01 *Debra Allonby v. Accrington & Rossendale College*, [2004] ECR I-00873, 11, 35
Case C-232/09 *Dita Danosa v. LKB Līzings SIA*, [2010] ECR I-11405, 11
C-274/99P, *Connolly v. Commission* [2001] ECLI:EU:T:1999:102, 46, 47
C-303/05 *Advocaten voor de Wereld VZW*, ECLI:EU:C:2007:261, 55
C-341/05 *Laval un Partneri Ltd v. Svenska Byggnadsarbetareförbundet, Svenska Byggnadsarbetareförbundets avdelning 1, Byggettan and Svenska Elektrikerförbundet* ECLI:EU:C:2007:809, 50
C-275/06 *Productores de Música de España (Promusicae) v. Telefónica de España SAU*, ECLI:EU:C:2008:54, 108
C-346/06 *Dirk Rüffert v. Land Niedersachsen* ECLI:EU:C:2008:189, 50
C-438/05 *The International Transport Workers' Federation and The Finnish Seamen's Union v. Viking Line ABP and OÜ Viking Line Eesti* ECLI:EU:C:2007:772, 50
C-51/08 *European Commission v. Grand Duchy of Luxemburg* ECLI:EU:C:2011:336, 50
C-94/07, *Andrea Raccanelli v. Max-Planck-Gesellschaft zur Förderung der Wissenschaften eV*, [2008] ECR I-05939, 35
C-553/07, *College van burgemeester en wethouders van Rotterdam v. M.E.E. Rijkeboer*, ECLI:EU:C:2009:293, 108
C-92/09 and C-93/09, *Volker und Markus Schecke GbR and Hartmut Eifert v. Land Hessen*, ECLI:EU:C:2010:662, 108
C-131/12, *Google Spain SL, Google Inc. v. Agencia Española de Protección de Datos (AEPD)*, ECLI:EU:C:2014:317, 108, 183
C-362/14, *Maximillian Schrems v. Data Protection Commissioner, joined party: Digital Rights Ireland Ltd*, ECLI:EU:C:2015:650, 108

C-434/16, *Novak v. Data Protection Commissioner*, ECLI:EU:C:2017:994, 123, 175
C-34/21, *Hauptpersonalrat der Lehrerinnen und Lehrer beim Hessischen Kultusministerium v. Minister des Hessischen Kultusministeriums*, ECLI:EU:C:2023:270, 133

ECtHR

Bărbulescu v. Romania (2017) App No 61496/08 (ECtHR, 5 September 2017), 40, 43
Danilenko and others v. Russia (2005) App No 67336/01 (ECtHR, 6 July 2005), 54
Demir and Baykara v. Turkey (2008) App No 34503/97 (ECtHR, 12 November 2008), 51, 52
Emel Boyraz v. Turkey (2014) App No 61960/08 (ECtHR, 2 December 2014), 55
Enerji Yapi-Yol Sen v. Turkey (2009) App No 68959/01 (ECtHR, 21 April 2009), 51
Florindo De Almeida Vasconcelos Gramaxo v. Portugal (2022) App No 26968/16 (ECtHR, 13 December 2022), 43, 84
Fuentes Bobo v. Spain (2000) App No 39293/98 (ECtHR, 29 February 2000), 45, 82
Handyside v. United Kingdom (1976) App No 5493/72 (ECtHR, 7 December 1976), 41, 46
Heinisch v. Germany App No 28274/08 (ECtHR, 21 July 2011), 46, 47
Herbai v. Hungary (2019) App No 11608/15 (ECtHR, 5 November 2019), 47
Hrachya Harutyunyan v. Armenia (2024) App No 15028/16 (ECtHR, 27 August 2024), 47
I.B. v. Greece (2013) App No 552/10 (ECtHR, 3 October 2013), 55
Kharlamov v. Russia, App No 27447/07 (ECtHR, 8 October 2015), 47
Klass and Others v. Germany, App No 5029/71 (ECtHR, 6 September 1978), 44
López Ribalda and Others v. Spain (2019), App Nos 1874/13 and 8567/13 (ECtHR, 17 October 2019), 43, 78
Malone v. the United Kingdom (1984) App No 8691/79 (ECtHR, 26 April 1985), 41
Marunić v. Croatia (2017) App No 51706/11 (ECtHR, 28 March 2017), 47
National Association of Teachers in Further and Higher Education v. UK (1998) App No 28910/95 (ECtHR, 16 April 1998), 51
Niemietz v. Germany (1992) App No 13710/88 (ECtHR, 16 December 1992), 39
Schuth v. Germany (2010), App No 1620/03 (ECtHR, 23 September 2010), 48
P.G. and J.H. v. the United Kingdom (2001) App No 44787/98 (ECtHR, 25 September 2001), 39
Roman Zakharov v. Russia (2015), App No 47143/06 (ECtHR, 4 December 2015), 44
Runkee and White v. UK (2007) Apps Nos 42949/98 and 51134/99 (ECtHR, 10 May 2007), 55
Satakunnan Markkinapörssi Oy and Satamedia Oy v. Finland (2017) App No 931/13 (ECtHR, 27 June 2017), 39
Sidabras and Dziautas v. Lithuania (2004), App Nos 55480/00 and 59330/00 (ECtHR, 27 July 2004), 40
Sunday Times v. the United Kingdom (1980) App No 6538/74 (ECtHR, 6 November 1980), 41
Szima v. Hungary (2012) App No 29723/11 (ECtHR, 9 October 2012), 48, 91

Thlimmenos v. Greece (2000) App No 34369/97 (ECtHR, 6 April 2000), 55
Vellutini and Michel v. France (2011) App No 32820/09 (ECtHR, 6 October 2011), 45
Vogt v. Germany (1995) App No 17851/91 (ECtHR, 30 November 1995), 45

Table of Legislation

International Treaties

Treaty of Versailles (Society of Nations), 27-29
Convention C001 (ILO), 27, 29, 212
European Convention on Human Rights (ECHR), 8, 12, 13, 28, 32, 36-56, 58, 59, 80, 82, 84, 85, 86, 88, 90, 91, 93, 96, 99, 119, 197, 210, 212, 213
Convention for the Protection of Individuals with Regard to Automatic Processing of Personal Data (Convention 108, CoE), 96-98, 120

EU Law

Primary Law

Charter of Fundamental Rights of the European Union (EU) (CFREU), 12, 13, 32, 37-39, 41, 45-54, 56, 58, 79, 82, 84, 86, 88, 90-93, 121, 139, 197, 210, 212, 213
Treaty on European Union (EU) (TEU), 32, 37, 38, 54, 58, 139, 163
Treaty on the Functioning of the European Union (EU) (TFEU), 103, 140

Secondary Law

Council Directive 89/391/EEC of 12 June 1989 on the introduction of measures to encourage improvements in the safety and health of workers at work, 117, 118
Directive 95/46/EC of the European Parliament and of the Council of 24 October 1995 on the protection of individuals with regard to the processing of personal data and on the free movement of such data, 4, 5, 8, 95, 98-100, 103, 115-119, 126, 129, 167, 170-172
Council Directive 2000/43/EC of 29 June 2000 implementing the principle of equal treatment between persons irrespective of racial or ethnic origin, 48, 53, 90, 178
Council Directive 2000/78/EC of 27 November 2000 establishing a general framework for equal treatment in employment and occupation, 37, 48, 53, 87, 90, 178
Directive 2002/14/EC of the European Parliament and of the Council of 11 March 2002 establishing a general framework for informing and consulting employees in the

European Community – Joint declaration of the European Parliament, the Council and the Commission on employee representation, 156, 178

Directive 2006/54/EC of the European Parliament and of the Council of 5 July 2006 on the implementation of the principle of equal opportunities and equal treatment of men and women in matters of employment and occupation (recast), 87

Regulation (EU) 2016/679 of the European Parliament and of the Council of 27 April 2016 on the protection of natural persons with regard to the processing of personal data and on the free movement of such data, and repealing Directive 95/46/EC, 3-5, 8, 10, 13-14, 16-18, 65, 87, 89, 95, 103-136, 149, 156-159, 165-185, 190-191, 194-196, 198-202, 206-207, 213-219

Directive (EU) 2016/943 of the European Parliament and of the Council of 8 June 2016 on the protection of undisclosed know-how and business information (trade secrets) against their unlawful acquisition, use and disclosure, 55

Regulation (EU) 2019/1020 of the European Parliament and of the Council of 20 June 2019 on market surveillance and compliance of products and amending Directive 2004/42/EC and Regulations (EC) No 765/2008 and (EU) No 305/2011, 155, 195

Regulation (EU) 2019/1149 of the European Parliament and of the Council of 20 June 2019 establishing a European Labour Authority, amending Regulations (EC) No 883/2004, (EU) No 492/2011, and (EU) 2016/589 and repealing Decision (EU) 2016/344, 220

Directive (EU) 2019/1152 of the European Parliament and of the Council of 20 June 2019 on transparent and predictable working conditions in the European Union, 178

Directive (EU) 2019/1158 of the European Parliament and of the Council of 20 June 2019 on work-life balance for parents and carers and repealing Council Directive 2010/18/EU, 87

Directive (EU) 2022/2555 of the European Parliament and of the Council of 14 December 2022 on measures for a high common level of cybersecurity across the Union, amending Regulation (EU) No 910/2014 and Directive (EU) 2018/1972, and repealing Directive (EU) 2016/1148 (NIS 2 Directive), 65, 83

Regulation (EU) 2024/1689 of the European Parliament and of the Council of 13 June 2024 laying down harmonised rules on artificial intelligence and amending Regulations (EC) No 300/2008, (EU) No 167/2013, (EU) No 168/2013, (EU) 2018/858, (EU) 2018/1139 and (EU) 2019/2144 and Directives 2014/90/EU, (EU) 2016/797 and (EU) 2020/1828 (Artificial Intelligence Act), 5-6, 9-10, 13-14, 16-18, 61, 129-130, 137-166, 184-185, 187-191, 194-196, 199-200, 206-207, 214-219

Directive (EU) 2024/2831 of the European Parliament and of the Council of 23 October 2024 on improving working conditions in platform work, 9, 11, 13-14, 17-18, 129-130, 186, 203-206, 218-219

BCLR - BULLETIN OF COMPARATIVE LABOUR RELATIONS

Vol. Author/Title/Year/ISBN

1. Roger Blanpain, *Individual Employment Contracts: Collective Agreements,* 1970.
2. Roger Blanpain, *Social Planning,* 1971 (ISBN 90-312-0018-2).
3. Roger Blanpain, *Guaranteed Income Funds,* 1972 (ISBN 90-312-0019-0).
4. Roger Blanpain, *Employee Participation at the Level of the Enterprise,* 1973 (ISBN 90-312-0020-4).
5. Roger Blanpain, *Vastheid van Betrekking: Staking en Bezetting,* 1974.
6. Roger Blanpain, *Labour Law and Industrial Relations (International Bibliography),* 1975 (ISBN 90-312-0023-9).
7. Roger Blanpain, *Multinational Enterprises,* 1976 (ISBN 90-312-0024-7).
8. Roger Blanpain, *Worker's Participation in the European Company,* 1977 (ISBN 90-312-0044-1).
9. Roger Blanpain, *Women and Labour,* 1978 (ISBN 90-312-0077-8).
10. Roger Blanpain, *European Conference on Labour Law and Industrial Relations: Multinational Enterprises,* 1979 (ISBN 90-312-0091-3).
11. Roger Blanpain, *Job Security and Industrial Relations,* 1980 (ISBN 90-312-0147-2).
12. Roger Blanpain, Greg Bamber & Russell Lansbury, *Technological Change and Industrial Relations: An International Symposium,* 1983 (ISBN 90-312-0205-3).
13. Roger Blanpain, James Janssen van Raay & A. Moulty, *Worker's Participation in the European Community: The Fifth Directive,* 1984 (ISBN 90-654-4187-5).
14. Roger Blanpain, *Equality and Prohibition of Discrimination in Employment,* 1985 (ISBN 90-654-4215-4).
15. Roger Blanpain, *Restructuring Labour in the Enterprise: Law and Practice in France, F.R. of Germany, Italy, Sweden and the United Kingdom,* 1986 (ISBN 90-654-4283-9).
16. Roger Blanpain & E. Kassalow, *Unions and Industrial Relations: Recent Trends and Prospect: A Comparative Treatment,* 1987 (ISBN 90-654-4294-4).
17. Roger Blanpain & Marco Biagi, *Trade Union Democracy and Industrial Relations,* 1988 (ISBN 90-654-4394-0).
18. Roger Blanpain & Jelle Visser, *In Search of Inclusive Unionism,* 1990 (ISBN 90-654-4439-4).
19. Roger Blanpain, *Flexibility and Wages: A Comparative Treatment,* 1990 (ISBN 90-654-4461-0).

20. Roger Blanpain, Stephen Frenkel & Oliver Clarke, *Economic Restructuring and Industrial Relations in Industrialised Countries,* 1990 (ISBN 90-654-4488-2).
21. Roger Blanpain & Friedrich Fürstenberg, *Structure and Strategy in Industrial Relations,* 1991 (ISBN 90-654-4559-5).
22. Roger Blanpain, Amira Galin & Ozer Carmi, *Flexible Work Patterns and Their Impact on Industrial Relations,* 1991 (ISBN 90-654-4572-2).
23. Roger Blanpain, *Workers' Participation: Influence on Management Decision-Making by Labour in the Private Sector,* 1992 (ISBN 90-654-4600-1).
24. Roger Blanpain, Brian Brooks & Chris Engels, *Employed or Self-Employed,* 1992 (ISBN 90-654-4613-3).
25. Roger Blanpain & Tiziano Treu, *Industrial Relations Developments in the Telecommunications Industry,* 1993 (ISBN 90-654-4642-7).
26. Roger Blanpain & Marco Biagi, *Industrial Relations in Small and Medium Sized Enterprises,* 1993 (ISBN 90-654-4696-6).
27. Roger Blanpain & Marco Biagi, *Participative Management and Industrial Relations in a Worldwide Perspective,* 1993 (ISBN 90-654-4769-5).
28. Roger Blanpain, Jacques Rojot & Hoyt N. Wheeler, *Employee Rights and Industrial Justice,* 1994 (ISBN 90-654-4804-7).
29. Roger Blanpain & Ruth Ben-Israel, *Strikes and Lock-Outs in Industrialized Market Economies,* 1994 (ISBN 90-654-4841-1).
30. Roger Blanpain, Kazuo Sugeno & Yasuo Suwa, *The Harmonization of Working Life and Family Life,* 1995 (ISBN 90-411-0064-4).
31. Roger Blanpain & Laszio Nagy, *Labour Law and Industrial Relations in Central and Eastern Europe,* 1996 (ISBN 90-411-0298-1).
32. Roger Blanpain, *Labour Law and Industrial Relations in the European Union,* 1997 (ISBN 90-411-0527-1).
33. Taco Van Peijpe, *Employment Protection under Strain,* 1998 (ISBN 90-411-0528-8).
34. Roger Blanpain, Takashi Araki & Ryuichi Yamakawa, *The Process of Industrialization and the Role of Labour Law in Asia,* 1999 (ISBN 9-041-1104-7-X).
35. Roger Blanpain & Marco Biagi, *Non-standard Work and Industrial Relations,* 1999 (ISBN 90-411-1117-4).
36. Roger Blanpain, *Private Employment Agencies: The Impact of ILO Convention 181 (1997) and the Judgment of the European Court of Justice of 11 December 1997,* 1999 (ISBN 90-411-1118-2).
37. Roger Blanpain, *Multinational Enterprises and the Social Challenges of the XXIst Century: The ILO Declaration on Fundamental* Principles *at Work, Public and Private Corporate Codes of Conduct,* 2000 (ISBN 90-411-1280-4).
38. Roger Blanpain, Ryuichi Yamakawa & Takashi Araki, *Deregulation and Labour Law: In Search of a Labour Concept for the 21st Century,* 2000 (ISBN 90-411-1370-3).
39. Roger Blanpain, *The Council of Europe and the Social Challenges of the XXIst Century,* 2001 (ISBN 90-411-1543-9).

40. Roger Blanpain, *On-Line Rights for Employees in the Information Society, Use & Monitoring of E-Mail & Internet at Work*, 2002 (ISBN 90-411-1626-5).
41. Roger Blanpain, *The Evolving Employment Relationship and the New Economy: The Role of Labour Law & Industrial Relations*, 2001 (ISBN 90-411-1691-5).
42. Roger Blanpain, *Involvement of Employees in the European Union, Works Councils, Company Statute, Information and Consultation Rights*, 2002 (ISBN 90-411-1760-1).
43. Michele Colucci, *The Impact of the Internet and New Technologies on the Workplace: A Legal Analysis from a Comparative Point of View*, 2002 (ISBN 90-411-1824-1).
44. Roger Blanpain, *White Paper on the Labour Market in Italy: The Quality of European Industrial Relations and Changing Industrial Relations*, 2002 (ISBN 90-411-1841-1).
45. Roger Blanpain, Russell D. Lansbury & Young-Bum Park, *Impact of Globalisation on Employment Relations: A Comparison of the Automobile and Banking Industries in Australia and Korea*, 2002 (ISBN 90-411-1850-0).
46. Roger Blanpain & Antoine Jacobs, *Employee Rights in Bankruptcy: A Comparative-Law Assessment*, 2002 (ISBN 90-411-1942-6).
47. Roger Blanpain, Takashi Araki & Shinya Ouchi, *Corporate Restructuring and the Role of Labour Law*, 2003 (ISBN 90-411-1949-3).
48. Roger Blanpain, *Collective Bargaining, Discrimination, Social Security and European Integration*, 2003 (ISBN 90-411-2010-6).
49. Roger Blanpain & Luis Aparicio-Valdez, *Labour Relations in the Asia- Pacific Countries*, 2004 (ISBN 90-411-2239-7).
50. Roger Blanpain & Ronnie Graham, *Temporary Agency Work and the Information Society*, 2004 (ISBN 90-411-2252-4).
51. Roger Blanpain, *The Actors of Collective Bargaining: A World Report*, 2004 (ISBN 90-411-2253-2).
52. Roger Blanpain & Michele Colucci, *The Globalisation of Labour Standards: The Soft Law Track*, 2004 (ISBN 90-411-2303-2).
53. Roger Blanpain, Takashi Araki & Shinya Ouchi, *Labour Law in Motion: Diversification of the Labour Force & Terms and Conditions of Employment*, 2005 (ISBN 90-411-2315-6).
54. Roger Blanpain, *Smoking and the Workplace*, 2005 (ISBN 90-411-2325-3).
55. Roger Blanpain, *Confronting Globalization: The Quest for a Social Agenda*, 2005 (ISBN 90-411-2381-4).
56. Roger Blanpain, Thomas Blanke & Edgar Rose, *Collective Bargaining Wages in Comparative Perspective: Germany, France, the Netherlands, Sweden and the United Kingdom*, 2005 (ISBN 90-411-2388-1).
57. Roger Blanpain & Anne Numhauser-Henning, *Women in Academia & Equality Law: Aiming High - Falling Short?*, 2006 (ISBN 978-90-411-2427-6).
58. Roger Blanpain, *Freedom of Services in the European Union: Labour and Social Security Law: The Bolkestein Initiative*, 2006 (ISBN 978-90-411-2453-5).
59. Roger Blanpain, Frans Pennings & Nurhan Sural, *Flexibilisation and Modernisation of the Turkish Labour Market*, 2006 (ISBN 978-90-411-2490-X).

60. Roger Blanpain & Boel Flodgren, *Corporate and Employment Perspectives in a Global Business Environment*, 2006 (ISBN 978-90-411-2537-X).
61. Roger Blanpain, Shinya Ouchi & Takashi Araki, *Decentralizing Industrial Relations and The Role of Labor Unions and Employee Representatives*, 2007 (ISBN 978-90-411-2583-3).
62. Roger Blanpain, *European Framework Agreements and Telework: Law and Practice: A European and Comparative Study*, 2007 (ISBN 978-90-411-2560-4).
63. Roger Blanpain, Jim Kitay, Leanne Cutcher & Nick Wailes, *Globalization and Employment Relations in Retail Banking*, 2007 (ISBN 978-90-411-2620-1).
64. Roger Blanpain, Russell Lansbury, Jim Kitay, Nick Wailes & Anja Kirsch, *Globalization and Employment Relations in the Auto Assembly Industry: A Study of Seven Countries*, 2008 (ISBN 978-90-411-2698-6).
65. Roger Blanpain & Michele Tiraboschi, *The Global Labour Market: From Globalization to Flexicurity*, 2008 (ISBN 978-90-411-2722-8).
66. Roger Blanpain, Michele Colucci & Frank Hendrickx, *The Future of Sport in the European Union: Beyond the EU Reform Treaty and the White Paper*, 2008 (ISBN 978-90-411-2761-7).
67. Roger Blanpain, Linda Dickens, *Challenges in European Employment Relations: Employment Regulation, Trade Union Organization, Equality, Flexicurity, Training and New Approaches to Pay*, 2008 (ISBN 978-90-411-2771-6).
68. Roger Blanpain, Hiroya Nakakubo & Takashi Araki, *New Developments in Employment Discrimination Law, 2008* (ISBN 978-90-411-2782-2).
69. Roger Blanpain, Andrzej Marian wiątkowski, *The Laval and Viking Cases: Freedom of Services and Establishment v. Industrial Conflict in the European Economic Area and Russia*, 2009 (ISBN 978-90-411-2850-8).
70. Roger Blanpain, William Bromwich, Olga Rymkevich, Silvia Spattini, *The Modernization of Labour Law and Industrial Relations in a Comparative Perspective*, 2009 (ISBN 978-90-411-2865-2).
71. Roger Blanpain, Juan Pablo Landa & Brian Langille, *Employment Policies and Multilevel Governance*, 2009 (ISBN 978-90-411-2866-9).
72. Roger Blanpain, European Works Councils; *The European Directive 2009/ 38/EC of 6 May 2009, 2009* (ISBN 978-90-411-3208-6).
73. Roger Blanpain, William Bromwich, Olga Rymkevich & Silvia Spattini, *Labour Productivity, Investment in Human Capital and Youth Employment: Comparative Developments and Global Responses*, 2010 (ISBN 978-90-411-3249-9).
74. Greg J. Bamber & Philippe Pochet, *Regulating Employment Relations, Work and Labour Laws: International Comparisons between Key Countries*, 2010 (ISBN 978-90-411-3199-7). General Editor: Roger Blanpain.
75. Roger Blanpain, Desislava Nikolaeva Dimitrova, *Seafarers' Rights in the Globalized Maritime Industry*, 2010 (ISBN 978-90-411-3349-6).
76. Roger Blanpain, Hiroya Nakakubo & Takashi Araki, *Regulation of Fixed- Term Employment Contracts*, 2010 (ISBN 978-90-411-3356-4).

77. Roger Blanpain, William Bromwich, Olga Rymkevich & Iacopo Senatori, *Rethinking Corporate Governance*, 2011 (ISBN 978-90-411-3450-9).
78. Roger Blanpain & Frank Hendrickx, *Labour Law between Change and Tradition: Liber Amicorum Antoine Jacobs*, 2011 (ISBN 978-90-411-3424-0).
79. Roger Blanpain, Thomas Klebe, Marlene Schmidt & Bernd Waas, *Trade Union Rights at the Workplace*, 2012 (ISBN 978-90-411-3460-8).
80. Roger Blanpain, William Bromwich, Olga Rymkevich & Iacopo Senatori, *Labour Markets, Industrial Relations and Human Resources Management: From Recession to Recovery*, 2012 (ISBN 978-90-411-4004-3).
81. Roger Blanpain, Hiroya Nakakubo & Takashi Araki, *Systems of Employee Representation at the Enterprise: A Comparative Study*, 2012 (ISBN 978-90-411-4080-7).
82. Roger Blanpain & Frank Hendrickx, *Temporary Agency Work in the European Union and the United States*, 2013 (ISBN 978-90-411-4769-1).
83. Roger Blanpain, Toker Dereli, Y. Pınar Soykut-Sarıca & Aslı en-Tabaı, *Emerging Patterns of Work and Turkish Labour Market Challenges under Globalization: Readings on Labour and Employment Relations*, 2014 (ISBN 978-90-411-4983-1).
84. Roger Blanpain, Pablo Arellano Ortiz, Marius Olivier & Gijsbert Vonk, *Social Security and Migrant Workers: Selected Studies of Cross-border Social Security Mechanisms*, 2014 (ISBN 978-90-411-4770-7).
85. Roger Blanpain & Nikita Lyutov, *Workers' Representation in Central and Eastern Europe: Challenges and Opportunities for the Works Councils' System*, 2014 (ISBN 978-90-411-4746-2).
86. Roger Blanpain, Ulla Liukkunen & Chen Yifeng, *China and ILO Fundamental Principles and Rights at Works*, 2014 (ISBN 978-90-411-4984-8).
87. Roger Blanpain, *The Use of Languages and Employment Relations*, 2014 (ISBN 978-90-411-5606-8).
88. Roger Blanpain, Hiroya Nakakubo & Takashi Araki, *Protection of Employees' Personal Information and Privacy*, 2014 (ISBN 978-90-411-5608-2).
89. Roger Blanpain, Jan Wouters, Glenn Rayp, Laura Beke & Axel Marx, *Protecting Labour Rights in a Multi-polar Supply Chain and Mobile Global Economy*, 2015 (ISBN 978-90-411-5662-4).
90. Roger Blanpain & Stefania Marassi, *Globalization and Transnational Collective Labour Relations: International and European Framework Agreements at Company Level*, 2015 (ISBN 978-90-411-4748-6).
91. Roger Blanpain, Frank Hendrickx & Petra Herzfeld Olsson, *National Effects of the Implementation of EU Directives on Labour Migration from Third Countries*, 2016 (ISBN 978-90-411-6257-1).
92. Roger Blanpain, Frank Hendrickx & D'Arcy du Toit, *Labour Law and Social Progress: Holding the Line or Shifting the Boundaries?* 2016 (ISBN 978-90-411-6747-7).

93. Roger Blanpain & Frank Hendrickx, *Reasonable Accommodation in the Modern Workplace: Potential and Limits of the Integrative Logics of Labour Law*, 2016 (ISBN 978-90-411-6258-8).
94. Roger Blanpain, Frank Hendrickx & Bernd Waas, *New Forms of Employment in Europe*, 2016 (ISBN 978-90-411-6239-7).
95. Roger Blanpain, Frank Hendrickx, Hiroya Nakakubo & Takashi Araki, *The Notion of Employer in the Era of the Fissured Workplace: Should Labour Law Responsibilities Exceed the Boundary of the Legal Entity?*, 2017 (ISBN 978-90-411-8470-2).
96. Elena Sychenko, *Individual Labour Rights as Human Rights: The Contributions of the European Court of Human Rights to Worker's Rights Protection*, 2017 (ISBN 978-90-411-8629-4).
97. William Bromwich & Olga Rymkevich, *Improving Workplace Quality: New Perspectives and Challenges for Worker Well-Being*, 2017 (ISBN 978-90-411-8628-7).
98. Sarah De Groof, *Work-Life Balance in the Modern Workplace: Interdisciplinary Perspectives from Work-Family Research, Law and Policy*, 2017 (ISBN 978-90-411-8630-0).
99. Sylvaine Laulom, *Collective Bargaining Developments in Times of Crisis, Second Edition*, 2025 (ISBN 978-94-035-0628-9).
100. Frank Hendrickx & Valerio De Stefano, *Game Changers in Labour Law: Shaping the Future of Work*, 2018 (ISBN 978-90-411-9953-9).
101. Ivana Palinkaš, *The Legal and Institutional Framing of Collective Bargaining in CEE Countries: Between Europeanisation and Decentralisation*, 2018 (ISBN 978-90-411-9199-1).
102. Jeremy Waddington, *European Board-Level Employee Representation: National Variations in Influence and Power*, 2018 (ISBN 978-90-411-9202-8).
103. Jan Pichrt & Kristina Koldinská, *Labour Law and Social Protection in a Globalized World: Changing Realities in Selected Areas of Law and Policy*, 2018 (ISBN 978-94-035-0093-5).
104. Matthew W. Finkin, *American Labor and the Law: Dormant, Resurgent, and Emergent Problems*, 2019 (ISBN 978-94-035-0654-8).
105. Giuseppe Casale & Tiziano Treu, *Transformations of Work: Challenges for the Institutions and Social Actors*, 2019 (ISBN 978-94-035-0891-7).
106. Miguel De la Corte-Rodríguez, *EU Law on Maternity and Other Child-Related Leaves: Impact on Gender Equality*, 2019 (ISBN 978-94-035-1452-9).
107. Valeria Pulignano & Frank Hendrickx, *Employment Relations in the 21st Century: Challenges for Theory and Research in a Changing World of Work*, 2020 (ISBN 978-94-035-1764-3).
108. Matteo Bottero, *Posting of Workers in EU Law: Challenges of Equality, Solidarity and Fair Competition*, 2021 (ISBN 978-94-035-2860-1).
109. Bernd Waas & Christina Hießl, *Collective Bargaining for Self-Employed Workers in Europe: Approaches to Reconcile Competition Law and Labour Rights*, 2021 (ISBN 978-94-035-2373-6).

110. Mathias Wouters, *International Labour Standards and Platform Work: An Analysis of Digital Labour Platforms Based on the Instruments on Private Employment Agencies, Home Work and Domestic Work*, 2022 (ISBN 978-94-035-4024-5).
111. Luca Ratti, *In-Work Poverty in Europe: Vulnerable and Under-Represented Persons in a Comparative Perspective*, 2022 (ISBN 978-94-035-4996-5).
112. Silvia Rainone, *The Role of the Court of Justice in EU Labour Law: A Case Study on the Transfer of Undertakings Directive*, 2023 (ISBN 978-94-035-2896-0).
113. Frank Hendrickx, Elena Gramano & David Mangan, *Privacy@work: A European and Comparative Perspective*, 2023 (ISBN 978-94-035-3106-9).
114. Elena Sychenko & Adalberto Perulli, *Employment Law and the European Convention on Human Rights: The Research of the Recent Jurisprudence of the ECtHR Related to Employment Law (2017-2021)*, 2023 (ISBN 978-94-035-3556-2).
115. Ilda Durri, *Casual Work Arrangements and Platform-Based Work: The Casual Work Agenda as a Way to Enhance the Labour Protection of Platform Workers*, 2023 (ISBN 978-94-035-3107-6).
116. Charalampos Stylogiannis, *Collective Labour Rights for Self-Employed Workers: A Human Rights-Based Approach of Platform Work*, 2023 (ISBN 978-94-035-0667-8).
117. Heather Kurzbauer, *Employment Vulnerabilities in the World of Orchestral Musicians: Symphonic Metamorphoses*, 2023 (ISBN 978-94-035-2737-6).
118. Natalie Videbæk Munkholm, Vincenzo Pietrogiovanni & Karsten Engsig Sørensen, *Managers in European Law: Rights and Duties of Executive and Non-executive Managers in a European Perspective*, 2024 (ISBN 978-94-035-3286-8).
119. Frank Hendrickx & Christina Hiessl, *The Meaning of Work: A Labour Law Perspective*, 2025 (ISBN 978-94-035-0579-4).
120. Bernd Waas, *Restrictions on the Right to Strike: International Law and National Laws in Europe*, 2025 (ISBN 978-94-035-2519-8).
121. Łukasz Pisarczyk, Barbara Surdykowska & Piotr Grzebyk, *European Framework Agreements from the Perspective of Central and Eastern European Countries*, 2026 (ISBN 978-94-035-4409-0).
122. Michele Molè, *Monitored at Work: The Legitimate Exercise of the Employer's Monitoring Power in the Age of Artificial Intelligence and the Internet of Things*, 2026 (ISBN 978-94-035-4426-7).

